Directing and Producing for Television

Fourth Edition

Directing and Producing for Television

A Format Approach

Fourth Edition

Ivan Cury

ELSEVIER

AMSTERDAM • BOSTON • HEIDELBERG • LONDON
NEW YORK • OXFORD • PARIS • SAN DIEGO
SAN FRANCISCO • SINGAPORE • SYDNEY • TOKYO

Focal Press is an imprint of Elsevier

Focal Press

Focal Press is an imprint of Elsevier
30 Corporate Drive, Suite 400, Burlington, MA 01803, USA
The Boulevard, Langford Lane, Kidlington, Oxford, OX5 1GB, UK

Notices

Knowledge and best practice in this field are constantly changing. As new research and experience
broaden our understanding, changes in research methods, professional practices, or medical treatment
may become necessary.

Practitioners and researchers must always rely on their own experience and knowledge in evaluating and
using any information, methods, compounds, or experiments described herein. In using such information
or methods they should be mindful of their own safety and the safety of others, including parties for
whom they have a professional responsibility.

To the fullest extent of the law, neither the Publisher nor the authors, contributors, or editors, assume
any liability for any injury and/or damage to persons or property as a matter of products liability,
negligence or otherwise, or from any use or operation of any methods, products, instructions, or ideas
contained in the material herein.

Library of Congress Cataloging-in-Publication Data
Cury, Ivan.
    Directing and producing for television : a format approach / Ivan Cury—4th ed.
        p. cm.
    Includes bibliographical references and index.
    ISBN 978-0-240-81293-9 (alk. paper)
    1. Television–Production and direction. I. Title.
    PN1992.75.C87 2010
    791.4502′32—dc22   2010033486

British Library Cataloguing-in-Publication Data
A catalogue record for this book is available from the British Library.

ISBN: 978-0-240-81293-9

For information on all Focal Press publications
visit our website at www.elsevierdirect.com

Printed in the United States of America

10 11 12 13   10 9 8 7 6 5 4 3 2 1

Dedicated to the ones I love . . .
        who surely include Barbara, James, Joanna, Peter, and Alex.
        And now Dorothy, Matthew, Kate, Julian, Annabel, Michelle,
        Max and Beatrice. . .as well as Chloe & Maisy

Table of Contents

Preface and Acknowledgments

FROM THE FIRST EDITION

Since the age of ten, I've been working in radio, television, movies, and theater. Many people helped me along the way—some inadvertently, like the producer who fired me a few days after telling me that the scene I had just directed was "filled with missed opportunities." At that time I hadn't even considered that such a possibility existed. Since then, I've made it a habit to reflect on my work and be sure that I don't miss any opportunities. I tell you this with the hopes that *you* will be prepared to avoid missed opportunities.

This book focuses on the kind of television that is produced with multiple cameras and is switched or cut as the program is happening. That includes most news and panel programs, daytime dramas (soap operas), live events such as political conventions, sporting events, many concerts, demonstration programs, and infomercials. No matter what format is discussed, the emphasis of this book is primarily on the director's role and, as is the case in many formats, on the producer's role as well.

The first edition of this book was written at a time when television was an analog-based medium. The second and third editions addressed the advent and acceptance of the digital revolution. This edition updates the production changes that the digital era has brought in. In speaking about those changes, Andrew Setos, president of Engineering at the Fox Entertainment Group, put it very succinctly: "We are no longer medium based. ...We're now file based." The consequence of that move has had a profound effect on how programming is transmitted and edited—in fact, on how it looks.

New procedures, new software, and new ways of working must be updated. Color bars are a good example of this. While they are still used to match cameras, they're no longer a part of the program package, and the director no longer needs to wait 30 seconds before putting up a slate and then counting down. Directors working on news programs may no longer be working from a script. Instead, they're working off the same teleprompter that's being used by the talent, which now also includes the cues for graphics and other inserted material.

Yet, with all that the new technology has brought about, the basic information in this book has remained very similar to the same basic information as appeared in the first edition. A panel program needs a rundown/routine and solid questions. The guests have to be seated in a way that makes it easy for the crew to shoot and be consistent so the audience understands the panelists' relationship to one another. A scaled ground plan (1/4":1' in America) and the shooting script for a dramatic program are not apt to change very much whether the program is recorded in an analog or a digital medium.

This edition strives to address those new issues. I've also added material that I believe should have been included from the very beginning. This includes examples of different script formats and a glossary of terms used in America and Great Britain.

THANKS

Perhaps more than anyone else, textbook authors owe monumental gratitude to a great number of people. Thanks must go to those at Focal Press who were involved with the book itself; Marie Lee, who first accepted the book, and Elinor Actipis, who has overseen the last editions. I thank Michele Cronin, who's been my direct contact for this edition, and Julie Trinder, who is the foreign rights coordinator.

Special thanks to Ken Hall for his contributions about broadcasting in the United Kingdom and for his outstanding work on the glossary that appears in this edition.

Thanks to those who have been particularly involved with and very helpful throughout this edition:

Steve Binder

Lisa Diane Cox—KTLA

Eric Feder—E! Entertainment

Christi Dean/Alissa Vasilevskis—Avid iNEWS

Michael Fierman

Nick Helton—KET

Price Hicks

Bryan Johnson—The Film Syndicate

Dan McLaughlan

Rodney Mitchell—Directors Guild of America

Steve Paino—Total Production Services

Howard Ritter

Michael Wheeler

Alejandro Seri—Final Draft

Andy Setos—Fox Television

Joe Tawil—Great American Machine

Victor Webb—KCBS

Mark Zucker—Sony Pictures

The students and faculty at California State University, Los Angeles

My wife Barbara, who read this through three prior editions and who read it yet again, offering invaluable help and support, and did so lovingly, patiently, expertly, and professionally.

I'm sure there are others to whom I owe my deepest gratitude but have inadvertently left out. I know later I'll wonder how I could possibly have forgotten all the help and advice they gave me. I hope they have a terrific sense of humor and will forgive my lapse.

Thanks, too, to all those who made the past editions possible:

California State University, Los Angeles: Chey Acuna, Alan Bloom, Tony Cox, Chiz Herrera, Glendal Way-Agel

Focal Press: Cara Anderson, Tammy Harvey, Terry Jadik, Maura Kelly, Kevin Sullivan, Christine Tridente, Diane Wurzel

Fox Television/Sports: Marvin Kale, Andy Setos, Jerry Steinberg

MJA Advertising: Jordan Morganstien, Florence Plato

Phoenix Editorial: John Crossley, Lisa Hinman, Matt Silverman, Cathy Stonehill

The Men's Wearhouse: Richard Goldman, Jayme Maxwell, Matt Stringer, George Zimmer, Joel Asher—Joel Asher Studio

William J. Bell, *The Young and the Restless;* Stephen Blum; Dan Birman from Daniel H. Birman Productions; Jack Brown from Jack Brown Productions; Gil Cates from Cates Doty Productions; Joe Cates from Joe Cates Productions; Peter B. Cury; Christine Chapman-Huenergardt from Chapman/Leonard; Tom Lord from KNBC; Alena Majerova from Technocrane; Stuart McGowan from Noodlehead Network; Spruce McCree from Crosscreek Television Productions; Art Namura from Loyola-Marymount College; Gerald Ruben from KTLA News; Olaf Sauger from Newsmaker; Doug Smart from Oswego State University of New York; Jim Stanton from JimmyJib; Shelly Yaseen from Dubs Inc.; Victor Webb from KCBS.

Thanks to all the students who offered advice and who caught mistakes of one sort or another: Karan Bedi, Rebecca Gonek, Veasna Him, Joe Stearns, and Darren Ward.

Thanks to friends, family, and past reviewers: James Cury, Henry Feldman, Marilyn Frix, Cynthia Gotlewski, Alex and Michelle Gorodetzki, Mike Greene, Tommy Ilic, Felix Lidell, Joanna Harris, Sandy Jacobsen, Michael Jaye, Gloria Johnston, Kit Lukas, Jody Price, Barry Schifrin, Cathy Schifrin, Eileen Berger Sheiniuk, Gene Sheiniuk, Barbara Spector, Gerald Weaver, Dan Wilcox, and Paula Woods.

chapter one

Introduction

The most important thing about being a director is having a job.

—Eric Von Stroheim

I begin this book with Von Stroheim's quotation because I once heard that the first thing you read is the thing that sticks with you the most.

THE DIRECTOR/PRODUCER'S JOB

In order to get and hold jobs, you will surely have to get along with others. We do not work alone. Directing is an interpretive rather than a creative art. Writers, painters, composers, sculptors, and architects are all creative artists. Creative artists work alone. They work alone on a blank screen, a blank piece of paper, a canvas, with clay, carving out a hillside . . . whatever. If they are composers, ultimately they'll need musicians to make the music happen. In the same way, playwrights and screenwriters need producers, directors, actors, and crews, who are the interpretive artists that make their productions come to life.

The playwright, who is the creator, has an idea for a story. It's filled with different characters, and the playwright knows how those characters are supposed to behave. Later, the director comes along with a somewhat different interpretation of the characters and explains that vision to a casting director. At the casting session, an array of actors take a stab at how they feel the characters should be played, and none of the actors' choices is the same as what the director or casting director imagined, or what the author imagined, or what some other actor imagined. Each interpretation is based on the life and experiences of whoever is doing the interpretation. It's never the same experience for any two people.

As director/producer, we have to choose one of the actors and try to mesh his or her idea of the character into what must evolve into a single, cohesive production. Inevitably, our choices are based not only on who's best but also on who's available, or who's affordable; sometimes the choice is based on friendships and debts.

Along the way we have to answer questions about our choices. We answer questions from the cast and the crew. We have to make instant interpretations and get all the people involved to do what we want. Money alone doesn't buy that, nor does cajoling, bullying, reasoning, or even love. But somehow, if the project is to be completed, we must find a way to bring the parts together.

Whether our work revolves around drama or documentaries, we have a better chance of getting all those parts to work together if we've anticipated as many questions as possible. Since knowing all the answers is impossible, we have to make do with *trying* to answer all the questions. Once there's a considered solution to the anticipated questions, it becomes easier to deal with unavoidable last-minute new information and the sudden "stop-the-presses" emergencies. We have the foundation to make whatever changes are needed, when they're needed.

This book strives to make you aware of the homework needed in almost any multiple-camera television shoot and in some single-camera shoots. The emphasis is on the "director/producer" rather than the other way around, because the material presented here is aimed at the director's preparation. The producer is included because the functions of director and producer are often interrelated, and because the producer's decisions often have a direct influence on the director's work. This book does not deal with the director's aesthetic, psychological, or artistic preparation.

It does not deal with the producer's business skills, such as acquiring rights, making deals, and managing a company. The text is aimed at providing answers to what's needed once a project is sufficiently in place to begin planning for the hands-on part of the production. Sometimes knowing what the hands-on part will be helps in arriving at sound aesthetic, psychological, and artistic decisions.

Time management is another topic that this book doesn't really cover, even though it is vital and needs to be addressed. Far too often projects that could have been successful, and even those that should have been, fail because of bad time management. For most people, long and late hours are not nearly as productive as a more considered allocation of time. The work that gets done in the two hours between 2 A.M. and 4 A.M. can usually be done in a half hour that starts at 9 A.M. The project that is started two days before it's due and is then rushed through preproduction, production, and postproduction almost always is finished with two kinds of problems that everyone recognizes: those that were really an inherent part of the production and those that were created by bad time management. The director/producer is responsible for managing his or her own time and the crew's time well and with respect.

Some of the information presented in the first few chapters of this book holds true for all types of productions. For example, a quarter-inch ground plan is used in both panel shows and dramas. Additional material on quarter-inch ground plans is covered in Chapter 4, Panel Programs and is then modified somewhat in Chapter 6, Scripted Programs. If you want to know more about the preparation required for a particular format, such as scripted dramatic programs, you can go to the chapter on that format and find information specific to it.

One thing that should be understood early on is that different markets in the United States, as well as production facilities in Canada, the United Kingdom, and other countries, have different rules and customs regarding job descriptions and working procedures. The standard operating procedure at a major network affiliate will differ from what can be expected at a local station in a smaller market. Many of the tasks will be the same—somebody has to run the audio board—but many phases of the operation are different. The network will require makeup and a makeup artist; a local station may not use any makeup at all. In the same way, the functions of the director and producer are apt to be very different in different markets. In New York, directors may not switch their own programs, but that's common practice at most stations outside of the major markets.

Even within the same market, different stations have different contracts that mandate the way one

must work. Inevitably the important things remain the same. At every station there is a meal break . . . and every station has cameras, and talent, and deadlines, and so on.

TELEVISION FORMATS

It seems to me that there are ten formats that make up the basis of television programming—although because we are *creative* interpretive artists, it's inevitable that someone will think of an eleventh soon. Perhaps reality programs might be considered a format unto itself rather than a documentary. In the meantime, these ten are a good start. Game shows aren't covered in this text, but the production of game shows calls on skills that are inherent in the other formats that this book *does* cover. Sports broadcasting is covered, in a limited way, in the chapter on Remote Broadcasting, Chapter 11.

This book begins with the simplest material and format, and then progresses to more complicated material. When I started working as a director, I was fortunate to spend a year directing a nightly news/panel show. This was the way many directors were "brought along" at the networks and stations. It made sense, because a panel show is often just two people talking to each other over a table. Dramas, too, often have two people talking to each other over a table. The instincts developed in cutting a talk show are exactly the ones to call on when directing scripted drama.

First Big Divide

Most of the material presented here is about switched or edited multiple-camera television, but in some formats single-camera techniques are essential. Where that's the case, you'll find material about single-camera production.

Second Big Divide

There are ten types of formats, but there are two basic kinds of programs. In the first, there is no script. There is no telling who will say what when, but as directors we must be prepared for anything. We become good journalists. These programs are:

1. Panel shows: *Meet the Press*, etc.
2. Demonstration programs: cooking shows, infomercials, etc.

3. Game shows: *Deal or No Deal, Jeopardy, Wheel of Fortune, Family Feud, The Price Is Right,* etc. In the UK: *1 vs. 100, Who Wants to be a Millionaire?,* etc.
4. Live transmissions: election day coverage, State of the Union addresses, etc.
5. Sports: baseball, basketball, and football games, etc.
6. Documentaries: *Scared Straight,* news, and magazine show packages, as well as single-camera "reality" programs such as *Survivor,* etc. In the UK: *Big Brother.*

In the other major category, programs are scripted or scored, such as the following:

7. News/wraparound: Everything from the morning to the late-night news and the "ins and outs" of programs like *60 Minutes* or *Today,* etc. In the UK: *The One Show, ITV This Morning,* etc.
8. Dramas (comedy and tragedy): Sitcoms such as *Glee, The Office,* and *30 Rock,* and daytime dramas such as *The Young and the Restless,* etc. In the UK: dramas may include *Doc Martin, Dr. Who,* or *The Bill;* daytime dramas may include: *EastEnders, Coronation Street,* etc.
9. Music/variety programs: *American Idol, Dancing with the Stars,* and *America's Got Talent,* etc. In the UK: *The X Factor, Britain's Got Talent,* etc.
10. Performance and Kinetic art.

Some of these formats are related. They all borrow techniques and skills from one another, so it's common to see music video techniques in dramas and documentary techniques in the news. For example, hospital and police dramas tend to borrow from a cinema verité style that came out of documentary technique; documentaries shot for the Olympics are filled with music video imagery and editing techniques. The formats that seem naturally aligned are:

- Panel programs and demonstration programs
- Music and drama
- PSAs/commercials (which may be like a drama, a music video, or a documentary)
- News and wraparound programs and documentaries

It's important to realize that these formats are all related. The techniques for shooting two people talking over a table are the same for a two-person interview show and a restaurant scene in a daytime drama. As a director I've used the same demonstration fundamentals to show a heroine's new engagement ring in a docudrama as those used to show a Chinese *gamelan* orchestra for a documentary on music for children. Those demonstration fundamentals are seen nightly in commercials that "demonstrate" the sponsor's product. It's usually considered easier to direct programs in which you don't have a script. What the director must set up is a "foolproof" method of covering the action—no matter what happens. News programs that have scripts are subject to change—even while on the air.

The director needs to be able to switch from the techniques used with the regular news format and script to shooting without any script the moment a breaking news story occurs. Some directors are better at this than others. Scripted programs, on the other hand, require a specific plan and a specific look. The artistic demands on the director are usually greater in scripted formats, as you'll see when we examine the homework needed for these two kinds of productions.

BASICS FOR ALL FORMATS

No matter what kind of program you're working on, there are a few major considerations that are important to all formats:

- A scaled ground plan
- Cross-shooting
- The 180-degree rule
- The rule of thirds
- Conventions

For the purposes of this text, three cameras are used in almost all cases. In actual production one might find productions using only two cameras or, more likely, four or more cameras.

The Scaled Ground Plan

The ground plan of the set, or studio floor, is a kind of map. It's an aerial view of the set drawn as if the mapmaker were high above the set looking straight down on it. The plan of the set is usually drawn to quarter-inch scale in which one-quarter inch equals one foot. Other scales such as 1:50 or 1/50th are used in United Kingdom. This tool is referred to as the "floor plan," "ground plan," or "set plan." At smaller stations and at some schools it is sometimes relegated to a few minutes of discussion, but at all networks, at most top 100 stations and occasionally at even the smallest station, the ability to read and relate to this standard tool is a must. In practice, if you're working at a smaller station that uses the same news set and the same interview set for many years, there may be no occasion to read a ground plan. However, as soon as something is built, reading scale plans becomes mandatory. Quarter-inch plans are usually the scale of choice. The fact is that reading and understanding a ground plan is as important to directing as reading and understanding a map is to flying an airplane. Although it's entirely possible to fly around a home airport during the day in good weather without knowing or understanding maps or instruments, as a pilot, it is very limiting.

At some stations director/producers draw plans, and sometimes elevations, to scale. Elevations are plans in a side view. This is to inform a crew about a location or to have a construction crew build or amend a set. At networks and larger facilities, designers and art directors design sets and draw plans and elevations. In order to understand what they're telling us, we have to be able to use the tools of their trade. This means being able to read quarter-inch plans and other scale drawings. We also need to be able to draw to scale in order to make overlays to be specific about what we want.

The set designer, who designs the walls and major set pieces, and the art director and property crew, who dress the set, will want to know if we want a three-foot desk or a four-foot desk. They don't care which one we ask for; they have both. They'll deliver almost anything at the networks and at lots of smaller stations, too. The question is, what—*exactly*—do you want?

Fortunately, working with scaled plans is simple. Unfortunately, taking the first steps at doing the work yourself is often terrifying; you simply have to learn it. You only have a small piece of paper in which to represent a room or a large area somewhere, so you need to substitute inches, or millimeters, for feet or meters. Each linear foot in a room or area may be represented by one-quarter inch. If a doorway is 3 feet wide, it is represented by 3 quarter-inch units. A 12-foot wall is 12 quarter-inches, and 12 quarter-inches equals 3 inches. So a 12-foot wall is represented in a quarter-inch ground plan by a line 3 inches long. Walls, step units, and major pieces of furniture that are included in the ground plan are drawn to the same quarter-inch scale. Sometimes minor pieces, such as an important telephone or light switch, may be indicated, but most decorations, such as lamps, pictures, dishes, and so on, are not indicated on the ground plan.

If you use anything other than a scaled ground plan, such as sketches or freehand drawings, you can fool yourself into accepting solutions that look nice on paper but don't actually work when you finally arrive at the set.

Assume that you're directing a daytime drama or a sitcom, or for that matter any production with a new set. The first thing that will be delivered to your door is the script and the quarter-inch ground plan. Reading it carefully helps you to establish relationships within the room. For example, if a refrigerator is drawn so that it is one inch from the kitchen table, it means there are four feet from the refrigerator to that table. From that you can tell that an actor will need two steps to go from the refrigerator to the table. In fact, no matter what action is supposed to take place at that location, you can know what will and what won't work. A careful reading of a quarter-inch ground plan might tell you that an area of the kitchen has enough room for an actor to bring food from the refrigerator to the table with ease, but that there isn't enough room to have three cast members stand side by side.

Art supply stores, architectural supply stores, many college bookstores, and office supply stores sell quarter-inch graph paper (Figure 1.1) and templates of household furniture and other household objects, such as sinks, refrigerators, and so on (Figure 1.2).

A handy shorthand exists for indicating the basic elements of an area in a plan. The plan shows the placement and size of walls, stairs, and other architectural elements. The plan uses symbols to indicate furniture and accessories, such as chairs, couches, stoves, and sinks, as well as such significant elements as mirrors, phones, bars, and so on. Figure 1.3 shows the bare walls of a typical living room set. The part at the bottom is left open. It represents an imaginary fourth wall. This is where the cameras are, and they are shooting through that imaginary fourth wall. Since the construction crew won't make it, we don't indicate it. For that same reason cameras are not indicated on the ground plan. It's a good idea to start examining rooms and objects and trying to figure out their dimensions. You can count ceiling tiles, which are usually 12″ by 12″, or 9″ by 9″, to see how big the rooms are. Bread boxes are about 15 inches long. A man lying on the ground is 6 feet long . . . give or take 6 inches.

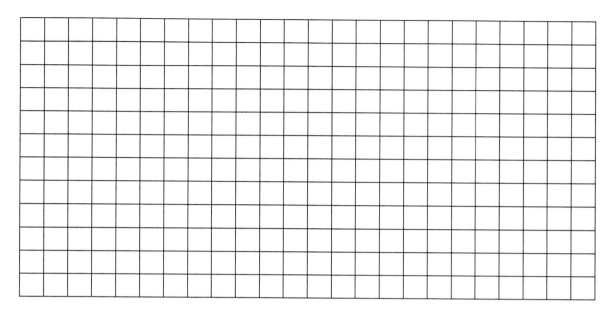

Figure 1.1   An example of quarter-inch graph paper. Each box is one-quarter inch by one-quarter inch and represents one foot in quarter-inch scale. It is noted on plans with "1/4"=1.0"."

Theatrical doors and television doors are almost always hinged upstage and open onstage. This arrangement allows the person behind the door to be seen when the door opens. If the door were hinged downstage, the audience would be unable to see who was there when the door opened. If it were hinged downstage, opening and closing the door would be awkward (Figure 1.4). *Upstage* is toward the back of the set. *Downstage* is toward the front. This comes from a theatrical tradition dating back to a time when the stage really sloped uphill toward the back. Centuries ago, part of the audience stood to watch a performance. The only way to see the performers at the back of the stage, over the heads of the performers in the front of the stage, was to build a stage with an "uphill." That tradition lives on.

A window piece, or "window flat," is often a "plain flat" that has a hole cut in it, with a window and its casement set into the hole. Where the window is set in differently, a different inset would be noted on the plan (Figure 1.5).

When drawing a table, we draw a figure with four sides. When drawing a couch or a chair, we draw three sides and leave one side open, or lighter, to indicate the direction of the couch or chair. One sits into the open side (Figures 1.6 and 1.7). While the ground plan from *The Young and the Restless* (Figure 1.8) has a great deal more detail than the plan in Figure 1.7, the similarities should make

reading both the simple plan and this more detailed work easy.

By its nature, the ground plan maps out some very specific information about the people who will inhabit the set. If it is a talk show, we know it is just that from the opening shot. If it is a living room, we get to know a lot about the people who live there just by looking at the room. Is there an armoire and a tea cart? If so, it's not likely to be a student's apartment.

In designing the set, the first consideration has to be architectural integrity. Imagine that you have before you a quarter-inch scale drawing of the bare walls of a living room. The back wall is 4 inches (16 feet), and the side walls are 3 inches (12 feet). If there is a window on each side wall, the audience may not know what's wrong, but something will nag at them. They may not stop and ask how it's possible to have windows on opposing walls, but the question is legitimate and the answer is simple: it's not possible.

Only one-room cabins or a very odd room that juts out from a building could possibly have windows on opposite walls. If you make it part of a set, the audience will probably accept it, but you're asking them to suspend their sense of reality. You're asking them to accept an anachronism. It's as out of place as an electric clock in an old-time Western or a bank calendar in King Arthur's court.

Figure 1.2 A typical quarter-inch household furniture template. This one is from Template Designs. The furniture represented in this or similar templates is readily available. Its scale is 1/4″=1.0″. Along the side of the template is a ruler marked off in quarter-inch increments.

Figure 1.3   A drawing of the bare walls of a typical living room set (not to scale).

By the same token, an 8-by-12-foot room will tell its own story. Is there only a couch and coffee table in the room? That lets the audience know that the room is incomplete. They'll want to know more about why there is so little furniture in the room. Is it a student's home that has only a few pieces of furniture because that's all the student can afford? Or is it the newly furnished home of someone who is quite wealthy? The choice of furniture may tell us the answer. That means that what you put in the room and where you choose to put it will have some bearing on the audience's understanding of the characters.

In real life, a couple goes apartment hunting. They find an apartment, which is surely architecturally correct, and they soon move in. The choices they make about how and where to decorate that apartment tell us something about who they are and what may happen in that room. Our television design must reflect those considerations.

Let's consider a panel show. Is there a desk? A couch?, A production area, and a band area? If so, we know it's not someone's living room. It's more likely a variety/panel program. Are there posters and pennants on the wall behind the desk, or is the desk backed with a drop that indicates a night urban scene? The first is probably a student production or a production aimed at a student audience. The second is probably a network program.

Custom, too, affects parts of the ground plan. One time when I was directing a daytime drama, I had to block a newly married couple into their honeymoon bed. The couple, a doctor and a nurse, had met while at work in a midsized community somewhere in the heart of America. My episode took place on the second night of their marriage in

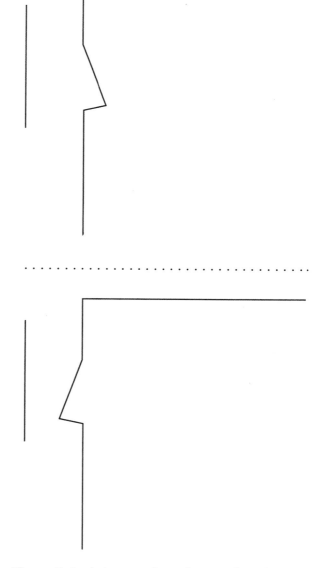

Figure 1.4   A drawing of two doors. Both are hinged upstage. The one on the top is hinged to open onto the set. The one on the bottom is hinged to open off the set (not to scale). The drawing includes a "backing flat" so the audience doesn't see backstage when the door is opened.

their new home. Another director directed the couple's first night together. He had to decide who slept on which side of the bed. I tried to call and find out what he had decided to do, but I couldn't reach him. I was in the middle of preparing my script (paper blocking) and had to direct the show the next day. I had to make a blocking decision

Figure 1.5 This drawing of a window piece indicates the casement and the amount of room it will take on both sides of the wall flat into which it is set (not to scale).

Figure 1.6 Two representations of a couch and a coffee table. The top one is a simplified version of the bottom one (not to scale).

immediately. Should the man be on the left or on the right? There was no right or wrong in this, but I was going to have a lot of last minute reblocking to do if the other director recorded the first episode with the man on the left and I chose right.

Then I remembered that there is a kind of unwritten custom in which the man sleeps closest to

the door. This is done ostensibly to protect his wife from any harm. It's an old custom—a little like the custom that says, "The gentlemanly thing to do is to walk on the side of the street closest to the gutter [so the woman doesn't get hit with garbage that is flung out of an open window]." Based on that old-fashioned principle, which was better than nothing, I made my decision. It turned out that I was right. Later, I got to ask the other director if he had made his choice based on the same custom. He had.

This is a long, but I hope interesting, way of saying that the room, as represented by the ground plan, has its own kind of life. As the director or producer, it's essential that you be in tune with what the floor plan represents. If the woman in my example had been closer to the door than the man, there are few in the audience who would call it peculiar, but it would have been an untrue moment for that rather old-fashioned couple. I think there is a limit to how many lies you can tell an audience.

Cross-Shooting

"The eyes are the mirror of the soul." We want to look into the speaker's eyes—*both* eyes. Traditionally, the cameras are set up numerically left to right. The camera on the far left is *camera 1*, *camera 2* is in the middle, and *camera 3* is on the right. Additional cameras continue be counted from left to right as much as possible. This means that the simplest configuration for shooting two people breaks down to:

Camera 1 shoots the person on the right.

Camera 2 shoots both people.

Camera 3 shoots the person on the left.

Essentially, camera 1 and camera 3 shoot across each other's line of view—in other words, they cross-shoot. Any other way yields profile shots where we do not look into the speakers' eyes (Figure 1.9).

The 180-Degree Rule

Between the two talkers there is an imaginary line called the "line of 180 degrees." The audience, which is represented by all three cameras, must be kept on one side or the other of the talent on the set. More specifically, we need to draw an imaginary line between the axis of action or interest and

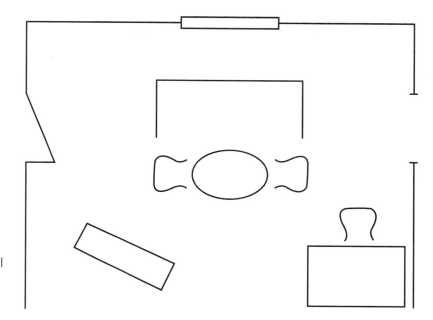

Figure 1.7 This plan indicates a living room. We'll use it later when we discuss working on drama (not to scale).

the audience, and stay on one side or the other of that axis. If you cross the line, with even one camera, you're apt to mix up the audience. We'll discuss this in more detail in Chapter 4.

Rule of Thirds

Probably the most popular "rule" about composition is called the "rule of thirds." It's used by photographers, painters, and graphic artists, as well as by television directors when their canvas or screen is in 4:3 aspect ratio. Essentially, this suggests that the page, or screen, should be divided both horizontally and vertically into thirds. This makes for nine boxes. Important elements of the composition should be placed with reference to these imaginary lines. Practically speaking, this has evolved so that when one is shooting someone looking directly at the camera, they are usually placed head-on *centered* and in the middle of the frame, with their eyes along or near the first imaginary line, as shown in Figure 1.10a. At all other times they are placed *off-center*, with their eyes along or near the same first imaginary line, as shown in Figure 1.10b.

Some Conventions

Conventions are a part of every format and are probably found in all theatrical endeavors. In Japanese Kabuki theater, there's a custom in which the property people wear black, and the audience

agrees to not see them. The prop handlers, dressed in black, come and go on stage. They change scenery. They remove and replace props—and it is as if they were never there.

Western television has customs and conventions, too. Sometimes they are invoked. Sometimes they aren't. For example, in our video shorthand, a dissolve, in which one image superimposes itself over another, means a change of place or time. Imagine a close-up of a weeping heroine. With tears streaming down her cheeks, she closes her eyes. The picture dissolves to that same heroine, but this time she's running through fields of tall grass, hand in hand with the now hospitalized hero. That dissolve told us, "At an earlier time. . . ." It's almost as if someone had said those words. The dissolve can stand for "meanwhile" or "but remember earlier" or "in another part of the world, this parallel action is taking place." Audiences have learned to accept that convention (Figure 1.11).

Within every format are specific conventions unique to that format. For example, if the same dissolve is used in a musical number, it is not taken to mean that there is a change in time or location; rather, it is simply a "soft way" of getting from one shot to another. No literal comment is being made, and custom informs us of that, too.

Inventions, Innovations, and Trends

Some inventions, innovations, and trends have affected all stages of production and are significant

Figure 1.8 This quarter-inch plan is from a production of *The Young and the Restless*. Courtesy of Columbia Pictures.

Figure 1.9 This living room ground plan is unlike "real" ground plans in that the cameras and people are included (not to scale). They have been added to this plan to indicate which camera would shoot which character. Note that the lines drawn from camera 1 and camera 3 cross; this is called *cross-shooting*.

to all formats. A brief look at some of those historically significant inventions, innovations, and trends may help us understand how we came to our current production techniques and what we might expect in the future.

The earliest documentary, for example, was simply a camera placed near railroad tracks. A train came into the picture. That was it. It was a "document" of that event. For years, the essence of documentary filmmaking consisted of placing the camera in a locked-off shot in front of whatever was happening.

Surely one of the most important advances in the history of production is the invention of the "pan head," a device that allowed the camera operator to move the camera smoothly in a horizontal plane and follow action rather than have to wait for things to happen in front of the lens. In postproduction, similar innovations were helping to change the way we would see things. Two shots were put together to help tell a story, and the idea of montage and its relevance to storytelling was born.

Technical Advances

These are some of the major advances that have shaped our concept of production:

Light, Inexpensive Gear. Unlike video cameras, film cameras tend to be heavy. Film cameras have to accommodate many moving parts. Film passes behind the lens of all motion picture systems. The camera itself has to hold the film in a light-tight case. It also has to hold the mechanism that moves the film, frame by frame, in precise alignment, at a precise and constant speed. All that tends to make for a camera heavier than the lightweight electronic-chip boards of tape or digital cameras. The film camera operator has to be able to see through a small viewfinder and make fine movements with the lens while carrying that heavy camera. Although most video cameras do attach the recording unit to the camera, the recording deck doesn't necessarily have to be attached to it. When we first walked on the moon, the receiver and tape deck were on Earth, while the camera was on the moon transmitting the

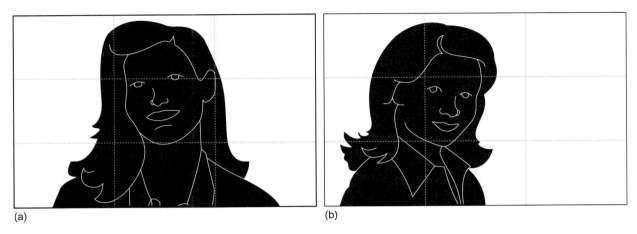

(a)   (b)

Figure 1.10 (a) The woman is framed in the center of the frame, talking directly to the camera/viewer. (b) The woman is framed off-center, talking to someone on the right. If we were shooting the person she's talking to, we'd frame her in the same relationship to the nine boxes, but she'd be framed on the right, looking left.

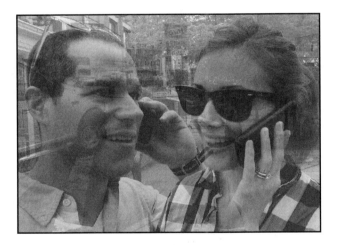

Figure 1.11 An example of a dissolve using the same shots as is used in the split screen. Notice that the backgrounds seem to bleed through.

pictures. That portability has translated into remarkable images that we now take for granted, including live pictures from the moon and from the ocean floor, from the drivers' seats of cars racing at Indianapolis, or from the helmets of people parachuting out of planes.

Film versus Tape. The advent of low-cost, easy-to-use tape changed the very nature of production. Before the arrival of tape in the late 1950s, the only way television viewers could see what was happening was either through a live feed or through film. The live feed took time to set up, was limited by access to transmission lines, and was limited further by how long on-site cable runs could be. Film, on the other hand, was not limited by transmission or cable needs, but it took time to see because it had to be processed and then edited. Editing film could become very complex, particularly if lip-syncing (in which we see lips moving and hear those words being spoken) was needed. For a while, the only way programs could be recorded was to "kinescope" them. Kinescopes were films that were taken by shooting a monitor as a program aired. The process accommodated the 525 lines needed for transmission but tended to squash the top and bottom of the picture, and they still had to be developed and handled like film. Then came tape. One could play it back immediately. At first, tape couldn't be edited, but there was no need for processing, as was the case with film. Like film, it could be bicycled around the country at a time when there were no nationwide transmission lines. Editing, however, was another matter, and for a long time editing tape was difficult. At best it was strictly linear in nature. The discussion of the role of editors in Chapter 3 outlines the history of editing. It's enough to say that various inventions and innovations made videotape editing somewhat easier to accomplish, but there were no visible frames, as was the case in films, and it was still a linear process in which it was impossible to move shots or scenes around randomly.

The Digital Revolution. One of the greatest revolutions in production stems from what has come to be known as the "digital revolution." Both audio and video were recorded as digital information, and that allowed for a much more facile manipulation of the information. The director and producer had instantaneous random access to what had been recorded, rather than linear-only access.

Tape to Hard-Drive.   The newest change is advertised as "tapeless," in which recordings are made on static digital hard drives. Apart from more convenient access, the digital hard drive also requires a lot less physical storage space, which is a tremendous advantage to major broadcasting and production facilities.

Additionally, the move to digital recording and editing has had an impact on the price of production and editing gear. As the cost decreases, there is a greater increase in the accessibility of both production gear and editing programs. With that accessibility the doors are opened to more directors and producers and to new approaches in production. Another way in which the digital revolution has had an effect stems from a 1997 FCC decision in which broadcasters were given a wide broadcast spectrum so they could transmit material digitally alongside their analog broadcasts. The benefits of transmitting digitally and in high definition include the following:

- Capability of transmitting more material on the same bandwidth
- Capability of cleaner pictures and audio
- Possibility of interactivity

At the time, the FCC also mandated a slow integration of digital broadcasting starting with the top 10 markets and moving on to the top 50 markets and finally mandating that by 2006 all broadcasting would be digital. The year 2009 became the new date for implementation of that requirement.

High Definition and 4/3 versus 16/9.   With the advent of digital television, new high-definition formats became available. With the advent of high-definition television, larger TV sets became more readily available, and they offer new aesthetic and creative opportunities. The traditional screen ratio was 4 long by 3 tall. Now the new screen ratio is 16 long by 9 tall. Directors and producers are finding that they need to produce broadcasts that can air and be appealing in both formats at the same time.

New Conventions

Currently, we see many more edits during camera movement than was once thought appropriate. There are purposeful jump cuts and shots that

Figure 1.12   An example of a typical split screen.

would have been previously thought of as "bad angles" and so on. The style seems to offer a greater urgency to the message and a new, freer way of presenting material. Perhaps it is due to the greater accessibility to editing tools and a need to break from traditional conventions. In fact, breaking from conventional editing ideas tends to create its own statement. It's as if we're saying, "Hey, we're breaking the rules. We're revolutionary. This is new! You gotta watch!"

Along the way, a new editorial language is being built. At one time, only linear editing, in which a story was laid out in chronological order, was acceptable. Then nonlinear "dynamic editing" emerged. With nonlinear editing it's much easier to tell a story by manipulating the pictures to lead the viewer to a particular point of view. The acceptance of new editing conventions makes it easy to juxtapose images, manipulate the speed of montage, and distort the sense of order to make a point. If we see a man approach a woman and a gun and then a knife, and finally a noose pop into his hand in a series of fast edits, we expect that mayhem is about to occur.

There are other conventions as well. Some wipes, for example, have conventions associated with their use. In early filmmaking, a split screen was often used to indicate simultaneous action. A halfway split screen was used to show two characters speaking to each other on the phone (Figure 1.12). Similarly, a convention was invoked to indicate a geographic direction. On a map, west is on the left and east is on the right. A plane flying from screen left to screen right meant the plane was going from west to east, which matched the convention we carried over from reading maps.

There is one final convention: Quality Control (QC). At its most basic it means that before a production is considered final there is almost always a last check to make sure that the audio and video are clean of glitches, and unexpected errors, and that the product is air-worthy or ready to be shown.

OVERALL SCOPE AND PLAN OF THE TEXT

As you read the rest of the chapters in this book, the fundamentals outlined here will remain the same. You'll need to read and write quarter-inch scale drawings. You'll need to understand about cross-shooting and the 180-degree rule. Last, you'll need to be aware that each format has specific conventions pertinent to that format alone; these specific conventions will make up at least a part of the material in each chapter.

REVIEW

- Directing is an interpretive rather than a creative art.
- High on the list of director's skills is time management. The director/producer is responsible for managing his or her own time and the crew's time both well and with respect.
- Different markets have different rules regarding procedures, but the tasks remain the same no matter where a production is mounted.
- Television productions are broken down into filmed, recorded, and live productions.
- Television productions may be broken down into either single-camera or multiple-camera productions.
- Whether single or multiple camera, all television productions can be broken down into one of two major headings:
    1. Those that occur as the production is being done, in which it is assumed that the director will have a plan for capturing the moment.
        a. Panel shows
        b. Demonstration programs: cooking shows, infomercials, and so on
        c. Game shows: *Jeopardy, Deal or No Deal,* and so on
        d. Live transmissions: elections, sports, and so on
        e. Multiple-camera documentaries and the packages in wraparound-style news magazines
    2. Those that are scripted or scored, where it is assumed the director will have a specific plan.
        a. Drama
        b. Musicals
        c. News/wraparound programs
        d. Performance art/commercials
- Significant fundamental rules relate to the following:
    1. The scaled ground plan, which is a kind of aerial map of the set or location in which small units are used to indicate larger units. In quarter-inch scale, each quarter-inch represents 1 foot.
    2. Cross-shooting in panel programs and dramas, in which the "outside," or the far left and far right, cameras shoot across each other's line of view in order to look directly into the talent's eyes. If they did not cross-shoot, they would get profile shots.
    3. The 180-degree rule, in which an imaginary horizontal line is drawn between the talent and the cameras. The talent must stay on his or her side of the line and the cameras on their side. Otherwise, participants or characters who are relating to each other appear on the screen to be facing in the same direction.
- There are many types of television conventions, which act as a kind of visual shorthand:
    1. *Upstage* refers to the part of the set that is away from the cameras, toward the back of the set, and *downstage* is toward the cameras.
    2. Dissolves that can be used to indicate a change in space or time.
    3. *Wipes* have been used to split the screen and indicate that scenes are taking place simultaneously—a split-screen phone call, for example.
    4. Black is used to signify the end of a scene.
    5. A picture of a plane flying from west to east is shown going from screen left to screen right, which mimics the layout of west and east on a map.

- Several major advances have shaped our concept of production:
  1. Light, inexpensive gear
  2. Tape over film
  3. The "digital revolution"
  4. Hard drive over tape
  5. FCC mandates for digital broadcasting
  6. High definition
  7. 16/9 versus 4/3 screen ratio
  8. Quality Control (QC)

- The following changes in style have been made:
  1. More edits during camera movement than was once thought appropriate
  2. Editing conventions:
     a. Images are juxtaposed.
     b. The speed of montage is manipulated.
     c. The sense of order is distorted to make a point.

## chapter two

The Facility

Understanding the demands of the various television formats is essential to effective television production techniques. Equally important is an understanding of the facilities and the personnel who assist in productions. No two crew members or facilities are alike. However, all formats, from panel programs to musicals, require crews and facilities. There will have to be a set, or a location, and it will have to be lit. The production will require camera operators, audio technicians, stage crew, and many of the people discussed in Who's Who, Chapter 3. Although this chapter focuses on studio production, much of the material is generic to location production (discussed in Chapter 11) as well. This chapter and Chapter 3 examine what you can expect from the most expensive top-of-the-line production center and crew complement. It would be most unusual to encounter this kind of facility and crew on a first job or at a learning facility. Furthermore, there is no single production that would require everything outlined in these chapters, nor any one facility that would offer all the gear and personnel outlined here, but some part of the material is essential to all productions. Understanding the many options available may suggest creative solutions to particular production problems.

A producer friend of mine who had just finished some preproduction work with his lawyer remarked that one of the signs of good producers is not that they know all there is to know about the legal aspects of producing, but that they know when they need a lawyer. The same is true for working in a studio and running the crew positions. You don't have to know how to run a camera, but you do need to know what the camera can do and who does it. This knowledge will contribute to a reasonable and concerned relationship between you and the crew and make for a better production.

Most directors and producers who work in network broadcasting don't know how to operate most of the gear used to produce the programs they oversee. At the unionized networks and facilities, directors and producers aren't allowed to handle any of the equipment. At most local stations, in contrast, directors and producers can, and usually do, handle the equipment. In either case, directors and producers need to know about their studios and studio operation.

Whether you're a student, a staff producer, or a freelance director/producer, you're going to have to evaluate a studio at some time in your career. Mostly the choice of studio will be based on what facilities are available or what the budget allows. A close look at the facility and the needs of your production can increase the likelihood of success by helping you tailor your needs to what the facility has to offer.

PARTS OF ANY FACILITY

To evaluate how suitable a studio is for multiple-camera television, director/producers should consider the three areas that make up every facility:

- The physical studio—where the production is shot
- The control room—where audio and video signals are channeled and where the lighting board may be housed
- The support areas—where the facility's office, storage, and preparation areas are housed

The Studio

The studio can be anything from a bare-wall studio, called a "four wall" (Figure 2.1), with no engineering or craft gear included, to a complete studio with

Figure 2.1 A bare, four-wall studio, which could be used for either single-camera production or multiple-camera production, with a remote truck serving as the control room.

everything that is required for the most elaborate production.

The Control Room

The control room at a network or university usually contains all the video and audio equipment one needs for a production, including the audio and video controls, and sometimes a lighting board (Figures 2.2, 2.3, and 2.4). It also has room for some, and sometimes *all*, of the following:

1. The producer
2. The director
3. The associate producer
4. The associate director
5. The production associates
6. The technical director
7. The video operator
8. The senior audio technician
9. The lighting director
10. The production manager
11. Network executives—professors
12. Guests, including agents, managers, publicists, media representatives, and friends and family

The control room sometimes houses the playback and record equipment. Sometimes several rooms are linked together by doors or sliding panels, and the area may then be defined as a "control area." The doors allow support personnel such as the video operator or lighting director to talk to their crews without creating a noisy central area. In some facilities,

(a)

(b)

Figure 2.2 (a) A small university control room. In the foreground are the audio board and a CD control. At the console in the background, reading from left to right, are some built-in tape decks, camera monitors, line and "on-air" monitors, camera control units, a vectorscope, and, at desk level, a small switcher. Above the switcher to the right are two digital recorders. (b) The control room of a network operation.

however, all the functions are found in the same room. The control room is not necessarily a part of all studios. Some studios are designed to be used for film or single-camera operation. When this is the case, the control room and many of the functions and areas described in the support area will probably be absent. When such a studio is used for a multiple-camera shoot, a truck is usually brought alongside the facility, and the truck's control room is used as it would be at a remote location. For example, when men landed on the moon, the camera was on the moon and the control room was in Houston, Texas.

Figure 2.3 A close-up of the switcher in the control room in Figure 2.2a. Although small, it can super, wipe, key graphics, and handle limited chroma-key productions.

The Support Area

The support area almost always consists of

1. Offices
2. Restrooms

   It usually has some kind of:

3. Dressing rooms
4. Makeup rooms
5. Scene and prop storage areas

   Sometimes the facility will contain one or more of the following areas:

6. Scene and prop construction and paint areas
7. A "green room" where the talent waits prior to appearing on stage
8. An audience area
9. Separate restrooms for the audience
10. A lobby or large audience-holding area
11. A separate area for house or audience audio and light
12. Master control for transmission of audio and video signal
13. A receiving area
14. Operations room or area for recording and playing back digital media and tapes
15. Graphics room or area

It's important that director/producers know what facilities are needed if they are to produce the best

Figure 2.4 A larger production switcher. This switcher can perform all of the functions performed by the switcher in Figure 2.3, and can also affect, dissolve, or wipe from one level to the next. Larger switchers are capable of a greater number of effects. Some switchers are designed for editing and may be similar in appearance.

possible program. The script or format determines what's needed, but the available facility, whether available by choice or not, can have a profound influence on the look of the production. To understand how the facility affects production, we'll look at the studio, the support areas, and the control room in some detail, recognizing that each studio is different. Recognize, too, that the ability to make prudent compromises is an essential ingredient of good producing.

THE STUDIO

A good way to begin thinking about the studio is to envision a bare-walls studio. At some facilities producers may rent just a shell—the bare walls—and bring in a remote truck to serve as a control room. Often a facility that was originally intended to be used as a film studio is rented or converted into a multiple camera recording studio. The UCLA film school did just that when it expanded its television production facility. Because the bare walls are the beginning of the full-blown studio, it may be wise to examine the features of the studio in its simplest form. Every studio has six sides: the four walls, the ceiling, and the floor. In between the ceiling and the floor you're apt to find a grid, which is used to hang scenery, or, more often, lights. Each of these elements is significant to the production.

The Floor

Let's start with the floor. Is it level? If the production calls for smooth trucking shots, a smooth floor is a must. If you are doing nothing more than shooting products on a sweep table (which is described later), then the floor is not very important. The most common studio floors are made or covered with:

* Wood
* Linoleum
* Tile
* Poured concrete
* Carpet

Each of these has its benefits and drawbacks.

Wooden Floors

When television started, studio construction developed out of the traditions of theater and film. Both film studios and stage floors were made of wood. For that reason, many of the early studios designed or converted for television had wooden floors. Some of those studios are still being used, and new studios with wooden floors are still being built. Most of the time, new wooden-floored television studios had their start as some other kind of space, such as a schoolroom or office.

On the plus side, wood looks wonderful. Actors and dancers are particularly pleased with its feel. Because theater has a long history of using wooden floors, local theatrical supply houses usually stock specialty items that help preserve and enhance wooden floors. Relatively speaking, wooden floors are easy to repair. If sets are to be permanently set in place, stage braces can be used to save time in rigging. If a production is set in a concert hall, the floor is almost sure to be made of wood. Wood can also be a wonderful temporary surface. I have been "saved" on more than one occasion by bringing in a portable wooden floor. Once during a telethon that was being transmitted from an office with a carpeted floor, we laid sheets of four-by-eight plywood over the carpet and created an aisle on which a camera could truck. I've also used sheets of plywood to create a floor for dancers in tap-dancing programs and to create a dance area in ballet programs. I was glad to have the wooden floor because safety issues can arise when dancers are required to use a cement or concrete floor. In fact, the American Federation of Film and Television Artists (AFTRA) considers dancers working on a cement floor to be hazardous and requires hazardous pay if such a floor is used. Inevitably, dancers worked better on a wooden surface. They liked the "feel" of it, and were glad that we were sensitive to their needs. They also stayed on the wooden part of the stage, which meant they stayed within a very rigid and easily defined area of light.

However, the disadvantages of wooden floors outweigh the advantages for most in-studio productions. The cameras and cable are hard on the floor. Inadvertently, the camera equipment or sets and props cause some damage. The wood can chip and sometimes even separate, which leaves the surface rough. When cameras move, or "dolly," over the damaged floor, the picture becomes unsteady or jerky. A polished wooden floor can play havoc with the lighting. If the floor is in a facility that permits painting the floor, the chemicals in the paint may hurt the wood. Paint, screws, nails, and tape probably do the most damage to any floor surface, but they are particularly hard on wooden floors. Sometimes inexpensive gray duct tape is used in place of gaffer tape. Unlike gaffer tape, duct tape leaves glue on the floor when it's removed (Figure 2.5); the glue doesn't come off easily, and that's a good reason to ban duct tape from all studio floors. Paint can be kinder, but inevitably, after many layers of paint, chips appear. The chips get painted over, and soon the floor is filled with little mountains and valleys that make it impossible to make smooth camera trucking movements.

Figure 2.5 On the left is gaffer tape, which is strong and bears weight well. It is dull gray, so it is nonreflective, and it can be removed without leaving a residue. Duct tape, on the right, costs about a third or less, but it reflects light and often leaves a residue when removed.

Linoleum or Tile Floors

A surface made of linoleum or tiles is very smooth, but it is also susceptible to being gouged or chipped faster than either wood or concrete surfaces. Additionally, linoleum and tile may not take water-based theatrical paint very well. On the plus side, tiles are attractive and can be used in creative ways. Because they do not have to be permanently set, they can be placed in various patterns and then changed for specific uses. Many major musical productions use glossy black tile for the special black-mirror look it offers. Socks are placed over the shoes of the talent and crew during rehearsals.

One studio I worked in used chroma-key blue tiles to create virtual sets. They simply laid the tiles over a concrete floor whenever they needed to make the conversion; that way, any color, pattern, or image could be made to appear to be the flooring. On the whole, tiles can be good looking, but they are often flimsy and have relatively short lives in the studio.

Another material that is gaining popularity is called GAMFLOOR™, which is a self-adhesive thin vinyl floor covering that comes in 48-inch by 50-foot and 100-foot rolls. It comes in a variety of colors and can be painted over.

Poured Concrete Floors

Poured concrete has been popular in many newly built facilities. Concrete offers a smooth surface that can be painted and restored easily and that resists chipping and gouging. Although it's expensive to install, its upkeep is relatively simple. It shares, however, many of the problems common to wood and tile surfaces. Paint and tape on the floor create damage (although poured concrete handles paint better than either wood or tile). There are safety issues for dancers who work on concrete floors. Fastening theatrical sets to concrete floors would severely damage the floors. However, the poured concrete floor is the smoothest, takes paint the best, and lasts the longest. The smoothest and perhaps best floor is a concrete floor with a tile or composite surface. This combines the best attributes of both surfaces, although the surface will still need to be replaced after heavy use.

Carpeted Floors

Carpeted floors may be found in studios dedicated to the news or to other productions that are not apt to need smooth on-air moves. The surface looks good if shot, and it keeps the studio quiet during the on-air comings and goings of props, guests, newscasters, and various member of the crew.

No matter which studio you use, the chances are it will have a floor made of one of these surfaces. The important consideration regarding any aspect of a studio relates to the needs of your production. Invariably those needs include some aspect of the studio that you'd like to change but can't.

Walls

These are the key elements to consider in looking at the walls:

- The soundproofing and acoustics of the room
- The cyclorama, or "cyc"
- Portals—the doors and the access ports for cables and other external feeds

Soundproofing and Acoustics

The first and foremost priorities are soundproofing and acoustics. Of course, if the studio is needed simply for product shots, soundproofing isn't necessary, but if you're shooting *with* sound, you need a soundproofed studio to prevent external sounds from interfering. Beyond that, some facilities have acoustic problems that distort sounds. Given a simple project, most such problems can be overcome. If the project is more complex—for example, a music program—and you don't know the facility, an engineer ought to be brought in to make an evaluation.

The Cyclorama

If you need a cyclorama (usually referred to simply as a "cyc"), then nothing else will do. The cyc is an area that seems to blend seamless walls into a seamless floor and creates the illusion of infinity. It's often used as the backdrop for talk shows, dance shows, dream sequences, and on-camera narration. It can be made of either a soft curtain pulled taut, which is called a "soft cyc," or of hard wood or plaster, called a "hard cyc" (Figure 2.6). If the cyc is made of curtain, it is sometimes gathered in loose folds, which offers another kind of look.

On the floor of the studio, near the cyc, many studios have ground rows or coves. These curved units are one or two feet high. Lights are placed behind them to project up and onto the cyc so they "paint" the surface with light. The hope is that when properly lit, the coving will blend the floor into the cyc so no horizon line will be visible. The director must be sure that the transition from ground row to

Figure 2.6 This hard cyc is in the corner of the studio. The picture shows how it is built to merge with the floor. The curtain on the left of the picture is drawn around in front of the hard cyc to create a soft cyc.

cyc is smooth and that there is sufficient free floor area for the production. Obviously, a dance program is more likely to need a larger cyc area and ground row than a standup spokesperson in a commercial. If your project requires a specially painted cyc, you'll need to know about the house rules regarding painting and restoring the cyc and coves. It might be prudent, for example, to place a vinyl floor covering, such as the GAMFLOOR™, over the existing studio floor, paint that, and then remove it after the shoot. If the choice is to use lights to create color on the cyc, you need to make sure that there are sufficient lights and gels to "paint" the cyc and the ground row in a seamless blend. When a studio offers a combination of materials—soft cyc and hard ground row, for example—lights may be the most practical way to create a seamless blend.

Portals

Studio portals and doors are another area of studios that is worth considering. Are the "elephant doors" used for loading and unloading large enough for your set, or must sets be built in small parts off-site and then constructed on the stage? Are there enough doors to make access to the various departments easy? Are there sound-trap doors between the control room and the studio floor? Poor studio layouts can add time to a production schedule and be costly. Many studios offer other "outside" services, such as running water with a built-in kitchen set or special plumbing lines to bring in water for rain

effects and other water needs. Sometimes gas can be supplied for kitchen appliances or for fire effects. If your production needs any of these, make sure the studio has them and that the feeds are located in a part of the studio that is easily accessed. If the studio can't provide for those needs, address the problem early enough to find a way around the limitations.

The Grid

Although it's not necessary for directors and producers to know all about grid systems, they do need to know some of the basic ways in which lights are hung, focused, and controlled. They also need to know if the studio comes with a lighting package and power and, if not, how they will be supplied. Will a generator be needed, or is there some way to be billed for the electricity that's used?

In film, lights can be positioned from floor stands. In most multiple-camera television formats, that's impractical. Floor stands would get in the way of camera movement, so lights have to be hung. The relationship of the grid to the floor and to the ceiling is significant. A grid that is too low doesn't allow enough unobstructed room for the throw of the lights. Pictures may suffer because the angle and the intensity of the lights are too great. A fixed grid that is too high creates severe shadows. To avoid the shadows, separate vertical pipes are required so each instrument can be hung closer to the floor and the talent. Sometimes the grid is built very close to the ceiling, particularly in studios that are converted from other uses, such as classrooms or offices. When this is the case, the lights create excess heat at the ceiling, which can result in overheating the studio. Whatever the case, most film studios, as well as television studios, have provisions for hanging lights. There are a number of different systems that are used to hang and focus the lighting instruments. Since hanging and focusing lights takes time, a good system can be very cost-efficient. The two fundamental grid types are those that are fixed and those that move.

Fixed Grids (Dead Hung)

A fixed grid consists of a series of metal pipes suspended from the ceiling or running from the walls of the studio (Figure 2.7). The pipes that will hold the instruments remain at a specific height and are capable of bearing the weight of lighting fixtures and cables. Make sure the studio has sufficient pipes

Figure 2.7   (a) A fixed grid, with a few instruments in place. (b) A typical studio ladder on wheels used for adjusting lights hung on a fixed grid. Stepping on the first step activates a brake that locks the ladder in place. Once off the ladder, the ladder's brake can be released, and it can be repositioned.

for the production so instruments can be hung in the most efficient manner. Ladders and electric "lifts" may be required. Working with fixed grids takes more time than working with some of the other systems.

Flying Systems

A more costly, but more efficient, system for flying both lighting and stage gear is one that is movable (Figure 2.8). With this system, the pipes may be rigged on hand-operated pulleys, as they are in most older theaters, or they may be electrically run. Movable systems allow the pipes to be lowered to the floor or to a working height. Instruments are mounted at this convenient height and then plugged

Figure 2.8   A flying grid with one pipe lowered. The pipe is on an electrically operated pulley system and is rigged to stop at a working height for hanging instruments.

Figure 2.9   This green-bed system grid is part of a film studio. The catwalk surrounds the sets. Another walk is above the center of the studio.

in and hoisted to a mark above the stage floor, where they are focused.

Additional Hanging Systems

The film industry uses a system to hang lights called a "green bed" system. Essentially, this is an arrangement of wooden catwalks above the studio floor from which lights are hung (Figure 2.9). As television programs work in such facilities, many accommodations have been made. In some cases audio booms are rigged from the catwalks. Yet another system has evolved primarily for events like concerts and sporting events, such as boxing matches. In this system, modular trusses are prehung and brought into place. They are then hoisted up over the event and fine-tuned for the location.

Electric Outlets

It's important that the facility have sufficient and convenient outlets to furnish electricity to the lighting instruments. If sufficient outlets are not available, cable may have to be rented along with a kind of ultra-heavy-duty extension cord and a juncture called a gang box, or distribution panel, to fulfill the production's needs. This creates an additional cost or line item for the budget.

Circuits

Sufficient circuits, both those that can be dimmed and those that are nondimmable, are imperative. If a sufficient number of circuits are not available, unacceptable compromises may have to be made. For example, if you have only one circuit but many outlets, you have only one choice: either all the lights are on or all the lights are off. Dimmable circuits allow for lighting levels other than just on or off. Dimming the lights affects the Kelvin temperature— the "color temperature"—of the lights. As incandescent lights are dimmed, the color tends to get redder. A small amount of dimming, about 10 percent, usually doesn't seem to make much difference, but after that, the effect becomes discernible. Scenes can be white-balanced at lower light levels, however, and it's often easier to dim the lights than to scrim each instrument in a scene. Discharge lamps such as HMI (metal halide) lamps have a limited electronic dimming range—about 50 percent of intensity, or one f-stop. LED instruments bring their own set of controls, and as is the case with instruments from any facility, it's important to make sure that the production's needs and the lighting units available are appropriate.

The Ceiling

Usually directors and producers don't get involved with the ceiling or roof of the facility. Still, roofs can be significant. A tin roof on a rainy day, for example, may create audio problems. Also, some ceilings seem to retain more heat than others, which will affect both the hardware and the disposition of the crew and talent. Finally, the ductwork for air conditioning and heating can have an impact on the hanging of lighting units. Also, you must consider the heating and air conditioning. Is it sufficient for your production?

Sometimes the air flow can be too loud and needs to be muffled or deflected. The only solution may be to turn the units on and off between takes. You might also have to compromise your shooting schedule so the studio can cool off (or heat up) between takes. It's best to know about all the problems and compromises you will have to make *before* you begin. Where you have a choice, it's wise to ask the production's lighting and engineering crew to do a tech survey, evaluating the facility. Most of the time, even in the most expensive productions, choices are limited. The studio you'd like to use isn't available when you need it, it's inconvenient for your production, or there is some other factor that requires maneuvering. The question isn't whether or not you have to make compromises, but *which* compromises you have to make.

THE CONTROL ROOM

If you need a studio that has a control room and a complete studio package, you don't have to know the configuration of every item that is—or was—on the market. You do have to have some kind of idea about what you need. The answer is always to be found in an analysis of your script and, to a lesser extent, in the routine. Defining studio needs requires a knowledge of the details of your production. The routine has the broadest strokes; the script is apt to have the most detail. Most studios are at least minimally equipped, and you, or the studio, can buy, rent, or borrow specific gear.

Control rooms are often too small and frequently have minor glitches. There's no pencil sharpener, no coat rack, and sometimes no clock. The clock is almost always left out of edit bays serving clients. However, they are almost always a major part of the view in a local station or network suite. What all control rooms *do* have are two or three "boards" and audio and video monitoring systems, including the following:

- The audio console
- The video console, or switcher
- Sometimes, the camera control units

The monitors:

- TV monitors
- Audio speakers

- Various scopes or monitors that are graphic displays of signal performance
- Computer terminals

Audio Gear: Control Room

Some audio equipment is used on the studio floor, and some is used in the control room. Later in this chapter we'll examine the studio components. Control room facilities include an audio board and a public-address (PA) talk-back system linked to the studio floor, cameras, and sometimes remote sites, such as the makeup rooms, props, and so on. Audio recording and playback devices such as the following may also be present:

- A digital audio tape (DAT) deck or an audiocassette deck
- A CD player
- A turntable
- A ¼-inch tape deck
- Rarely, an old cueable broadcast cart that looks like an eight-track cartridge deck

There may also be the following:

- Cable hookup to an iPod® or similar device
- Computer-generated sound sources
- Computer editing capabilities

Additionally, various audio and video monitoring sources may be included. You can expect studio-quality speakers and, perhaps, a small and inexpensive speaker/monitor to simulate the sound as heard-at-home on a typical television set. There will be video playback devices as well.

The most important-looking piece of gear is probably the audio console (Figure 2.10). Almost all the rest of the hardware used by the audio department can be rented and installed easily. The function of the audio console or board is to gather and mix audio sources and then to feed that mix to some other destination or destinations. Here's how it works. Each source—there can be more than one at the same time, such as a microphone and a CD—is plugged into a separate channel or an audio pot, which controls the volume. The console may also allow for control of the highs, midrange, and lows of the source. Control of these properties is referred to as "EQ," which stands for equalization. The board can then output the channel or channels with or without EQ to any of a number of receivers. A

Figure 2.10 A stereo studio audio board.

receiver might be an audio or videotape, a hard drive, or even a radio station feeding a live stereo broadcast of the production. In its simplest form, the audio board takes a number of sounds from different sources, sometimes changes their sound characteristics, mixes them together, and finally records them or puts them on the air.

The director/producer's job is to determine whether the audio console and gear are adequate to the task. Sometimes you don't need a very scientific approach. If your production requires no more than an announcer and a CD, and the audio board has a lot of buttons and slides, the chances are the board will be adequate. If you have a complicated audio production that uses many sources for sound, you'll have to be explicit about your needs and ask the studio or your engineer-in-charge whether your production can work in the studio as it is. With sufficient advance notice, additional hardware can almost always be rented to augment the existing audio equipment. However, rental hardware is not always available when you need it, and the cost may need to be added to your budget.

Video Gear

The studio's video complement will include cameras, camera pedestals, and the heads on which the cameras are mounted. Video gear may also include video projection systems and character and graphic generators, and perhaps a video mixing board in the control room.

The Video Board

The function of the video board, or switcher, is to join various video sources into one picture and transmit that mix. A good example of the result of using a switcher can be seen on the nightly news. In order to have a picture of a newscaster and the graphic with the newscaster's name, you need three things: a picture of the newscaster, the video from a character generator or art card with the newscaster's name, and a device that will superimpose the graphics over the picture. That mixed picture can be sent to a live feed, as in a news broadcast, or to a videotape or hard drive. The video board performs all of these functions. When you walk into a control room, it's surely the most intimidating piece of equipment in the room—particularly if it's a big switcher. Large or small, however, it's really a simple piece of gear.

In the early days of television, the switcher was very simple. Explaining it from that simplified perspective may make the modern ones easier to understand. The basic studio had two cameras and a black generator. The director "faded up" from black to one of the cameras and then "took," or dissolved, to the other one.

Fading up from black occurs at the beginning of most programs and commercials. To "take," or "cut to," a camera means to put that camera on the air. In film terms it would be an edit. The fade-up from black is the way one gets to see the first shot of most dramatic productions. After that there's a "cut" to the next shot and succeeding shots.

When there were only two cameras in a studio, all the director could do was cut back and forth between the two cameras or dissolve between them. In a "dissolve," you see progressively more of a second picture until it takes over the frame. Sometimes, for a special effect, the switcher would be stopped midway through a dissolve to hold the two pictures on the air, in what is called a superimposition, or "super"—one image superimposed on the other. Essentially, it's what would be called a double exposure in film. It was a wonderful effect, particularly in musical numbers, and it is still used today (you can see an example of this in Figure 7.6). In those early days of television the only other technical effect was the fade to black at the end of the show—a practice still commonly in use.

One device—a little switcher—made these basic maneuvers possible. Early switchers had two sets of switches or buttons with a rheostat between them. The rheostat in the video switcher is like a fancy

Figure 2.11 The words "I guarantee it!" and the signature are keyed over the picture. If these words were a super, the letters would be more transparent, and their edges would be softer. Courtesy of The Men's Wearhouse.

light switch that gradually brings up the lights in a theater, only this switch gradually brings up a picture—usually from black. At the end of the program, the director would fade the picture ever closer and, finally, entirely to black. Today, the most sophisticated switchers do the same thing. For daytime dramas and sitcoms, that's really all that's needed, although modern switchers have many more options. In fact, today's switchers can do a lot of things that they couldn't do before.

One of the first improvements over the simple super was the "key." In a key, one source goes over another. That's almost always the way a person's name is handled when it appears in white letters in the lower third of that person's picture (Figure 2.11). Originally, a name was supered, and you could see the person's clothing through the white of the super. With a key, the letters seem to be placed on top of the person's clothing. As the switchers became more sophisticated, the white letters could be changed into any number of colors.

More sophisticated switchers allowed the director to wipe between sources and to hold a wipe midway. Holding a wipe midway created a split screen. This was a popular early convention, which was often used to show two people talking to each other on the phone as in Figure 1.12.

As switchers evolved, they offered the ability to mix many more sources in many more ways. Now video is digitized, and pictures can be made to appear to fly in from any part of the screen.

The picture can twist and fold over like a book. New switchers can zoom in and out on predetermined parts of pictures. They can highlight one part or another, and they can handle multiple sources at the same time.

Essentially, however, the switcher is used to select a particular source (a camera, for example) or sources (a camera with a super from a remote feed) from a wide variety of sources, including cameras, hard drives, videotape decks, remote feeds, graphics, and so on. It then mixes the sources into one picture and sends the mix to any of a number of different receivers, including "on the air," hard drive, videotape, or remote feeds.

As a director or producer, you need to know your production requirements. If you suspect that the switcher will be inadequate, you need to develop a fallback position. Most of the time, directors and producers run into trouble by requiring more from a simple switcher than it can do. To prevent this from happening, be very specific about what you intend to do. For example, you might say, "I will need a switcher that can handle a camera on the audience, super graphics, and then dissolve underneath the graphics to another camera, and then another and another. From that we need to dissolve to a remote feed that will require a key over it." One way to become articulate about specific needs is to imagine what you want to have happen and then say every part of it out loud. If the switcher can't handle your needs, get a new switcher or change your plans. For practice, try calling every video event in a news broadcast. Turning off the sound will help.

Video

At one time video operation was a part of all production, but with the advent of digital cameras and operation, the need for constant hands-on control of the video has diminished. It is still critical in some kinds of productions— for example, outdoor sporting events where contrasts may change suddenly. Where it is still a part of the production the video operation may be located in a different part of the building from either the control room or the studio. In some operations it's totally eliminated. Video, too, has a board or switcher that is dedicated to controlling elements of the video. Here a video engineer, surrounded by a number of instruments that help evaluate various aspects of the video (Figure 2.12), manipulates the picture prior to sending it to the switcher. Essentially, the video operator

Figure 2.12   Some of the scopes used by the video engineer to determine the parameters of the video signal.

enhances the picture through the use of several controls. It's here, for example, that one increases or decreases the amount of specific color, or chroma, in the sources—camera, film, remote feed, and so on—that are being sent to the switcher. The video operator can open or close a camera's iris to increase or decrease the amount of light that hits the picture chip or tube. In part, this manipulation of the picture is done to try to match the signals from many sources. Sources may appear different for a number of reasons: One camera may be older than another, or the cameras may have different kinds of lenses, and that can affect the picture. Each camera or source will probably render even the same pictures differently, and the video operation compensates for that difference.

Before charged couple device cameras (CCD) became as prevalent as they are now, a studio's cameras were lined up on various charts prior to each day's production and were matched by hand and eye. Now much of the matching of the outputs of cameras and most sources is done through digital technology. Usually, the intent of the manipulations is to be sure that the viewer is unaware of the differences between sources so a cut from camera to camera as well as to playback yields consistent picture quality.

Sometimes, however, the video operator is called on to do just the opposite and is instead responsible for distorting the picture in a way that enhances an effect. Once during a commercial I directed, we changed all the reds of a particular shade because a woman walked through the background wearing a very bright red dress. The system was told to read that shade of red as a dark wine, and the woman remained a part of the background, which is where she was supposed to be.

THE STUDIO COMPLEMENT

A multiple-camera studio usually comes with both the electronic and the stage (or theatrical) gear needed for a shoot. The electronic gear consists of video and audio equipment, including cameras; booms; microphones; a lot of cable for audio, video, and lighting; an intercom for the control room, the floor crew, and other areas of the facility such as makeup rooms; and audio speakers to the floor. The stage equipment consists of the materials needed to support props and lights, and sometimes paint and construction.

Camera Equipment

Cameras come in a variety of sizes and styles, and all cameras consist of three parts:

1. The lens
2. The camera body, where the light coming through the lens is translated into an electronic signal
3. The viewing system

The Lens
Lenses come in a variety of styles. Wide-angle lenses can have the characteristics of fish-eye lenses or simply show a very wide angle. Telephoto lenses can be long enough to shoot a close-up of a bird in a tree or the surface of the moon. Lenses are either fixed focal lengths or zoom lenses. Each of these lenses has specific characteristics that are unique and significant to the way things are seen and recorded. However, all lenses have certain characteristics in common. They all transmit light, determine how wide or narrow a view can be seen, and change the way foregrounds and backgrounds are perceived.

Zoom Lenses. Studio television cameras are almost always mounted with zoom lenses. A zoom lens allows the camera operator to appear to get closer to or farther away from the subject without moving the camera. The zoom lens may be manipulated manually. The camera operator moves the elements by hand or they may be servo controlled. In a servo-controlled

zoom lens, the servo control serves the same function as the camera operator's hand in a manual lens. Since it responds to an electric servo mechanism that is part of the zoom housing, it usually provides a smoother move than can be done by hand.

Fixed Focal Lenses. Fixed focal lenses "see" things in one of three basic ways. Within each of the three basic ways there are a number of different focal lengths, each with a different field of view:

1. Wide angle, which sees a wide angle and might be considered peripheral vision
2. Normal angle, which sees about what the eye would see without peripheral vision
3. Telephoto, which seems to bring things that are far away closer

The Camera Body
The camera body houses the electronics, the chips, or, in older cameras, the tubes that deliver the video information.

The Viewing System
The two kinds of viewing systems are the field configuration and the studio configuration.

Field Configuration. A viewing system designed for field use has an eyepiece that requires the operator to put his or her head directly to the viewing system. It closes out any light source that might make viewing difficult. Unless the entire unit is mounted on a crane that can support the camera operator and has a pusher, an eyepiece viewfinder limits the kinds of smooth trucking moves that are possible. However, a field-configuration viewfinder affords easy moves from one position to the next and can be panned, tilted, or zoomed. This kind of system does not work very well in the studio (Figure 2.13).

Studio Configuration. In a studio configuration, a small monitor takes the place of the eyepiece. Most of the new digital cameras use this kind of viewing system for cameras that are intended for field use. When this kind of viewing system is used in the studio, the operator usually works with a camera mounted on a pedestal or crane. The operator is required to be able to make smooth moves on the air that would be impossible if the operator's eye had to remain fixed to a viewfinder, so a monitor is used for viewing and is integral to the camera (Figure 2.14).

Figure 2.13   A Sony camcorder suitable for field work.

Figure 2.15   The simplest kind of wheeled production rig.

Figure 2.14   A Sony high-definition studio camera mounted on a Vinten pedestal and head.

Camera Mounts

Camera mounts are designed to hold the camera locked in one place and, when needed, to allow the camera to make steady movements. Mounts allow the camera to follow action up and down (tilt) and from side to side (pan). The three significant components of all studio camera mounts are the wheels, the body, and the head. Different mounts are designed for different kinds of cameras. Heavier cameras obviously need mounts that can handle heavier loads, while light cameras are unwieldy when mounted on large mounts. From top to bottom, the production rig's most basic setup (Figure 2.15) is:

A *camera, lens and viewfinder* sitting on top of . . .

a simple spring or friction *pan head* . . .

mounted on a *tripod* with . . .

three independent *wheels*.

The wheels and tripod are capable of moving ("trucking" or "dollying") the camera from one place to another. A tripod on wheels is not a configuration that would ordinarily be used for on-air moves. A spring-controlled head allows pans and tilts, but they are almost always jerky and uneven.

More expensive mounts have wheels that crab. A crabbed configuration allows the camera to scuttle across the studio floor like a crab on the ocean floor (Figure 2.16). This is done by having all the wheels geared to face in the same direction through a central control that is positioned by the camera operator. It allows the camera to glide in a seemingly effortless fashion in any direction. The counterweighted or hydraulic body allows the operator to move the camera up and down in place so the operator can "pedestal up" or down on the air. In this kind of configuration the head would probably be a fluid

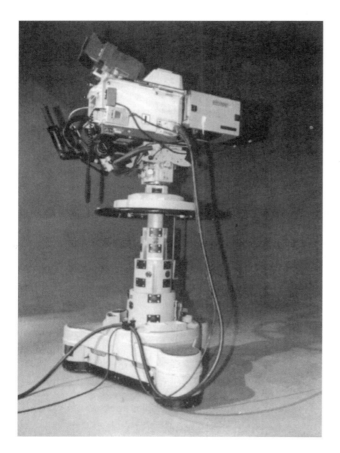

Figure 2.16 A more professional and costly pedestal and head.

Figure 2.17 A studio jib.

head, which allows for smooth pans and tilts. The entire system of counterbalances makes for graceful, effortless shots, no matter how heavy the camera may be. This kind of mount costs more than most family cars, but it does allow for very smooth moves. Where there is a great deal of movement in a set, a jib may be used.

Essentially the boom arm is a long pole with a camera on one end and a counterbalancing weight on the other. The boom is mounted on a pedestal and allows the operator to swing the camera in a wide arc, enabling high and low shots as well as sweeping lateral shots. Essential to its function is the ability to maneuver the camera from the counterbalance side of the boom. This is most often accomplished with a servo mechanism. Specific jibs are discussed in Chapters 7 and 11 (Figure 2.17).

In more and more television markets, cameras are robotic units. They do not require a dedicated camera operator, but one person can handle

anywhere from a few cameras to many. The operator is usually positioned either in the control room or someplace on or near the production floor. They have become ever more sophisticated and can get creative moving shots as well as static shots, although they are more limited than cameras operated by camera operators. The limitations are in the range of operation and in the smoothness of some moves.

Audio Equipment

Just as the control room has audio equipment specific to it, the studio itself has its own specific audio gear.

Studio audio gear consists of:

*   Microphones
*   Speaker systems
*   Cable and special gear

Microphones
Microphones are either unidirectional so they "hear" sound from only one direction, or omnidirectional so they "hear" sound from all around. Both types have advantages and disadvantages.

Omnidirectional Microphones. An omnidirectional mic "hears" sounds from all around. It might be useful in recording an orchestra from just one source. It can be effective when used by students who aren't very skilled and just want to hear what's happening on the studio floor. This kind of microphone will pick up a lot of ambient noise along with whatever is supposed to be heard, which may or may not matter. It is this kind of microphone that is built into most home video cameras.

Unidirectional Microphones.   A unidirectional mic hears sounds from a particular limited angle or area. It is usually the choice when skilled hands are doing the audio. Unidirectional microphones will reject sound that is off axis and thus will limit the amount of ambient noise that is recorded.

A third general category might be the bidirectional microphone. This type of microphone is a kind of unidirectional microphone that is limited to two "live" sides, which are usually opposite each other. Bidirectional mics were very popular in radio, allowing actors to work on both sides of the microphone while turning a deaf ear to the orchestra behind the actors. They can be used for cross-table interviews or for two-part vocal recordings.

Microphones come in a number of basic body types:

- Lavaliere mics, which are small, omnidirectional microphones, are usually pinned or clamped under or onto a guest's clothes or sometimes in the guest's hair; they are primarily used in panel programs.
- Hand or stand mics can be mounted on floor stands, desk stands, or on boom arms.
- Shotgun mics, which are always unidirectional, are usually mounted on booms and sometimes on cameras.
- Parabolic mics, which are always unidirectional, are almost always used outdoors to record sound taking place at a distance, as in sporting events, crowd scenes, and sometimes for documentaries.

Most microphones used in a studio are hard-wired. This means that a permanently attached wire goes from the microphone to a receptacle and into the audio board.

Sometimes wireless, or radio frequency (RF), mics are used. These come in a variety of shapes, although they are usually lavaliere or hand mics. These microphones use radio frequencies to transmit a signal to a receiver. The receiver's output is then wired into the audio board. Since RF mics don't have cords, they permit great freedom of movement. Singers often like to work with this kind of microphone. They may be subject to interference, however, and their battery sources can run out of

power at inopportune times if they are not carefully maintained.

The Intercom

Studio audio equipment also includes an intercom system, which facilitates communications between members of the production crew. At any moment in a production, the intercom may connect some or all of the following crew members:

1. The director
2. The members of the set, prop, and lighting crews
3. The lighting director and a separate line to that crew
4. The audio director, with a separate line to the boom operators and audio crew (this is usually a split feed that has the program feed in one ear and an audio director interrupt in the other)
5. The video operator
6. The camera operators
7. The stage manager

For news programs there might be a special intercom between the talent and the producer called an IFB, which stands for interruptible feed back.

In addition, the studio usually provides a speaker system from which the director or producer can address the studio floor from the control room. The same speakers might be used to feed audio to the floor from the audio booth. This might be useful to supply music to the floor for a dance program.

Cables and Special Gear

Studios usually have sufficient audio cable, but if an unusual number of sources are being used for a production, additional cable may be necessary. Certain audio requests will require special consideration. For example, special hookups are required to overcome electronic transmission delays when talent is situated on two different continents.

Camera operators who have to work next to loud live bands may need special headsets to block out the music so they can hear the director. Such headsets are not standard equipment, and it's the producer's or unit manager's job to know that unusual equipment must be specifically requested or supplied.

The best protection against emergencies is early and clear communication about the exact technical needs of the production. Explain precisely what you need, and you're more likely to get the right gear. Most of the time studios have a great deal more equipment on hand than any single production needs. This flexibility helps the studio serve many kinds of productions.

Telephones

Some productions use telephone communication as an integral part of their program. Special equipment allows callers to be heard in the studio by the host, talent, and studio audience, as well as by the home audience. This kind of production, referred to as "phoners," allows a wide range of guests from anywhere around the world, since all the guest needs is access to a telephone.

Stage Equipment

Stage gear includes all the hardware used for:

1. The stage itself, such as sets, dollies, rigging gear, and so on
2. Lighting, including the instruments and paraphernalia needed to hang and control the lights
3. Props, including all the hand and set props used in a production

Stage equipment also includes everything needed to maintain the basic elements of stage production. This includes not only sets but also the devices used to control set elements—things that are often taken for granted, such as:

4. Dollies to bring sets and heavy pieces on and off stage
5. Rigging gear to hold sets in place and to achieve some special effects
6. Hand and electric tools
7. Various kinds of chemicals for gluing, cleaning, and sometimes special effects
8. Marking tapes, chalk, paper towels, and other such expendables

Sometimes set construction is taken care of by the facility, although it is unusual to find that large an investment of staff, space, and materials in anything but a network, major-market station, or university facility. Most of the time, sets are constructed off premises and trucked in.

Construction

The process of having a set designed and approved is covered in Chapter 3, which discusses the various people with whom we work. For the moment, it's the construction itself that is of importance. Although the model used here is that of commercial broadcasting, the same material would be required for a university production using a theater or communication department's scene shop.

Whenever there's any kind of construction involved, off premises or on, small station or network, scheduling becomes critical. Time has to be scheduled to build and then tear down, or "strike," the set from the scene shop where it is constructed and painted. Additional time must be scheduled for shipping the pieces and assembling them on stage.

Whether on or off premises, the scene shop must have both adequate space and an assortment of tools available to build the sets. The shop needs enough space to lay out 4-foot by 8-foot sheets of 1/4-inch or 3/4-inch plywood, as well as longer pieces of wood. The shop will no doubt have a number of different kinds of saws, drills, and sanding tools, as well as a good-sized collection of small electric hand tools, from jig cutters and power screwdrivers to hand drills and sanders. It will also have a large collection of hand tools and fastening devices, from nails and bolts to staples and wire.

The director/producer doesn't need to know how to put together a set, but he or she does need to know how to read a 1/4-inch-scale plan or blueprint, as described in Chapter 1. The director/producer must learn to recognize quickly any ramifications suggested by the plan; he or she will have to deal with the set during the shooting and should be forewarned and prepared. For example, assume that a 1/4-inch ground plan shows a room that has a front door on the left wall and a back door on the right wall. If that wall measures 7½ inches in the plan, the director needs to know that the room is going to be 30 feet long. The shop will build the set just the way it's indicated in the plan. From a glance at the blueprint, the director/producer should realize that it will take a very wide shot to see both doors at the same time.

Building a new set is always challenging. The construction crew builds the basic set. The set-up crew then puts it in place on the stage floor and a paint crew stands by for touch-ups. The last step is dressing, or decoration. Every set seems to have its own special features. No one can foresee all the possibilities and challenges that will arise as the set is

Figure 2.18   This paint frame is 37 feet long by 17 feet wide. In this picture it's holding a 4-foot by 8-foot flat.

Figure 2.19   A rental exterior. Courtesy Stephen Blum, Los Angeles.

used. Invariably, you will wish you could make some small changes.

The best advice I ever had about set construction was to visit the shop while the set is still under construction to see how things look *before* the builders are absolutely finished and the set has been painted. No matter how good the plans, elevations, and sketches may be, the set always looks different as it grows in the scene shop. Sometimes things that were approved in plan look different at full scale, and it may be best to call for a change. Any changes you make once you're in the construction stage will be costly, but sometimes not making a needed change at this point can wind up costing even more.

Most scene painting is done in the shop. Touch-ups are done on the studio floor. Small theatrical "drops," such as a city scene or a garden outside a window, are usually painted at the shop or are part of the studio's stock scenery. Large painted backdrops (usually rented) need to be made on paint frames, which can be very large, as much as a few stories high; these are not usually found at studio facilities (Figure 2.18).

Before the set is brought into the studio, the floor is marked with tape to outline where it will go. Pipes are then lowered in from the grid to a tied-off height—about four feet from the floor—suitable for hanging lights (a "dead hung" pipe position). The lighting instruments are then mounted on the pipes at their approximate positions and taken up to the height at which they'll be used. The set is brought to the studio and assembled on the studio floor, and the walls are touched up. Drapery, carpets, and furniture are then brought onto the floor; some open space

must be saved for the lighting crew's ladders so the crew can focus their instruments and hang any special elements that have not been rigged. Once the lights are hung and focused, the ladders or movable scaffolding can be removed and the set dressed.

The set dressing includes both props and furniture. These major additions to the set include items such as rugs, curtains, bedding, and so forth, as well as pictures on the wall, false light switches, and other details. Prop dressing includes items that would more logically be considered hand props, such as telephones, dishes, flatware, desk items, and so on. If the show is to have any kind of ongoing life, the set and set pieces as well as hand props should be stored and secured near the studio.

Sometimes you can rent studio stock sets. In fact, there are some facilities that offer nothing but stock sets. The most commonly rented are kitchen sets, but living rooms, bathrooms, courtrooms, jails, diners, and airplane interiors are also frequently rented. Figure 2.19 is an example of a rental exterior. Figure 2.20 is an empty loft suitable for a dance studio or old-time light manufacturing location. The prudent director/producer will try to find a way to customize the stock set or location so it doesn't look familiar to the audience. This is done by painting and dressing the set in a unique way. Doing so, of course, may add cost to the rental because of the charges connected with making the change and then restoring the set to its original condition.

Figure 2.20 An empty loft. Courtesy Stephen Blum, Los Angeles.

Figure 2.22 Here, the sweep table has been raised.

Figure 2.21 A lucite sweep table in its shipping position.

Figure 2.23 A product on the sweep table. In production, the product would be lit, and since the table is made of Lucite, it might be lit from the bottom as well as the top.

Some studios specialize in the production of commercials. You could not expect to find a full range of sets at such facilities—there would be no jail or dorm room—but they are likely to have a really good, practical kitchen set. Commercial rental studios also usually offer excellent "limbo" looks. Limbo is the look of infinity that a cyc is supposed to invoke. When a cyc is lit, it gives what is usually referred to as a limbo look. If all the lights are turned off the cyc, the resulting black is sometimes still called limbo but more often "cameo" or "cameo black." Finally, commercial production houses often can supply two of the items most frequently used in

producing commercials: sweep tables and overhead light tents.

In its most common appearance, a sweep table is a long table, approximately 30 inches high by 4 feet by 8 feet on which a product is placed (Figures 2.21, 2.22, and 2.23). The table may be covered with a long roll of paper or fabric that sweeps up from the surface to the top of the camera's frame. Some sweep tables have lucite tops that can be underlit. The product will appear to be floating in a world that has no end. Cans of gasoline, boxes of toothpaste, and all manner of boxed and canned goods are photographed on sweep tables in consumer goods commercials.

A light tent is a paper or fabric tent into which a product is inserted—sometimes on a table made of frosted glass. There is a hole in the fabric through which the camera lens is inserted. The product may then be lit from all six sides. This eliminates any reflections of indications of the light source, and the product often seems to glow from within.

Lighting

In looking at a studio's lighting package, it may be best to start with the instruments themselves. There's apt to be a wide variety of instruments. While the director doesn't need to know the kinds of instruments that are available or their function, it is important to know something about the process of lighting for television. Whatever instruments are used, they have to be lamped, cabled, and fed to the dimmer panel. The dimmer panel is a kind of central clearinghouse for all the lights hung in the show. It allows the electrician to control the light sources from wherever they are plugged in. Each of the units will have to be focused. Instruments may be "ganged" or may work independently. If, for example, the illusion of a light turning on is needed, the lighting director might put two or three instruments on the same dimmer so they all turn on in unison and enhance the illusion of a single source. The light crew may also need to access lighting gear, such as:

- *Lighting stands and C stands.* These devices hold lighting instruments. Hardware—such as scrims, blacks, blackwrap, and flags (described following)—can be mounted on these stands and used to control the lights.
- *Scrims.* Scrims employ a diffusion material, usually white or opaque, made of "spun glass." At one time these were made with asbestos. Newer materials are now used, but the term persists. Scrims are used to soften the intensity of the light and are usually mounted in metal frames.
- *Nets.* A net is a diffusion material, usually black net or sometimes metal screen, used to diffuse light.
- *Blacks.* A black is a device, usually a square or oblong frame, covered with solid black cloth that is used to trim light beams. Sometimes flats made of black velvet or duvateen are used as blacks by both lighting and stage crews.
- *Blackwrap.* This is black opaque aluminum foil that is used to patch light leaks or shaped to make shadows, barn doors, and so forth.

- *Flags.* These are shorter pieces of mounted cloth or metal used to trim the edges of beams of light.
- *Reflectors.* These are devices that reflect light.
- *Barn doors.* These are metal flaps in front of instruments that look like actual barn doors and are used to trim the edges of the light beams.
- *Cookies.* Also called coo-koos, or cucaloris, these metal or wood templates are placed in front of instruments to create shadow patterns, often of clouds or leaves. The word *cucaloris* is a translation of a Greek phrase meaning "shadow play."
- *Ladders.* Ladders used in lighting are sometimes mounted on wheels.

Expendable materials used in lighting include colored gels or frost gels to "soften" the lights, electrical tape, gaffer tape, or blackwrap. Light and how it works concerns cinematographers, painters, art critics, and many of the people who work in film and television. Although the director/producer may not become personally involved in lighting a production or even a scene, he or she must know the fundamentals. The most basic lighting arrangement is called three-point lighting, and it consists of:

1. A key light, whose function is to illuminate the subject
2. A fill light, whose function is to fill in the shadows caused by the harshness of the single key light
3. A back light, whose function is to separate the subject from the back wall

Additional lights of importance are those that light the set itself.

The best advice I ever got on the subject of lighting was "Turn off all the lights, and then just turn on the lights you need."

Props

The two basic kinds of props are set props and hand props. These can be rented, bought, or made. Set props are items that dress a set, such as a jukebox, a bed, or a couch. Hand props are items that are handled by the talent, such as portfolios, guns, pens, and telephones. Props can further be categorized as those that are expendable and those that are not. Expendable props are items such as food that's eaten, cigars that are smoked, balloons that are broken, and so on. Reappearing props are items that are used frequently during a production, such as the Lone Ranger's silver bullets, a doctor's stethoscope, a police officer's badge, or, in any talk series, a color-coordinated leather portfolio that a host might use on camera to keep notes. These need to be maintained and kept in a secure area when they do not appear on camera.

Most programs have a group of set and hand props that appear on the show. It's wise to make sure that the items that are needed for your show can be stored when you're not shooting and accessed easily when you are shooting. Although major studios usually have a small selection of standard props, such as phones, desk sets, and some kitchen products, it's wise to bring your own props. Otherwise, you may find that the studio has a white touch-tone phone when your script calls for a black rotary one.

SUPPORT AREAS

The major areas that involve the director/producer are the studio floor and the control room. However, the support areas are just as important. A few other departments will need places to work, and if your production follows the usual course of events, you can expect at least a few last-minute minidisasters— and probably a major one or two. Suddenly there will be a need for three more copies of the routine. The makeup crew and the caterer (or pizza delivery) will need a place to set up. The talent will need a quiet place to go over the script. As things get more hectic, there will be a few dozen emergency calls to make. The band will have a new drummer or singer and will need a place to run through a couple of songs. When you first consider a studio, of course, the specific minor crises cannot be a part of the picture. However, a well-thought-out studio has support areas to handle all these needs.

To get an idea of a typical studio's support areas, imagine you are walking through a brand-new network facility. Clearly, not every production facility will have all the amenities outlined in the following overview of this television studio. However, many of the areas and needs will be the same—whether the studio is a major network or State University Studio One.

Entrance and Lobby

When guests arrive for a program, they need to know where to go. Sometimes they need to

meet outside of the actual studio for a while because another show is recording. Large groups of performers—bands or groups of dancers, for instance—may have to wait in some kind of holding area. That same holding area may later be used for the audience. If it's raining or particularly hot, or if instructions have to be given to a large group at the same time, it's nice to work at a facility that's set up for, or can arrange to accommodate, those large groups. Often the lobby is ideal for this, but it's important to let the studio know about these plans beforehand. If it's just a hallway outside the studio, it's wise to arrange ahead of time for chairs or benches and for someone from the program to act as a host for the program's talent. If it's office staff who will be helping out, let them know about your plans early enough so they can be prepared.

Office Space

Invariably phone calls will need to be made. While cell phones are handy, you're often forced to use studio phones for productions that take place at the studio. That's because studios may be insulated so that cell phones are out of service. You may discover that you have access to nothing more than a pay phone outside the studio; if so, you need to know that *before* you arrive . . . and bring a lot of change. Most studios have a mix of private lines, for which the production is charged, and perhaps a public pay phone or two.

Along with the phone lines, additional space will be needed to store small props, write cue cards, and discuss changes to be made in the production. A quiet area, away from the stage, is very important. The production offices, which are usually not near the studio floor, are intended for these kinds of activities.

Green Room

Directly adjacent to the stage floor, or as close as possible, is the green room (which may or may not be green). This is a holding area for talent just before they go on stage. It's where the producer, production assistant, or stage manager meets the guests and escorts them to the set. The term "green room" comes from an obscure theatrical tradition. One story is that because actors are there just before they go on stage and get attacks of stage fright or nerves, they're always a little green at the gills. This area needs to be soundproof so any talk and laughter taking place in the room can't be heard on the actual shooting stage. It should be large enough to hold all your production's guests and talent, which might include a football team, a children's choir, or the chorus from a Wagnerian opera. Sometimes green rooms are very well furnished, but at some facilities, only benches are used. The room should have a full-length mirror or two, since it's the last time the cast or guests will see themselves before going on camera. It also should have a few wastebaskets for the inevitable soggy tissues (from makeup and tears). Running water is an advantage, as is a refrigerator. Nearby vending machines become very popular if there's a large cast and a long rehearsal. Not all green rooms, however, are designed to accommodate crowds.

Dressing Rooms

Dressing rooms come in three basic varieties:

1. Chorus rooms, which are used to hold large groups of people
2. Star dressing rooms, which often have a small bathroom attached
3. Onstage quick-change dressing rooms. (This may be nothing more than a three-fold screen or a pair of two-fold stage flats shaped to form a small private room where quick changes can be made when an artist leaves the stage.)

Except for quick-change rooms, all dressing rooms should have seats, a ledge to hold makeup, and well-lit mirrors, preferably with a color temperature that's similar to that found on the stage. They also need to have an area to store clothes and personal belongings that are left in the room. Talent, guests, and contestants always appreciate a full-length mirror. A carpet is particularly welcomed by the cast so dressing, including changing shoes and socks, can be done without walking on a cold cement or tile floor.

Makeup

The makeup crew needs a place to work that has adequate seating and lighting. The makeup room ought to be close to the dressing rooms and stage. Sometimes that means accommodations for a men's chorus and sometimes for a simple two-person talk show. The needs of the program will determine what's essential. Usually, a two- or three-chair makeup room is available for major talent and an

Figure 2.24   A small, well-stocked makeup room, complete with a sink.

additional larger room for supporting cast. A large mirror facing the makeup chair or chairs allows the makeup artists to step back and see their work from a distance. The lighting for makeup chairs should be the same color temperature as is being used on the set. The makeup department also needs running water to clean sponges, brushes, and other tools and to mix some of the more exotic chemicals necessary for complex makeups. A barber's chair is a great convenience in the makeup room, although a tall director's chair is often used. Height is important; the makeup artist shouldn't have to bend over to apply the makeup. A rack to hold costumes and a full-length mirror for a last look at the total effect complete the requirements. Figure 2.24 shows a well-stocked network makeup room.

Hair

If extensive work is to be done with hair, a sink with running hot and cold water and a chair that tilts back and allows for hair washing are critical. A place to maintain wigs and hairpieces, as well as foam or wooden dummies for dressing the hairpieces, is also needed. There might be both standing hair dryers and blow-dryers.

Wardrobe

A major studio may have a special area for wardrobe in which costumes can be fitted, hemmed, seamed, stored, and pressed. It may have room for fittings, with three-way mirrors and a small stand so hems and trousers can be pinned. The room should be fitted with racks for costumes. It also should have an ironing board, an iron, and a steam iron. Presumably, the wardrobe crew will bring along their own tools and expendables, including needles, pins, assorted threads, scissors, and so on.

Schedules are required for makeup, hair, and costumes so rehearsals and tapings aren't adversely affected. The preceding categories support the personal appearance of the guests and talent, but another area of the studio support system is needed to run the stage area.

Master Control

Most facilities have an area that controls video and audio signals to air and that also houses the center's servers and perhaps some videotape decks. At television stations, both prerecorded and live programs and commercials are fed through master control. Programming that is to be broadcast is then fed to a transmission facility, from which the program is broadcast.

A video and audio library is often nearby. Program graphics, such as names of guests, show credits, and so on, may come from a character generator in the studio control room, a central area in the master control or tape room, or a separate "graphic area." More sophisticated graphics may be sent from an art department to the studio or to master control and then the studio. Almost all studios are digital now, with the exception of an analog playback machine or two.

Recording

In film, 35 mm and 16 mm formats have been the standard for many years. Digital media have taken the place of tape in almost all phases of television production. Production may be recorded on any one of a number of tape or hard-drive formats, with recognition that tapeless operation is or soon will be the norm. In the past, digital formats included Digital Betacam, DV Cam, and DVC Pro. A facility might also still have a cartridge machine that had been used for commercials or some Betacam SP, 1-inch, ¾-inch U-Matic, VHS, and SVHS machines for viewing.

Some programs record the show, or segments of the show, on both a master and a protection. Other programs record the output of each camera, called isos (as in ISOlated feeds), independently and edit the program later. Some programs record all cameras as isolated feeds and the switched feed as well.

Audiorecording may also be necessary, so the tape operation area may use a server, a DAT deck, or even a 1/4-inch or cassette deck. The audio facility will probably have a computerized suite for handling digital audio. As is the case in production, postproduction requires that if you know you're going to need a particular piece of gear, it's essential to ask about it and reserve it beforehand. The only thing for certain is that you can take almost nothing for granted.

Feeds

Outside feeds may come from a telephone line, a microwave, or a satellite. If feeds are needed, then arrangements need to be made in a timely fashion. Most of the time, the director and the producer don't get involved in how that happens but expect the engineering staff to handle that part of the broadcast requirements.

Library

The video/film and audio library used to be kept close to the control area. It was easier to get to any needed materials if they were stored nearby. Furthermore, the temperature demands for storing tape and film in a library were similar to those required for the tape operations area. Servers, on the other hand, require much less room than tape and can be accessed from anywhere on or off a facility. Nevertheless, there is still a need to maintain the old tape libraries, since archival footage is often still needed. This is particularly true for news programming, where stories may be reused. In the case of national disasters, where several days' worth of stories are created, accurate filing becomes very important. This is particularly evident when a specific element of the story is needed weeks or months later.

In the age of tapes, bar coding became a standard, and tapes were located based on the layout of the room and the shelves. With the advent of hard drives, material can easily be accessed, but locating a particular story still presents filing challenges.

Once, after returning from shooting a commercial on location, I discovered that someone at the editing facilities library had inadvertently taken recently shot material from our shoot and, although it was clearly

Figure 2.25 A videotape library with sliding shelves that holds an extensive backlog of taped materials.

labeled, was about to use it as stock for another job. At that facility it was common practice to reuse commercial stock, and they had a poor system, if any, for controlling the release of materials prior to reusing them. Needless to say, we did not work there again.

Library protection should also extend to maintaining the privacy of your material. If you're shooting Ford commercials, you probably don't want Chevrolet to have access to its competitor's newest campaign.

Last, the construction of the library or vault should afford protection in case of fire or other natural disasters. Undoubtedly, that protection comes with the understanding that there are limits to any protection. The needs of storage apply to digital media as well as to 1/4-inch audiotape, film, videotape, computer data, and occasionally slides. Figure 2.25 is an example of a well-designed tape library.

Telecine

Material that comes from a source that needs projection—films or slides—must be transferred before it can be integrated into a video program. Telecine is the area where this is done. The material is transmitted to a color-correction unit, either by direct scanning or through projection onto a cathode-ray tube, or scanned by a rotating camera, line by line. This allows for correction of the colors, hues, contrast, and luminance, and at times the framing. The output is transferred as the corrections happen. Commercial

production fine-tunes this process so each scene is analyzed and optimized, while stations tend to find a general level and use that instead.

Graphics

Electronic character generators and digital graphic devices may be used for nothing more than supering names, but they can be used for a great deal more. A character generator usually produces type and some print characters in different fonts, sizes, placement, and color, while a graphic generator is more often used to create whole frames of "art." These are usually frames scanned or imported from external sources or from computer-generated media.

Many productions require some way of letting the audience know who is speaking. Usually, white letters at the lower third of the screen indicate to the audience who is speaking, where they are, whether they are live, on location, and so on. Those words are "keyed" over the person who is speaking in type that is called "supers" (although they are really "keys," not "superimpositions"). At many stations, particularly in news operations, they are referred to as "identifiers" or "locators." They are generated from a character generator. Not all character generators are the same. Some handle type justification more easily than others. Some have a very limited number of fonts. Some older programs have a very limited number of "pages" that can be stored. It is wise to make the program's needs known early enough so a match can be made with the available equipment.

The more complicated graphic capabilities associated with state-of-the-art graphic installations are usually in the art department. These may include hardware and software from Silicon Graphics, Discrete Logic, Avid, and Quantel, with names such as "Henry," "Flame," "Deko," and "Inferno." More accessible graphics programs like Adobe Photoshop and Illustrator are also used. Although the art department is responsible for the graphics that appear on air, the same department may design program logos, stationery for the station, promotion material, and newspaper ads as well. The video graphics they prepare are a part of daily television fare, such as the still billboards for upcoming programs or promos for various commercial interests. Often segments within the news will display a story icon. A graphic representation of a fire, a child in a crib, or handcuffs, for example, is keyed or wiped in behind the newscaster. The graphic will be produced on a graphic generator fed to the studio or a frame storage device and then sent to master control or the studio.

The graphic is then integrated into the program through the technical director's switcher.

Graphics such as a panelist's digital photographs may be supplied to the facility as a file and then integrated into the program. The file can be delivered on a CD or even via e-mail. It's wise, however, to make sure that the quality of the file conforms to the station's "airworthy" requirements.

The Audience

Not all programs require an audience, but those that do will require support areas for them. The audience needs a place to gather before entering the auditorium. Audience members need restrooms that are separate from the backstage area. They need access to the auditorium in some way that doesn't bring them into contact with the cast. They need good sight lines, as does the lighting crew. The audience may also need a separate sound system to hear what's happening on stage. It's probably a good thing to provide a television monitor of the program as it's being recorded, since cameras, microphone booms, and crew members are often in the way of the audience's sight lines. You may also need "applause" signs. If you do, make sure the facility has them, or make them yourself, ahead of time.

Some facilities come with a staff of pages who take incoming phone calls on stage during rehearsals and can serve as ushers for the audience.

As the director/producer, you need to be sure that the facility can provide an adequate audience area with all the hardware needed to encourage the audience to respond in a positive manner. If not, you can lose a dramatic moment. I once directed a musical program in which the star sang a song and asked the audience to clap along while he was singing. When they didn't clap, we all knew it was because the audience sound system was so poor that they simply hadn't heard the request. We also knew that we had to make some changes in our production requirements, and we did.

Screening Rooms

Sometimes a facility will have screening rooms, which can be anything from an office or conference room to a small theater. Being able to view material in the screening room away from other distractions can be very useful, and it is surely a bonus to the director/producer. In the same vein, it is often very useful if the facility can provide a client's booth, where clients and guests can watch the program and be out of the way of a working crew.

Thus, the three areas of most significance to the director/producer are the control room, the stage, and the support area. A careful evaluation of the individual production's needs and a creative utilization of the capabilities offered by a facility can create a productive work environment and enrich the final production.

REVIEW

- The three areas that make up every facility are the physical studio, the control room, and the support areas.
- Every studio has six sides: the four walls, the floor, and the ceiling. The floor can be made of:
  1. Wood—It has a nice look and feel, but damages easily.
  2. Linoleum—It is smooth and versatile, but damages very easily.
  3. Tile—It is smooth and versatile, but damages very easily.
  4. Poured concrete—It is smooth and long-lasting, but costly and sometimes hard on performers.
  5. Carpet—It looks good and is quiet, but is difficult for camera moves.
- The key elements to consider in looking at the studio walls are:
  1. The soundproofing and acoustics of the room
  2. The cyclorama or "cyc"
  3. Portals—the doors and the access ports for cables and other external feeds
- The two fundamental grid types are fixed and flying systems.
- Control rooms have:
  1. An audio console
  2. A video console, or switcher
  3. Video, audio, and signal performance monitors, and sometimes . . .
  4. The camera control units
- Audio gear in the control room includes:
  1. An audio board
  2. Public address (PA) talkback to the studio floor, cameras, and sometimes remote sites, such as the makeup rooms, props, and so on

3. A digital audio tape (DAT) device and sometimes an audiocassette deck
4. A CD player
5. Possibly a turntable
6. Possibly a ¼-inch tape deck

- Probably also:
  7. Computer-generated sound sources
  8. Computer editing capabilities
  9. Additionally, various audio and video monitoring sources such as a turntable, an iPod port, and so on

- Video gear:
  1. A video mixing board in the control room
  2. Cameras, consisting of:
     a. The lens, usually a zoom lens
     b. The body
     c. The viewing system
  3. Camera pedestals, or jib, consisting of:
     a. The head mount
     b. The base and usually
     c. Wheels
  4. Heads on which the cameras are mounted, consisting of:
     a. A mounting plate
     b. Pan and tilt mechanism

- Video gear may also include:
  5. Video projection systems
  6. Character generator
  7. Graphic generators

- Audio gear in the studio consists of:
  1. Microphones, unidirectional and omnidirectional, and occasionally bidirectional hardwired and wireless. The basic body types are:
     a. Lavaliere
     b. Hand or stand mics
     c. Shotgun mics
     d. Parabolic mics
  2. Speaker systems
  3. Cable and special gear

- Stage gear includes all the hardware used for:
  1. The stage itself
     a. Dollies
     b. Rigging gear
     c. Hand and electric tools
     d. Chemicals for gluing, cleaning, and sometimes special effects
     e. Marking tapes and expendables
  2. Lighting
  3. Props

- Lighting gear consists of:
  1. Lighting instruments
  2. Bulbs
  3. Cable
  4. Lighting stands and C stands
  5. Scrims
  6. Nets
  7. Blacks
  8. Flags
  9. Reflectors
  10. Barn doors
  11. Cookies (also called coo-koos or cucaloris)
  12. Ladders
  13. Outlets
  14. Expendables

- The most basic lighting arrangement is called three-point lighting, which consists of a key light, a fill light, and a back light.

- The two basic kinds of props are set props and hand props.

- Three kinds of dressing rooms are:
  1. Star rooms for one or two people
  2. Chorus rooms for many people
  3. Onstage rooms for quick changes

- The support areas may include some or all of the following:
  1. Entrance and lobby
  2. Office space
  3. Green room or rooms
  4. Dressing rooms
  5. Makeup
  6. Hair
  7. Wardrobe
  8. Master control for transmission of audio and video signals
  9. Library
  10. Telecine
  11. Graphics
  12. Audience area
  13. Screening rooms

chapter three

Who's Who

This chapter covers the various jobs and personnel that are involved in the production of television programs. While it does not mention all the production jobs at every station, it probably includes a great many more kinds of jobs than are to be found at any one facility. Some of the positions, however, such as the camera operator, sound technician, director, and producer, are found at every facility.

There are differences in the level of skills needed at different levels of production, but the fundamentals remain the same. Some of the same jobs, skills, and personnel necessary for a student news production at a college facility are the same as those needed for a multimillion-dollar rock concert at a remote site. The difference lies in the level of skills required and creativity expected in executing the jobs.

In this chapter, we deal only with the people who come into direct contact with the director/producer during the working phases of preproduction, production, and postproduction. Others—those in sales, marketing, public relations, advertising, and so on—although essential in commercial television, are not covered in this book.

As a way of describing production jobs and their responsibilities, let's imagine a director/producer's final production meeting. While not all productions have such a meeting, they are common, and they are a good way to investigate who is going to do what in a production. Sometimes unusual circumstances cause job descriptions and job categories to change in midstream. For example, while I was a staff producer/director at CBS, a music reader suddenly became a conductor. That happened because one minute before going on the air—live—with a classical Christmas concert, the conductor had a heart attack, and the music reader was forced to take over. Most changes are not that dramatic. Nevertheless, there are times actors or directors are hired at the last minute and have no time to perform all the preproduction requirements. Directors then do the best they can with the situation as it is. The following is about normal circumstances.

PREPRODUCTION

By the time a project has been approved, there's a concept in place. It's going to be a musical, a sitcom, or a panel program; preproduction can now begin, and the team goes to work. Many phone calls and meetings precede a final, major production meeting. At this final meeting all involved with the production commit to what they anticipate is required from their areas and what they will deliver. Even recurring programs—such as sitcoms, daytime dramas, talk shows, and so on—have at least one such major production meeting a week. The goal is to keep up with the following week's out-of-the-ordinary demands. By the time the meeting is called, the director and producer should know almost all of the answers to the questions that will be asked by the participants. The value of the meeting is that everyone hears everyone else's plans. It's here that the lighting director may discover that he or she can't use red gels because the costumes were changed to orange at the last minute. Operations may discover that audio is planning something that contractually requires an extra crew member. These meetings are also valuable because problems may be revealed and then resolved in open discussion. It's a public forum for the production personnel regarding the specific production. Even in less rigidly organized situations—a cable program, a university or high school production—a final meeting to confirm everyone's expectations is a good idea.

The following people come to the preproduction meeting of a network program. Local programs have a shorter list, but the job functions are constant.

1. Executive in charge
2. Producer or show runner
   a. Associate producer/assistant producer
   b. Production assistant (possibly)
3. Director and his or her staff, including:
   a. Associate director (possibly)
   b. Stage manager, if the production has particularly difficult stage-managing demands—for example, a production with a large cast or unusual special effects, as in a magic show. Otherwise the stage manager would not ordinarily be brought in for the meeting.
4. Unit manager
5. Operations
6. Engineering, represented by the engineer-in-charge
7. Accounting (sometimes)
8. Set designer
9. Art director/set decorator (sometimes)
10. Lighting designer/electrician
11. Graphics (sometimes)
12. Makeup/hair (sometimes)
13. Wardrobe (sometimes)
14. Talent (sometimes)
15. Music (sometimes)
16. Special effects (sometimes)
17. Relevant guests, such as:
    a. Animal handlers
    b. Drivers
    c. Explosives experts
    d. Fan club representatives
    e. Greens people
    f. Martial arts experts
    g. Security

At a network or local station, almost all of the preceding would be working for the station. This is not the case for independent production companies. Major facilities that rent out both space and personnel may supply all the personnel or just the key personnel exclusive of the director, producer, and their staffs, and possibly some of the designers. Production costs are divided between "below-the- line" and "above-the-line" charges. These charges relate to both physical plant and hardware and personnel costs.

- *Below-the-line personnel* are those who are paid as part of the facilities budget. Their jobs are usually technical in nature. Below-the-line costs would also include the buildings, hardware, vehicles, and so forth that are part of the facility.

- *Above-the-line personnel* are those who are paid out of the production's budget; they are often thought of as being "artistic." Most often these are "freelance" employees who work on a variety of projects for different clients and producers. They are writers, actors, set designers, graphic artists, and so on. Apart from station-produced remotes, almost all of a remote crew's personnel are freelance. (Above-the-line costs would also include consultants, rentals, and any other out-of-pocket expenses.)

Following you'll find outlines of the job descriptions of everyone who is significant at the production meeting. You'll also find job descriptions of some who do not attend the meeting but are important to the production, such as executives—vice presidents, programming executives, or syndicators.

Confusion may result from the fact that while production requirements do not change, titles sometimes do from place to place, and situations invariably occur that have to be handled without regard to title. It doesn't matter, for example, whether it's the "executive producer" or the "line producer," the "show runner" or the "talent coordinator," who assumes responsibility for booking performers for a variety program, but if an act calls an hour before taping and explains that it is unable to appear, that act will have to be replaced. At that point titles do not matter. The executive producer may suggest a replacement or may leave it to the producer or to a talent coordinator, but a replacement will be needed, quickly.

The Executives

The executive is the liaison between the business end of the production and the creative end. However, executives are accountable to the organizations they represent. Although they often recognize that it's the creative side of the business that attracts viewers, they tend to operate in a way that they feel will be most advantageous to the organization. At best, there is a balance between the executive, the creative, and the production arms of the production. At the worst, the interaction is meddlesome and destructive. This part of preproduction is like any relationship. Ultimately, the goal is for the executive in charge, vice president, executive producer, show runner, station manager, syndicator, or professor to help the production so the product distinguishes the entire team. It's also important that the project make money, attract or retain viewers, or teach students.

The Executive Producer

Executive producers may have sold the program, or they may have been put in place by a network or station to oversee a particular program or series. They make the deal, set the spending parameters, and may have the final say over who is hired. They may also recommend particular facilities and personnel, and so on.

The Producer

The producers—executive producer, the series producer, line producer, or show runner—shepherd productions to completion. In some organizations the series producer handles the function of the executive producer.

Production Executive or Executive in Charge of Production

This individual has the greatest involvement with the financial state of the production. In some ways, the job requires the skills of a lawyer, accountant, or a production manager, but the scope implied by the title is greater. Executives in charge may negotiate rentals and draw up contracts. They usually have a large list of current resources, and they often offer creative solutions to production problems.

The Line Producer/Show Runner

The line producer or show runner answers to the producer, executive producer, and production executive. He or she manages the day-to-day operational problems and acts as the liaison for the executive producer. If the program is a daily program, one line producer may supervise Monday's program and then supervise it through the postproduction phase on Tuesday, while another producer takes over Tuesday's production. On a weekly program, two line producers may take turns; alternatively, one may manage all the in-studio affairs, while the other manages all the office and administrative tasks. *Show runner* is a term that is often used for sitcoms, while *line producer* is more often associated with episodic or filmed productions. However, there is no hard and fast rule for which title a program is apt to use.

The Associate Producer/Assistant Producer

In the academic community, the titles "assistant professor" and "associate professor" indicate rank.

In commercial television, the titles "associate producer" and "assistant producer" (AP) seldom do; instead, they designate different roles. The roles are determined on what seems to be a totally arbitrary basis by the producing organization.

In fact, sometimes either title is bestowed on cast members, editors, or writers—for special jobs being done or as a kind of payoff to soothe fragile egos or pad shallow resumes. More often, the AP works with the producer on specific parts of the program. The AP's job is to implement the producer's initiatives. Assistant or associate producers may be called on to make original contact calls or do the research to find particular people. They greet guests and take them to the stage manager, who in turn takes them to their assigned dressing rooms.

The room assignments are usually made in consultation with the producer or the producer's staff. That way the stage manager and the talent know one another, and the stage manager and the producers know where to expect to find the talent. In some contracts, the stage manager's "guest wrangling" function is a Directors Guild of America (DGA) requirement.

APs are often responsible for making sure contracts are completed and that the paperwork is properly filled out and filed. Additionally, they may call on contacts they have within the industry to help a particular production. Many APs in the freelance world handle only postproduction. Others specialize in keeping track of expenses, working closely with the unit production manager.

While I was at CBS, I worked on a "strip show," similar to *Oprah* or *Dr. Phil*. Essentially a strip show is a program that airs five days a week at the same time—that is, it's "stripped across the board" (from the way they appear on the program director's computer screen and schedule board at most stations). The way our show used APs is typical of this kind of program. Once a week at a concept meeting, the associate producers would pitch program ideas they thought they could produce. They explained why they thought a program was timely, whom they had contacted, and any special "perk" that might make the program interesting. Perks might include guest stars, free film footage, a performance element, or tie-ins of one sort or another. Others working on the program might be able to offer help. If the idea was accepted, the AP would be assigned a date for the program and be told to book the guests, write the questions, and present the package to the producer, who would make suggestions and offer direction. Last, the AP would present a final package to the host with the help of the producer. This included script notes, background or research notes, and particular perks for the program, among other things. On the day of the show, the AP was available to brief guests and make sure the elements of their segments or shows were ready for taping. On other days, they were busy putting together the next program or set of ideas.

On variety programs, APs may book guests (although that is more often the function of a talent coordinator), help create the routine of the show, take care of contracts, oversee certain parts of the production as assigned by the producer, back up the production assistant with notes, and assist in any other way they can—including going to the drugstore for aspirin.

The Production/Program Assistants

The two major kinds of production assistants (PAs) are "runners" and "booth PAs."

Runners

This kind of PA is usually in an entry-level position. Runners for the production are the "all other categories" of the production team. They make copies of show routines, scripts, budgets, and schedules; make coffee; and run errands for the production and sometimes for the producers. Sometimes they're called "gophers" or "gofers," as in "Go fer coffee" or "Go fer office supplies." They may do research for the production. Along the way they learn where to find essential production tools like the copier, the coffee machine, aspirin, and areas like the graphics area, editing, etc. They also learn who is responsible for different areas of the production, what they do, and how best to work with them. As they go about the business of "running" for a production, they become intimately knowledgeable about that production and the people who work on it. This may lead them to being offered the next kind of PA job.

Booth PAs

This is often the first promotion. Booth PAs log takes during taping and take edit notes. By the time a runner PA is offered this kind of responsibility, he or she usually has a clear understanding about how the particular program is put together. Booth PAs are often used at edit sessions to interpret notes. ("What did Hal mean when he said we should take

the first part of take 4 and cut back to 1? Was that camera 1 or take 1?") The parameters of the job change with the level of the production. In a network setting, many of the duties of the booth PAs are prescribed by DGA or other union mandates. A freelance syndicated program may be more demanding, pay less, and offer more opportunities for learning.

At the highest end, the booth PA acts as "script person," keeping careful notes for editing. They are counted on to be aware of minor events that can lead to great problems in editing. A typical problem would be an actor who had picked up a cup with his left hand in a wide shot. Later in the day the cup is in his right hand in a medium shot that's supposed to become the "buy" take.

A PA comes to the production meeting to take notes about the agreements made during the meeting. Additionally, the PA needs to find out about crew assignments and any other information that can be useful during the inevitable sudden emergencies that occur during all productions. PAs don't usually speak at these meetings. In fact, they soon learn that one of the things that is not welcome is another uninformed voice offering hopeful suggestions in a time of crisis.

The Director

While the producer is involved with what the program is about and who is on it, as well as how much it costs, television directors are responsible for maintaining the "look" of the show. It's only during the creation of a program, the pilot episode, that the directors input regarding "a look" may be sought. Whatever the case, network or local station, panel show or variety, directors are expected to make it look good and stay on schedule. What follows relates to the most basic requirements for any production.

Before the initial production meeting, the director will have had numerous meetings with the producer and the producer's staff regarding all the production elements of the program. The director will have covered the drafted routine of the show, the cast, the sets, and the lighting. The director also will have gone over all the preproduction plans. This usually includes the schedule for loading in, painting, lighting, and dressing the set. He or she attends the production meeting to get acquainted with those they have met only by phone to ensure that all foreseeable occurrences have been planned for and to resolve any conflicts among personnel or facilities. The director will be calling the shots when the actual production takes place.

The Production Manager

The production manager, sometimes called the unit production manager, is responsible for tracking costs and making sure vendors are paid. He or she is also responsible for updating the producer on costs and expenditures. In any production, there are real out-of-pocket costs versus book or transfer-of-fund costs. There are also projected versus actual costs, which must be kept current.

- *Below-the-line costs.* Stations have ongoing costs, such as hardware and crews. The building has a mortgage, and crews get regular salaries whether or not they work. In order to offset these costs, programs are charged fees. The program's production budget must reflect these operating costs. These below-the-line costs are sometimes called transfer or book costs; they are most significant to in-house programs, since there will be no actual transfer of money.
- *Above-the-line costs.* Producers who are renting facilities, however, must count the studio and its personnel as above-the-line costs or actual costs, because they will actually have to pay for these services. Actual costs are real costs and reflect real payments—to talent, to groups holding rights, to the studio and its personnel for their rental, and to any other group from which rented services or materials have been purchased.

The production manager, or sometimes the assistant or associate producer, must keep track of all of these costs. This is done by means of a production budget, which indicates the projected costs for each item used. As the production evolves, projected costs are compared with actual costs. The production manager may use many standard production budget templates, which, to be effective, should be very comprehensive. Movie Magic, Production Pro Budgeting, and Gorilla software offer popular film and tape budgeting programs. Excel spreadsheets are often constructed to accomplish the same tasks. The Association of Independent Commercial Producers (AICP) website also offers access to a number of vendors of scheduling and budgeting software. Many of the sites offer a trial package. Figures 3.1A and 3.1B are from Gorilla.

By the time of the production meeting, the production manager is well acquainted with the program and will have met with almost everyone else at the meeting. The production manager makes sure that no hidden costs inadvertently appear. He or she will also be responsible for making some "horse trades" in the budget so particular items can be had, ideally at the expense of others. A typical horse trade might be "I can get you the Chapman Crane for a day, but you've got to give up the fresh floral bouquet at the host's desk and use a house prop instead." It's up to the director or producer to accept or decline the trade.

Operations/Scheduling

At a network or local station, the operations department assigns the physical studio and hardware, as well as the engineering and stage crew to run it. They'll need to know the requirements of your program and will usually try to get the best studio and crew for your needs. If you are doing a simple panel program, for example, the chances are that you won't be assigned the largest sound stage or a lighting director who's best known for producing elaborate high-key gelled lighting effects. At a rental facility, the operations department is apt to supply the studio, a studio manager, and an on-site engineer who is familiar with the facility, while the production company hires the crew.

Wherever you're shooting, once you've chosen a day for the shoot, or preferably provided a choice of days, a dialogue will begin with the operations department. The operations room at many facilities looks like the Hollywood version of a war room, in which the general staff plots what to do while the planes are overhead. There are a number of different ways of handling the scheduling, and more often than not the schedulers use computer programs such as *ScheduleAll*. The programs emulate the old-fashioned white boards with markers or grease pencil boards. Facilities, studios, and edit bays are laid out on a template that overlays a calendar. It's updated as jobs and facilities are logged in—all in a variety of colors. The different colors usually correspond to stages of the job—for example, "Monday the 4th, Studio 1 on hold for Company X, second hold for Company Y. Monday the 4th to Wednesday the 6th, Studio 2 committed to Company Z."

3/23/2006

TOP SHEET

Budget for: Test	:
Budget Name: Test Budget	:
Test Project	:
	:
	:
	Subgroups displayed in this report:

Acct #	Category Title	Total
	ABOVE-THE-LINE	
101-00	STORY RIGHTS & EXPENSE	
102-00	SCENARIO	
104-00	PRODUCER	
106-00	DIRECTOR	
110-00	CAST	
111-00	EXTRAS	
	Sub Total	
	PRODUCTION	
112-00	PRODUCTION	
114-00	ART DIRECTOR	
115-00	SET CONSTRUCTION	
116-00	SET OPERATIONS	
117-00	SECOND UNIT & INSERTS	
118-00	CAMERA	
119-00	SOUND	
120-00	ELECTRICAL	
121-00	MECHANICAL EFFECTS	
122-00	DRAPERY	
123-00	SET DRESSING	
124-00	ANIMALS/ACTION DEVICES	
125-00	WOMEN'S WARDROBE	
126-00	MEN'S WARDROBE	
127-00	MAKEUP & HAIRDRESSING	
128-00	PROCESS	
131-00	PROPERTY	
140-00	PROD FILM & LAB	
141-00	STILLS	
147-00	TRANSPORTATION	
148-00	TESTS	
160-00	LOCATION EXPENSE	
170-00	MISCELLANEOUS EXPENSE	
178-00	AMORTIZATION	
179-00	RENTAL CHARGES & FEES	
	Sub Total	

Test Budget
Page 1

This report was created with Gorilla™
Licensee: Ivan Cury

Figure 3.1A A typical top page for a production budget summary. This is the "Top Sheet" to a sample program from Gorilla. It would be used to summarize the costs throughout the budget. There can be hundreds of line items to accommodate specific needs. A demo version of the program is available at their website at http://www.jungle software.com.

3/23/2006
ACCOUNT LEVEL BUDGET REPORT

Budget for: Test		:
Budget Name: Test Budget		:
		:
		:
	Subgroups displayed in this report:	

Acct #	Category	Account Title		Total
	ABOVE-THE-LINE			
101-00	STORY RIGHTS & EXPENSE			
	101-01	Story Rights		
	101-03	Royalties		
	101-05	Royalties		
	101-07	Story Abandonments		
	101-09	Abandoned Fringe		
	101-59	Amortized Series Costs		
			Sub Total	
102-00	SCENARIO			
	102-01	Writers		
	102-02	Secretaries		
	102-03	Exec. Story Consultant		
	102-08	Script Steno/Print		
	102-09	Script Photography		
	102-10	Writer's Travel		
	102-59	Amortized Series		
			Sub Total	
104-00	PRODUCER			
	104-01	Executive Producer		
	104-02	Supv. Producer		
	104-03	Associate Producer		
	104-04	Producer's Secretary		
	104-10	Producer's Travel		
	104-59	Amortized Series Costs		
			Sub Total	
106-00	DIRECTOR			
	106-01	Director		
	106-02	2nd Unit Director		
	106-03	Dialogue Director		
	106-04	Director's Secretaries		
	106-10	Director's Travel		
	106-59	Amortized Series		
			Sub Total	

Test Budget
Page 1

This report was created with Gorilla™
Licensee: Ivan Cury

Figure 3.1B This is the Account Level Budget Report from the same test budget supplied by Gorilla. This is just one of the pages in which the details get filled in. In this example the subheading for director, which is summarized in Figure 3.1A as a single "cost" 106.00, really encompasses six line items: 106.1 Director, 106.2 2nd Unit Director, 106.3 Dialogue Director, 106.4 Director's Secretaries, 106.10 Director's Travel, and 106.59 Amortized Series.

When you call Operations, they need to know:

1. The nature of the program; the format of the production.
2. What dates you have in mind and what alternatives are acceptable.
3. Which of their studios your production need to use—the large one with a hard cyc or the small insert stage that is sometimes used for news interviews.
4. How many hours your production will use the studio (including setup, production, and strike).

Then, at a local station, a network facility, or a facility that supplies crew, you will need to know:

1. THE CREW CALLS
   a. For how many hours do you require just a setup crew as opposed to a production crew?
   b. When should the paint and light crew come in? The engineers? Others?

At this point, Operations would begin to work out a plan based on your description of the production's needs. Its staff considers the studio hours you need to mount, rehearse, and shoot the production and the time it will take to strike the set and return the studio to its normal condition.

In working out a schedule, Operations is guided by the rules and conventions of the facility. Different production organizations have different requirements. While a professional, union studio works by one set of guidelines, student productions work with another. Students are constrained by school rules regarding the use of the studio, the willingness of others to help, and occasionally the availability of a pizza restaurant that's open late and delivers. Nonunion production facilities have their own sets of criteria for crews. Most of the tasks that have to be accomplished are the same everywhere. The three largest unions for television production crews that represent stagehands and engineers are:

- The International Alliance of Theatrical Stage Employees (IATSE)
- The International Brotherhood of Electrical Workers (IBEW)
- The National Association of Broadcast Employees and Technicians (NABET)

All union facilities, and many nonunion ones, maintain standards that are mandated by contract.

A simple example of these standards concerns lunches. Almost always, crew lunches can begin no sooner than two hours after the job starts and no later than six hours after the start. Second lunches must be taken no later than five hours after the completion of the first lunch. These rules are meant to ensure that management doesn't take advantage of the crew and that the crew gets a chance to get some food without being hassled. Once when I was a crew member on what turned out to be yet another all-night shoot, I came to love that rule. Later, as a director/producer, I wished for a little more flexibility.

As far as Operations is concerned, the engineering crew comes on duty after the stage crew. It can become quite a challenge to schedule lunches so a sufficient crew is available all the time. As a director/producer you become acutely aware of how time is used as you go through a 10-hour engineering day that doesn't actually give you 10 hours. Most studios (and common sense) require you to take five-minute breaks every hour. That's a total of 10 five-minute breaks a day, or 50 minutes, which leaves you 9 hours and 10 minutes in which to shoot. You lose an hour for lunch, which leaves you with 8 hours and 10 minutes to shoot. You lose at least another half-hour for Engineering check-in and setup at the beginning of the day and another half-hour after lunch, which leaves you 7 hours and 10 minutes in your 10-hour day to shoot your project. Even then, such a schedule works only if everything goes as planned. Counting the half-hour of wrap time, your actual time for directing and producing during that 10-hour day amounts to only 6 hours and 40 minutes. Obviously, even when working efficiently, it can be difficult to avoid expensive overtime.

Another rule—and one that always seems to be in transition—limits the number of jobs that any one person can do per shift. For example, the utility audio person can switch from pushing boom to sound effects during one eight-hour shift, but cannot switch to any other job or even return to the boom during that same shift. Recent contracts permit more changes as long as the change happens at a convenient time, such as during a recording stop or a lunch break. These kinds of contractual obligations are handled by the facilities operations manager, who must arrange for a studio and crew and have a firm grasp on the specific needs of each production prior to the production meeting. At the meeting, the details are agreed upon, and any potential contractual problems are addressed. These problems often come up in what appear to be simple asides such as "If you're not careful, that second lunch could get to be very expensive. You've got to take it no later than midnight and no earlier than 8:00 P.M."

Other production team members may participate by offering suggestions. They are trying to make sure that nothing has been overlooked. They might need more time for one job and less for another. For example, the set crew might ask for more time to rig some special effect, while the lighting director may explain that new blue gels will have been left in place after an earlier program, and thus, if your show can use a blue background, less time will be needed to gel the instruments.

Engineering

No matter where you work, you're likely to have an engineer who knows the facility assigned to your production: the facility's engineer in charge (EIC). Each facility has its own quirks, and the EIC can provide shortcuts, using his or her knowledge of the facility and the crew. Even if you bring your own crew, the rental facility expects you to use and pay for at least one of its personnel. This will be its in-house staff person, who knows the facility's strengths and weaknesses and the peculiarities of the facility's gear, personnel, and engineering policies.

Before the production meeting, it's usual for the director/producer and the unit manager to get together with the EIC and outline the demands of the production. The EIC wants an overview of the production in order to be able to make suggestions regarding the schedule and to have time to work out any unusual hardware needs or technical requests. Knowing the needs of the production allows the EIC to contact Operations prior to the meeting and make suggestions for crew assignments. For example, if your program requires complicated moves using a Chapman Crane or a jib crane operator, the EIC may try to get the facility's "A team," which is more proficient than the "B team."

During the production, the EIC will be the link between engineering gear, crew, and management. EICs help with last-minute requests and may be able to offer solutions to problems that arise during the production. In the event of some unavoidable engineering delay or "downtime," the EIC, along with the technical director (TD), may be called on to help arbitrate questions that arise. Downtime is any period when an unforeseen event hinders the production. Engineering downtime usually involves malfunctioning engineering equipment.

Accounting

Accountants are rarely present at production meetings unless there's some unusual aspect to the production. An example of a project that might require intense use of accounting is a phone-in response program, such as an infomercial, in which the facility's fees are based on responses to the production.

The Set Designer

The set designer is almost always present at the production meeting. Set designers usually provide the "look" of the production, although this function is sometimes performed by a set decorator or art director. At the most basic level, the set designer provides the shell into which the production is placed. One of the concerns of the set designer is the allocation of adequate time for the setup and dressing of the set. The look of the set and the time required to put it in place have an effect on others in the production team. The lighting designer, for example, needs to know where the set will be placed to make use of the cyc or perhaps instruments that are still hanging after an earlier production. Set designers also confer with other designers in the production, such as costumes and graphics, regarding color combinations and various matters of style.

Occasionally, the set designer merely takes set pieces from the facility's stock and arranges them. Even so, prior discussions are still important. It's advantageous to conduct those conversations at the facility, where you can see precisely what's available for the production. If the program is to be designed, the director/producer will already have met with the designer many times. A script or outline and sufficient time to look it over will be provided, and discussions about the style, deadlines, and cost of the project will ensue.

Some guidance regarding the feel of the project is also needed. As a neophyte director, I didn't know how to work with a designer; therefore, I virtually designed sets myself, leaving very little room for the designer to do the job. After working with a few good designers, I came to realize how important it is to leave the designing part of the project to them. Thereafter, I concentrated on describing a set's requirements in a way that helped the set designer do his or her work. Precise language is crucial to helping the designer provide the most appropriate set. I found it extremely important to define exactly what kind of program was being done, what physical needs the production had, and how the design could be placed into a larger context. For example, if I were directing and producing the pilot for a sitcom, I would have to say much more than just we need a living room and kitchen set. I would also describe how you got from the living room to the front door, how steps led to upper rooms, and how there had to be a doorway to a kitchen—which in turn needed to be practical and had to have a back door. I would describe associations the set should evoke—say, a lower-middle-class urban environment in the 1960s. I might go so far as to tell the designer that while the characters should not appear to be a "hippie family," hand-me-downs would be an easily accepted part of decoration. If possible, I would bring in pictures of similar sets or rooms. I might also bring in films, or videos or URLs of places that had a specific look that I wanted.

After some agreed-upon time, the designer presents concepts for the set. These presentations might include scale models, drawings, ground plans, and elevations (Figures 3.2 through 3.5).

Eventually, a design is accepted, and then it's sent out for bids. When the bids are in, some set adjustments are usually required in order to stay within the budget. It's important to know prices for various parts of the set so the inevitable compromises can be made. Once that's done, the designs are sent to the shop, and deadlines for the shop are established, as are any delivery requirements. The

Figure 3.2 A model of a theatrical set. Models for television sets are very similar. Courtesy of Glendale Way-Agel.

Figure 3.3 A sketch for a talk show.

Figure 3.4   This quarter-inch plan serves as a kind of aerial map of the set and therefore shows the tops and placement of major elements.

production manager or producer will be working with the facility to make sure the set can be constructed and can arrive when a crew can be scheduled to accept it and set it up.

Early in the production meeting, the quarter-inch ground plan is presented by the designer. It's drawn on a grid of the proposed studio. Elevations may also be shown, as well as a scale model or drawing of the set. The colors and color samples to be used are discussed, along with any special treatments required from lighting or costumes. The art director or set decorator may then pick up where the set designer has left off.

The Art Director/Set Decorator

At some facilities, the title of art director belongs to the person in charge of graphics rather than anyone

Figure 3.5 Some of the elevations for the set shown in Figure 3.4, showing the sides of the set.

involved with sets. At other facilities, the art director has the job of decorating the set. Sometimes set decorators work for the art director, and sometimes they work for the scene designer. The names and title are not really that important; what matters is that someone must take charge of creating the environment for the project. The set designer will design a set. The set will then be dressed with chairs and tables, light switches, telephones, and other props and accessories. Either the set designer does the whole job or somebody else comes in and does the dressing.

Usually, set decorators are also the "designers" and locators of props. In this capacity, they work with the scene designer to find whatever unique props or set pieces are needed. For example, they will find "that very special four-foot sofa" to be used in the porch scene, or they will come up with Wal-Mart's plastic glasses for the picnic scene, or, for that matter, Waterford crystal for a different kind of picnic scene. The choices set decorators make give a production its texture. The tastes and abilities of the set decorator have a great impact on the overall feel of the program. For these reasons, set decorators need the script as early as possible in the preproduction process. Like the designer, they need to confer with the director to get a sense of the production. They need to have ample time to review scripts and their notes, to create prop lists, and to make the phone calls, online enquiries, and personal sleuthing that may be necessary to locate specific items. A shooting schedule helps them plan for rental pickups and returns, which may add to cost-effectiveness.

Set decorators also work with Operations or with the facility's unit manager to make sure that deliveries can be accommodated and props can be stored properly. Usually, they make no presentation during the meeting but instead take notes and answer questions regarding their area of the production.

The Lighting Designer

Lighting designers (LDs) design and implement the lighting for the production and do the following:

1. Draw up the plans for placement of instruments
2. Specify types and wattage of the instruments
3. Indicate any special notes regarding the lights

Once the instruments are hung, the LD supervises the focusing of the lights. The head electrician oversees the following:

1. The pipe rigging
2. The hanging of the lights
3. Patches for the lights
4. Scrimming and gelling where necessary

Scrim is a material used to diffuse light. A gel is colored material placed in front of a lighting instrument to change the color of the light. Moonlight might be blue, for example, or a nightclub might have many colors for effect.

Before the preproduction meeting, the lighting designer receives a marked script and ground plan from the director. From that ground plan the LD creates a lighting plot and a course of action for the lighting crew. The ground plan is marked to indicate all the talent blocking (see Figure 6.3), and the script is marked to indicate any lighting effects that need to be prepared. This might include practical lights in a bedroom, the glow from a fireplace, lightning, or a pool's reflection. Sometimes the lighting designer will "double-hang" an area to achieve two different effects in the same place or to have a second solution in place before a potential problem arises.

At the preproduction meeting the lighting director outlines the amount of time required to light the show. The process of basic lighting, which means selecting instruments and hanging them, begins once the floor is marked, the pipes are rigged (if necessary), and the instruments are put in place. When the set is up, in place, and painted (but before it's dressed with furniture), the crew mounts ladders and aims and focuses the instruments. Some lighting jobs can be done while the set is being put up: cutting gels and putting them into gel holders or rigging the special-effect lights. Coordination of such tasks should have been worked out in phone calls prior to the production meeting but will probably be finalized at the meeting.

Optional Attendees

Others who may attend the production meeting are people involved in specialized areas. Graphics is a good example. It's unlikely that someone from the Graphics area would attend a production meeting for a daytime drama or a sitcom. That's because so few graphics are used in that kind of production. However, a Graphics staff member might attend a meeting revolving around a graphics-intensive program, such as a game show, a sports/news wrap-around program, or a commercial in which graphics were important.

Graphics

If the program requires special graphics consideration, then it's reasonable to expect the graphic designer to be present at the production meeting. On a game show or at an election special, for example, instantaneous computer graphics will probably be needed. A representative from Graphics attends the production meeting and outlines the approach to any problems and special needs he or she might have. At other times, specialists such as representatives from firms specializing in instant computer graphics might be hired and attend the meeting.

Makeup and Hair

Almost all programs require makeup. It may be an "imagined" need, but it's important nevertheless. At the most fundamental level, makeup may be no more than a powder base intended to make people look the way they would appear outside a studio with artificial television lighting. On another level, being made up is a somewhat unique and positive experience. In the makeup room the guest is a celebrity. For a panel program or any similarly uncomplicated format, the makeup and hair stylist does not need to attend a production meeting, although this might change in more elaborate productions. If extraordinary time or facilities are required, as in a production with a chorus wearing body makeup, the makeup and hair stylist should be available. It's wise to have the makeup personnel determine how much additional time they will need; their needs may affect the production's scheduling. The same is true for work with prosthetic pieces, such as false noses, scars, and so on, as well as with wigs and other hair-related items. Such work requires scheduled meetings for talent fittings and for director/producer approval.

Wardrobe

Productions with large casts or with particular wardrobe needs require special consideration. Such wardrobe needs arise in productions requiring unusual or specific costumes (such as antique or period costumes), breakaway costumes, or specially rigged costumes. As in the case of makeup and hair stylists,

these require fittings and approval. It's best to confer beforehand with either the costume designer or the wardrobe personnel to decide whether their presence at the production meeting is essential.

Talent

Usually, on-camera talent doesn't need to attend the production meeting. However, talent that brings some unique aspect to the production, such as a magic act or a tumbling or acrobatic act, might be asked to attend so everyone can verify that the facility will provide for any special needs. Ideally, the director/producer will have put the act in touch with the right people ahead of time.

Music

If the project is musical in nature—a concert, a musical commercial, or any program that requires music, either live or recorded—the music director or the road manager of a musical act such as a rock group or traveling jazz ensemble should attend the production meeting. The music director or road manager can answer questions about the placement of the musicians, the amount of time needed for orchestra setup, kinds of microphones that will be used, audience speakers, and systems of foldback. Foldback allows the musicians to hear voices over the volume of the instrument they're playing. The drummer can hear the singer, for example, over the sounds of the drum set, and so on. This is particularly necessary with musicians who do not have extensive experience working in television. I have had a difficult time convincing acts who are used to working in nightclubs that what worked there will not work in the TV studio. Specifically, they have been unwilling to reroute their audio feeds to accommodate both the clean track needed for television and the specialized audio effects that they had used for the live audience during their performances. That meant that it was impossible to get a clean audio track for a postproduction "sweetening" session. During an audio-sweetening session, which is essentially a sound-mix, various tracks can be manipulated. One voice can be emphasized over another or over a master music track. Specific instruments or tracks can be emphasized, reverb or delay can be added, and so on. This is important when an act's audio is okay for the studio audience but "muddy" and unsuitable for the small speakers used in TV sets. If the music is prerecorded and needs to be played back to the floor, questions regarding playback format can be answered. The preproduction meeting is an ideal forum to answer questions regarding postproduction sweetening sessions.

Special Effects

Special effects come in five basic forms: mechanical, electrical, chemical, optical, and digital.

- *Mechanical effects* are a part of live action and include breakaway anything: chairs, beds, cars, and so on. It includes physically creating wind, rain, fog, snow, clouds, and so forth. It also involves things like shattering glass and rigged tricks—like shoes that allow a performer to lean at 90 degrees or an apparatus for flying people in and out of a set.
- *Electrical effects* are any effects that require electricity but not matters of lighting. While directing *The Doctors*, I needed to show that a fire was starting at a circuit breaker, so Special Effects rigged a dummy circuit box that sparked on cue. Another example of electrical special effects is work with a remote electronic trigger. When the trigger is attached to a flip pad, small items (for example, a stuffed frog) can be made to jump on cue. A flash pot can achieve the visual illusion of an explosion. Audio then adds the sound.
- *Chemical effects* include fire, smoke, chemicals that change color, food illusions, and so on.
- *Optical effects*, which may be considered to be photographic effects, are special effects using mirrors, special filters, or lenses.
- *Digital effects* are effects that can be achieved digitally, usually in postproduction. Digital effects may be used to place actors, props, or sets against different backgrounds or to change or enhance video or audio.

Many other specialized effects exist as well. Weapons, fire, use of gas, rain effects, and others may require licensed personnel. These specialties raise the issue of safety on the set, as well as liability for the production company and for the facility. When these kinds of effects are needed, it's necessary to inform the facility and the production manager or engineer in charge. The special-effects specialist or department should be invited to attend the meeting and explain any relevant issues concerning the particular effect to be used. Presumably the director/producer will have spoken to the special-effects crew and will have coordinated with all the necessary departments.

Guests

Others attending the production meeting might include relevant guests, such as the following:

1. Animal handlers
2. Drivers
3. Explosive experts
4. Fan club representatives
5. Greens people
6. Martial arts experts
7. Security
8. Stunt coordinators

The production meeting is a poor time to discover major imminent production problems, particularly those that require long discussions with a particular area or that demand negotiations or calls to outside sources. Yet, all members of the production team must come out of the meeting knowing their responsibilities during the actual production. In order to make sure that happens, the director/producer must see to it that the right participants have been invited so no issues are overlooked and the important questions have been answered *before* the preproduction meeting begins. That way the meeting may serve to give all departments an overall view of the various elements of the production.

PRODUCTION

After the preproduction meeting is finished, after the set is up and lit, after the phone calls and various alarms and false alarms have been dealt with, the day finally arrives when actual production begins. A lot of new people become involved. In order to see how the director/producer interacts with them, let's imagine that we're beginning a production at a rental facility, and we'll assume it's a well-equipped local television station. The people we work with will fulfill the same jobs whether the production takes place on a college campus or at a network flagship studio.

Productions always have people who represent the following areas:

1. Reception (office staff, friends, or crew position at a school or university)

2. Studio manager (staff technician at a school or university)
3. Engineering crew (crew position at a school or university)
4. Technical director (crew position at a school or university)
5. Cameras (crew position at a school or university)
6. Video (crew or staff at a school or university)
7. Audio (crew position at a school or university)
8. Stage manager (crew position at a school or university)
9. Prop crew (crew position at a school or university—sometimes the stage manager)
10. Stage crew (crew position at a school or university—sometimes the director/producer)
11. Light crew (crew position at a school or university—sometimes the director/producer)
12. Paint crew (crew position at a school or university—sometimes the director/producer)
13. Talent, including chorus, extras, and so on
14. Graphics (crew position at a school or university)
15. Makeup/hair (crew position at a school or university—sometimes the producer/director and sometimes a friend who's good at it)

Reception

The first place where guests interact with your production is reception. This is where they find out what studio to go to or where they are held until they're called. Sometimes the reception area also serves as the conduit for phone messages. Whether you're getting help from a rental facility or from the academic staff, it's wise to give the reception area or phone page a list of the people involved in your production. Indicate who is talent and who is production staff. An alphabetical listing makes it easier for the person acting as receptionist to know what to do when people show up at the front desk and when calls come in. If there are special instructions—for example, "We're expecting a FedEx package; we need it as soon as it arrives"—you should be sure to leave a note with the receptionist or phone page. When it's time for lunch or a break, their replacements can step in and substitute without any problems. It's a good idea to let the PA know when the replacement takes over so they can confirm any special directions. Establishing a positive relationship with the staff at the reception area often leads to a positive impression with your talent and guests as they arrive.

Studio Manager

Often there's a studio manager who maintains the physical plant. At a rental facility, that may include everything from security and janitorial services to receiving and billing. At a local station or school, those tasks would be handled by someone else. At rental facilities and at stations, the studio manager represents the facility's interests should there be any damage caused by the production. The studio manager also oversees any "givens" from the facility. If, for example, the floor is to be painted by the production house, the studio manager may be the one to hire the painter and arrange for the purchase of paint and the rental of fans to help the paint dry quicker. Usually studio managers know their facilities very well, and they often have a wonderful list of sources that can be a great help to a production company. Most of the time, they can't get to production meetings because they're overseeing other productions at the time, so it's best to keep them updated on the details of your production.

Engineering Crew

The engineer in charge (EIC) is the link between management and engineering, and between engineering and the production team. EICs spell out contractual obligations and represent management's engineering interests during the production. Although they are part of the facility's staff, I've found when experiencing engineering problems that EICs try to find solutions and arbitrate questions in an honest and fair way. The technical director is the direct engineering link between the director and the crew. A typical studio engineering crew consists of the following:

1. A technical director
2. Two, three, or four camera operators (and/or robotic cameras)
3. An audio mixer

Sometimes any combination of the following is also included:

1. A program recorder/playback operator
2. One or two boom operators
3. One or two boom pushers
4. A sound effects person

5. One to four utility/cable persons
6. A crane operator
7. A crane boom person
8. A jib crane operator/cameraperson
9. A video operator

Here's what the first four of these crew members do.

Technical Director

At some stations, particularly in local markets, the director serves as the technical director (TD). In major markets this is a crew position, in which the TD is responsible for the crew. The TD oversees the technical quality of the production and maintains engineering standards. The TD sits next to the director and runs the special-effects generator or switcher. The TD routes incoming signals and takes, wipes, or dissolves feeds from cameras, graphics, playback, or remote sources. The director or associate director readies each shot or source before it is taken or put on the air, which alerts the crew to the next event. The technical director does the actual job of pressing the button that puts the source on the air or commits it to tape or disk. In many programs, TDs are also responsible for special-effects generation through their switcher. They insert keys, both black-and-white and color or chroma-key, as well as wipes, fades, and dissolves. With digital effects, this can also include positioning and flying video in and out, rotating it, and creating the myriad optical/electronic special effects we've seen in news programs and music videos. Often TDs are the ones who remind the director/producer when it's time to take a crew break. The TD may have to exercise judgment as to when a shot is ready to be put on the air. Sometimes in the heat of the moment the director will call for a shot that's not ready; the camera may be out of focus or on the wrong person, even though it is the right time to ask for the shot. The TD is wrong if he or she puts a fuzzy picture on the air, but also wrong if he or she doesn't follow the director's commands. In the largest sense, there's no right or wrong about how the TD should act at such times. Ideally, logic and sensitivity will prevail once the moment has passed. Needless to say, that's not always the case. Professionally speaking, the crew should not be asked to make such decisions. The director should ask for the shot when it's ready and should have arranged things so it *is* ready when it's needed.

Camera Operators

The camera operators focus, zoom in and out, tilt, pan, "boom" up and down, and truck their cameras. In a professional operation, under ordinary circumstances, camera operators work without assistants. In a production that uses a script or score, the camera operator works from a shot list (Figures 3.6 and 3.7), which is a list of the shots assigned to that particular camera, according to the process described in Chapter 6. The operator is expected to get and repeat the same shot through rehearsals and recording or air. Better camera operators create better shots from the terse directions they are given. They do this by shooting from high or low angles, by creating moves, and by other interpretive camera work.

Figure 3.6 Cameras mounted with holders for the shot sheets. Courtesy of the Chapman Company.

Figure 3.7 Three-by-five cards taped to the camera are simply a different way of mounting camera shot lists.

For example, if an actor is entering the room and crosses to a desk, the camera operator will be asked to "carry the cross." Some operators will simply pan the movement; others may choose to truck with the cross. The trucking move will bring the camera and pedestal from one side of the set to the other, which enhances the feeling of movement as objects in the foreground will pass in front of the lens. Both are acceptable ways of "carrying the cross," but the latter is a more exciting shot. (A wise director might ask for a truck and explain the move in the first place rather than just ask the camera operator to "carry the cross.")

In programs where there is no script or score, the camera operators are expected to understand what's needed and get shots for the director. However, each camera still needs an assignment. In a panel show or segment, the director might assign camera 1 to the host, while camera 2 gets a cover shot, and camera 3 "shops around" for whoever is talking. It's expected that camera 3 will not quickly pan to the next person to talk as soon as it happens; instead, the camera person would wait to lose the tally light and then pan. Tally lights are the red lights on top of the cameras and in the viewfinders. When a particular camera is selected by the TD at the special-effects generator, the tally light for that camera is illuminated, signaling that it is "on." At the very least, the camera operator would make an unhurried clean pan or widen out to include whoever is now talking.

Audio Mixer

The audio department is responsible for the sound. That means that its personnel select the mics to be used, unless a preference is specified by the director or producer. The audio crew is responsible for laying out the cables, dressing them so they don't become distractions, and placing microphones. When shooting a drama, the audio crew must take lighting into account before choosing the best location for the booms. Minimizing boom shadows is essential. In a drama, at least two booms are used so the actors appearing in the same scene can walk away from one another and still be "on mic." For a musical production, the audio department chooses mic stands and the kinds of mics to use for the different instruments. It also determines whether pads, which restrict the amount of sound picked up by the mics, are necessary. During the actual production, the audio mixer operates the audio console and

either mixes while the program is being recorded or aired or sends the audio signal to be recorded at an optimum level for postproduction editing and sweetening. There may be a crew working with the audio mixer to set up the program and additional audio crew members to run more complicated programs. This is particularly likely if the program involves music or sound effects.

Dramatic programs, such as daytime dramas and sitcoms, require boom operators who operate the boom microphones. The boom is a movable stand on wheels with an arm that can swing the microphone out to the actors and then manipulate the "on-axis" position of the microphone to get the best sound from the actors. Often the operator sits on the boom stand. A boom pusher is employed to adjust the placement of the boom during a scene and to push the boom from set to set.

Video Operator

The video operator is responsible for the visual quality of the pictures. In order to ensure consistency, the Society of Motion Picture and Television Engineers (SMPTE) has set standards that govern much of the look of television as we know it. Until the advent of digital medium, all productions that were recorded on tape were required to provide the following:

1. A minute for wraparound
2. At least 30 seconds for "bars and tone"—to set standards
3. Either black with original footage following or, more likely,
4. A slate—to confirm what's on the tape
5. Countdown—from "10" backward to "3" to preview video and audio for the last seconds prior to the program's actual start
6. Two seconds of black—to avoid inadvertently airing the last part of the countdown
7. Program

Once programs were recorded digitally, the requirements changed. Bars and tone were still used but not for on-air playback. Bars and tone are now used for camera and audio control.

————

Each of the bars in "bars and tone" is a different color representing the television standard for primary and secondary colors. They are fed from a color-bar generator that has been set to SMPTE standards. Cameras can then be set to the color bars by the video operator to ensure consistency of color. The tone standard—a high, somewhat piercing sound—was recorded at a zero reading on the VU meter in analog format and at −12 db in digital format. (FinalCut uses −12 db, and this has become a kind of standard. A standard of −13 db and other alternate, locally agreed-upon standards are substituted at various national and international facilities.) For editing purposes the tone is used as a guide for matching recorded levels. In a digital environment the program package is handled as if it were a text file. It's given a name, and it is assumed that by the time it's ready to be aired, the video and audio quality of the package is airworthy. There's no wraparound or countdown. Whatever video or audio corrections were needed had to have been acted upon in the recording or editing stage. Data material regarding the program that is readable from the server but not-for-air accompanies the file for most programs. This allows those playing back the production to verify the file to be aired. Nevertheless, readable program slates are often found at the beginnings of some programs so stations airing the program can verify that the program they are about to air is indeed the particular episode that is called for. During the recording, the video operator manipulates the camera controls in order to make any of a number of adjustments to the video. Ideally, all the cameras are recorded at their full potential, and all the cameras will look matched. As a director/producer, you don't need to know how to do this, but you do need to be sure that someone is monitoring quality control while the program is being recorded—usually the video operator for video and the audio engineer for audio.

Although digital monitors with plasma or LCD screens are less prone to variances than older, tubed analog monitors, the monitors in the control room are probably not totally accurate representations of the colors that are being recorded. The most accurate rendition of the pictures and the colors is usually found at the video operator's workstation. The quality of the picture is an area of production that requires a certain amount of trust because not all the monitors match. Some monitors are older than others, some have parts that have burned out faster than others, and so on.

Once when I was working on a commercial project, an advertising executive came into an adjoining editing suite. In his hand was a bottle of pink Pepto-Bismol, which he placed on top of the monitor in his editing bay. "This is what Pepto-Bismol looks like. I want this television monitor to show me this color when my product comes on the screen." The engineers arranged for that to happen, but that was the only room in the facility that showed the bottle in that particular shade of pink. Since not all monitors are matched, every other monitor in the building showed some other shade of pink. Certainly, television sets at home each had its own version of pink. You want the best-quality picture to be recorded and transmitted. The director/producer has very little choice but to trust that the video operator's monitor is a true representation of what's being recorded.

Stage Manager

Stage managers are the director's representatives on the floor. They are responsible for having the cast and crew ready when needed, and they must serve as links from the control room to the floor. The stage manager may also serve as a link with management. On large productions, the stage manager's work is often broken up, so there are a first, a second, and a third stage manager (or more). A typical example might be an awards presentation in which there is:

1. A stage manager for arrivals
2. A lead stage manager who might be responsible for stage left
3. A stage manager for stage right
4. A stage manager for the backstage dressing room and public relations area

Essentially, stage managers deal with four different groups: the production group (the director/producer and his or her staff), the stage and technical crews, the talent, and management.

1. The Production Group. Contractually, the stage manager serves the director/producer, transmitting instructions to the floor and interacting with the stage and technical crew, the talent, and management. However, the stage manager's ability to function is often dependent on those for whom he or she works, and the job can become difficult if the chain of command is broken.

For example, problems can arise when producers or clients deal directly with the talent and fail to communicate through the director and stage manager. When the talent acts on the instructions of the producers or the client, chaos can ensue. Producers and clients who create such situations are usually not aware of the ramifications of their instructions; usually they are unaware that graphics and audio, not to mention the cameras, may be committed to other tasks and need time to accommodate any new material. It's best to have a single chain of command and stick to it. The safest line for that chain is one in which the director gives commands to the stage manager and everyone else. Those commands may have come originally from the producer, the client, or someone in between, but at least the director will be in a position to anticipate anything that might require additional action.

2. The Stage, Technical, and Engineering Crews. The stage crew consists of the following stagehands and engineers:

- A *stage crew* is responsible for loading in, setting up, and running all operations and effects of the set. This crew is responsible for running the show. For example, that might mean dropping in the chandelier in *The Phantom of the Opera* or flying (or letting in) a backdrop for a tap dancer. On a revolving stage they might hand-rotate an entire stage setting, with actors or singers in place. In some organizations the setup crew might be a different crew than the running crew.
- A *paint or construction department* is responsible for keeping the set looking good and in working order. It provides such services as paint touch-up or repair to the set, including creating new material when needed, such as adding bracing to some part of the set that suddenly requires additional support.
- A *property, or "prop," department* is responsible for both set props and hand props.
- An *electrical department* is responsible for lighting and for electrical feeds to any part of the set. This includes power for everything from instruments with amplifiers to "hot" lines for practical electrical appliances and special effects.
- *Special-effects crews* work in mechanical, chemical, optical, or electrical special effects.

The engineering crew may report to the stage manager as well, although most of the time the technical director is the one who keeps in touch with members of the engineering crew. The stage manager may be called in when the crew is on a break or when guests or outside artists are working on the floor in some technical capacity—such as when musical acts use road technicians to achieve musical or digital audio effects during a performance.

3. The Talent. By Directors Guild of America (DGA) contract, the stage manager assigns makeup rooms. This is done so the talent can be located quickly. Since it's the stage manager's responsibility to make sure that the talent is alerted prior to being needed on stage, he or she must be able to contact the talent at any time should the need arise.

4. Management. A good stage manager knows the rules governing the facility's operations. As a stage manager at WNET in New York long ago, it was my job to urge guests not to continue conversations on the studio floor after the program was finished. By contract, the stagehands were not allowed to leave the facility until the floor was clear. Guests enjoying after-show chitchat could have innocently incurred thousands of dollars of overtime while the crew waited for them to finish talking. In a similar way, the stage manager may remind a visiting production crew about upcoming breaks and may help plan the best times to take them.

In any event, the stage manager must be a tactful but firm individual who's aware of what's happening in the production. Even the simplest relay of commands requires tact; a director's command to "tell that fathead to sit down" is better relayed as "Sir, would you please sit down now?"

Sometimes a stage manager's hurried note can help save a performance, as was the case when a stage manager alerted me to the fact that the artist who had just been announced and was about to start singing was drunk and had his fly undone. We shot him above the waist, and instead of looking drunk, he looked pensive and very moved by what he was singing.

Throughout the process, the stage manager needs to be attentive to the specific needs of the cast, crew, production staff, and management.

Stage Crew

The stage crew takes care of all the operational aspects of running the show. They load in and strike the set. This means they accept the set, read the plans, mark the floor—*usually* under the supervision of the scene designer—and then reconstruct it on the floor, in place. They help with any kind of minor construction corrections that have to be made. They run the set once it's up, which means taking care of any effects that are part of the set, such as opening and closing the set-piece elevator doors in an office hallway set.

Sometimes jurisdictional questions regarding effects arise. For some time while I was on staff at a local New York television station, we were unable to use a new electronic/mechanical slate because of jurisdictional issues. The question was, should the slate be considered "electric" and be run by the NABET/IBEW crew, or was it "mechanical" and therefore run by the IATSE stage crew? (We used a chalkboard slate for years.)

The crew's size is determined by either the minimum that is required for the studio or, more likely, by that moment in the production where the greatest number of stagehands are needed at the same time. Once during a beauty pageant a producer complained about the large number of stagehands he was forced to use. It was then pointed out that there was a moment in the live event where the crew had to lift a car and walk off with it during a 30-second break. Most of the crew did very little before or after that activity, but all of them were needed for that one brief moment.

Paint Crew

The paint crew is usually associated with scene construction facilities. Networks may have scenic painters/artists on staff, but most television programs don't have a permanent standby paint crew for productions. It's too expensive. When a set has just been moved from the paint shop, it's customary to have a scenic artist on call for touch-ups. That's because in moving from the scene shop to the studio floor, one can expect at least minor paint damage to the set. After that, a paint crew is occasionally brought in for touch-ups for sets that require them.

In New York and Los Angeles, I have worked with scenic artists who have been enormously skilled in painting surfaces to resemble marble, terra-cotta, and various kinds of wood. As might be expected, the very good artists are expensive and need to be booked in advance. The director/producer seldom works directly with these artists, but in the course of time, their contribution to a program is clearly perceived, and the wise director and producer keep a file of freelance artists—both those who are skilled and those who are problems.

Prop Crew

Ordinarily, the prop crew consists of a property head and a crew of as many assistants as are necessary. They maintain specific, regularly used props and a collection of generic, often-used props (such as phones and file folders), and they acquire and rig special props for each production as needed. They may also cook and prepare food used on camera, although that may mean nothing more than reheating a cafeteria meal.

Sometimes both outside and inside crews are required. The outside crew works with vendors and rental houses outside the studio, while the inside crew takes care of the running of the show. In theater companies and productions in cities, the property department usually keeps track of local antique shops, secondhand shops, and specialty shops that will rent props for theatrical, television, and film use and can help locate specific props.

In most cases, "outside packagers" have their own property chiefs who work with the studio crew. Directors and producers in an organization work with whoever is assigned. This is one of the times it's particularly useful to be on good terms with the operations personnel who assign studios and crews and to take advantage of the talents of particular crew members. The best property heads want to read the script as early as possible and then translate what they read into a list of what's needed. They also maintain a list of sources and offer helpful suggestions. Some prop crew members are experts in one field or another, and it's helpful when someone who is sensitive to your needs can come on the show.

Light Crew

The lighting designer designs the lights for the program. To do so, he or she arranges an overlay to the quarter-inch ground plan that notes:

1. The kind of instrument to be used
    a. Fresnel—the industry standard, used as a spot or flood
    b. Ellipsoidal Reflector spotlight (Liko, etc.)— a hard-edged instrument trimmed to illuminate very fine areas, used with metal cutouts (cukoloris) to create shadows; clouds and leaf patterns are typical.
    c. Scoop—a soft light for general illumination, usually to light the set

d. Softlight—a large instrument providing soft, diffused, almost shadowless light
e. LEDs multiple-source hard light. Short throws. Excellent on camera. Good for mixing color on cycs. Claimed high efficiency—no heat.
f. Fluorescent soft diffused, hard to control
2. The wattage of each instrument
3. The position of each instrument on the pipe from which it is hung
4. The direction in which the instruments are to be hung
5. The function of each instrument (sometimes omitted)

The head electric or lighting-board operator arranges the patches or plugs for the instruments.

Once the basic set is in place and the lights are hung, the lighting crew begins focusing. First, an instrument is spotted and centered on the particular portion of the set it lights. Then it's flooded to whatever degree the designer thinks is appropriate. The edges of the beam are trimmed with "barn doors"—metal attachments that cut the light off in a straight edge; lights on such areas as doors, windows, or the edges of sets can then be set to conform to the specific areas they are meant to light. The instruments may then be scrimmed with scrim material (a spun-glass type of material that softens and diffuses the lights) or metallic screens. Scrimming lowers the foot-candles of light that reach the set without reducing the color value of the light. Lights that are too bright are scrimmed so they don't create "hot spots" (unnaturally bright areas) on the talent or on set pieces. Shadow cutouts or cukolorises would be added during this phase of the lighting to create shadows, such as clouds in the distance, a leaf pattern outside a window, venetian blinds, and so on. Most of the time, the director/producer of multiple-camera television productions has very little to do with this phase of the production. In some markets, however, director/producers light their own shows.

Talent

All performers who appear on or off camera are referred to as "talent." That includes actors and actresses, singers, musicians, acrobats, stunt personnel, hosts, narrators, professors, generals, and even trained seals, to name but a few. The word is not generally used when referring to guests and contestants; they just remain "guests" and "contestants."

While they are connected to the program, they all need a place to stay when they're not being used. The stage manager has to know how to locate them. As the link between the talent and the production company, the stage manager will try to accommodate all requests that the producer may make, including those for special handling. The stage manager is required to act tactfully. However, directors and producers also have to be aware that there are times when the talents' demands exceed what a stage manager can reasonably provide.

Choruses, Extras, Family and Friends, and Animals . . .

Apart from the groups just mentioned, stage managers often must work with a variety of other people, including managers and agents. Others, who may not be aware of the demands of the studio, include the talent's family and friends, inspectors of one sort or another, as well as animal handlers and their animals (from tarantulas to elephants), members of a chorus, social and religious groups, and extras. When the director/producer knows that any of these people will be visiting, it's wise to let the stage manager know as early as possible so any special needs may be met. Everyone should realize that such groups may require more time and handling than those who are more familiar with the workings of a television production.

Graphics

Graphic artists, or "image editors," work with and create images that serve as icons or logos for programs or events. They also create the type style for supers, which adds essential information to the video. Typically, this is the type that indicates the names of talent or lets the audience know whether an event is happening live or was taped earlier. A production may require that a graphic artist or a character-generator operator be either in-studio or on call. News programs may have regular graphic artists as well as character-generator operators assigned. They may also use graphic programs built into editing packages.

As soon as possible, the graphic artist or character-generator operator needs a list of the graphics required, including the names and titles or artwork.

They input the information or artwork, a logo or icon, and check it before the program—ideally without time pressure, although that may not be possible on news broadcasts. In the case of end-credits, it's best for the producer to indicate the order in which the graphics are to appear and which ones are to appear on-screen at the same time. By contract, the director and writer get full-screen credit. Usually, the director's credit must appear as either the last title before the program or the picture begins or the first title at the end of the program or picture. Others involved in the production may share the screen, or they may be part of a roll, or crawl. The sooner that information can be made available, the easier and more accurate the job will be. Whenever possible the graphics should be checked and double-checked before they are put on the air. I was once responsible for using a lower-third super that identified Senator Jacob Javits as a Democrat from New York. In fact, he was a Republican, and I, as the director, should have caught it.

Makeup and Hair

The most usual function of makeup is to make the talent look "normal." In fact, the talent is being seen under unusual circumstances. It's far from "normal" to deal with set lights, the television process itself (two dimensions, lens distortion, etc.), and the realities of performing or being interviewed. At the least, powder removes the shine of oils on normal skin, which are unduly emphasized under bright lights and the scrutiny of close-ups.

However, makeup often exceeds what would be considered normal and actually enhances the way performers or guests look. Makeup is not plastic surgery, though. There is a limit to what can and can't be done. Some people have natural features that can be enhanced with makeup; others don't. Director/producers may wish to leave the makeup artists to their own devices, or they may have definite ideas about "the look" they are after. If so, discussion with the makeup artists and hair stylists becomes important. At the very least, the director/producer will want to know how to create a schedule so the talent will be ready on time. I used to estimate that when there were no special requirements, women needed 30 to 60 minutes for makeup and men needed 10 to 20 minutes. If special requirements existed, such as prosthetic pieces—like a false nose, scars, Mr. Spock's elongated ears—more time would probably be needed. Makeup artists and guests will vary.

Makeup is often a quiet place for the talent. The talent can't talk because moving the face might interrupt the makeup process. It can be a very stress-relieving area. There are some times, however, when the director or producer must interrupt that stillness and give simple instructions regarding the program, such as "You're on in the second half of the show. Michael, the stage manager, will escort you from the green room during a commercial break."

Many celebrities insist on bringing their own makeup artists and expect the production to pay for this. Sometimes that's a good idea, and sometimes it's not. The celebrity's personal makeup artist is apt to know how best to work with the celebrity; also, having friendly faces around makes the celebrity feel at ease and indulged. Both of these attributes may work well for the production. However, if the makeup artist is unable or unwilling to work within the production's demands, problems may ensue. The issue of which makeup artists will be used should be discussed when the talent is booked.

POSTPRODUCTION

If the production will be edited, it usually enters the postproduction stage once the bulk of the production has been shot. The director/producer becomes involved with considerations about postproduction long before the actual process begins. However, in some formats, notably commercials, the director may not be involved in the editing phase. Postproduction activities vary from format to format: dramas are handled differently from documentaries, single-camera is different from multiple-camera editing, and so forth. Those differences greatly affect the way one shoots. In shooting for the single-camera format, for example, the camera operator and director/producer allow enough head and tail at the end of each shot to create a choice of in and out points. In multiple camera production, there may be no easy in or out; it's prudent at the beginning or end of the program to shoot multiple cutaways intended strictly for the editing process. This means, for example, "nodders" for talk shows (discussed in Chapter 10), applause shots for musical programs, and cutaways or coverage for news and documentaries. Other chapters of this book cover the various aspects of postproduction for each format.

The following individuals are involved in the postproduction process:

- The account executive/sales
- The scheduler
- Reception
- The librarian
- Shipping
- The editor, graphics, and assistants
- The sound mixer

The Account Executive/Sales

If the director/producer is working in-house—and "in-house" can mean anything from a network production to a high school facility—there usually won't be a sales department dedicated to a production. At best the director/producer will negotiate with either operations or engineering, and they don't usually interact with their colleagues in a customer-service-style relationship. Student/faculty relationships are equally unlike the salesperson/customer relationship.

Sales representatives or account executives at a typical postproduction facility will want to impress the director/producer with the advantages of working at their facility rather than at someone else's. They can be expected to point out the highlights of their facility, including rates, availability of special gear, and exceptional personnel.

Choosing among facilities is often difficult because there are so many intangible factors. For example, facility rates are almost never based on the same total package. One production facility will include graphics as part of the edit package, while the next will charge for it. One facility will have the latest, greatest switcher, while the next will have last year's. These things may or may not affect the rates. Usually the producer, not the director, has to make a decision, based on the specific needs of the specific program. Once those needs are clearly defined, decisions regarding when and where to edit may be easier. If it's determined that a facility can't do a desired kind of wipe or special effect, you may still want to use that facility and find a creative way around the problem.

Account executives, sales representatives, or their staffs may offer advice about where to go for facilities or personnel they are unable to provide. For instance, they might suggest a graphics house if there isn't one on the premises. They'll certainly try

to help in any way they can, but apart from advice, their help is limited to offering the use of office facilities: the phone, a copier, or a refrigerator filled with refreshments for the clients. If you're doing your own editing, they may have a staff member who can offer advice. If you're working at a station or network or in any situation in which there is someone else doing the actual hands-on editing, the editor is the main source of assistance.

Scheduling

The edit session requires scheduling. The scheduler needs to know the date and time that you want to begin your edit session. That slot may not be available, so it's good planning to have a few alternative dates and times in mind. The scheduler needs to know which facilities will be required and the number of hours you need. You might need a complete edit suite for a full day but other facilities for the latter half of the day. Some facilities bill out their graphic package on an "as-used" basis. Others include that in the suite. Knowing which way you are going to be billed allows you to schedule your time in the suite in the most economical way.

Reception

As is the case with the production facility, it's wise to provide the reception area with a list of the people who will be with you in the edit suite.

Library

Once there is a substantial amount of material to be edited or shipped or if your production requires archive materials, the librarian becomes very important. A production may have started with three Beta masters, but chances are they soon included a variety of different viewing copies and then some audio layoff tapes, submasters, and graphic files—any or all of which may be needed now for a current production. Any help you can offer the librarian is greatly appreciated, and that help usually means complete, consistent, and accurate labeling, including relevant names, codes, and dates.

Shipping

A printed shipping list and shipping information, including your company's airbill number (which allows the facility to ship things at your expense) or instructions, can make the shipping part of your production go smoothly. A file or disk with the same information may be appreciated, but provide it in a format compatible with the shipping department's system.

The Editors and Editing

Editing History

This book is primarily about programs that are produced using multiple cameras. For the most part they require either very little or no editing. Nevertheless directors and producers have to edit. This brief history may help explain some of the reasons we edit as we do.

Originally television was live. The first way of recording television was on film and was called "kinescope." The kinescope was shipped by mail, which was the way programs were seen in different parts of the country. Videotape first aired in 1957, and it greatly improved the quality of playback. Editing tape grew out of the tradition of audiotape editing. Videotape, which was 2 inches wide, was physically cut, spliced, and handled in much the same way editors handled quarter-inch audiotape. A major complication to that was that the sound and the picture were a half-second, seven and a half inches, apart. A mechanical tape counter, which was not very accurate, tracked the tape's position.

The first improvement was editing by creating a new master from a playback. The edit point was found using a tone on a cue track to find a repeatable edit point. The first improvement of that was Editec, which was released in 1963. It allowed the editor to control a frame shift of the point.

In 1967 the Society of Motion Picture and Television Engineers (SMPTE) standardized 30-frame code for editing, allowing access to specific addresses on a tape and making consistent edits in a linear fashion possible. It became the standard for computerized editing.

The state of editing today has been radically changed by the acceptance of digital media. With digital media editors have the ability to edit any part of the production's video or audio. Sought-after material can be found and manipulated almost instantaneously. Video can be resized, recolored, repositioned, or replaced. Audio can be removed, sweetened, and replaced with frame accuracy. Tape is being replaced by hard drive and solid-state media.

Editors

There was a time when editors worked for a facility. In fact, the quality of the editor or editors was what attracted clients to a particular postproduction facility. Every postproduction facility offered two things: the use of their hardware—the newest switcher or the most up-to-date film-to-tape transfer system—and, more important, the facility's editors, playback operators, maintenance crew, and CG or graphics operator. Facilities that offer full-service editing are still quite common, but there are many more freelance editors who work at any one of a number of different facilities, including client offices or their own home.

Wherever the editing is done and whoever does it, the process is very similar. Field acquisition material—mostly material that has been shot on a memory stick, DV-Cam, DVC-Pro, Beta XD, or Blue Ray—is transferred ("recorded," "pushed," "ingested") to a server at an ingest station and then handled as a file by the editor. The process is not yet entirely solid state, but it is becoming ever more tapeless.

As a director/producer, you'll most likely be editing yourself, working with your own editor, or using the editor who works for the facility, or a free-lance editor at a rented facility. You need to make sure that you bring all the necessary elements to the edit. You can begin creating a checklist of those elements prior to the edit. Getting help from an editor prior to the actual session may not be as easy as it seems. If the editor is busy, he or she may be working through an answering service while editing someone else's job and thus not available for impromptu discussions on the particulars of your edit. You will need all the materials necessary for the compilation of the production, including the following:

1. The source material memory stick, DV-Cam, DVC-Pro, Beta XD, or Blue Ray original material to be sent to the server
2. Audio tracks on media that can be addressed by the editing system
3. Graphic material on media that can be addressed by the editing system
4. A decision list, with the "in" cue and "out" cue for every edit, based on viewing of the original materials
5. A list of the credits in the order they are to be arranged, with an indication of framings and checked spellings if that is to be added in the editing process

The Sound Mixer

The sound mixer is responsible for the final audio for the production. In some formats this is simple, as when there is only a sync sound track and a music or sound-effects track. If such is the case, the program or commercial may be mixed during the edit. If a more substantial mix is required, a sweetening session is necessary. In that case, all the audio elements and notes pertinent to the production must be assembled prior to the session. Once the session has begun, the audio will be laid off to a multiple-track recorder or computer, and each element will be added, piece by piece, at the standard baseline setting for digital recording. Later, a second pass will be used to emphasize one element or another. The master audio will then be mixed down and laid back to the master.

MANAGEMENT SERVICES

In addition to the people involved in the preproduction, production, and postproduction processes, the director/producer will encounter many others:

1. Agents and managers (your own or those representing the talent you hire)
2. Accountants and lawyers (yours or your talents')
3. Public relations, publicity, and advertising executives

As a director/producer, you work with the media on your own behalf, on behalf of the production, and on behalf of the talent involved in your production:

4. *Music licensing personnel.* In music licensing, you may work with someone who helps you find specific music and someone who helps you acquire the rights to that music. It may be the same person. The fundamental issue is that if your production is to have public showings, you must have the rights to any music you use. This requires rights from the composer or copyright holder and the talent.
5. *Stock footage licensing personnel.* The same provisions as for music licensing are mandatory here. Most stock-footage houses charge for viewing and then charge per second of material used, based on the kind of usage.

The rates charged for commercials airing nationwide, for example, are higher than the rate charged to a local station. Some of the issues surrounding stock footage are covered in Chapter 7.

6. *Caterers.* Most of the time, the facility at which you are working has arrangements with a caterer, has its own kitchen, or offers a handy supply of menus from nearby restaurants that will deliver. On network and local programs, staff directors, producers, and the rest of the staff take a break and buy their own meals. On programs where there is visiting talent and on-location shoots, a budget item is mandated to provide lunch or dinner. In most student projects, feeding the talent and crew is an important line item in the budget.
7. *Transportation personnel.* If there is any major trucking that has to be done—of set pieces, instruments, gaffer rigs, and so forth—you may be required to hire union teamsters. Productions also use vans and let production assistants transport talent from hotels and crews to locations.
8. *Location services staff.* Location services arrange either a portion or all of the services required for location shooting, which may include:
   a. Location scouting and securing of the location. Some homeowners or locations charge a great deal per day. Location fees can vary from a few hundred dollars to many thousands of dollars a day. (Whatever the cost, location owners are very particular about the condition in which the locations are left after the shoot.)
   b. Security at the location
   c. Acquisition of permits
   d. Arrangements for catering
   e. Arrangements for housing and transportation en route to and from the location
   f. Arrangements for housing and transportation at the location
   g. Cleanup after leaving the location. (It's important to be specific about what the location service will and will not supply. Details about the cost of each phase of the service are essential.)
9. *Insurance agents and their staff.* Insurance for a shoot can be expensive. A great deal of

unusual gear comes in and out of a location, cables are laid across the floor, hot instruments surround the shooting area, and accidents often occur. The location becomes a high-risk area. Insurance premiums reflect very valid concerns regarding location work.

10. *Union and guild members.* If you work on a production that has workers represented by unions or guilds, ask the facility or the unit production manager about the specific contractual obligations that may affect your production schedule. Find out what the problems may be before they occur and arrange to work around them.

Along the way to completing a production, the director/producer will work with a great number of people, all of whom make a unique contribution to the project. Recognizing their specific needs and helping them do their jobs by giving them the information and the time they need helps to ensure a high-quality production.

REVIEW

Preproduction

People who are involved in making a television production:

1. Executive in charge: final responsibility for the program or series
2. Producer and line producer: runs the day-to-day program
3. Associate producer/assistant producer: assists the producer/line producer
4. Production assistant: takes notes, assists producers
5. Director: responsible for the production of the program, including blocking and calling shots
6. Associate director: readies shots, responsible for timing
7. Stage manager: the director's voice backstage and onstage
8. Unit manager: tracks costs and makes sure vendors are paid
9. Operations: assigns facility and, sometimes, crew
10. Engineering, represented by the engineer in charge: facilitates all engineering needs, both hardware and personnel
11. Accounting (sometimes)

12. Set designer: designs the set and may dress it
13. Art director/set decorator (sometimes): dresses the set
14. Lighting designer/electrician
15. Graphics
16. Makeup/hair
17. Wardrobe
18. Talent
19. Music
20. Special effects
21. Stage crew
22. Paint crew
23. Prop crew
24. Animal handlers
25. Drivers
26. Explosive experts
27. Fan club representatives
28. Greens people
29. Martial arts experts
30. Security

Production

Production costs are divided between "below-the-line" and "above-the-line" charges. Productions almost always have people who represent the following areas:

- A technical director: responsible for the crew, video, and engineering standards
- Two, three, four, or more camera operators (camera operator for robotic cameras)
- An audio mixer: responsible for all sound

Sometimes, any combination of the following is also included:

1. A sound-effects person
2. One to four utility/cable persons
3. A crane operator
4. A crane boom person
5. A jib crane operator/cameraperson
6. Stage manager: the director's representatives on the floor. They deal with four different groups:
   a. The production group (the director/producer and his or her staff)
   b. The stage and technical crews (engineering and set, paint, property, electrical and special-effects crews)
   c. The talent
   d. Management

7. Prop crew: prop crew acquires or makes props and runs props for the program
8. Stage crew: responsible for the set
9. Light crew: the lighting designer designs the show. He or she arranges an overlay to the quarter-inch ground plan, which notes:
   a. The kind of instrument—fresnel, liko, scoop, and so on
   b. The wattage of each instrument
   c. The position of each instrument on the pipe from which it is hung
   d. The direction in which the instruments are to be hung
   e. The function of each instrument (sometimes omitted)
10. Paint crew
11. Talent including chorus, extras, and so on
12. Graphics
13. Makeup/hair

Note that actual program slates are often found at the beginning of programs. Embedded slate data are always present. Using viewable slates is a particularly good idea for series productions so those airing the program can verify that the program they are airing is indeed the particular episode that is called for.

Postproduction

The people involved in the postproduction process are:

1. The account executive/sales
2. Scheduler
3. Reception
4. Librarian
5. Shipping
6. Editor, both online and offline
7. Graphics and assistants
8. Sound mixer

Editing History

• Grew out of tradition of audio editing. Videotape that was 2 inches wide was physically cut, spliced, and handled in much the same way as quarter-inch audiotape. A mechanical tape counter tracked the tape position.

• The first improvement was editing by using a tone on the cue track to find a repeatable edit point.

• Editec allowed for a controlled shift of the point.

• Society of Motion Picture and Television Engineers (SMPTE) standardizes 30-frame code for editing.

• Digital video: any part of the production's video or audio can be found and manipulated almost instantaneously. Video can be resized, recolored, repositioned, or replaced. Audio can be removed, sweetened, and replaced with frame accuracy.

In addition to the people involved in the preproduction, production, and postproduction process, the director/producer will encounter many others:

1. Agents and managers
2. Accountants and lawyers
3. Public relations, publicity, and advertising executives
4. Music licensing personnel
5. Stock footage licensing personnel
6. Caterers
7. Transportation personnel
8. Location services staff, including:
   a. Location scouting and securing of the location
   b. Security at the location
   c. Acquisition of permits
   d. Arrangements for catering
   e. Arrangements for housing and transportation en route to the location
   f. Arrangements for housing and transportation at the location and sometimes cleanup after leaving the location
9. Insurance agents and their staff
10. Union and guild members

chapter four

Panel Programs

Many people start their television directing careers by directing panel programs. These are the kinds of programs that are sometimes referred to as "talking heads." They make up most of the work seen on Sunday mornings at the networks and on public-access channels. They're probably the most popular and certainly the cheapest kind of programming to produce. Knowing how to shoot them well makes working in other formats easier because although the preparation for other formats is different, the conventions governing panel programs are the same as those for shooting any kind of conversation or discussion. Those conventions include discussions in a drama, a sitcom, or simply the banter associated with a late-night talk/variety program. These are the elements you need to know in order to be properly prepared:

1. Preproduction—routine or rundown
2. The ground plan and setting
3. The seating arrangements—180 degrees or 360 degrees, with:
   a. One host and one guest
   b. One host and more than one guest
4. Production—rehearsal:
   a. The procedure for rehearsing a panel show
   b. Timing the program
   c. Shooting options
5. Postproduction, editing—transcript

Preproduction starts with an outline, a ground plan, and a setting. The easiest way to approach the panel show is to imagine that there is just a host and a guest sitting in the limbo of a studio. The limbo, or "cameo black look," is very popular in low-budget television all-talk programs. It consists of two or more people sitting in a studio, surrounded by black curtains (cameo black) or a colored cyc, usually a pink or blue cyc (limbo).

Historically, a cyclorama, or cyc, was used in the theater to give the illusion of sky. In both theater and in television today, "cyc" refers to a large wall or curtain that is usually white so it can be lit, but it can be black, too. It's used as a neutral background.

Sometimes the terms limbo and cameo are interchanged. Whichever term is used, the intention is to create a background that is as neutral as possible. Occasionally, light slashes or hanging artwork is used to give accents to the background.

Usually three cameras are used to photograph the participants. Traditionally, one camera shoots the host, one camera shoots the guests, and one camera—the one in the middle—shoots the wide shots. Figure 4.1 shows how that looks as a ground plan. When people are seated, their eyes are approximately three and a half feet from the ground.

A standing cameraperson has to stoop to keep the lens of the camera on a line with the eyes of the panelists, who are seated on chairs on the floor of

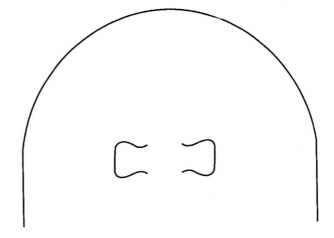

Figure 4.1 A typical ground plan for two people in a "limbo-look" set (not to scale).

the studio. Having the lens at eye level with the panelists is important because eyes are often revealing, and we are used to talking to each other that way. Having to stoop to get a shot becomes uncomfortable for camera operators. Inevitably, the cameras get raised to a height convenient for shooting instead of remaining at the best height for communicating. The usual solution to this problem is to place the chairs on a platform so that eye level is raised to an easier shooting position. Most panel programs are shot on a one-foot riser for just this reason. The ground plan is then changed to include a one-foot riser, as seen in Figure 4.2.

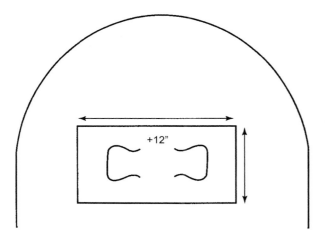

Figure 4.2 This is essentially the same ground plan as in Figure 4.1, but in this plan a one-foot riser or platform has been added to bring the eye level of the guests up to a convenient lens line. This information is indicated by the box drawn around the two chairs and the "+12"" (not to scale).

SEATING ARRANGEMENTS

The two seating arrangements that are used most often are 180 degrees, in which the participants are seated in a straight or slightly curved line, and 360 degrees (in the round). If more than two panelists are involved, they can be seated in four ways: 180 degrees—host at the end (either the right or left side of the panel); 180 degrees—host in the middle; 360 degrees—host in the audience; and 360 degrees—host surrounded.

Each of these formats has advantages and disadvantages. The 180-degree choice keeps the panelists on one side of an imaginary line and the cameras on the other side. When that relationship is maintained, the audience keeps a clear perspective of where things are. This imaginary line is called the line of 180 degrees (Figures 4.3–4.11).

If the director does not maintain the integrity of that 180-degree relationship, the screen direction of the panelists gets confused, and as a result, the audience sees close-ups of panelists who appear to be talking to the other members' backs instead of their faces.

Imagine a classroom in which a teacher stands at the front of the room and points to a door at his or her right. To all the students, the teacher would appear to be pointing left. If the students got up and got behind the teacher, they would agree that the door was to the right. If the line of 180 degrees is broken, each camera cut makes it appear that the cameras are jumping in front of and behind the teacher. The audience can't tell if the teacher is looking left to right or right to left. The screen direction becomes confusing because the shots are cut from one side of the line to the other.

GROUND PLAN AND PICTURES OF A TYPICAL PANEL PROGRAM

Figure 4.3 This ground plan of a panel talk segment (not to scale) shows the placement of cameras for a production that uses the convention of the line of 180 degrees. Ordinarily, cameras and their placement would not be indicated on the ground plan, nor would there be chair numbers. A "+12"" would be indicated on all the plans through Figure 4.14.

Figure 4.4 This ground plan (not to scale) includes the position of camera 2.

Figure 4.5 The photograph shows how the scene as indicated on the ground plan would look from camera 2's position.

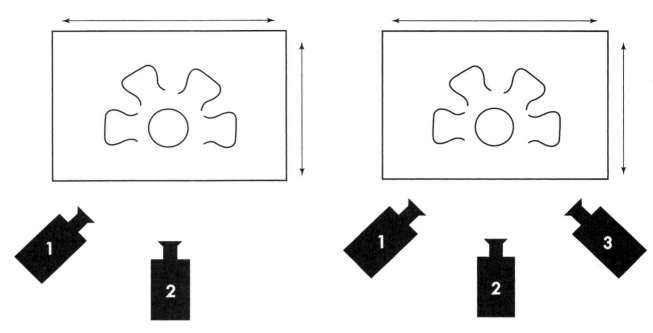

Figure 4.6 This ground plan (not to scale) includes the positions of both camera 1 and camera 2.

Figure 4.8 This plan (not to scale) indicates the third camera as it should be placed to shoot this program in the traditional 180-degree format.

Figure 4.7 The photograph shows what camera 1 would see from the position indicated on the ground plan. In this case, the camera has a cross two-shot to the host, seated in chair 4, talking to the woman in chair 1.

Figure 4.9 This is what the woman in chair 1 would look like as she talks to the host in chair 4. Note that the host (in Figure 4.7) appears to look from right to left. In this picture, because the line of 180 degrees has been maintained, the woman looks back at her, facing left to right.

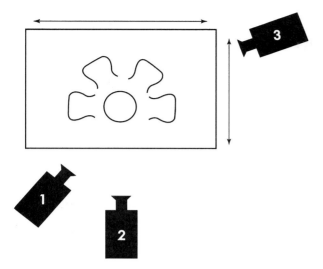

Figure 4.10 In this ground plan (not to scale), camera 3 has broken the line. It is upstage of the line of 180 degrees, which is an imaginary line that passes between the downstage characters.

Figure 4.11 This shows camera 3's picture from the position indicated on the ground plan. Because the camera has broken the line of 180 degrees, the host (as seen in Figure 4.7) and the guest (as seen here) face the same direction, which is not at all what the picture from camera 2 shows the audience.

SEATING ARRANGEMENTS AND CAMERA COVERAGE

180 Degrees with the Host at the End: Pros and Cons

When the host is seated at one end of the panel, the panelists usually look to that end to answer the questions posed by the host. Shooting this way usually

yields the most head-on shots. Assume we are using the ground plan shown in Figure 4.12. Although numbers do not appear on the ground plan, it's convenient for the director and camera operators to agree that the chairs are numbered from left to right, chair 1 through chair 4. In this system, the name or function of the person sitting in a chair is unimportant. For this program, the host happens to be in chair 4; the guests are in chairs 1 through 3.

This kind of ground plan is the basis for almost all nighttime talk/variety shows that are shot in the traditional 180-degree format. The host—from David Letterman and Jay Leno going back to Johnny Carson, Jack Parr, and Steve Allen—traditionally sits at the end of the panel. The difference is that those in the seating positions 1 through 3, or however many people are on the set, are usually seated on a couch, and the host is at a desk in what would be chair 4. Guests are brought onto the set, they chat awhile, and then each moves one slot down to allow the next guest to talk in close proximity with the host. This seating arrangement keeps the host in a commanding position. The panelists form a united front, responding to the host. On most of the popular panel/variety programs, the host's home-base area is on the audience's left side of the stage and is shot by camera 1. This means that the last camera that needs to leave the chat or "home-base" area to get to the "production area" is camera 1, the host's. While being seen on camera 1, the host can say, "And now, here's [the next guest]."

Camera 3 will have left the talk area and be ready in the production area, usually at the audience's right, to get the first shot of "the next guest." Camera 1 is also the first and the easiest to break back to the host after a production area performance is completed.

Each camera in a panel program has a specific function. The director needs to be able to show the

Figure 4.12 This ground plan (not to scale) indicates a numbering system for the seating arrangement.

audience a close-up of whoever is talking. That's usually done with camera 3, on the far right. A wide shot that emphasizes the relationships of the guests and shows any action that may be happening is also necessary. That's covered by camera 2, in the middle. The guests are all laughing, for example, or somebody does something that needs to be seen; they stand up and dance, or pull a rabbit out of a briefcase. The wide shot is called a "cover shot," since it covers the action. In a star vehicle, a close-up of the star is also a cover shot. No matter what happens, we want to see how the late night show's host reacts; that's usually on camera 1. In a symphony orchestra, the wide shot of the orchestra and the close-up of the conductor are both cover shots. On a panel program, or the panel portion of a talk/variety program, the camera setup and shooting pattern are likely to play out something like this:

- Camera 1 has a close-up of the host. Assuming the host is a star, or at the very least represents the viewer, a cutaway to the host is almost a cover shot for the program. However, that same camera can be used to single out a strong panelist who for some reason turns away from the host. Sometimes panelists begin to ask questions on their own or turn and directly answer remarks made by someone else on the panel or in the audience. In this case, camera 1 may leave the host and get a shot of the panelist. When that happens, camera 2's cover shot becomes very important.
- Camera 2 has a wide cover shot, in which we see everything.
- Camera 3 covers whoever responds to the host.

Shooting 180 Degrees with the Host at the End

A typical shooting scheme for a sequence might be like this:

- Camera 1 is "on the air" as the host asks a question.
- Camera 2 then is put on the line as the first panelist, whoever that is, responds, giving camera 3 an opportunity to find out which panelist is speaking and get the shot.
- At the end of a sentence or phrase, the director cuts away from the wide cover shot on camera 2 and puts camera 3 on the line, which has now had time to find the shot, find focus, and frame the shot.

Creative directors seek out and use other shooting schemes. For example, in the same five-person panel, an alternative approach might be:

- Camera 1 gets a single shot of the host but is prepared to widen to a wide shot, holding the host at the far end of the shot.
- Camera 2 gets the two people in the center.
- Camera 3 gets the two people at the camera left end of the set.
- The host asks a question, and camera 1 widens out to a cover shot. We can then cut to either camera 2 or 3 on a two-shot and zoom into whichever panelist is talking.
- The entire sequence can then be shot in two shots that zoom to the speaker.

A "two-shot" is a picture that includes two people in it. Sometimes it is a "flat" two-shot. A flat two-shot usually shows two people in profile; it is as if you were standing at the center of a table at which two people were playing chess. Another kind of two-shot is a "cross two-shot," sometimes called an "over the shoulder" shot. It features one of two people; it's what you might see if you were standing behind one of two chess players and looking at the other one. The ideal is to have the appropriate shot on the air, as if the entire production were scripted and the director had planned every shot.

180 Degrees with the Host in the Middle: Pros and Cons

In the second seating arrangement, the host is in the middle and is featured, while the guests are on either side, seated in a line (Figure 4.13). This type of setup is used in many political debates. The guests may feel more "on display" because of the seating arrangement, but they will be seen in profile when they respond to the host.

Shooting 180 Degrees with the Host in the Middle

Camera 2 has a close-up of the host seated in chair 3. It can also have a wide shot that includes the host. Assuming the host is a star, or at least represents the viewer, a cutaway to this camera is almost always a cover shot for the program. That same camera can be used to single out panelists, but for the most part it is limited to the cover shot of the host or the wide shot.

Camera 1 or 3 has a cover shot—down the line—which is a wide shot from either side, down

Figure 4.13 This ground plan (not to scale) offers seating for four guests and a host, but by placing the host in the middle chair, chair 3, the guests are likely to look upstage when answering questions. Pictures of the guests will have more profiles than a seating arrangement with the host at either end.

the line of the guests. These cameras also get singles or two-shots of the person who is speaking. Camera 1 covers the camera-right panelists (chairs 4 and 5), and camera 3 covers the camera left panelists (chairs 1 and 2).

A typical shooting scheme for a sequence with a host and four guests might be something like this:

- Camera 2 is on the line with the host, who asks a question. The camera can justifiably zoom out to a wide two-shot or cut to:
- Camera 1, which has a two-shot camera-right of the host, or
- Camera 3, which has a two-shot to the left of the host.

An entirely different approach would be to:

- Cut to camera 1 or 3 on a wide shot, and then either zoom in to whoever is talking or use the other camera to cut to a single.

- Once one camera is committed to a close-up of a panelist, any one of the remaining cameras has to get a wide shot. The remaining camera can get singles.

360 Degrees—Host Surrounded: Pros and Cons

Shooting "in the round" (Figure 4.14) creates a more intimate feeling among the guests, and there is no apparent star. Everyone's seat appears to be equal, and when sitting in the round the guests may feel that the cameras have been shut out. The guests may be more open in airing their feelings in conversation. Of course, the cameras have not been shut off, and the director will still make choices that favor one panelist or the host over the others. However, the perception the guests get from sitting in the round can result in an easier give-and-take, a more interactive conversation. This seating arrangement almost always forces the director to break the line of 180 degrees, so when cutting from close-up to close-up, guests appear to be talking to the backs of one another's heads. If this happens early enough in the interview, the audience usually accepts the convention and doesn't mind the unusual results.

Shooting 360 Degrees

Camera 2 has a close-up of the host. It can also have a wide shot that includes the host, all of the downstage guests (chairs 1 and 5), and parts of the other two guests not hidden by the downstage guests. As in the other scenarios, we can assume that the host is a star, or at least represents us, and a cutaway to this camera is almost always a cover shot for the program. That same camera can be used to single out panelists in profile, but for the most part it's limited to the host or the wide shot.

Camera 1 has a shot of guests 4 and 5 and can shoot them in either a two-shot or singles. Camera 3 has a shot of guests 1 and 2 and can shoot them in either a two-shot or singles. Both cameras 1 and 3 have wide shots, which are similar to each other. A typical shooting scheme for this setup is similar to the one in which the host is in the center. A sequence might be:

- Camera 2 is on the line with the host, who asks a question. The camera can justifiably open to a wide two-shot or cut to either:
- Camera 1, which has a two-shot, camera right of the host, or

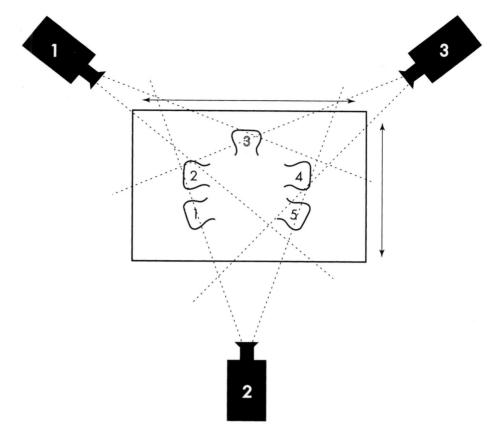

Figure 4.14 A ground plan (not to scale) for a panel segment in which the host is in chair 3—the center. Camera positions are indicated for shooting this kind of seating arrangement while shooting "in the round"—360 degrees. Chairs 1 and 5 might be placed so they are more directly facing the host, but the cover shot would not be as strong.

- Camera 3, which has a two-shot, to the left of the host.

An entirely different approach would be to do the following:

- Cut to camera 1 or 3 on a wide shot, and then either zoom in to whoever is talking or use the remaining camera, not on the host, to cut to a single.
- Once the camera is committed to a close-up of a panelist, one of the remaining cameras has to get a wide shot, and the other one can get singles.

PROGRAM ROUTINE

A program that consists of a standard opening and close and two people having a conversation may not regularly publish a "routine." Almost all other programs do create and distribute a working routine, sometimes called a program rundown. Essentially, this is a skeletal outline of the program. It's made available as a text file, readable by monitors appropriately placed or as a hard copy. It shows six important items:

1. A segment number
2. *Who* appears in the segment
3. *What* the segment is about
4. *Where* the segment takes place
5. How long the segment lasts—the running time
6. How far into the show we should be when the segment is over—the cumulative time

Here's a concise program routine, followed by an analysis of some of the significant factors involved in its creation. At one time material to be aired might have been "rolled in" from a tape deck or film chain. The tape playback would have been labeled VTPB, for videotape playback, and the film would have been labeled SOF, for sound on film. Now material to be aired is delivered as a file from a server. The change in the "delivery system" of openings, closings, or internal program packages doesn't affect the way the director or producer constructs, rehearses, or shoots the production.

PROGRAM NAME—DATE—EPISODE #

#	Description & Location	Run Time	Cumulative Time
1.	Tease Intro (Host VO @ Home Base over SLUG 1 @ Master Control	:30	
2.	SLUG 2—Program Opening Animation @ Master Control	:30	1:00
3.	Host & 3 INSIDE THE WHITE HOUSE @ Home Base Tom Jones: Press Secretary Mike Smith: Reporter *Star Journal* Kate Lang: League of Women Voters	7:00	8:00
4.	Commercial Break 1 (@ Master Control)	2:00	10:00
5.	Host & 4 INSIDE THE WHITE HOUSE II @ Home Base: Adding Jane Murray: *Gotham News*	6:30	16:30
6.	Commercial Break 2 (@ Master Control)	2:00	18:30
7.	Host & 2 RE: CHILDREN & THE NEWS @ Production Area Dr. John May Dr. Alice May	6:30	25:00
8.	Commercial Break 3 (@ Master Control)	2:00	27:00
9.	Wrap & Tease @ Production Area	:30	27:30
10.	Credits—Graphics over Production Area	1:00	28:30

Here's that typical routine with notes to explain some of its ramifications:

#	Description & Location	Run Time	Cumulative Time
1.	Tease Intro (Host VO @ Home Base over SLUG 1 @ Master Control	:30	

This means that the first item is a "tease" for the show, designed to grab viewers and keep them watching. The Description & Location column indicates that it will feature the voice of the host coming from the Home-Base area. The voice will be heard over pictures coming from a server located in Master Control (VO is an acronym for voice-over). Under Run Time we learn that the segment will last 30 seconds; because this is the first item on the routine, there is no Cumulative Time.

#	Description & Location	Run Time	Cumulative Time
2.	Slug 2 Program Opening Animation @ Master Control	:30	1:00

Item #2 consists of SLUG 2. It is the program's opening animation and comes from Master Control, although it will be started from our control room and aired through our switcher. The Running Time of the animation is 30 seconds; combined with the 30 seconds of the tease, that yields a Cumulative Time of 1 minute. Item #2 consists of slug 2. It is the program's opening animation and comes from a server. Almost all stations will have transferred the opening—in this case a film animation—to a file that would then be inserted from the server as the production was being recorded.

#	Description & Location	Run Time	Cumulative Time
3.	Host & 3 INSIDE THE WHITE HOUSE @ Home Base Tom Jones: Press Secretary Mike Smith: Reporter *Star Journal* *Kate Lang: League of Women Voters*	7:00	8:00

Item #3 consists of the host and three guests who will be talking about something called "Inside the White House." The three guests, itemized in the routine, will be seated in the Home-Base area, per the director's instructions. The host's seat and the way in which

guests are seated will probably be part of the show's conventions—as it is on The Tonight Show, *for example. Which guest sits where will still need to be specified. Usually this seating is based on a sketch or information given to the stage manager during rehearsals. The segment will go on for 7 minutes.*

This segment should then be finished 8 minutes after the program goes on the air.

The associate director (AD) is responsible for timing the program at many stations. At local stations, the director must perform this task while directing the program. If this were a morning show that began at 9 A.M., the AD might use either a stopwatch or the clock to time the show. If the AD used the clock, he or she would know that at 9 o'clock and 30 seconds the animation should begin airing. At 9 o'clock and 8 minutes, the first talk segment should be ending. In order to do that, the AD will have to give the host time-cues. In this case it will be easy, particularly if the AD works backward.

If segment three is supposed to be over at:

9:08:00 (9 o'clock and 8 minutes), then at

9:07:30 (9 o'clock, 7 minutes, and 30 seconds)

the host must see a cue of "Thirty Seconds."

At 9:07:00 (9 A.M. and 7 minutes) the host gets a "One Minute" cue.

At 9:06:00 (9 A.M. and 6 minutes) the host gets a "Two Minutes" cue, and so on.

The cues will be given to the host by a stage manager, sometimes called a floor manager. The stage manager gets directions from the director or AD and with hand signals indicates how much time is left in a segment. Sometimes time cards—cards with "3," "2," "1," ":30," and "Cut" or "Finish" printed on them—are used in place of hand signals. Usually only the last 3 minutes of a segment are timed out for the talent. During the running of the program, the AD may discuss time with the producer.

Directors usually don't participate in the discussion because they are involved with the shooting. The producer may wish to change the timings within a segment, depending on how well the segment is going. The AD will have to make the time adjustments to the entire program while it's on the air or being recorded. This will mean shortening or lengthening one segment and making up the time in another. The AD will get approval from the producer regarding the new lengths of the segments and then have the stage manager show time cues at the new appropriate times.

#	Description & Location	Run Time	Cumulative Time
4.	Commercial Break 1 (@ Master Control)	2:00	10:00

This is the first commercial break. It will be inserted at Master Control. If this is a program for a network or for syndication, the chances are that there will be a "show logo graphic" inserted from the control room during the two minutes of the break. Any Master Control airing the program could use this as a cover should there be any problem with the commercial slugs as the program airs. Slugs are usually commercials or public service announcements that are "rolled or slugged into" the show. They are put on the air in the "commercial slug" or "commercial slot" that was left in the program.

#	Description & Location	Run Time	Cumulative Time
5.	Host & 4 INSIDE THE HOUSE II @ Home Base: Adding Jane Murray: Gotham News	6:30	16:30

This item also takes place at Home Base. One person will be added to the panel of three, which means there will be a panel of four guests and a host. She will probably be added to the end of the panel and will be put in place during the commercial break.

#	Description & Location	Run Time	Cumulative Time
6.	Commercial Break #2 @ Master Control	2:00	18:30

This item will be handled like Commercial Break #1. During this commercial break, the cameras will go over to the production area and set up for the next segment.

#	Description & Location	Run Time	Cumulative Time
7.	Host & 2 RE: CHILDREN & THE NEWS @ Production Area Dr. John May Dr. Alice May	6:30	25:30

In item #7 the cameras will take up new positions, in which the seating for the host is part of the show convention for the production area. The guests'

seating will be spelled out during the rehearsal, as it was for item #3.

#	Description & Location	Run Time	Cumulative Time
8.	Commercial Break #3 (@ Master Control)	2:00	27:00

This commercial is handled as are the others.

#	Description & Location	Run Time	Cumulative Time
9.	Wrap & Tease @ Production Area	:30	27:30

Rather than returning to the Home Base, the host will conclude from the production area, where the last interview was done.

#	Description & Location	Run Time	Cumulative Time
10.	Credits—Graphics over Production Area	1:00	28:30

Credits graphics will be superimposed—or more properly, keyed—over the Production Area. There are often contractual credits that must be granted. At a station that is a signatory to a Directors Guild of America contract, for example, the director must get full screen credit as the last credit before the production begins or the first credit at the end of the program.

The producers and associates will use the routine to schedule guests' arrivals. They'll be considering last-minute preproduction meetings and other day-of-production needs. Women's makeup, for example, usually takes longer than men's, which affects the guests' scheduled arrival times.

The hair and makeup department will need to know who needs to be made up first. They'll need to know that the guests in the White House sequence are to be done before those in the sequence regarding children. Wardrobe may be standing by for any last-minute fixes such as pressing or other clothing-related issues. The stage manager assigns dressing rooms. This is done in conjunction with the producers so everyone knows where to find each guest. The wise director/producer introduces the guests to the stage manager as soon as possible. That way, if the guests need something while the program is on the air and the director/producer is not available, they know that their contact is the stage manager. The stage manager will also need to bring the guests to Makeup and to the studio floor in time for the shoot; therefore, he or she needs to know who's who and where everyone is. Graphics will use the routine, as well as a graphics list, to confirm the needed identifiers and spellings. Audio needs to know how many mics to place in each area and will have to decide what to do when the fourth guest, Jane Murray, enters the set during Commercial Break #2.

Props will need to know how many chairs are needed in each area and must be alert for the stage manager's cue that a commercial break is in progress and that it's time to bring in the additional chair. During the running of the program, the associate director (AD) might remind the stage manager about the addition of the chair. The AD would have written a note on the commercial page for this item to alert the stage manager if needed. Lights will be able to tell which areas get lit, when they get lit, and whether or not booms are present. Booms will affect the lighting because they throw shadows, and a different lighting plan might need to be used.

During the running of the show, the AD will use the routine to confirm time-cues to the host. The AD will confer with the producers during the running of the segment to determine whether a particular segment should be lengthened or shortened. If segment 3 is going well, for example, it might be extended to 7 minutes and 30 seconds instead of just 7 minutes. If this happens, one of the other segments will have to be shortened by 30 seconds. Last, the director needs the rundowns as a fast way of remembering who is in which segment, in which area the segment takes place, and the approximate length of each segment.

SCRIPT FORMAT

For the most part paper scripts have been replaced with computer terminals, and the director and crew work from the files displayed on those terminals. The outline is similar to that used by news organizations. Typical computer-generated news outlines are shown in Figures 9.1 and 9.2. The director of these programs uses the teleprompter copy, which now includes graphic directions, in order to cut the show. Regardless of whether one uses a paper or computer outline and script, the needs are the same. What follows are the rules that govern a paper script.

Some specific script-formatting rules govern the preparation of scripts for multiple-camera productions:

1. All multiple-camera television scripts are written on 8½-by-11-inch pages.
2. All scripts have a one-inch margin on the left so the script can be placed into a ring binder, if needed.
3. All scripts have a three- to four-inch margin on the right for director's (or crew's) notes.

Several other features are standard:

4. A script is always written in upper and lower case, except for directions, which are always in UPPER CASE.
5. Pages are always numbered and always at the upper right.
6. Each page of the script is keyed to the program routine. The item number appears at the top left or center of the page.
7. Scripts are always double-spaced.
8. Revisions are indicated on all new pages with date and time. Different-color pages are often used for each new revision. While the industry does not uniformly color-code revisions, script colors and revisions were standardized by various television production organizations.
9. Color-coding has been used on the *Academy Awards* broadcast, most network news programs, CNN, and many independently produced programs.
10. This is the American Association of Producers color code for revision order:
    a. White (blue for commercials)
    b. Pink
    c. Yellow
    d. Green
    e. Goldenrod
    f. Salmon
    g. Taupe
    h. Cyan

The following script and ground plan (Figure 4.15) are based on the preceding routine. Explanations of terms and acronyms are included in square brackets, but these would not appear in an actual script.

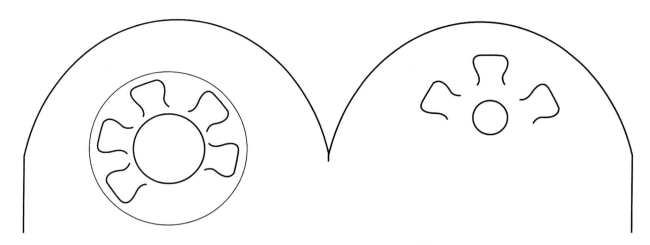

Figure 4.15   A simplified ground plan (not to scale) for this production.

ITEM #1—:30

Host (VO)

The White House stands as a symbol of America and is recognized by people of all nations. The power of that image and the weight of pronouncements from the White House are of great importance to all of us.

We thought it might be wise to examine how news gets reported from the White House. How manipulated is the press, and what are the consequences of a public that has been given only managed news?

SLUG 1—(MOS) :30 Footage of the White House

[MOS means "no sound." It is an acronym for either "minus optical sound" or "mit out sound." The latter definition is the best known and is attributed to an unknown film editor. It was a joke made at the expense of one of the 1930s German film directors, probably Eric Von Stroheim. SOF stands for "sound on film."]

Video OUT-Q

Still of White House fades to blk [black]. [An Out-Q is the last thing seen or heard in a segment. It serves as a cue for the next event.]

ITEM #2—:30 Slug 2 (MC) [Master Control]   **pg. 2**

Program Opening Film   SLUG 1—(MOS) :30 Footage of the White
Animation   House

Audio OUT-Q   Video OUT-Q
Music fades   Pix of State Capitol—fades to blk.

ITEM #3—7:00 (Home Base)   **pg. 3**

INSIDE THE WHITE HOUSE

Host:

When the announcer says, "And now this
just in from the White House," or "According
to White House sources . . . ," we really listen.
The power of the White House is enormous.
The events reported from there, or what we
are led to believe happens there, are usually
very important. How accurate is the reporting
from the White House? How accurate can it
be?

We've brought together a number of
people who have some definite ideas
about this question.

Tom Jones has been the press secretary to
the White House for the past three years.
Before that, he was a writer for the *Washington
Eagle* for almost five years. He came to
know politics through his early days as a
Senate page.

ITEM # 3 (continued)   **pg. 4**

INSIDE THE WHITE HOUSE

Mike Smith is currently the national reporter for the *Star Journal* and has been covering the Washington scene for almost 20 years. His weekly radio show is syndicated to over 300 radio stations across the country.

Kate Lang is president of the League of Women Voters. She's written articles on how to get the facts behind the facts and is currently writing a novel about a reporter's investigation of events at the White House.

INTERVIEW

1. According to the *Star Journal*'s article, we are being duped by the White House.
2. Is that true?
3. How can that happen?
4. If the electorate doesn't get truthful information, what are the ramifications?
5. What is the relationship between the press and the press secretary?
6. How does that affect the news we get?
7. How does the White House prepare for press conferences?
8. Comment on press leaks? How do they happen?
9. Explain how are they handled?

OUT-Q

Host: Thanks. . . . We'll be right back with a surprise guest.

ITEM #4—2:00—Commercial Break 1 (MC)   **pg. 5**

ITEM #5—6:30 (Home Base)   **pg. 6**

INSIDE THE WHITE HOUSE II

Host: Joining us now is a writer whose perceptions of the news have been a part of our city for a long time now. She's the senior editor at the *Gotham News,* Jane Murray. Ms. Murray is the recipient of a Pulitzer Prize in journalism for her work on the link between tabloid journalism and juvenile delinquency.

INTERVIEW

1. How do senior editors find out what's really happening in the field?
2. What can they do about misinformation and deception?
3. How do they manage their reporters away from home?
4. Recount of preproduction interview question re: Tall tales told to Jane.
5. Reporters' comments on relationship to home editor.
6. Can you get the "real story"?
7. Is deception "in the air"? How? Examples.

OUT-Q

Host: Thanks. Coming up next: What do kids think?

ITEM #6—2:00—Commercial Break 2 (MC) **pg. 7**

ITEM #7—6:30 (Production Area)   **pg. 8**

RE: CHILDREN & THE NEWS

Host: We tend to think that the events regarding news
and its coverage have no effect on our children.
Disputing that claim are our next two guests.

Dr. John May is a practicing child psychologist. He is
currently the senior resident in child psychology at
Gotham Municipal Hospital.

His wife is Dr. Alice May, who is codirector of the Child
Psychology department at Gotham Municipal.

With her husband, she is the author of *Children and the
Truth*, which deals with children's perceptions of reality.

INTERVIEW

1. Is there any documented proof of a relationship
   between truth in the media and children's
   psychological problems? If so, what?

ITEM #7 (continued) (6:30)   **pg. 9**

RE: CHILDREN & THE NEWS

2. You recently completed a study of TV viewing on child behavior. Could you explain what your findings show about children and the news?

3. What relevance does this have (if any) to press releases from places such as the White House?

4. Is there any clearinghouse for material that children ought to be watching? What? Where? How can parents get in touch?

5. What would you advise parents regarding the issues of truth in reporting? Watching TV? Reading newspapers? Other sources?

OUT-Q
Host: Thanks. . . . We'll be right back after these messages.

ITEM #8—2:00—Commercial Break 3 (MC)   **pg. 10**

ITEM #9—:30 (Production Area)   **pg. 11**

WRAP & TEASE

Host:

Well, that's it for today's show. We hope you enjoyed the different opinions expressed. We look forward to seeing you tomorrow.

Tomorrow, we'll look into friendship in the new millennium. There's a fortune cookie out there that says, "A friend is a gift you give yourself." Have you given yourself that kind of a gift lately? Have we been shortchanging ourselves? Are friendships still as important as they always were? In today's society, is there such a thing as a real friend? Looking at some of the stories in the news one might well ask, "Do I dare get to know my neighbor?"

See you tomorrow.

ITEM #10-1:00 (Graphics over Production Area)   **pg. 12**

1.

Our City

_____

2.

Hosted by

Pat Thomas

_____

3.

Directed by

Hank Fields

_____

4.

Technical Director

Matt Gatlin

_____

5.

Cameras

Eric Feder

Mike Greene

Rod Munoz

_____

ITEM #10 (continued) (Graphics over Production Area)   pg. 13

6.

Audio

Drew Daniels

Video

Tomi Ilic

———————————————

7.

Stage Manager

Alex Gorodetzki

Graphics

Peter B. Cury

———————————————

8.

Associate Producers

James Oliver

Joanna Harris

———————————————

9.

Production Assistants

Nancy Katz

Elizabeth Harris

Michelle Pigot

———————————————

ITEM #10 (continued) (Graphics over Production Area)   **pg. 14**

10.

Produced by

Barbara Harris

_____

11.

A Station Production

Each segment had at least a page dedicated to it. Segments that required more than one page spilled over to the next page. For example, segments 3 and 10 each needed more than one page. The script is formatted this way to keep segments together. "Used" pages can be thrown away while "on the air." This allows the director to start each new event with a clear page. Once the routine and script are finished, copies are delivered to those who need them.

A hard copy of the script may be distributed, or a copy of both the script and the routine is made available as a file and is readable from monitors appropriately placed for:

a. The host
b. The producer
c. The director
d. Standards and practices or Legal Affairs (at some stations)
e. The station's files

Just the routine goes to:

f. The technical director
g. Playback
h. The audio chief
i. The stage manager
j. The graphics department
k. The head of props
l. The head of lights
m. The makeup department
n. The hair department
o. The wardrobe department

If there is a hard copy of the script, the director usually marks his or her script to indicate when and where each camera will be put on the air. Since this format is mostly spontaneous, the director's marking will be limited. However, the director will still be able to use the script and rundown to accomplish a number of tasks during the rehearsal. He or she will want to make sure that the playback (or the "file") for the tease is ready, that it really does run 30 seconds, and that the OUT-Q is accurate. It is a good idea to preview everything before putting it on the air. If this were to be run in a computerized environment, there would be no marked script, but the prompter would be checked for accuracy, and the items would be run in the same manner.

REHEARSAL PROCEDURE

Eventually it would become time for a FACS (sometimes spelled FAX) rehearsal. This is a rehearsal in which the program uses the full facilities (FACS, for short). During that rehearsal, a number of things will have to happen:

- The guests will need to be briefed by both the producers and the host.
- Makeup will need to have time to work on the guests.
- The director will want to see what the guests look like and what clothes they've brought to the studio.
- Whenever possible, it's a good idea to run through all the parts of the program that are scripted, with either the actual guests or with stand-ins sitting on the set.

There is an agenda for the rehearsal. Each member of the crew will be making sure that his or her contribution is ready. While the producer is concerned with the program content and with interacting with the guests, the director has a different, more technical, agenda. Here are the director's concerns during the rehearsal by item number in the routine.

Item #1

The director will learn that the host's microphone has, in fact, been laid out and is working. The director wants to check on all the elements that are to be inserted into the program. Does the technical director have control of the right server or playback source? Is the timing accurate, or has that been checked earlier? Is there a "pad" at the end, or does it fade out or pop out? Is the OUT-Q as indicated? Does the copy fit well? Should the host be cued to read immediately after the fade-up, or should some of the package play out first? (A "fade-up" is an illusion in which a picture appears from black. Almost all programs and commercials "fade up" from black and then dissolve to black when they are finished.) Is there audio on the package? Is there a music bed? (A "music bed" is a piece of music that plays throughout a segment. It may be given more or less presence under narration or a soundtrack, but it is always there.) Might one be appropriate, and, if so, is one available?

Item #2

If this is a regularly presented program, the director is probably quite familiar with the opening. It probably originates as a digital file, either from a server or an assigned playback device. Where that's the case a button is pressed and the file plays. While film is no longer apt to be used as a regular part of a broadcast, guests still bring in old film clips, and student film festivals regularly appear on air, so directors need to be aware of the problems that go along with the airing of such materials. The first choice would be to transfer the film to a server and call it up from the server.

Where actual film of any kind is used, the director needs to be sure that the technical director has control of the film chain (a device for showing 16 mm or 35 mm film or slides on the air), that the right film has been loaded onto the right film chain, and that the film is heads-out, with the leader showing in the preview monitor. "Heads out" refers to the way film is wound on a core or reel. When it's heads-out, it's wound so the beginning of the film is at the beginning of the core or reel, ready for air. If it is tails-out, the back end or tail of the film is the first thing that would pass through a projector. After a film has been projected, it's tails-out until it's rewound. If film is to be aired, the director would need to be sure that the projection gate was clean, and that there were no "hairs in the gate," which refers to film emulsion or dust inadvertently deposited at the film projection gate as a film is being shown. It often looks as if there were a hair wriggling across the screen when it's projected. Last, one would want to make sure that the sound from the film chain was okay.

Item #3

Running the introductions to the piece with either the actual guests or with stand-ins can catch a number of problems before they happen. By now we know that the mic for the host works. This is the time to test the rest of them. The camera operators will have a chance to see who gets what chair and when, particularly in the introductions. If there are a lot of moves for the camera operators, this is the time for them to learn how much time they have for each move. As you look at the seated stand-ins, take a moment to consider the lighting. Make sure that there are no unusual shadows (as from booms) or hot spots.

We know the host is in chair 5 on camera 1, and the first person introduced is Tom Jones, in chair 1. The easiest way to do the introductions is to cut to camera 3 on chair 1 and then pan right to each of the guests as they are introduced. After the last guest is introduced, the director cuts to camera 2 for an establishing shot so the audience can see the relationships of the panelists.

The following alternative plan has a somewhat brisker pace. It requires the camera operators to know how much time they have to "set" a shot. In this scenario, after the host (in chair 5, on camera 1) introduces the first guest, the director cuts to camera 3 on chair 1. The director then cuts to camera 2 for chair 2's introduction. Meanwhile, camera 3 can set up on chair 3. At the appropriate time, camera 3 is put on the air, and camera 2 goes to chair 4. Finally, camera 2 can pull to a wide shot, or camera 3 can be taken with a wide establishing shot. One purpose of the rehearsal is to give the camera operators a chance to learn the system that will be used for the introduction. It also affords the director and the lighting director the opportunity to make sure the lights are in the right place. If you don't check light placement, it's all too easy to find yourself with a problem that could have been solved. I experienced a minor disaster once while directing a panel program when I didn't get to see one woman on camera prior to shooting. Her hair was styled high on her head. The first time I saw her on camera was when we were on the air. Her hair threw a shadow directly across the host's face, and there was nothing I could do about it at that point!

It would be most unusual to rehearse the questions. Usually, questions can be discussed in broad terms among the host, the producer, and the guests, but the actual wording of the questions is typically saved for the taping to preserve spontaneity.

The last thing to do at rehearsal is to find out if the OUT-Q is as written or will be ad-libbed. It seems like a small thing, but there is a problem with a host whose tags are not definitive: "We'll be right back . . . So don't go away . . . There's plenty more . . . So stay tuned." Any one or a few of those phrases could have been the last line. The danger is that if the host says "We'll be right back" and then pauses, the director may command a fade to black, only to discover that the fade is happening as the host starts to say "So don't go away . . . There's plenty more . . . ," and so on. The director needs a very specific phrase for the OUT-Q.

Item #4

During the commercial break of item #4, guests will be brought to the set. They will be seated and miced. This need not be rehearsed, but it would be wise to make sure that everyone agrees on how each new guest will be brought onto the set. Is the stage manager ready? Is a stagehand with a chair standing by? Is there an audio assist to put on a lavaliere microphone if needed? (A lavaliere is a small microphone that is meant to go unnoticed. It is usually slipped onto the edge of a jacket or dress and serves as the microphone for seated guests.)

Item #5

At this point the director will want to make sure that there's a chair for the new guest and that the microphone is working. Since the material is scripted, the director will want to "walk it through" with the cameras. Coming out of the "break" of item #4, the first shot will probably be on the host, in chair 5 on camera 1, as the introduction of Jane Murray begins. As Ms. Murray is introduced, the director cuts to camera 3 on the last chair over. Then, to reestablish the seating arrangement, a cut to a wide shot on camera 2 would be appropriate. Once again the director checks the OUT-Q at the end of the segment.

Item #6

During commercial break #2, the director reassigns the cameras to positions in the production area, making sure that the cameras can reach the right spot in the two-minute break allowed.

Item #7

This segment is handled in the same way as the other interviews, with checks for lighting and audio, and with confirmation of the OUT-Q.

Item #8

Another commercial break is taken.

Item #9

This segment is read through, since its timing is critical to getting the program off the air at precisely 28 minutes and 30 seconds after it started.

Item #10

This segment is for the program credits. One minute of credits is really quite long but may be acceptable in some productions. The last item in a production is often designed to be flexible so the credits can go by quickly or slowly. Sometimes a standby "short credits" is kept ready to accommodate a production that ran too long. The total time of credits designed to run 1 full minute ought to have a comfortable 5-second swing either way—they can run either 55 seconds or for 1 minute and 5 seconds. The director runs the credits to make sure that they are all there, in the right order, and spelled correctly.

THE SHOOT

Soon after the rehearsal, the crew gets set for the taping. First, a brief period is set aside to confirm all the last-minute changes that will have been made. These changes may mean extending an interview or adding questions that have become more relevant after the latest meeting with the panelists. It will include a touch-up for makeup. It may include different graphics or additions or deletions to the script. Meanwhile, the crew will make their last check-ins with Master Control, confirming that they are still receiving the studio's signal and that the facilities will remain with the program through the scheduled time.

Once the show is on the air, the director will be involved with the "look" of the show. The producer will consider that, too, but will be more interested in the content of the program. Should different questions be asked? If so, they may be posed either directly through an earphone that the host wears or by a note sent via the stage manager. If the information will affect the direction of the program, the producer will inform the director. A typical note: "The host is about to ask chair 4 a question that's a real *killer*!"

At major stations and the networks, changes in the running time of segments are of little importance to the director, since the producer, associate director, and stage manager run that part of the production. However, at most stations the director is responsible for time-cues as well as the shooting of the program.

Even when the director is working with an AD, he or she still needs to hear the time-cues that are sent to the host. It could be awkward to start setting up an elaborate combination of shots with the host's camera tied up on a wide shot and then find there are only 30 seconds left in the interview. Whether the director or the AD keeps track of the time, the back timing remains the same. The "back timing" is done by giving time-cues during the running of the program so the program can be completed in exactly the right time. During segments it means getting each segment off after using up only the time allotted for it. At the end of the program it means getting the program off on time. It's not unusual to hear the director or AD counting out the show at the end of the program: "Thirty seconds and six credits left, 25 seconds and five credits left," and so on.

An example of the use of back timing an element to get a program off the air smoothly occurred regularly on the nightly news magazine program on Channel 13 in New York. The program was designed to end with the music fading out. In order to achieve that, I had the audio engineer "dead pot" the music (start the music but keep the volume at zero) 3 minutes and 28 seconds before the end of the program. (Three minutes and 28 seconds was the total length of the music cue.) Somewhere, about 3 minutes after I had started the music, right after the host signed off, we faded up the remaining time of the music cue for our credits, and when the music ended (3 minutes and 28 seconds after I had started it), the program went off the air with the music nicely back-timed and fading out.

Most panel programs don't get edited. When they do, all the relevant personnel get together to create the editing log. This usually involves the following members of the staff.

- The director
- The producer
- Whoever is responsible for notes (such as the production assistant)
- Whoever is responsible for logging tapes used and running the edit session (usually the associate director)
- Anyone whose expertise is needed to create an accurate edit log. (This might mean an expert who had appeared on the program or musicians who might be needed for scoring.)

Whenever possible this is done while the material is fresh. If the editing is to be extensive, a written transcript of the material that had been ad-libbed by the panelists is made.

In almost all editing situations, some math will be needed. The math used for television is related to problems in time. Time is base 60, not base 10, as in dollars and cents. It means that we need to deal with 30 frames to a second, 60 seconds to a minute, 60 minutes to an hour, and 24 hours to a day. This is harder to read about than to do!

Inevitably there comes a moment when a segment in a production is too long, and a portion must be removed. The producer says something like, "We've got that 7-minute and 12-second segment with the song in it. Let's remove the song. It runs 2 minutes and 43 seconds. What'll we have left?"

The part of the problem that you don't run into with dollars and cents is subtracting a high number that needs to be handled in base 60 (seconds) from a low number of seconds. For example:

7:12—The length of the segment
−2:43—The length of the song to be deleted

The easiest way I have found to do that is to change the top number. In this example I borrow a minute, or 60 seconds, from the 7. The 7 then becomes a 6, and I add those 60 seconds to the 12 seconds, so it becomes 72 seconds. Then it's easy to subtract:

6:72—The length of the segment
−2:43—The length of the song to be deleted

Once the program is over, the producer, or part of his or her staff, will leave the control room to thank the panelists and escort them out of the studio. While that part of the production staff is engaged in good-byes, others are working on the editing journals. Meanwhile, the technical crew will check the recorded tape or file for technical quality, and the stage crew will wrap the camera cable and wrap up the studio, including the lights and props.

REVIEW

- Panel programs are almost always shot either observing the line of 180 degrees or in-the-round 360 degrees.
- Many panel programs are shot with the guests sitting on platforms so the eyes of the talent are on a line with a standing camera operator.

- The simplest shooting plan has:
  1. A camera on the left shooting close-ups of those on the right
  2. A camera in the middle shooting a wide shot
  3. A camera on the right shooting close-ups of those on the left
- Another type of shooting sequence features "two-shots," in which two people are seen at the same time, and the camera zooms in to whoever is speaking.
- Almost all programs have a working routine, sometimes called a "program rundown." This is a skeletal outline of the program. It is used by most of the different departments involved in producing the production.

Whether in hard copy or text file, each separate element of the program is assigned:

1. A segment number
2. A place where the segment takes place
3. Who appears in the segment
4. A very short explanation about what the segment is about
5. The running time/how long it lasts
6. The cumulative time/how far into the show we should be when the segment is over

In a typical network or syndicated panel production with a full staff, the routine or rundown is made available as a text file readable by monitors appropriately placed or as hard copy and is distributed to:

a. The host
b. The producer
c. The director
d. Standards and practices or legal (at some stations)
e. The station files
f. The technical director
g. Playback or Operations
h. The audio chief
i. Stage manager
j. Graphics
k. Head of props
l. Head of lights
m. Makeup
n. Hair
o. Wardrobe

- For the most part paper scripts have been replaced with computer terminals, and the director and crew work from the files displayed on those terminals.
- Where hard copy is used, specific script formatting rules govern the preparation of scripts for multiple-camera productions:
  1. All multiple-camera television scripts are written on 8½ -by-11-inch pages.
  2. All scripts have a one-inch margin on the left so the script can be placed into a ring binder, if needed.
  3. All scripts have a three- to four-inch margin on the right for the director's (or crew's) notes.
  4. A script is always written in upper and lower case, except for directions, which are always in UPPER CASE.
  5. Pages are numbered at the upper right.
  6. Each page of the script is keyed to the program routine. The item number appears at the top left or center of the page.
  7. Scripts are always double-spaced.
  8. Revisions are color-coded, or at least indicated on all new pages with the date and time of the revision
- Each segment has at least one page dedicated to it.
- During rehearsals the director checks all the elements that can be checked. This is done by actually looking at or listening to each element as it appears on the rundown or script.
- Acronyms and phrases from this chapter:

MOS	minus optical sound
SOF	sound on film
FAX/FACS	facilities
VO	voice-over
VTPB	videotape playback
Heads out	The way film needs to be in order to be projected
Hair in the gate	Emulsion or dust deposited on the gate as the film is projected. It appears as a wriggling hair on the screen.

chapter five

Demonstration Format

The demonstration format, a kind of "show and tell," has been a part of television since its very early days. It includes productions ranging from a food channel production that "shows and tells" how to cook, to segments on late-night television where the host shows album covers, funny pictures, funny headlines, and so on. Much of the production in corporate videos is created using demonstration formats. Googling "how to" gets over a billion hits. All how-to productions, which are show-and-tell in nature, are very direct in what they're trying to accomplish. They tell a story with a beginning, a middle, and an end. They're video cookbooks, and they say, "Here are the ingredients. These are the steps needed to combine the ingredients. This is what it finally looks like." Each step along the way requires the director/producer to arrange for the audience to see only the most relevant material—at just the right time—for just the right *length* of time needed to tell the story.

Until you become involved with an actual production, this seems like an easy program to produce and shoot. In fact, it is—but only if great focus and care are given to each detail in the preproduction stage. It's just because it *does* seem so easy that so many problems can arise. It's one of those cases where the devil is in the details. Rehearsing each little step of the program and being sure about the details may seem foolish, but it's essential. It's the same whether you're working on the smallest scale with the simplest material or on a major production at a major facility.

DIRECTOR IN CONTROL

One of the first rules to be learned is that, wherever possible, the director should retain full control. This may seem more aggressive than polite, but it's critical. "Taking control" means the director has to accept responsibility for the production and find the best way to get what's needed to make the program a success. It doesn't mean either "be tyrannical" or "be nice." In fact, when directors try to "be" anything, they usually fail. It's only when they try to make something happen, in the most straightforward way, that they achieve success. The chances of success are greatly enhanced if the director knows what needs to happen next and then takes control of it.

Just how necessary it is to retain control became clear to me when I directed a program in which a guest had a slide projector and explained a trip he had taken. (Today, he'd probably be using a computer with a PowerPoint demonstration.) He ran the slide projector from the set, and I had a camera on the screen. The audience saw each new slide when he thought it was best. The kindest way to phrase the result is to say that he and I had different ideas about timing, and he did love his slides. Thereafter, I insisted that guests with slides review the slides with me and then give the slides to *me,* after which I would give them to our projectionist and offer a monitor to the guests that showed nothing but the slides. I would change the slides on the air when I thought the story needed the next visual. The tempo picked up considerably, as did the interest of the audience. The director's need to control the action remains the same whether its slides or PowerPoint. Of course, on most late-night programs it's the star who controls the tempo of showing items. Fortunately, most stars have a highly developed sense of timing.

It's also important to keep control of the "showing part" of the demonstration program. The dreaded uncontrolled moment happens when a guest holds up some small item that demands a close-up. Invariably it's held up in the air and waved around as the desperate cameraperson tries vainly to find focus for the close-up. Most of the directors and celebrities who work in the demonstration format have found specific places on the set where items that are to be shown are placed. This allows the close-up camera to zoom in to that spot and find its focus even before the first item is put in place.

Whether it's a program or a segment of a program, there must come a time when the director/producer talks over what's to happen during the production. If it's a demonstration program, a "routine" or "rundown" is created to outline what's seen, when it's seen, and how long each segment will appear on the air. There may be no written routine for the material within each segment, but the components are thoroughly worked out, and the outcome produces a firm idea of exactly what, where, and when each item will be shown. This will help the director/producer get appropriate wide shots to show all the action—and very specific shots in the close-up.

SHOW-AND-TELL MATERIAL: A GUIDELINE FOR CREATION

The following is a general guideline to creating show-and-tell material.

Preproduction

1. Coordinate pictures with ideas.
2. Create a routine.
   a. A written long routine for the program
   b. A short routine, or outline, for showing things within each segment. It should be based on some overriding idea: the order of construction, a chronological order, the size of objects to be shown, and so on.
3. Rehearse the demonstration at home or at the office and then again in the studio.
   a. Create a format that limits the way in which material will be shown, and rehearse the demonstration. Take no shortcuts—rehearse it *all!*
4. Use the real thing as often as possible, or use props that are very similar to the real thing.
5. Discover special needs.
   a. For the camera: lenses, filters
   b. For audio: sound effects, music
   c. For the stage: props, graphics

Production

1. Limit the area where material is to be shown.
2. Create strong time-cues.
3. Limit the focus of the talent—that is, "Look at camera 3, show to camera 2."
4. Holding small objects in the air makes it impossible for the camera operator to accurately focus on the object being shown, so show prearranged material in only one of the following ways:
   a. *Panning*: Show prearranged material panning left to right (or right to left)
      OR
   b. *Marked spot*: Show preset objects on a "marked" spot. Remove the first object and replace it with the next item to be seen.

Coordinate Pictures with Ideas

The most essential part of demonstration programs or segments is that they tell a story. *Telling* is the important thing. The *showing* is what makes the telling better. Organize the material. Start with an idea, and then illustrate it. Wonderful items with very little connective thread make for dull viewing.

I used to direct three shows every Monday for the National Educational Television channel in New York. The program was called *New Jersey Speaks for Itself*. It was designed to let people in the metropolitan area know about what was happening in New Jersey. Invariably, one of those shows would feature a guest who was going to demonstrate something for us. If the guest was not prepared, it was difficult to create a half-hour production that was even adequate. The problems I encountered there continued to arise each time I worked in this format, whether it was on an infomercial, a game show segment, or with student production.

Guests on my program took on nightmare qualities when they arrived at the studio carrying everything they owned relating to the topic they would address. They had carloads of material for segments that were supposed to last a maximum of 12 minutes. They had no idea how to show their material, what to say, or where to put it. Moreover, they usually came late, so they couldn't rehearse, and they had been so busy they hadn't had time to return phone calls to discuss the project. Equally unpleasant were guests who arrived just as late, just as unprepared, and had no more than half a dozen vertical, unmounted pictures with which they expected to fill the same 12 minutes.

Clearly, the best guests, and thus the best programs, were those with which there had been some communication and preparation. Better guests brought in objects that related to a story. Each item they intended to show would help the viewer understand more about the story.

If the story is a how-to piece, then each item that's shown should build on the preceding one. There should be a rehearsal, not just a "talk-through," beforehand to work out exactly what visuals apply. If the piece is one in which varieties of the same thing are shown—hand-carved ducks, for example—then one ought to find a unifying theme that links each piece in a logical way—for example, "Here are ducks from the East Coast; here are ducks from the West Coast" or "Here are big ducks; here are little ducks." They might organize the material to show the works of one artist and then the works of the next, or different schools of carving, or even ducks through the ages. Almost anything would be acceptable that coordinated an idea with the pictures.

Create a Routine

Whether directing a segment or a program, you need to create a routine. Imagine you're working with me on that WNET production that used hand-carved ducks as a show-and-tell/demonstration segment. On that episode I was able to have a preproduction meeting with the guest. We arranged to show the ducks chronologically from the earliest carvings to the more modern ones, and since there were a large number of works, we organized them further by sculptor. The program had the following routine:

New Jersey Speaks for Itself—Date—Episode

#	Description & Location	Run Time	Cumulative Time
1.	Opening animation @ Master Control	:30	
2.	Host with Bob Zee re: N.J. Election @ Home Base	7:00	7:30
3.	Host lead to PSA @ Home Base	:30	8:00
4.	PSA @ Master Control	1:00	9:00
5.	Host and Duck Guest @ Home Base	1:00	10:00
6.	Duck Display @ Display Area	7:00	17:00
7.	Host thanks and Tease panel @ Home Base	1:00	18:00
8.	PSA @ Master Control	1:00	19:00
9.	Host and four re: Summer Fun @ Home Base Annabel and Julian Cury Bea and Max Gorodetzki	7:30	26:30
10.	Host wrap @ Home Base	1:30	28:00
11.	Closing credits over duck display	:30	28:30

Rehearsal

Items 1 through 5 were somewhat standardized and would be rehearsed later, following the example used to rehearse a panel program. Item 6, the duck display, is listed in the program routine as a simple line of copy; nevertheless, there was a kind of subroutine that had to be constructed with the guest. It had to be a complete and repeatable outline of how things were going to be shown.

One of the first considerations in creating the routine is time. The allotted time for item 6 is 7 minutes. That needs to be broken down. There's a teaching trick that's useful here: first you tell the students, or in this case the audience, what they're going to see, then you show it to them, and then you tell them what they've seen. If you accept that, then 30 seconds are needed to introduce the way in which we'll see the ducks, and at the end we'll need another 30 seconds to summarize what we've seen. That leaves just 6 minutes for the actual demonstration. If things are rushed so each duck is seen and discussed for just 15 seconds, there's enough time to see four ducks per minute. We have 6 minutes. Four ducks per minute, times 6 minutes equals 24 ducks—maximum. It would be prudent to have a few "standby" ducks in case the guest whizzed through the display, but there isn't time for a lot more. Once you break that down for a guest, he or she can begin to arrange the material to suit the needs of the program.

Through our initial discussion, the guest was able to decide that the best way to show the duck carvings was in chronological order, showing one or two examples from selected artists, starting with antiques from the early 1900s.

Once guests are prepared, they can work out the specifics on their own. They should be encouraged to go home and go through every step of the presentation, using all the props exactly as they intend to use them on the program. We *don't* want them to write and memorize a script, because that might get stilted. We *do* want them to be very familiar with every part of the presentation and tell us what we have to know. Later they'll bring the material to the studio or an office for a rehearsal.

The Real Thing

Once when I was directing a daytime drama, in the days when one taped as-if-live, and with just 10 minutes to go before we taped, I was told that the program was short. We needed to stall by at least 2 minutes. The story line was that some of the regulars were leaving their old home to move on to a new place. I suggested that the stagehands put a bunch of old props in a box—things like old ice skates, a stethoscope, a lamp, and so on—and wrap the box. The actors would open the box and make up stories about the props for the required 2 minutes. There was no time to rehearse.

So we tried it for the first time on the air. Naturally, reality bit me. Everything worked fine except the wrapping paper. It sounded like a forest fire every time the actors touched the stuff. If there had been time to rehearse, I would have eliminated the wrapping paper. There usually is some little unimportant detail that reveals itself only as you work the piece under real conditions, even in a demonstration program.

Of course, there are big differences between rehearsing at home or at an office and rehearsing at the studio. Even if the guests are diligent and rehearse on their own, they still need a studio rehearsal. They need to become familiar with all the little changes that are part of the studio setup. The table will be different. The space they have to work in will be changed. Apart from their own contribution to the program, they'll have to know how the show runs. Will they walk from the discussion area to the production area on the air or during a commercial break? Where is the production area? How will they know when to begin? What does the display area look like? Where can they store props? They may have discovered some of the things they're going to need when they rehearsed at home. Confronting the actual set and props makes a big difference. That can be done without an engineering crew, but someone from the crew should be available to supply props that suddenly become needed— a blue cloth to cover the gray countertop so there can be contrast with a gray duck, for example.

At the studio, the guest should be escorted to the set. Enough time should be scheduled for a rehearsal. The guest should be given a copy of the routine to see how he or she fits into the program. It would be best if the guest sees the home base set and the presentation area and then sets up the needed demonstration props as soon as possible. While the guest is setting up the ducks in the presentation area, you can explain the workings of the program. The guest needs to know that after the chat with the host, he or she will be invited to walk over to the display area and show some examples of duck carvings that have already been set up.

Once the display area is set up, you can begin a small "walk-through." The director needs to arrange the move from one area to the next. It's sometimes difficult to spell out things you feel are obvious, but this is one of those times where Murphy's First Law prevails: "If it can go wrong, it will." Take nothing for granted. Everything should be spelled out for the guest. The less initiative the guest has to take, the more professional the program will look.

Start at the home base area. This is what the guest will do on the program. During taping, the host would invite the guest to show the ducks. The host would continue to talk as the guest stood up and walked over to the display area. During this rehearsal the director would set a path for the guest so the walk to the display area doesn't interfere with the on-air shot of the host. Once the guest was in place, the stage manager would "okay" the host. That would be the cue for the host to say something like "Well, let's see what you've brought us." After that the guest would begin, with no further cue. It's wiser to arrange for the guest to get a word cue to begin from the host rather than taking a cue from the stage manager. It should seem natural to the guest.

One time I had an awful moment in a program I directed when a stage manager threw the guest a cue to begin, only to have the guest whisper, on camera, "Now?"

Guests sometimes are embarrassed at how much time it takes to do something that seems so simple. They can get the mistaken impression that you are unsure of them or even that you think they're stupid—outcomes to be avoided. They become embarrassed about keeping the host waiting around for them. So it's easier to rehearse the moves without the host and to create an atmosphere that conveys "This is the way things are done in television." Once the rehearsal begins, the director creates a lead-in line and makes sure the guest understands that those are the exact words that will be the cue to begin. It's imperative that the host says only those words. Guests will need to be rehearsed long enough to feel comfortable with all the new things that are happening around them. Another rehearsal, this one with the host, will familiarize the guests with the host's delivery instead of the director's.

Display Area

The display area we used in *New Jersey Speaks for Itself* was a special table on wheels. It was very much like the one that's used by many network talk show hosts. It's the familiar table they wheel into the production area to show small products—to demonstrate the latest gadget or to cook something on an electric skillet. The tables are usually 36 inches high by 18 inches wide by 48 inches long; the important thing is that it be tall enough so the working surface is about waist high. That made it easy to show items, and it was not too high for a camera to be able to shoot down into a bowl, to see jewelry laid out on a surface, and so forth. The table was only 18 inches wide, but we had a larger board to place on top of that when necessary. If it had become much wider, it would have been awkward to use. The table was covered in front. It had a shelf that left about 18 inches of storage space underneath the top surface. If there was an overflow of props, we also had other standby tables we could press into service, including a bridge table, a typing table on wheels, and even the end tables from the guest lounge in the studio.

THE DEMONSTRATION

Showing things can be accomplished in one of two distinct ways. I usually chose one of them for our guests during our first discussions so they could try it during their rehearsals at home. Two ways of showing things were created to ensure that an article is never shown suspended in the air while being held in the guest's hands. Rather, whatever is to be shown is left in a fixed place so a camera operator can find focus on a stationary object.

1. *Panning*: The articles to be displayed can be prearranged on the table in a line so the guest can point them out one by one. Essentially, the "close-up camera" pans from left to right. This method is especially useful when you have just a few items and you want to show the stages of development or when you feel that a pan rather than a cut-back to the guest will be more suitable.

2. *Marked spot*: A spot is found on the display table, and each item to be shown is placed on that spot. When a hand comes into the frame to move it, the director cuts to a wide shot. The item is removed and replaced by the next item, all in a wide shot. Then the director cuts to a close-up again. The camera operator getting the

Figure 5.1 (a) In this demonstration program, the presenter is talking to camera 3 and is showing a feature on a lighting unit to camera 2, which is getting the close-ups. (b) This is what camera 2 is shooting. (c) This is the picture from camera 1's position, which includes the host and the demonstration as seen from the discussion area. (d) This is the way the demonstration looked on the monitors in the control room. Camera 1 covered the host and the demonstration, while camera 2 got close-ups and is seen in the preview monitor. Camera 3 was "on the line."

close-ups finds focus on a preset, innocuous mark—a short white thread or a small pencil mark—and simply waits for the next item to arrive on that mark (Figures 5.1a–d).

This is the way every nighttime host shows pictures, headlines, album covers, and so on: the host places the item to be shown on the "show-and-tell mark." This is one of those things that is easy to explain to a guest, and most guests are happy to oblige, but somehow they don't. While they understand the idea in discussion, when the actual moment

comes to demonstrate, they forget everything they've been told. Instead, they reach down, pick up the object, and float it around in the air, while the camera crew tries vainly to help. The rehearsal affords the director an opportunity to work with the guest on this seemingly unimportant but critical facet of presentation.

Let's assume we decide to show the ducks one at a time, and the first duck to be shown is preset on its mark. The rest of the ducks are lined up on a shelf underneath the display area—left to right—in the order in which they will be seen. Off to the right of the display area is a bridge table, where the guest places the ducks after they've been seen.

During this walk-through the director tries to anticipate any problems that might arise. While directing this episode, I realized at this point in the rehearsal that the tabletop we had in place was too gray and that the ducks were not standing out very well in black and white, or even in color. So we placed a different-colored cloth over the table to enhance the contrast for our viewers and went on with the rehearsal. A printed pattern would have been totally unacceptable because it would have created a confusing picture.

The issue of contrast in showing things is very important. Some years later, after having directed *New Jersey Speaks for Itself*, I was working on a daytime drama that had a scene in which a gun was being shown in close-up. The black gun was being handled by a man wearing black gloves and a dark sweatshirt. The gun didn't show up well at all. I remembered the time I had spent working in show-and-tell programs, and the gloves were changed to a lighter color to stand out against the dark sweatshirt. After we made that change, the black gun was much easier to see.

Once the show-and-tell area is set, the guest runs through his or her presentation. This allows the director to discover glitches that might show up later as surprises. Is a special lens needed? An extra table? Some graphic that might be useful and made on the spot? Was there some music or sound effect in our library that might enhance the presentation? Watching the guest go through the presentation gives the director the opportunity to call on his or her knowledge of the medium to enhance the guest's presentation and, ultimately, make it more appealing to the audience. There is the added benefit that rehearsing on the actual set usually helps the guest feel more at ease.

In *New Jersey Speaks for Itself*, there were a few moments when we were to see extreme close-ups of the ducks, and a macro lens would have been useful. Since a macro lens was part of the camera complement, it was easy to use. I only needed to know when to switch the lens and then when to switch back. As we rehearsed the presentation, it became clear that the guest had no idea of running time, so we arranged to have the stage manager show the guest some time-cues. Because this program used many "amateur" guests, we had taken special precautions in giving them time-cues. We made 8-inch by 10-inch cardboard cards with

the numbers 5, 3, 2, 1, and 30, and the word "Finish" (instead of the traditional "Cut"), and we used the cards rather than the usual hand signals. Before we began the rehearsal, I usually explained that guests were to end their sequences gracefully. They could say any ending they wanted—even something like "Well, that's all the time we have. I hope you've enjoyed it," and so on—as long as the very last words were "Thanks for watching." I had learned about the pitfalls of abrupt endings long ago when I showed a guest a "Cut" sign and he stopped talking in midsentence! I also reinforced the importance of using the words "Thanks for watching" as an end cue. Without specific words, there's no telling how many false endings we might have.

A stage manager was at the rehearsal to rehearse cues and to become a familiar presence to the guest. Once the director/producer had left the floor, it was important that the guest look to the stage manager for direction. The guest went through all of his presentation without the host or cameras. The stage manager showed the time-cue cards, indicating how quickly that first card would appear. Most guests were surprised to discover the realities of working with actual times. For some quite suddenly, and for others after what seemed an eternity, there were 5 minutes left, then 3 minutes left, then 2 minutes, 1 minute, 30 seconds, and then the "Finish" card.

It would take about half an hour to rehearse the 7-minute piece. The first 5 minutes were spent setting up the area. Five minutes were needed to introduce the guest to the television terms he needed to know. He had to learn to talk to camera 3 and show things to camera 2, the close-up camera. I provided the guest with a monitor that showed only the close-up of the ducks (the output of camera 2) but not the guest. I didn't explain the reasoning behind this and was perfectly happy if the guest simply took it to be some special television mystery. In fact, seeing oneself on a monitor can be very distracting, and an amateur guest may lose his or her train of thought and become flustered.

Each time we came to something that was out of the ordinary, we went over it until the guest felt comfortable. We barely got through the full rehearsal of the duck presentation before it was time to rehearse the show with the host and cameras. Although I intended to move briskly through the talk segments of our program, rehearsing no more than the "in" and "out" of each segment, I expected to do a real-time rehearsal with the show-and-tell segment.

Had the duck segment been done with our host, or with anyone who was familiar with the demonstration format, we would have used considerably less rehearsal time. A program dedicated solely to a show-and-tell production—a cooking program, for example—might take much more time to rehearse, depending on the nature of what was being cooked and what was available in the studio. Were the program to revolve around expendables, such as the food on a cooking program, it would be prudent to have enough supplies for at least a run-through, a dress rehearsal, and a taping or two.

SINGLE-CAMERA DEMONSTRATION PROGRAMS

The material we've looked at so far has been produced with a multiple-camera format. A great deal of demonstration production, however, is produced using single-camera techniques. The production steps are essentially the same for both single- and multiple-camera formats. Both formats involve preproduction, production, and postproduction phases.

In both single-camera and multiple-camera production, it's essential to:

1. Create an outline.
2. Develop a script.
3. List the production's needs—talent, locations, props, equipment, and so on.
4. Develop a timetable, with deadlines.
5. Work out a budget.

There are some script format differences, however. In fact, there are distinct script formats for:

1. Multiple-camera television
2. Single-camera film or television
3. Audio-video/commercials
4. Theatrical productions

Appendix 1 has examples of these script formats.

In a multiple-camera production the director/producer's job is to arrange the material so the action can be covered no matter what the guest says. In a scripted single-camera production we know what will be said, and we are expected to be more specific in choosing *what* is seen and *when* it is seen. Therefore, the production and postproduction for a single-camera scripted production follows the steps used in a scripted format, which allows for more specific choices. Ideally, whether using a single-camera or multiple-camera format, the director/producer should have enough expendable demonstration material—foods, liquids, clay, and so on—for a rehearsal, the production, and a pickup or two, at the very least. Pickups are shots or sequences of shots that repeat, or pick up, a particular event in a production. A close-up of an egg being cracked in a video about making scrambled eggs might become a pickup shot if the original egg made a mess in the close-up during taping.

Finally, it must be recognized that there are some productions that don't fit into any "standard template." But most productions *do* get produced following similar plans because it tends to be the most efficient way to work.

REVIEW

1. The director must retain as much control of the program as is possible.
2. Pictures and story should be coordinated.
3. Find a common thread.
4. Create a routine for the program and a "subroutine" for the demonstration.
5. Even if the guest is very familiar with the material, it should be rehearsed as a demonstration before it gets to the studio. Use the same props or very good substitutes for those that will be used in the production.
6. Rehearse in the studio and identify any special needs, such as filters, music, props, or graphics.
7. Demonstrate items by:
   a. Marked spot: placing them on a prearranged spot
   b. Panning: lining them up and panning
8. Rehearse the talent so they do not hold objects up in the air, as your camera operators will not be able to find focus if they do.
9. Consider the background of the material that will be demonstrated. Make sure that it helps in the display. It's usually best when it offers contrast that will look good in both black and white, and color. A printed pattern should be avoided.

10. Were the program to revolve around expendables, such as the food on a cooking program, it is wise to have enough supplies for at least a run-through, a dress rehearsal, and a taping or two.

- There are distinct script formats for:
  1. Multiple-camera television
  2. Single-camera film or television
  3. Audio-visual/commercials
  4. Theatrical productions
- The time line for a production includes the creation of:
  1. An outline
  2. A script
  3. Lists of production needs
  4. A time table with deadlines
  5. A budget

chapter six

Scripted Format

The conventions we now use for shooting multiple-camera television come from the early days of live television when directors were imported from the theatrical community. The skills they had learned in the theater were effective when it became necessary to put dramas and scored musicals on the air. They found the stage managers prompt book particularly valuable (Figures 6.1A and 6.1B). In fact, the procedures and the script markings we now use for "a line cut" or "cutting" a television show—daytime dramas, some sitcoms, classical music, operas, ballet, and theatrical productions—are very similar to the notations used by stage managers in the theater.

As in the theater, the functions of the director and the functions of the producer are quite different. There is no single example that will cover all productions, but for the most part, the producer is more involved with legal and management issues, while the director works with the script and actors or musical elements, as well as with the crew.

DRAMA

If you direct drama of any kind, then you work with actors. There are lots of books and theories dedicated to the working relationship between the director and the actor. The ones I have found most helpful are *An Actor Prepares* and *Building a Character,* both by Constantine Stanislavski (also spelled Konstantin Stanislavsky), and *The Art of Dramatic Writing* by Lajos Egri. Almost all the books that deal with working with actors stress the need for relaxation, concentration during the scene, acceptance by the cast of the given circumstances, and clear-cut goals for each part of the scene. They also stress the need for truth and

honesty on the part of the director and actors; they offer techniques for the actors and director to find an inner approach to the drama.

This inward-looking approach is perhaps the most difficult part of the director's role. It demands the insights of a psychological analyst and the personality traits of a benevolent despot. *The Art of Dramatic Writing* is particularly helpful in analyzing the construction and intent of a play. Although these parts of the director's work are essential, they are not a part of *this* book. The material covered in this chapter deals with the mechanics involved in the working relationship among the talent (actors, musicians, and dancers), the crew, and the director/producer. These considerations often color the artistic choices that are made.

It's easier to learn the mechanics of the director's job if you assume the performers will have been cast to type. In fact, for the most part, typecasting is the order of the day. Actors are usually hired because they "are" the part. This makes the actor's and the director's jobs much less complex. At most network and major stations, the director doesn't make the final casting decisions and usually doesn't have sufficient rehearsal time to "work with the actors" on acting problems. Typecasting eliminates most acting problems. Working on the mechanical aspects of scripted programs, such as daytime dramas or sitcoms, is still daunting. It may also be the most fun. The hard part is the enormous concentration and organization it takes to make all the elements come together in the brief and expensive time that's allowed for each production.

If a program takes the best director eight hours to shoot, that is all the time that will be available. Taking more time is a waste of money. Reserving too little time means the project won't get completed.

KNIGHT OF THE MIRRORS

Look! Dost thou see him? A madman dressed for a masquerade! Q 62

(Quixote attempting to escape, finds himself facing still another
mirror)

Look, Don Quixote! See him as he truly is! See the clown! Drown,
Don Quixote. Drown - drown in the mirror. Go deep -- deep -- the
masquerade is ended!

(Quixote fall to his knees)

Confess! Thy lady is a trollop, and thy dream the nightmare of a
disordered mind!

DON QUIXOTE

(Dazed and in desperation)

I am Don Quixote, Knight errant of La Mancha...and my lady is the
Lady Dulcinea. I am Don Quixote, knight errant...and my lady...my Q 63
lady...

(Quixote falls to the floor and is silent)

KNIGHT OF THE MIRRORS

(Removing the casque from his head)

It is done! Q 64

SANCHO

(Thunderstruck)

Your Grace! It is Doctor Carrasco! It is only Sanson Carrasco!

DR. CARRASCO

Forgive me Senior Quijana. It was the only way. Q 65

(The lights change back to the prison. The Captain of the
Inquisition steps forward)

CAPTAIN

Cervantes! Prepare to be summoned! Q 66

CERVANTES

By whom? (AS JUDGES APPR. TOP-O-BRDG.) Q 67

CAPTAIN

The Judges of the Inquisition. Q 68

Figure 6.1A A page from the prompt book for *Man of La Mancha*. It shows the cues as they appear on the stage manager's script. The cues in the prompt book indicate that after a particular word or visual cue, some event will be called for by the stage manager. In the same way, the directions in a television director's marked script indicate where and when a command will be given. From *Man of La Mancha*, used with author's permission. © 1966 by Dale Wasserman.

KNIGHT OF THE MIRRORS
Look! Dost thou see him? A madman dressed for a masquerade!   *Q 62*

(Quixote attempting to escape, finds himself facing still another
mirror)

Look, Don Quixote! See him as he truly is! See the |clown!| *Q62.5* | MIRR BALL |
Drown, Don Quixote. Drown - drown in the mirror.
Go deep -- deep -- the masquerade is ended!

(Quixote fall to his knees)

Confess! Thy lady is a trollop, and thy dream the nightmare of a
disordered mind!

DON QUIXOTE
(Dazed and in desperation)
I am Don Quixote, Knight errant of La Mancha...and my lady
is the Lady Dulcinea. I am Don Quixote, knight errant...
and my lady...my lady...   *(AS Q FALLS)   Q63*

(Quixote falls to the floor and is silent)

KNIGHT OF THE MIRRORS
(Removing the casque from his head)
It is done!   *Q 64 |5|*

SANCHO
(Thunderstruck)   *RAIL- MIRR.BALL ↑*
Your Grace! It is Doctor Carrasco! It is only Sanson Carrasco!

DR. CARRASCO
Forgive me Senior Quijana. It was the only way.   *Q 65*

(The lights change back to the prison. The Captain of the
Inquisition steps forward)

CAPTAIN
Cervantes! Prepare to be summoned!

CERVANTES
By whom?

CAPTAIN
The Judges of the Inquisition.   *Q 68*

(FOLLOW) WNCH#2 BRDG.STAIRS ↓

Visual   *(AS STAIRS TOUCH FLOOR) Q 69*

Figure 6.1B   Note that this page is the same as Figure 6.1A, except that the lighting director has eliminated cues 66 and 67. The stage manager leaves the numeric holes in the sequence, and no shifting of the remaining cues takes place. This is handled the same way in television.

The director knows that everyone watches the clock and the budget, as well as the production itself. The director is on the line to deliver. If you can do the job and do it well, there's a definite sense of accomplishment and fun.

A 60-minute daytime drama (a soap opera) really has just 44 minutes of material to be shot. The rest of the hour is commercials, station breaks, and credits. There is only one long 12-hour day in which to shoot the material. An hour program may easily have 500 to 600 shots. Sitcom episodes run for approximately 22 minutes to make up a 30-minute program. They rehearse for one week and may have anywhere from 200 to 400 shots. Multiple-camera scripted sitcoms are limited in the amount of actual shooting hours they may use, because they work before live audiences, which demand real-time performances. Sometimes two or more separate performances, such as the dress rehearsal and the actual performance, are edited together. Often the total number of hours allowed for work on the production of a sitcom or other television program is limited because children are in the cast. The laws regarding the number of hours a child can work are very strict. Rehearsal and shoot times for them are specifically prescribed.

At best, a cast with children must complete its production in a single eight-hour shoot day. The director of scripted material must be very prepared, and the three things that can help him or her to do that are conventions, the ground plan, and the shooting script.

CONVENTIONS

One of the foundations of our theater is the idea of an imaginary fourth wall. The actors pretend there is a fourth wall and everything they do happens behind it. The pretense is that there's no audience out there squirming and laughing. The audience pretends right along with the actors, and we all accept the magic that lets us see through the wall. It's a convention. Television audiences accept this convention and many others as well. In television, a dissolve from one scene to the other indicates that there has been a change in place or time. If a couple embraces and the camera pans off into the fireplace, we assume that they're going to continue the embrace and that we're going to give them some privacy. One of the most traditional conventions is

that a scene starts with an establishing shot and then as the action gets more intense, the camera comes closer. These and other conventions, some of which are cultural, are important to the creation of a shooting script.

Conventions that are a part of our cultural heritage, such as "ladies go first" through doors or the clinking of wine glasses in a toast, must become a part of the way we present material. Nevertheless, a close look at the way television handles conventions would show that they are constantly being broken. Which conventions will be broken and why are regular considerations of the director. Sometimes a break in conventions signals that some event represents an important moment. It's as if the director were saying, "You see, this is so important I'm not even taking time to put the camera on a tripod to show you this." (This may well be the birth of the shaky hand-held look.) "I'm starting with a close-up of the phone and not showing you a wide shot with Heather, the character who is now speaking, because it's the phone that really sets the scene. After all, we all know that Brad may call Heather at any moment . . . or, then again, maybe not!"

At WNET, the public broadcast station in New York, we indicated the shots framing by body position. A shot would be called for as "head to toe" (which meant include everything from slightly above the head to slightly below the toes), "knees" (which meant include everything from slightly above the head to the knees), waist, chest, shoulders, or chin. At other stations, less precise terms, such as *wide shot, close-up*, and so on, were often used. When these less precise terms are used, it becomes important to find out exactly what the framing would be for a wide shot or a close-up. The problem is that "close-up" may mean a chest shot at one studio and a shoulder shot at another. Figure 6.2 shows an example of a marked shooting script. (You can see a marked script for a musical production in Chapter 7.)

Other conventions set out guidelines for actors' movements (that is, blocking) and combinations of shots. Most programs demand the appearance of some kind of action. When daytime drama first came to television, blocking was minimal. A character would enter a kitchen, and the dialogue and action would be restricted to such exchanges as "Hi, Madge, I'm so glad you came over. Sit down, have a cup of coffee, and let's talk about the horrible troubles Ashley and Brian seem to be having." They then sat and talked.

#6030

PROLOGUE - SCENE TWO

NICK/SHARON HOUSE - NIGHT

(OPEN TIGHT ON A DECEMBER CALENDAR AS FEMALE

HAND COMES INTO PICTURE, DRAWING A RED X THRU

THE SQUARE FOR DEC 31. PULL BACK TO REVEAL A

REFLECTIVE SHARON, STARING THOUGHTFULLY AT

THE CALENDAR AS SHE AND WE HEAR NICK'S VOICE)

                    NICK (O.C.)

    Why so serious?

(SHE LOOKS UP TO SEE NICK AS)

                    SHARON

    Nick! I was just thinking.

                    NICK

    Obviously not happy thoughts.

                    SHARON

    No, no. That's not true. I'm just

    thinking back, because it's the last

    day of the year.

                    NICK

    I can't believe it. A few more hours

    and this year is history.

                    SHARON

(WARM, REFLECTIVE SMILE AS SHE REACHES OUT,

TAKES HIS HANDS)

    It's been quite a year for us, hasn't

    it?

                    NICK

    The best year of my life.

Figure 6.2 A page from a shooting script for *The Young and the Restless*. The director's marks are similar to those used on other programs. The letter *H* in some of the shots stands for "Hold" and indicates that the shot is the same as the preceding shot. The handwritten notes at the top of the page are instructions for the stage crew. Other notations found in the dialogue (such as "at stairs" or "x in a bit") are stage directions intended for the actors. They are placed in the shooting script at the moment in which the action is to be performed. Reprinted by permission from Columbia Pictures Television.

It's not that way anymore. Now we have daytime dramas and sitcoms that require the look of dramas, with genuine conflict revealed through the dialogue and action of the characters. The blocking in each scene has to emerge from the inner conflict of the situation. Since a daytime drama is produced every day, some conventions for handling the blocking evolve for each program. For example, there was a time on some daytime dramas when scenes almost always started with a wide sweeping shot. After that, there were many extreme close-ups. That convention probably evolved because shooting the actors in extreme close-ups gave the illusion of extreme drama. It also meant less blocking, less camera rehearsal, and fewer chances for camera-framing errors.

The convention continued, and soon after a few extreme close-ups, one could expect a medium or waist shot in which someone walks, agitatedly, into a new two-shot and then turns around to respond . . . in a new close-up. From there on, in that convention it's ever-tightening close-ups, until the next revelation or emotional crisis. Other conventions deal with the handling of cameras and switching or editing. Traditionally, a zoom or any movement of the camera or lens must be motivated. There are three classic motivations for zooms, which you can remember with the word *CAD*.

C = Curtain, the beginning or end of a scene. The zoom acts as a "curtain" for the scene. It also may set up the scene. If the scene starts on a close-up of the telephone and then widens out to see "our hero" staring at the phone, we know something important involving a phone call is about to happen or has just happened. At the end of a scene, when the heroine leaves in a huff, we can expect to zoom in to the hero's face as he clenches and unclenches his jaw.

A = Action taking place on screen. A boy enters the room in a waist shot and then walks to a desk, and we see that there is a girl in the room. She is sitting in a chair at the desk. In order to not lose sight of the boy, the camera pans with him as he walks and then is forced to zoom out from the single shot of the boy to become a two-shot that includes the girl. We'll see more of this scene later.

D = Drama, dramatic moments in the scene. In daytime drama this "zoom in" usually occurs at least once a scene. It is a kind of punctuation

mark, as if to say, "Well, what do you think about that?" Once the actor's blocking is set, writing the shots in some form that can be duplicated is the key ingredient to effective shooting. That's where a ground plan and shooting script become indispensable.

THE GROUND PLAN

The ground plan is a quarter-inch map of the set. The director uses it to determine where things are in the set and to communicate that to the rest of the crew. It shows, in very clear terms, the actual relationship between elements of the set. In practice, it lets a director know how many steps a character will need to get from one place to another. It also indicates the location of key scenic and prop elements for the director and for various crews.

The set crew uses the ground plan to place the set and then to place major props in it. The prop crew sets pieces based on notes on the ground plan. The lighting department uses the ground plan to indicate what areas have to be lit and how. Elements of it can be quickly rearranged, if need be, by indicating the changes on the ground plan. That's very useful because something invariably comes up at the last minute that requires minor changes in the set.

Prior to rehearsal, the director will mark a copy of the ground plan for the lighting director (Figure 6.3). The lighting director (LD) will need to know the areas in which characters will walk, which way they will face, and whether they will be sitting or standing. The LD also notes from the ground plan what special lighting requirements may be needed for each scene. Typical concerns might include a scene requirement that the bedroom lights be practical. The director has created action—"business"—in which the lights will be turned on during the scene. The LD knows that this will require brighter wattage in the lamps so the bedside lamps can be seen over the bright set lights. It may also necessitate some special instruments to give the illusion that there is a change in the room lighting because the bedroom lights have been turned on.

Perhaps the director will want to arrange for mood and will ask, for example, that the hospital corridor be overly bright. Often notes become quite extensive. For example, an LD's ground plan might have to indicate that the director intends to start scene four with a pull-back from a blue moon

Figure 6.3   The director has marked the character blocking into this coffee house set so the LD can place instruments for the characters. Note that "night" is noted on the plan. Note too that this illustration is *not* to quarter-inch scale. Courtesy of Columbia Pictures.

shadow coming through the kitchen window and falling onto the kitchen floor. During the pull-back a burglar's shadow will need to be included, and so on. The LD will incorporate the director's notes, as indicated on the ground plan, into the overall lighting plan for the program.

THE SHOOTING SCRIPT

Presumably, if you can plan ahead to get exactly what you imagined, your shooting is apt to be more precise than it would be if you improvise. A repeatable plan is, obviously, more consistent. The shooting script is the single most important element to making the shooting plan repeatable and reliable. It's unlike the "dialogue" script in a number of ways. The original dialogue script contains the text of the script and may include some directions. At first it may be written in any way the writer chooses. Although it may include locations, it does not contain any shots, and it is not yet a shooting script. The shooting script, on the other hand, is formatted in a very strict manner. The following is the format for multiple-camera television, shot live or on tape. Filmed and theatrical productions use a somewhat different script format, as shown in Appendix 1.

1. It is *always* typed or printed.
2. It is *always* on 8½-by-11-inch paper (*never* on legal-sized paper). It fits into binders better that way and is easier to carry.
3. All the pages are numbered in the upper right-hand corner.
4. All the revisions are labeled with the date, and sometimes even the time, of the revision. Often revisions are copied on different-colored paper so the production team can be sure that it is dealing with the most current edition of the text.
5. There is always a one-inch margin on the left and at least a three-inch margin on the right. It is in this right-hand margin that the director marks the shots.
6. Unlike single-camera productions, in which dialogue may be single-spaced, the dialogue for multiple-camera productions is always double-spaced. This creates room on the page to make write-in changes and is easier to edit. Dialogue is set in upper and lower case. Instructions are all upper case, as are the names of the characters. This style makes it

easy to distinguish dialogue from the author's instructions during a taping.

7. Stage right and left are indicated as seen by the camera, not by the actors' right and left. The actors' stage right and stage left refer to the actors' right and left when they are on stage looking at the audience or camera. The actors' right and left are exactly opposite of camera right and left.
8. Lines finish at the bottom of the page. They are rarely broken so a character starts speaking at the bottom of one page and then continues on the top of the next. Only in the case of very long speeches is this page break allowed. This is done so the director doesn't turn the page and find a fast camera call at the top of the page.
9. The way one marks the text is essentially the same on all programs. Each director or program may have a distinct style, but the distinctions are usually inconsequential, and the key elements remain the same, no matter who is directing. The key elements are as follows:
   a. How the shot is put on the air; the default is a "take" or a cut. The shot may also be put on the air as a fade-up, (or fade in) a dissolve, or a wipe. In all but the "take," the duration of the change is of great importance.
   b. The camera
   c. The shot number
   d. The character
   e. The framing
   f. The development of the shot
10. Directors mark the script in pencil because there will be inevitable changes, and pencil marks can be erased. On network daytime dramas and sitcoms, the marked pencil script is then copied. On short scripts the associate director (AD) remarks the script so he or she can make any erasures along with the director.

Pencil Exercise

What follows is the traditional way of working on productions that are shot and edited "live" and yield what is referred to as a "line cut." Other ways of working exist, and these will be discussed later in this chapter.

Many of the problems that are typical to a drama are incorporated in the following "pencil exercise." Once you have gone through it, compare the notation with the notation in Figure 6.2 from *The Young and the Restless.*

Allen Fletcher, who was a professor of acting and directing at Carnegie Mellon University and later one of the directors of San Francisco's American Conservatory Theater (ACT), attributed this exercise to Stanislavski of the Moscow Arts Theater. This introduction may have been a joke on the students, but the exercise was useful then and is still being used. Changing the lines almost never works. Invariably, a more exciting script takes concentration away from the dynamics and mechanics of the exercise. The idea is to make up your own plot and set it to the lines of the exercise.

Full Script for the Pencil Exercise

PENCIL EXERCISE/SCENE ONE—ACT ONE

FADE IN

THE SCENE: WHEREVER YOU WANT IT TO BE

> BOY:

I'm looking for my pencil.

> GIRL:

Yes.

> BOY:

I lost it.

> GIRL:

Yes.

> BOY:

Have you seen it?

> GIRL:

No.

> BOY:

I thought I left it here.

> GIRL:

No.

Marking the Blocking

In my plot, the boy enters a room looking for his pencil. The girl, who is already in the room seated at a desk, acknowledges his presence but pays little attention to him. Finally, she responds to him and locates his pencil behind his ear.

For the purpose of this exercise, start with the ground plan shown in Figure 6.4, which is a living room. There's a door that swings in at the upper left side of the set, through which the boy will enter. He'll cross to the girl, who is seated at the downstage right desk. Down left (camera left) is a small bar. ("Downstage" is toward the cameras, and upstage is toward the back wall or curtain.)

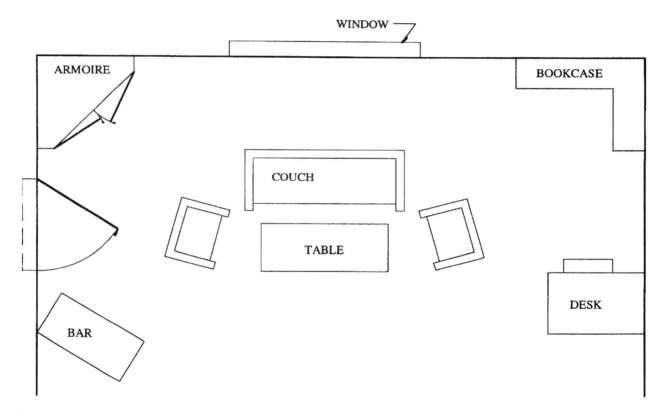

Figure 6.4   A designer's rendition of the plan for the pencil exercise. Reprinted by permission from G. Shizuko Herrero.

I . Actors blocking and Stage Managers cue. NOTE: NO CAMERA BLOCKING

*PENCIL EXERCISE/SCENE ONE - ACT ONE

FADE IN

THE SCENE: WHEREVER YOU WANT IT TO BE

Q Boy (handwritten)

BxToG (handwritten)

                    BOY

I'm looking for my pencil.

The first thing the director does is to mark out all the characters' blocking on the script. I use a colored pencil (usually red) to indicate the characters' movements, or blocking. These notations are placed in the script at the precise points where the blocking is to occur. Red pencil stands out during blocking rehearsal, and the instructions are easy to find. I also use the letter "x" to mean the word "cross." Sometimes that refers to actors' blocking: "Boy x to Girl" means "The boy crosses over to the girl." At other times "x" refers to camera directions: "This is a 'x2,' or a 'cross two-shot.'" A cross two-shot is sometimes referred to as an over-the-shoulder shot.

For the sake of this exercise, let's assume that the first thing to block is the boy coming through the door on the left and crossing to the girl (Figure 6.5). Ordinarily all the actors' blocking would be done first, and then the camera blocking would be done. It will be easier to enter the subsequent blocking as it occurs. Here is how the first part of the actors' blocking would look and be marked (see Pencil Exercise II).

- The first mark is a cue to the stage manager to start the action. The stage manager's cue to the boy must happen *before* the scene begins so the boy can be in motion (making his cross) as the scene fades up.
- The actor's blocking would probably have been written first, since we deal with the actors before the cameras. The actual marks on the script are put in place where the action is to occur. I mark the action in a colored pencil so it will stand out on the page and not get confused with any other kind of instructions. Red marks refer to character blocking, and black pencil refers to cameras. Colored pencil marks are not an industry standard.

Figure 6.5 This is the framing for shot #1. The boy is in a waist shot ready to cross. His blocking "B x to G" and the cue for his entrance are noted in the script. A line has been drawn down the side of the script, which sometimes helps locate a shot when it's needed quickly.

II. PENCIL EXERCISE/SCENE ONE - ACT ONE

FADE IN

THE SCENE: WHEREVER YOU WANT IT TO BE

BOY

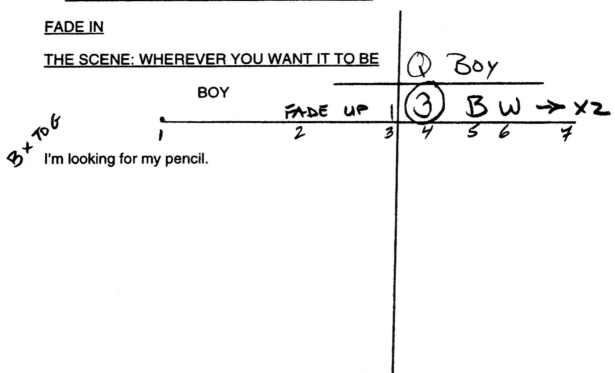

I'm looking for my pencil.

Pencil Exercise II shows how camera shots would be added to the already actor-marked shooting script.

1. When the shot is taken (in this case not a word cue but action)
2. How the shot is to be put "on the air" (it will fade up)
3. The shot number
4. The camera
5. The character
6. The framing
7. The development within the shot

Everything about the shot is indicated on the shooting script, as if the shooting script itself were a time line or map of the individual events that make up the scene. All the director's shot choices must indicate seven things:

1. *When the shot is taken.* In this case the shot has to "fade up" rather than be "taken." The convention is that the scene "fades up" just as the action or line begins so the scene goes on the air as the action begins. We don't want to fade up and see an actor waiting for his cue.

Therefore, the actor is cued *before* the fade-up, and the director watches the monitor to be sure that the action has started before commanding the fade-up.

2. How the shot is to be put on the air. Usually there is no mark, which indicates that the shot is a take. If the intention is to go from one picture (or black) to another with a fade-up, a wipe, or a dissolve, *that* is noted on the script. If there is no notation, the assumption is that the shot is to be a take.

3. *The shot number.* Each shot is numbered. The shot numbers are used by several different people to keep track of where they are in the script. These people are:

   a. *The associate director.* The AD's function is much like that of a stage manager in the theater. ADs are responsible for readying upcoming events, such as the next shot, a light cue, a prop cue, a sound effect, and so on. They do this through a closed-circuit intercom system that connects the control room, the cameras, and other "as assigned" locations: the audio booth, the light booth, sound effects, and so on. Sometimes the AD wears a headset, and sometimes there is an open mic in the control room. Headsets are worn on the floor. At the as-assigned positions, crew members may use either headphones or speakers, depending on need. The numbered shots help keep the AD and the technicians at the right place in the script. In television, this function is assigned to an associate director. In film, the directors work with an assistant director. Assistant directors may perform some tasks that are similar to those of associate directors, but essentially, assistant directors work in film and are not as involved with setting up shots. Instead, they serve as liaisons among the director, the cast, the crew, and management—notably the unit production manager.

b. *The technical director.* A technical director (TD) is responsible for the technical aspects of the program and pushes the buttons or fader bars, at the director's command, to put the cameras "online." Although the TD listens to both the associate director's "readies" and the director's "takes," the TD sometimes keeps a step or two ahead by using his or her copy of the numbered script. Under some contracts the TD doesn't get a script but works from the AD's and director's calls instead.

Conversely, there have been contracts under which the director isn't allowed to talk to the crew. The director lets the TD know, via the shooting script, what is expected; the TD then acts as if he or she were the director of photography on a film-style shoot. That way, it's the TD who readies every shot; during actual production the director simply calls the takes. Later in this chapter we'll look at the more traditional control room operation during a taping.

c. *Camera operators.* Camera operators use the shot numbers to keep track of their shots. Each camera operator has a shot sheet, which contains a list of only his or her individual shots. In a way, it's a personalized script for each camera's performance.

d. *The edit suite.* Additionally, the shot numbers will be used when the program is edited. It's much easier to say, "Use shot #320 from the third take" than to say "Use the shot of the boy that comes after he crosses to the girl and says, 'I'm looking for

my pencil,' in the second scene of the fourth act from the third take."

4. *The camera to be seen.* The camera number of the camera to be used is circled or written larger than any other mark on the script so it really stands out. It's made particularly distinctive because the director may be looking at a monitor, thinking about a note, or concerned about some other part of the production and needs to return to the script quickly. The large camera numbers stand out and help the director, associate director, and technical director find their places in the script.

5. *Who is seen in the initial framing of the shot.* This notation limits the starting frame of the shot to whoever or whatever is supposed to be in the shot when it first goes on the air. It is what the camera operator sees in the frame just before the shot is taken. In this case, the first shot should only include the boy. Later, we'll see the girl.

6. *How they are seen.* In our example, the camera operator knows that the initial shot is of the boy. How we expect to see the boy—the framing, whether it is a head-to-toe shot, a waist shot, or a chin shot, for instance—is very important. It is therefore indicated in the shooting script and is part of the notation for the shot sheets for each camera. When the director says "take," it's expected that the camera operator will have framed the shot as it had been planned and rehearsed. Once the shot is on the air, it may well be changed by action, but at the instant before the director calls for the take, to put the shot online or on air, the director expects to see the shot framed as had been planned. In the first example, the shot started as a waist shot of the boy and changed when the girl came into the picture.

7. *What developments will happen in the shot.* It's expected that the camera operator will maintain the director's framing. If the character moves and there's no indication of a change in framing, the shot, as noted, will be held. Sometimes, however, that's impossible. In our example, if the boy crossed so he was standing near the girl, it would be impossible to hold the boy in a waist shot without having a very badly framed shot in which the bottom of the frame held only the top half of the girl's head. If the director expects a change in framing or knows that new framing must happen, the new framing

II. Actors blocking and Stage Managers cue. NOTE: NO CAMERA BLOCKING

*PENCIL EXERCISE/SCENE ONE - ACT ONE

FADE IN

THE SCENE: WHEREVER YOU WANT IT TO BE

Ⓠ BOY

BOY. *FADE UP* | *③ BW —> X2*

BXTOG

I'm looking for my pencil.

will be noted for the camera. In our example, the boy, first seen in a waist shot, brings the shot to a cross two-shot. By using the zoom to widen with the boy's cross, the camera operator will hold the boy, then include the girl, and hold focus throughout. It's expected that the camera operator will know the conventions and will understand that the two-shot develops only as the girl appears in the viewfinder. Focus will be held because the lens has widened, which automatically increases the depth of field and the apparent depth of focus.

Marking the Cameras

Since cameras are usually located on the floor in numerical order, we can assume they'll be lined up with camera 1 on the left, camera 2 in the middle, and camera 3 on the right (when looking from the perspective of the audience, not of the actors). Because the boy will be facing camera 3 as he enters from the upstage door, camera 3 is probably the best choice for our first shot. Once the girl comes into view, the shot will have to widen and become a "cross-two" (or over-the-shoulder) shot so she will be included in the frame (Figures 6.6 and 6.7).

In the early days of television, camera 2 might have been used to give us a wide establishing shot. It would have to be very wide as the scene started, and our cast would appear very small on the screen. There are three ways our boy can enter and speak: (1) he can speak and then cross (x) to the girl, (2) he can x while speaking, or (3) he can x and then speak.

Deciding which way is best involves a fundamental premise about handling blocking for the camera. By a process of elimination, the third choice will probably be the best choice. Here's why. If we choose the first option, in which he speaks and then crosses, the cross becomes a "stage wait." The audience wants to know who he's talking to and what's going on. If you don't supply the answers immediately, the audience loses interest, unless there's a very provocative first line. Furthermore, if the audience waits, they'll get to see the room as he crosses, and then they'll come upon the back or profile of

the girl, who will now be in the foreground of camera 3's shot. At this point, the audience will need a moment to register the fact that there is someone else in the room. They see it's a girl, but now they want to know who she is. What is her relationship to the boy? Did he act threatening or loving? Is she an older woman? Is she his mother or his girlfriend? One picture does tell a lot, so these questions would be answered in a lot less time than it takes to read this. Since the boy has spoken already, we leave the audience no time to digest the information about the room or the girl because we need to cut to the front of the girl for her response. At best, everything will feel rushed.

Similar problems can arise in the second option, in which the boy crosses and speaks at the same time. In the third option, which is the best, the boy crosses, and the audience sees the room without a stage wait and without any other action happening. Meanwhile, they can wonder about the boy. Who is he? Where is he going? What will happen? Then the audience sees the girl and finally hears the question. By this time, we are ready for the next shot, and there is no sense of being rushed.

Now let us say we want to see the girl as she takes her line (Figure 6.8). Our cue to take the shot will be the end of the boy's line. If we "take one," which is shot #2, then we will be showing the girl when she speaks (see Pencil Exercise III). At the end of the boy's speech (camera 3 was online), we can assume that the girl will react to the boy's entrance. She would now be looking at the boy. Camera 3

Figure 6.6   A part of shot #1. The boy is crossing to the girl; it's evolving into a two-shot.

Figure 6.7   The final framing for shot #1. The boy has arrived at the girl's desk.

III.*PENCIL EXERCISE/SCENE ONE - ACT ONE * (Shot #2 of the girl)

FADE IN

THE SCENE: WHEREVER YOU WANT IT TO BE

FADE UP

BOY

I'm looking for my pencil.

GIRL

Yes.

has a shot that features the boy and therefore is the poorest choice if we want to see the girl. That leaves us a choice of either camera 2 or 1. The camera that sees her best and represents the boy's point of view is camera 1, so we'll use that. We would say, "Take one," where "one" refers to camera 1.

The framing for the shot will be determined in part by the position of the boy next to the girl. We are obliged to use a cross two-shot, because the boy's body would get in the way of all but a very tight close-up of the girl. Tight close-ups (shoulder or chin shots) are usually considered inappropriate so early in the scene, since nothing of great importance has happened yet. The convention is that this kind of shot is saved until later in a scene, at a moment of high drama. Furthermore, the preceding

shot ended in a cross two-shot. To match that, and to maintain a neutral look at this early stage of the play, we would want to see the girl in the same cross two-shot. Therefore, shot #2 will happen immediately after the boy's line is finished. It will be on camera 1 and will be a cross two-shot.

The convention regarding framing for two-shots is that they are always assumed to be as tight as they can be without looking uncomfortable. Otherwise, the director will specify either a "one and a half," which crops the downstage person in half, or a loose two-shot. If the scene calls for a very wide two-shot, the director would try to find some elements of the picture to use as a reference for the framing—for example, "Frame from the edge of the desk to the doorway."

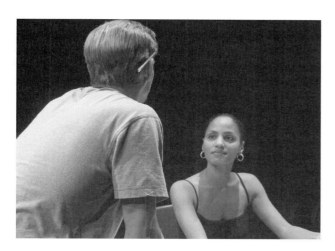

Figure 6.8 Shot #2. A cross two-shot in which we see the girl across from the boy.

IV. Boy's first response to the girl. Shot #3 carries boy to bar.

<u>*PENCIL EXERCISE/SCENE ONE - ACT ONE</u>

<u>FADE IN</u>

<u>THE SCENE: WHEREVER YOU WANT IT TO BE</u>　　　Ⓠ BOY

　　　　　　　　　　　　FADE UP　　1　③ B W ⇒ X2

　　　　　　　　BOY

ʒ x TO 6　　I'm looking for my pencil.　　　　2　① X2

　　　　　　　　GIRL

　　　Yes.　　　　　　　　　　3　② 2 SHOT ⇒ HOLD BOY

　　　　　　　　BOY

✗ TO BAR　　I lost it.

At this point there are a lot of options for the scene. Since this is just an exercise, we can play out a few of them. One of the "givens" is that we should probably feature the boy right after the girl says her first "Yes" on camera 1. Initially, one might think that it would be best to show a close-up of the boy at this time, but the camera that would do that is camera 3. The only thing that has happened since camera 3's last shot is that the girl said "Yes." Prior to that, camera 3 was left with a cross two-shot. It was originally focused on the boy when he was across the room at the doorway. It held focus on the boy's cross by widening. Widening made use of the greater depth of field inherent in a wide shot. If we now tried to use camera 3 to get a close-up of the boy, we'd probably find that the camera operator didn't have

sufficient time to refocus for that close-up. (See Pencil Exercise V for the notation to implement these decisions.) We could go to camera 3 for the same cross two-shot that it had, or we could go to camera 2. Camera 2 has a profile of the boy. I decided to use camera 2 in a flat (rather than a cross) two-shot, have the boy make a cross to the down left (camera left) bar, and then speak.

The shot starts as a two-shot (Figure 6.9), holds the framing on the boy at the knees, and loses the girl on the boy's cross. I would be careful to make this two-shot a loose two-shot so it looked different from the cross two-shots from cameras 1 and 3 (see Pencil Exercise IV and Figures 6.7–6.10). This would also make holding the boy's cross easier for camera 2's operator.

Figure 6.9 The initial framing for shot #3: a shot of the girl and the boy in a flat two-shot, as seen from camera 2's position.

Figure 6.10 The way shot #3 develops. Camera 2 is holding the boy, so this is a continuation of the same two-shot. We are seeing it as it evolves into a single shot of the boy.

V. Adds shot #4 = x2 shot to girl with boy at bar

*PENCIL EXERCISE/SCENE ONE - ACT ONE

FADE IN

THE SCENE: WHEREVER YOU WANT IT TO BE — Ⓐ BOY

FADE UP 1 — ③ BW → x2

BOY

B X TO G — I'm looking for my pencil. — 2 ① X2

GIRL

Yes. — 3 ② 2 SHOT → HOLD BOY

BOY

X TO BAR — I lost it. — 4 ① X2

GIRL

Yes.

Now that the boy is at the bar, we have to reacquaint the audience with the geography of the room. The audience needs to know how far apart these two people are. Is he so far away that he cannot touch the girl? Is the girl close enough to the bar and the boy that one withering glance would stop him from getting closer? What is their relationship to other objects in the room? Therefore, a two-shot is needed. She's going to speak. She's on the right of the set, relating to him on the left of the set. Camera 1 sees her best. It's her camera in this instance, and it has a nice angled cross two-shot (Figure 6.11 and Pencil Exercise V).

Figure 6.11   Shot #4. This cross shot to the girl comes from camera 1, which also shows the boy searching for his pencil at the bar.

VI. Boy's blocking and shot #5. Brings the boy back to girl as in shot # 1

*PENCIL EXERCISE/SCENE ONE - ACT ONE

FADE IN

THE SCENE: WHEREVER YOU WANT IT TO BE　　Ⓠ Boy

FADE UP　1　③ BW → X2

BOY

I'm looking for my pencil.　　2　① X2

GIRL

Yes.　　3　② 2 SHOT → HOLD BOY

BOY

I lost it.　　4　① X2

GIRL

Yes.　　5　③ BW → X2

BOY

Have you seen it?

It's now time to bring the boy back to the girl. Essentially, we use the same convention that we used to bring him through the door in shot #1 (Figures 6.12 and 6.13). First mark his cross in pencil where it happens, and then mark the shot (see Pencil Exercise VI).

Figure 6.12   The initial framing for shot #5: the boy at the bar, as seen from camera 3.

Figure 6.13   Shot #5 as it developed. The shot continues, and the boy arrives near the girl. It resembles the end of shot #1.

VII. Shot # 6. This is a flat two shot.

*PENCIL EXERCISE/SCENE ONE - ACT ONE

FADE IN

THE SCENE: WHEREVER YOU WANT IT TO BE   Ⓐ BOY

                                    FADE UP 1 ③ BW → X2

                    BOY
Bx TO G
    I'm looking for my pencil. _____ 2 ① X2

                    GIRL

    Yes. _____ 3 ② 2 SHOT → HOLD BOY

X TO BAR   BOY

    I lost it. _____ 4 ① X2

                    GIRL

    Yes. _____ 5 ③ BW → X2

                    BOY
Bx TO G
    Have you seen it? _____ 6 ② 2 SHOT

                    GIRL

No.

                    BOY

I thought I left it here.

                    GIRL

No.

Shot #6 could be a cross two-shot of the girl, a single of her, or a two-shot (see Pencil Exercise VII).

In reality, we probably have too many shots for this little scene, so to keep it simple, we'll hold the flat two-shot until the end (Figure 6.14).

Figure 6.14   Shot #6, a flat two-shot from camera 2. It's wide enough for the audience to see the action at the end of the scene.

VIII. Adds Girl's blocking and reaction shot words.

*PENCIL EXERCISE/SCENE ONE - ACT ONE

FADE IN

THE SCENE: WHEREVER YOU WANT IT TO BE

① BOY

FADE UP ① ③ BW → X2

Bx to G

BOY

I'm looking for my pencil. 2 ① X2

GIRL

Yes. 3 ② 2 SHOT → HOLD BOY

X TO BAR

BOY

I lost it. 4 ① X2

GIRL

Yes. 5 ③ BW → X2

Bx TO G

BOY

Have you seen it? 6 ② 2 SHOT

GIRL

No.

BOY

I thought I left it here.

GIRL

No. → GETS PENCIL
FROM BEHIND BOY'S EAR 7 ③ B SH
PENCIL IN FOREGROUND

Ø BLK

In my scenario the girl notices the pencil behind the boy's ear right after she says her last "No" (see Pencil Exercise VIII). She reaches up and holds the pencil in front of his face. He, of course, looks and feels foolish (Figure 6.15).

Our shooting script must reflect that. The strongest elements that prompt a change of camera angle are the end of a sentence or a change in idea or action. Sometimes the director's whim or emotional state may be the reason for a change in camera, but cutting to the word or deed that is happening on camera seems more helpful and appropriate. Therefore, we mark the girl's action in our shooting script, which shows the audience a wide enough shot to indicate that some special action has taken place. The special action is her getting the pencil from behind the boy's ear. We may not see the pencil yet, because it is so small in comparison to the rest of the screen. We also want to see the boy's reaction to this turn of events, so we will use her action as a cue to cut to the last shot in the episode, which is a shoulder shot of the boy's face with the pencil in the girl's hand in the foreground.

The last mark on the script stands for "dissolve." The shorthand "dissolve blk" means dissolve to black.

SHOT SHEETS

Once the shooting script of the shots used in the pencil exercise is set, shot sheets need to be made for the cameras. These cards or tear sheets are mounted on each camera and indicate each camera's shots. Figures 6.16, 6.17, and 6.18 show examples of the shots used in the pencil exercises.

During the running of the program, the AD calls out every "stand by" for the talent and effects

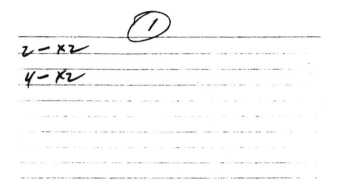

Figure 6.16   A shot sheet for the pencil exercise for camera 1. It shows only camera 1's shots.

Figure 6.17   A shot sheet for the pencil exercise for camera 2. It shows only camera 2's shots.

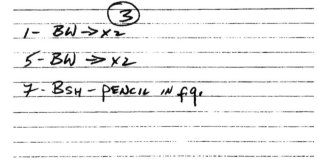

Figure 6.18   A shot sheet for the pencil exercise for camera 3. It shows only camera 3's shots. While the shot is supposed to be a shoulder shot, what's provided is wider than a shoulder shot in order to include the important pencil, and it would be acceptable.

Figure 6.15   Shot #7, the final shot in the piece. It's "the curtain," in which we see the boy reacting to the revelation about his pencil.

and "readies" the shots. The AD will say something like "Stand by to cue the boy. Ready to fade up camera 3—shot 1." The director will then say "Cue the boy," and when the director sees that the boy has begun to move, the director will continue by saying, "Fade up 3." Once the shot is on the air, the AD readies the next shot: "Ready 1, shot 2"; "Stand by the snow effect"; and so on. The AD readies a shot or action only after the director has "taken" the prior readied shot or action. Too many "readies'" or "readies" that are given too early, only lead to confusion. The camera and shot number are the key elements in the "readies." Note, however, that in the first example the AD asks for a "fade up"; otherwise a "take" is assumed. That information is also indicated in the readying. At some stations and on some occasions, the AD defines the shot as well as gives the shot number ("Ready to fade up camera 3—shot 1, the boy at waist. It will become a cross two-shot"), but that makes for a lot of chatter on the intercom. The predominant style of readying shots uses nothing more than the camera number and the shot number. On some programs, only the shot number is readied. The director may either snap his or her fingers to take the shot or call out the camera number . . . *not* the shot number.

The assumption is that the camera operator will have the shot set before the director calls for it. The AD serves as a backup, making sure that each camera operator is ready with the next shot to be called. In the unlikely event that an operator is unprepared, it's the AD's responsibility to alert the cameraperson.

Experienced camera operators understand shooting conventions as well as the director does, and they know what shot will be called for. Often the shots in a scene are the same. That is, there will be matched close-ups on cameras 1 and 3. At other times, specific shots have to be filed in short-term memory because they really are different. For example, camera 1 might spend most of a scene on just the same "held" chest shot of the heroine. These might be alternated with chest shot "holds" of the

hero on camera 3. Then, for just one shot, camera 1 is responsible for getting a close-up of something that's mentioned in the dialogue—perhaps a gun in a drawer or a wedding ring on an end table. At such times, the shot number is a handy device to remind the camera operator of the upcoming "odd" shot.

On a daytime drama, the crew usually comes in at 7 A.M. and each writes out his or her own shot sheets. The AD meets with the crew in the control room and reads the shots from the director's shooting script. The AD will call out the shot number, the camera, and the shot directions—for example, "Shot 1 camera 3, boy waist becomes a cross two. Shot 2 camera 1, a cross two. Shot 3 camera 2, a two-shot that holds the boy."

Meanwhile, the director is on the floor, going over the blocking with the actors. During the camera blocking rehearsal, there will probably be additions and deletions to the shots. Additions are handled by inserting the shot at the right place on the script and adding a letter to the shot.

Let us say, for example, that we want to insert a look that passes between the girl and boy prior to her first line. In actual production this would be far too busy a scene if all this were done in the first few shots; it is simply an example of how the shots would be inserted. We would indicate it as shown in Pencil Exercise IX.

The shots would be added before shot #3 and called 2a and 2b. Usually when an "a" shot is added, a "b" is almost always added, too. It takes us back to where we were before the cutaway was inserted. The girl says her line, and the scene proceeds. In the control room, the director will have to be in tune with the actors and their rhythm in order to call for the shots at the right pace. In this case, holding the first cutaway on the line for too long means that the girl will start to speak while the shot is on the boy; if it is too fast, we'll wonder why the girl doesn't speak. Because these shots come together so quickly, the AD would ready this flurry of shots in one burst by saying, "Ready shots 2 a, b and 3—cameras 3, 1, and 2."

IX. Insert shots 2a and 2b

*PENCIL EXERCISE/SCENE ONE - ACT ONE

FADE IN

THE SCENE: WHEREVER YOU WANT IT TO BE

(handwritten: ① BOY)

(handwritten: FADE UP 1 ③ B/W → X2)

                    BOY

(handwritten: BY TOG)   I'm looking for my pencil.

(handwritten: 2 ① X2)

(handwritten: 2A ③ X2)

                    GIRL

(handwritten: 2B ① X2)

Yes.

(handwritten: 3 ② 2 SHOT → HOLD BOY)

(handwritten: X TO BAR)

                    BOY

I lost it.

x. Delete shot number two.

<u>*PENCIL EXERCISE/SCENE ONE - ACT ONE</u>

<u>FADE IN</u>

<u>THE SCENE: WHEREVER YOU WANT IT TO BE</u>   ① BOY

          BOY   FADE UP 1 | ③ BW → X2

B X TOG

   I'm looking for my pencil.

           GIRL

Yes. _____ 3 ② 2 SHOT → HOLD BOY

TO BKR

X I lost it.

When we delete a shot, the number is simply dropped from the script. If we decide to delete camera 1's first shot (SHOT #2) because camera 2 already has a two-shot, we would simply erase rather than cross out shot 2 on camera 1. We erase the shot instead of crossing it out because everything will be shot in real time. Neatness makes it easier to find one's place. It would look like Pencil Exercise X. The AD would first ready shot #1 and then ready shot #3.

REHEARSAL ROOM

Rehearsals are handled differently for sitcoms than they are for daytime dramas or, for that matter, for long-form productions such as recorded theatrical stage presentations. Special programs that decide to air dramatic productions "live" have even more elaborate and complex rehearsal structures. Other long-form productions that might require special rehearsal procedures would be original video productions designed for industrial, educational, or network broadcast. Furthermore, various production facilities have their own conventions and requirements. However, the function and goals of the rehearsals are the same, no matter how they are done.

The function of a first rehearsal in a rehearsal room is to establish a unified approach to the scene and to block the scenes. It is important that everyone agrees about what each scene is trying to say. Ideally, this is achieved through discussion and work on the scene's relationship to the play and to the background and goals of the characters in the scene. In many cases, this is where most of the dialogue between the director and the actors takes place. Blocking and stage business is also worked out in the rehearsal room.

In network practice, particularly for ongoing sitcoms or daytime dramas, there is a very restricted amount of time allowed for preparation. Allowing too much time wastes money, and too little time thwarts the production. Usually, the actors have been working at the part or a similar one for years, or they've been hired because they are right for the part and will fit in easily. The function of the rehearsal room, then, is to block the play: to assign all business or actions, such as phone calls, where to eat while the other person is talking, how to handle the gun, and so on.

At first—early in the day for a daytime drama or early in the week for a sitcom or long form—the director has time for some passing remarks about the play and quickly gets to the blocking. Since drama revolves around conflict, most scenes have an element of chase to them, in which one character pursues another. Ideally, the blocking subtly mirrors the inner life of the scene. The television director often creates a blocking pattern that uses the depth of the set rather than working in a flat plane to achieve a more active and dynamic look.

On a daytime drama, there is barely time to walk the actors through the blocking. Often a director will just sit with them in a rehearsal room or on the set and dictate blocking in the same way that the AD is dictating shots in the control room.

STUDIO WALK-THROUGH

The next phase of rehearsal takes place in the studio with full facilities. Sometimes all of the studio rehearsals are done from the control room. I prefer to walk through the first rehearsal on the floor. The objectives of this rehearsal are:

1. To see each shot on camera
2. To change what needs to be changed as soon as the need for change appears
3. To confirm each shot with the camera operator, associate director, and anyone else who will be affected by the change.

Being on the floor helps the director see any impediment outside the camera's view. For example, I once blocked a scene that took place along a path in a park. In the rehearsal hall I had placed the actors in a spot near a convenient chair that was standing in for a tree. Once on the studio floor, it became apparent that the boom microphone had to swing from one side of the real tree to the other to cover both actors. That was a very difficult task for the boom operator. A small blocking adjustment was made in which both actors simply took one small step to the left, and the scene was much easier to do.

Whether or not the director works from the floor, the AD readies the shots, and the director calls the takes. Any changes or corrections needed are made immediately, with the director, TD, AD, and camera crew logging them as they occur on their own scripts or shot sheets.

STUDIO RUN-THROUGH

The run-through is the next phase of the rehearsal procedure. It's designed to see how the various shots work when the scene is run at full speed. Is there time to make a particular fast series of shots, or do compromises have to be made? The run-through, as opposed to the earlier walk-through, requires that the director keep a pencil in hand and make notes of problems when they occur. Stopping to correct things as you go along at this juncture would only defeat the purpose of this rehearsal. The director would then have to take the rehearsal back and try to get up to speed again. Either a production assistant (PA) takes notes on the fly, or a tic mark is placed on the script where a problem arose. Such a mark is usually sufficient to jog one's memory.

After the problems are corrected, a dress rehearsal is held. This serves as a kind of proof that the production is ready to be taped. During this rehearsal, the cast and crew are making sure that last-minute changes can really work, and they are becoming familiar and comfortable with the material.

Opinions vary widely on whether it is a good idea to tape the dress rehearsal. Many sitcoms and daytime dramas do so, and their actors are used to working with that kind of schedule. I have found, however, that taping "the dress" doesn't work with everyone. Some artists give a better performance when they know "this is it." If you elect to tape the dress, the function of a dress rehearsal is subverted for them. Once the artists know the dress is being taped, they give "a performance" and may have little left for a second take. If they don't know they are being taped, they may be pacing their performances for the take, and you may not get the best performance from them. Also, they may not trust you after that. Whether it is good practice to tape the dress will depend on the artists and the way they work, as well as on such production considerations as studio time constraints, other actor conflicts, and so forth.

RECORDING/LIVE

Finally, when it's time for the performance to begin, the action in the control room starts with the director asking that the first scene be readied. The TD and LD alert their crews, and the AD makes sure that the "floor" is ready to begin by asking the stage manager to stand by for a recording. At this time, the stage manager either confirms that the floor is ready or explains the delay. Once the floor is ready,

the AD "readies" the record. The director commands "Record." Engineering confirms the record, and the AD readies the first shot. The director asks the AD to count down. Usually this count begins at five: "Five, four, three, two, one."

The stage manager will have let the actors know that the recording has begun and will then count down with the AD from five to two. "One" will not be said aloud on the floor because the microphones on the floor may be open. Once number one in the countdown is uttered by the AD, the director commands the first readied item. For our pencil exercise scene, the director cues the boy; this is relayed by the stage manager, and the director looks at the monitor to make sure the boy is indeed walking. The command is then given to fade up camera 3. We then fade up on the boy in the process of making his cross to the girl. The AD then readies the next shot, camera, and number.

The camera operator is able to check on what that shot is supposed to be.

The director calls for the second shot on camera 1 after the boy says the word "pencil."

The TD presses the button that puts that camera on the air.

In more complicated productions, the AD or director may remind the cameras of difficult moves coming up. For example, the AD might say, speaking to camera 3, "Okay 3, here comes that tricky shot #97 where you carry Ashley over to Brian and then dump to Tanya." It's better if the director and the AD refer to the characters' names, not the actors' names, and refer to camera numbers, not camera operators.

If you try this pencil exercise, you may find that shooting the scene is easier if the actors take long pauses between the lines during the first stages of the camera rehearsal. After a while, they can come up to normal speed, but it can be quite a surprise to discover how fast things need to happen in the control room.

REHEARSAL SCHEDULES

Daytime Drama Rehearsals

Daytime dramas rehearse and shoot in two basic ways.

* *Programs in which the program is shot through from beginning to end.* In this style of work,

there is usually a morning rehearsal in a rehearsal hall while the set is being dressed. Then the cast and production staff rehearse with cameras, going through each scene. This is followed by a dress rehearsal, which may be taped, followed by the actual scheduled taping. In some programs, pickups, or re-dos, of scenes are done on the spot. In others, the pickups are all done at the end of the day.

• *Programs that are shot out of order to accommodate sets or scheduling problems.* An altered sequence might mean shooting all the living room scenes first, then all the hospital scenes, and so on. In some cases, programs are shot out of order to accommodate members of the cast. In this style of shooting, the actors are called in and rehearse in the order in which the production will be taped. Each scene is then blocked and taped in place in the studio. The entire production is then put together in the editing room. If two studios are used, as is the case with *The Young and the Restless*, sets that are finished in the first part of the day can be reset for the next day, while the second round of sets is being used. Additionally, all the actors appearing in one location are finished after their scenes are completed.

Sitcoms

The production techniques used in the multiple camera production that are common to live performances, daytime dramas, and some sitcoms come from our live theater heritage. In the traditional television model, a scene or an entire play is performed with few stops, and the production is recorded using a number of cameras whose output is edited through a switcher as the event is happening. The director calls for whatever camera he or she feels is most appropriate, and the technical director switches to that camera's output. It then goes directly to air or to a recording with all the edits in place. That cut is called a "line cut." However, over the years a number of new ways of working have evolved, fueled by technical advances.

Another style of working in sitcoms is the "quad-split." The first wave of television sitcoms in the early 1950s were 15-minute programs shot live with a line cut in the same way that all live dramas were shot. The first big switch in shooting dramas for television occurred with the *I Love Lucy* show, which used multiple cameras and shot the entire program as a whole. However, it was shot entirely on film. To do so, it invented techniques that would be particularly suited to the needs of a film production. It used three (later four) Mitchell BNC 35 mm cameras mounted on four-wheel McCallister crab dollies, with three crew members per camera to produce the program. A camera operator viewed the material through the viewfinder and adjusted the framing, a focus puller pulled focus at each new spot that had been marked on the floor, and a dolly grip moved the dolly from mark to mark. A camera director, usually an associate director or technical coordinator, cued camera changes based on line or action cues. Filmed sitcoms, both multiple-camera and single-camera, and "live" sitcoms filled the airwaves. The live programs were often kinescoped and were bicycled or mailed around the country. (Kinescope was a kind of filming that was done by shooting a live performance off a television monitor.)

Once tape was available, many of the major sitcoms continued to be shot on film, but a great number also were shot on tape as if they were live. In 1975 the *Barney Miller Show*, which was recorded on tape, went on the air produced by Danny Arnold and directed, for the most part, by Noam Pitlik. One of the technical hallmarks of the production was that although it was shot on tape rather than film, the output of *all* the cameras was recorded. The viewfinder images were sent to a quad-split screen that showed the output of all the recordings, and the final production was entirely postproduced. Today, quad-split shooting is the preferred way of working for most sitcoms. The traditional McCallister dollies have been replaced with studio peds, and the BNC cameras are now the latest studio high-definition digital cameras.

The format for shooting scripts in a production using the quad-split technique is different from that used for a line-cut production. Shooting scripts for quad-split productions must indicate each camera's assignment. Presumably, those assignments will ensure coverage of all the action. Figure 6.19 is an example of a shooting script for a pencil exercise shot with multiple cameras using the quad-split technique. Figure 6.20 shows the viewing system for cameras in a quad-split production.

While there may be some differences in the working style of each show, the process is essentially the same. For three days the director works with the cast in a rehearsal hall or on the actual set. The blocking and business that will be part of the production are worked out, as are various issues having to do with the inner life of the production.

Then on the fourth day the crew meets with the actors, and individual scenes are worked out. In the quad-split method a camera coordinator or assistant director maps out the camera's assignments in conjunction with the director. The actors rehearse the scene, and their positions and the cameras' are both marked. The four cameras, named A, B, C, and X, go through their assignments, and the output of their cameras is seen in a quad-split screen. (Letters are used instead of numbers, and because "D" sounds too much like "B," the "X" is used. Then, too, the story goes that in the early days of filmed sitcoms, it was unusual to have an EX-tra camera, hence the name "X.") Usually, the outside cameras "A" and "X" get close-ups, and the inside cameras "B" and "C" get cross two-shots or simply wider shots. The director and producers watch the quad-split and make sure that all the action is covered. Where a second setup is needed for extreme close-ups or special props or business, the scene is shot again with a second set of marks for the cameras.

One of the new models in production techniques comes from working with partially scripted material. This style of work has become popular in producing sitcoms, such as Larry David's *Curb Your Enthusiasm*. The director sets up angles and works with the cast and crew but doesn't work from a shot-by-shot script. Instead, each camera's output is recorded and the entire program is edited in postproduction.

Sitcom Rehearsals

The first three days of rehearsal for both line-cut and quad-split rehearsals are the same. During "camera days" the procedures differ. Ad-libbed productions vary in their procedures depending on location or studio operation, as well as cast and production company demands. In any event, the number of hours one can work is limited if children appear in the program, and they almost always do. A typical week's rehearsal for a line-cut or quad-split sitcom might go something like this:

Mon. Rehearsal Hall or Studio

- 9:00–10:00
  Production meeting with the executive producer, producer, director, and all creative department heads for a page-by-page breakdown of technical requirements.

- 10:00–12:00
  Read-through with actors, writers, producers, and network/studio representatives. The show is timed,

and there may be some discussion about the parts being played by this week's visiting actors.

- 12:00–1:30
  Lunch for the cast, while the director, writers, producers, and network representatives discuss what will have to change on the basis of the first reading. This may lead to notes to the director as to which scenes might best be rehearsed while new scenes are being written.

- 1:30–5:00
  Discussion of the scenes and some blocking. Since new scenes will be written, it is pointless to become too fixed in the blocking. Meanwhile some wardrobe fittings may be scheduled.

Tues. Rehearsal Hall or Studio

- 10:00–12:00
  Read through the new scenes or lines, discuss what the changes imply, make any necessary changes to those scenes that had been blocked on Monday, and start to block the new material.

- 12:00–1:30
  Lunch for the cast. Meetings with props/costumes/lights/sets and the director.

- 1:30–5:00
  Continue blocking the show. At the end of the day there will be a run-through for the producer and writers.

Wed. Rehearsal Hall or Studio

- 10:00–12:00
  Finish blocking the show. There may be many new pages of material that will be on different-colored paper to alert everyone of the most up-to-date revisions.

- 12:00–1:30
  Lunch for the cast. (If rehearsal has been held in a rehearsal studio rather than on the set, the director visits the shooting set.)

- 1:30–3:30
  Work on specific scenes that seem to need work.

- 3:30–4:30
  Run-through for the network/studio executives, the producers, and writers. The cast is released, and discussions ensue as to what changes might be made to enhance the production.

LINE-CUT CAMERA REHEARSAL/SHOOT DAYS

Thurs. Studio—Rehearsal with Facilities and All Crews

- 10:00–12:30
  Give out new pages and begin blocking the show shot-by-shot for cameras. There are two steps to this. First, during this rehearsal the camera operators stand

near their cameras with individual shot-sheets showing just their assigned shots in hand. The actors perform the scene, and the AD calls out the shot numbers so each camera operator can see what his or her shots will be. At this stage in the rehearsal the crew is learning the show, and the actors are not "performing" but merely indicating what the action will be. The scene is then rehearsed either from the floor, shot-by-shot, or from the control room. A different work method has the director immediately working from the control room in the style most often used in daytime drama

- 12:30–1:30
  Lunch for everyone. That's because this is a rehearsal day with the full technical and stage crew. It's best to have everyone—cast, crew, and producer's staff—available at the facility at the same time. For this reason, the lunch break is taken at the same time by everyone. The director might confer with the producer and writers, but those discussions would not be noted on the schedule. Friday's lunch, on the other hand, where performance becomes more important, would include notes to the cast and therefore is included on the call sheets.

- 1:30–5:00
  Finish shot-by-shot blocking of the show. Finish the day with one very rough run-through for the network, the writers, and producers.
  After this run-through the actors are released, and the network, producers, writers, and director confer about the run-through.

Fri. Studio with Full Facilities

(Full facilities are required on Friday but not Thursday because Friday is the record day. Full facilities would include tape machines or server availability for recording, as well as specific gear, such as a warm-up comedian's microphone. It would also include personnel related to the audience, such as pages and audience staff. These would be scheduled in at the appropriate time.)

- 10:00–12:30
  Give out new pages, based on the rough run-through. Run show at speed.

- 12:30–1:30
  Lunch and notes.

- 1:30–2:30
  Run program.

- 2:30–3:00
  "Dress audience" arrives.

- 3:00–4:00
  Record dress.

- 4:00–5:00
  Dinner—"record audience" arrives.

- 5:00–7:00
  Record show and pickup shots. There are two kinds of pickup shots. In both cases the shot is done after the scene is recorded and then edited into the show. The first kind of pickup shots involves those that are planned. This would be a shot of a prop or a setup that might be risky if not handled separately. An arrow hitting the bull's-eye might well be a pickup shot, as would a pie in the face on a close-up. Other pickups revolve around props. The heroine takes off her wedding ring and leaves it on the night table, the gun is left in the drawer, and so on. The close-up is then shot as a pickup and put into the show later. The second kind of pickup is a shot or series of shots inserted to cover a mistake that happened during the recording.

QUAD-SPLIT CAMERA REHEARSAL/SHOOT DAYS

Thurs. Studio—Rehearsal with Facilities

- 10:00–12:30
  Give out new pages and begin blocking the show shot by shot for cameras.
  A. Show & Mark: As with the line-cut rehearsal, the camera operators stand near their cameras with individual shot-sheets showing just their assigned shots in hand. The actors perform the scene. As they move through their positions, their place on the studio floor is marked by the stage managers, using different-colored tape for each character. The AD calls out the shot numbers so each camera operator can see what their shots will be.
  B. Camera Block: Once a scene is blocked, the actual cast, the "A" team, is released, and the "B" team or stand-ins walk through the scene, going from mark to mark. The camera's positions are marked at this time. The boom operators, or "boomers," map out their positions and strategies as well.
  C. Run-Through: Once the cameras are marked, the scene is rehearsed with the "A" team.

- 12:30–1:30
  Lunch for everyone, with conferences as needed.

- 1:30–5:00
  As is the case with the line cut, the director completes the shot-by-shot blocking of the show. The day's work is finished with one very rough run-through for the network, the writers, and producers.
  After this run-through, the actors are released, and the network, producers, writers, and director confer about the run-through.

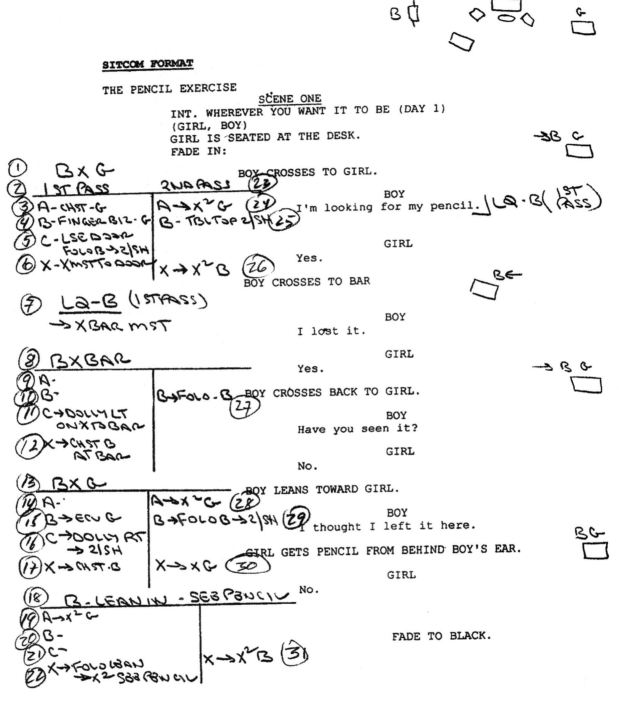

Figure 6.19 An example of the pencil exercise prepared as if it were to be shot using the quad-split technique. In this version of the "pencil exercise," the boy has a move before each line. He enters and crosses to the girl. His next move is to the downstage bar. His third move is back to the girl, and finally he leans in toward her and says his last line. She then locates the pencil behind his ear and gives it to him. The circled numbers have been added by the author to explain the markings. On the right side of the page the director has sketched the action. Marked script courtesy of Howard Ritter. *See the screen box on page 151 for an analysis of the shooting script notes.*

Sitcom Script Analysis

1. Blocking note: (Blocking notes are placed above the T) The Boy (B) crosses (x) to the Girl (G)
2. The "T" indicates there will be two passes for the scene. The first pass, items 1–22, is on the left side of the T, and the second pass is on the right side of the T.
3. A camera: Chest shot of the girl
4. B camera: Finger business. (The girl will be drumming her fingers on the table as the scene starts.)
5. C camera: Loose on the door—follows boy to a 2 shot
6. X camera: Cross master to door
7. Line Q (on first pass) B camera sets up a master shot across the downstage bar just a beat after the girl says her first "Yes."
8. Blocking note boy crosses to bar.
9. A—Holds shot
10. B—Holds shot that is now the cross-master over the bar
11. C—Dolly left on the boy's cross to the bar
12. X—Chest boy at bar
13. Blocking note: Boy crosses back to the girl.
14. A—Holds shot
15. B—Extreme close-up of the girl
16. C—Dolly right get a 2 shot
17. X—Chest boy
18. Blocking note: Boy leans in to girl. Girl will find pencil.
19. A—Cross 2 to girl
20. B—Hold shot
21. C—Hold shot
22. X—Follow hand to a cross 2—see pencil
23. Second pass. Once there is a "buy" take for the first pass, the actors would re-do the scene for these additional shots.
24. A—Cross 2 shot favors girl
25. B—Tabletop 2 shot
26. X—Goes to a cross-two shot favors girl
27. B—Follow boy
28. A—Goes to cross 2 shot favors girl
29. B—Follow boy to a 2 shot
30. X—Cross shot to girl
31. X—Cross shot to boy

During the second pass, the C camera might be used as an alternate coverage camera for the boy.

Fri. Studio with Full Facilities

- 10:00–12:30
  Give out new pages, based on the rough run-through. Run show at speed. Record special insert shots if they are required.

Figure 6.20   A cameraperson's working view of a set using the quad-split method. In the upper left is a "smart lens" reader that lets the camera operator know where the camera is focused and the depth field at that point. To the right of that is the viewfinder, marked for 4/3 and 16/9 formats. Under the viewfinder is a holder for the shot sheet. Hanging off to the right is a quad-split screen that shows what each camera is shooting.

- 12:30–1:30
  Lunch and notes.
- 1:30–2:30
  Run program.
- 2:30–3:00
  Dress show audience arrives.
- 3:00–4:00
  Record dress in show order so the audience can understand the program and laugh at the appropriate time. Scenes may be repeated. Executives and writers will be taking notes, which will be given to the director during the dinner break. The director will then give the notes to the cast.
- 4:00–5:00
  Dinner—air show audience arrives. Notes to cast.
- 5:00–7:00
  Record show in show order, repeating material if necessary.

SCORED MUSIC

Concerts, classical music, popular music, and jazz, as well as opera and musicals, all work from scores. Dance productions, too, may work from scores. Even if you can't read the musical score or dance notation, you can still mark a kind of shooting script that makes it possible to be at the right place at the right time by following this procedure.

1. *Get your own copy of the score.* Assign each bar a number. This is exactly what the conductor has done. Find a consultant who can read a score and who will be willing to work with you. Often the musicians or conductor will be happy to help you find an appropriate person.
2. *Analyze the music* with your consultant so you know where a theme begins and which instrument picks it up next, as well as what voices or instruments respond and where.
3. *Mark the cameras* with shot numbers on the score, just as you would with words on a script.
4. *Listen to a recording* of the piece along with your consultant. Have the consultant count down to each shot. The music may be recorded at a different tempo than your performance, but your rehearsal time with a recording will help compensate for your inability to read the score yourself.

Rehearsals for scored music are very much like rehearsals for a daytime drama. However, in some ways it's easier to shoot a Beethoven symphony than a soap opera. In the symphony everyone is seated. If you've done your homework, you know which instrument plays next, and you can be there with the right camera.

One major problem for directors when working with an orchestra is the expense of bringing an orchestra together. There are many players, and they all have to be paid. Anything the television producer can do to lessen the total cost, without lowering quality, is a plus. For orchestral work, it is wise to go to the orchestra rehearsal at their rehearsal studio after having confirmed with the conductor that your marked copy of the score is correct—that it matches the score the conductor is using and that your bar or score markings match the conductor's. This is done so during the rehearsal when, for example, the conductor suggests that the orchestra "Pick it up at letter 'E,'" your copy of the score matches his, and you can get to letter "E" as well as the orchestra can. Mentally review the shots as the orchestra rehearses. If the orchestra repeats a part, imagine what the other cameras can see and either convince yourself that your choices are the best or make the necessary changes.

When the orchestra finally rehearses on the studio floor or concert hall stage, call your shots along with the orchestra. If there is something that has to be changed, stop and make the changes as soon as there is a break in the music; ask the conductor for a moment or two if you must. There may or may not be a dress rehearsal; your preproduction work needs to have been adequate. One nice thing about this kind of performance is that the director can always cut to either a wide shot of the orchestra or a close-up of the conductor; they are always working. The shot may be weak, but it isn't wrong, and it's been used to cover a lot of mistakes.

DANCE SCRIPT

I have found that the best way to work with dance is to create a script of what the dancers are doing. It doesn't matter if what you write isn't exactly "dancerly" as long as you understand what is happening. My notes usually read something like this:

Boy enters upstage left and jumps around to downstage center.

He pirouettes a couple of times.

He falls to the floor.

He gets up.

He goes down.

He lies down on the ground.

A girl enters upstage right and slinks down to the boy.

She dances around him.

Then a lot of dancers enter from down right and left.

That might not be beautiful prose, but it allows you to mark cameras on what is now a shooting script. You can then time the music, even if it's just a rehearsal piano you've recorded, and create a "timed script" that will help determine whether your camera movement ideas and cutting will work.

:00–:30	Boy enters upstage left and jumps around to downstage center.
:30–1:15	He pirouettes a couple of times.
1:15–1:20	He falls to the floor.
1:20–1:25	He gets up.

1:25—1:30 He goes down. He lies down on the ground.
1:30—1:45 A girl enters upstage right and slinks down to the boy.
1:45—2:05 She dances around him.
2:05—2:30 Then a lot of dancers enter from down right and left.

Rehearsing

The rehearsal schedule for dance is dependent on the scale of the production and on the budget. The rehearsal steps for dance are the same as they are for a daytime drama. You have to create a script, and then you need a chance to mark it and test it while the dancers dance. You want to create an opportunity in the studio that allows the camera operators and the rest of the crew to learn their parts, just as they would if they were working on a drama.

REVIEW

- The three things that help the efficiency of the director are:
  1. Conventions
  2. Ground plans
  3. Shooting scripts
- The blocking in each scene has to emerge from the inner conflict of the situation.
- Traditionally, the zoom or any movement of the camera or lens must be motivated.
- The three classic motivations for zooms and other camera movement are (CAD):
  1. *C—Curtains:* The beginning or end of a scene
  2. *A—Action:* Action taking place on screen
  3. *D—Drama:* Dramatic moments in the scene
- The ground plan is a quarter-inch map of the set. It shows in very clear terms the actual relationship between scenic elements of the set.
- The typed format of a shooting script follows the following rules:
  1. It is always typed or printed.
  2. It is always on 8½-by-11-inch paper.
  3. All the pages are numbered.
  4. All the revisions are labeled with the date of the revision and sometimes even the time of the revision.
  5. There is always a one-inch margin on the left and at least a three-inch margin on the right.
  6. The dialogue is always double-spaced.
  7. Dialogue is set in upper and lower case.
  8. Instructions are all upper case, as are the names of the characters.
  9. Stage right and left are indicated as seen by the camera.
  10. Lines finish at the bottom of the page.
- Everything about a shot is indicated on the shooting script as if the shooting script itself were a time line or map of the individual events that make up the scene. A marked script serves a number of different members of the production crew. The notation tells:
  1. When the shot is taken (usually a word cue, but sometimes action)
  2. How the shot is to be put "on the air"— cut, dissolve, or wipe
  3. The shot number—for reference
  4. The camera—which one
  5. The character—the person or thing we see in the picture
  6. The framing—how the person or thing we see is framed
  7. The development within the shot—what, if any, development will happen in the shot
- Each element of the shot notation is essential to the way the program looks. Often the notation serves a variety of uses. Shot numbers, for example, are used by the AD, TD, and camera operators during the production and by the postproduction crew in the edit suite.
- Action should be marked in the script where it occurs, in the same way that shots are indicated on a shooting script when they occur.
- The audience needs time, however brief, to accept new information, such as the fact that there is someone else in the room.
- Framing a shot is best done by finding visual key points in the frame. The key points may be some part of the body, such as the chest and head (called a *chest shot*) or the knees and torso (called a *knee shot*) of a character or some element of the set. That way the operator has a visual image to which he or she may return.
- The director's plan must give the operator time to prepare the shot.
- When characters move within a setting, the audience needs to be reacquainted with the

geography of the room and with who is where in it.

- Dramatic development is one of the best reasons for a change of camera framing.
- Shot sheets are prepared so each camera operator has a list of just those shots for which he or she will be responsible.
- Once camera rehearsal has started, additions to the shooting script are handled by adding a letter to the number. Deletions are handled by simply dropping the shot and leaving a "hole" in the numeric count. (For example, if shot #3 is dropped, the count goes 1, 2, 4, 5, etc.)
- The functions of rehearsal are to achieve predetermined goals:
  1. In the rehearsal room one seeks to agree on performance and to block the production.
  2. The goals of the first facility rehearsals are:
     a. To see each shot on camera
     b. To "set" each shot
     c. To change what needs to be changed
  3. The goal of the first "run-through" is to see how the various shots work when the scene is run at full speed.
  4. The dress rehearsal serves as a kind of proof that the production is ready to be taped. It allows the cast and crew to rehearse any last-minute changes.

- When shooting, it is clearer to everyone if the director and the AD use the characters' names and camera numbers instead of the actors' names and camera operators' names.
- Three styles of shooting multiple camera comedies are:
  1. Line cut
  2. Quad-split
  3. Ad-libbed
- When shooting scored music:
  1. Get your own copy of the score. Assign each bar a number.
  2. Find someone to analyze and work on the score with you if you can't read music.
  3. Analyze the music so it will make visual sense.
  4. Mark the cameras with shot numbers on the score.
  5. Rehearse by listening to a recording. Work with your consultant if you can't read the score.
  6. A wide shot of the orchestra or a close-up of the conductor are both appropriate cover shots.
- When shooting dance:
  1. Create a script of what the dancers are doing.
  2. Block the script as you would a drama.
  3. Rehearse with a recording and a stopwatch.

chapter seven

Music

Musical production for television can be categorized by three different criteria:

1. Types of material
   a. Scored material—classical music, theatrical performances, some concerts
   b. Improvised material—rock and roll, jazz
2. Types of performance
   a. Live performance—concerts, variety programs, specials
   b. Edited performance—any kind of material
3. Types of production
   a. Single-camera—any of the preceding; most music videos and most shorter pieces
   b. Multiple-camera—any of the preceding; most concerts and long-form productions

We'll start by examining a multiple-camera special, one that does not allow for a lot of postproduction. It's the kind of program *TV Guide* might describe as "a tribute to the many styles of music to be found in America." A program like this, which encompasses different kinds of material and performances, offers a look at a broad range of production problems and techniques. Additional material concerning remote variety specials and concerts is presented in Chapter 11. At one time the production would have been shot and would have a minimum amount of editing. Most specials today would have the output of each camera recorded, as well as a line-feed, and the editing would be extensive.

PREPRODUCTION

Most director/producers will be involved in non-union situations at some time or other. Whether the production has a union crew or a nonunion crew, and whether it has a big budget, a low budget, or none at all, the director's/producers' concerns are the same. There are times when a nonunion crew can function more effectively than a union crew; however, in order to examine what I believe to be the most thorough and professional method of production, the material in this chapter assumes that work is being done with professional union crews in major studios, venues, or locations, with permits for all shooting.

Music programs are put together in several different ways. One is a highly edited program, in which each act is shot on separate days and each segment is composed of many edited parts. Alternatively, it might be a *Saturday Night Live* kind of program that is actually live or a program from the Kennedy Center that is recorded live but is subject to editing.

In order to explore as many kinds of musical productions as possible, let's assume that you're going to produce and direct a one-hour "shot-as-live" music special with a number of different kinds of performances. It's expected that the final production will be completed in the edit suite. Each act will be rehearsed separately, and an audience will be present for many of the numbers. In a case like this, we'll encounter the preproduction steps needed to facilitate any kind of musical production.

Our program starts with the talent. Assume that we're based in a major television market such as Los Angeles or New York City. A legal team has been assigned to handle music clearances and contracts, and staff members will arrange for travel and lodgings for the acts. If the program is to have a large audience and will air as a network production rather than in a local market, the legal matters will

155

be significant. Under most circumstances, preproduction will involve the following activities:

1. Getting the talent—recognizing that there will be last-minute additions and deletions
2. Creating a routine for the program
3. Creating a rehearsal schedule for the program
4. Creating a shooting schedule for the program
5. Rehearsals
6. Prerecordings

This make-believe program leaves out a lot of wonderfully talented acts. It's designed to set up and answer the most common production problems for most popular musical formats, from single-camera to multiple-camera and from popular music to classical music. For example, the location preparation for this network program is the same as it would be for a location piece headed to MTV or a college music video assignment. Our program, *Variety America*, is about the variety of music in the United States. We'll be shooting it live from Nashville. Since the performances demonstrate a number of musical styles, they'll demand different approaches to the audio setups and rehearsals. This imaginary program (with only two commercial breaks, which is unusual) consists of the following:

- *Big band* that works from a score, has a vocalist, and then a choir
- *Acoustic star*, a single performer, singing with an acoustic guitar
- *Living legend*, another performer singing with an acoustic guitar and needing the same

microphone setup as the acoustic star. These two will sing a duet.
- *String quartet*, a classical music quartet that also works to score
- *Broadway star*, a single performer working to both lip-sync and track
- *Jazz family*, a jazz group that will be improvising much of what they play
- *Jam*, all-out, with many audio sources

The routine for our program is on page 159. Figure 7.1 shows a similar routine used for the *International Emmy Awards* program, and Figure 7.2 shows the Oscar rundown. Note the similarities between these two rundowns, even though they were created by different producing organizations many years apart. A computer printout of this year's *Academy Awards* broadcast would yield the same information in a similar configuration. The form in Figure 7.1 is slightly different from the one I use. By the time the final routine is in place, page numbers and other relevant information are included. Note the similarities and differences between the rundown in Figure 7.2 and our imaginary program. The *International Emmy Awards* program is in a later stage of development; it has more complete notes about each item, space for adjusting proposed times (which they label as "cum," for cumulative), and the actual times they will need to deal with while the program is on the air or in the edit bay. The important elements in all of them, however, are an item number; a description of the segment, including who's in it, what it's about, and where it takes place; a segment time; a cumulative time; and a show or actual time.

Rev: **20-Nov-95**

23RD INTERNATIONAL EMMY AWARDS
• RUNDOWN •

20-Nov-95
8:15 - 9:45 PM EDT
LOC: Hilton Hotel - NYC

ACT #1

Item# Description	Page #	Segment	Cume	Actual	
1. **SHOW OPEN/INTRO TOM ROGERS - VTPB/MATTE** • International Council Logo • 23rd Int'l Emmy Logo Fly-in • Sponsor Billboard Fly-in (VTPB: SOT) (Announcer VO)		0:57	0:00:57		
2. PRESIDENT'S OPENING REMARKS/ INTROS LAYBOURNE (Anncr VO, Pres. Int'l Council: Tom Rogers)		01:00	0:01:57		
3. CHAIR'S OPENING REMARKS/ INTROS ANIMATION PKG (Anncr VO, Gaia Chair: Geraldine Laybourne)	(3)	05:00	0:06:57		
4. **ANIMATION PACKAGE-VTPB** VTPB/SOT	(4)	04:11	0:11:08		
5. **PETER USTINOV WELCOME** **& INTRO SUSAN SULLIVAN**	(5)	01:30	0:12:38		
6. **AWARD #1** **ARTS DOCUMENTARY** a. Present Award (Susan Sullivan) MUSIC: Playon (ATPB) VTPB: Nominee Pkg (Sot)(2:36) NOMINEES: 1) "BOOKMARK: SEX LIES & JERZY KOSINSKI" (UK) 2) "A SHORT FILM ABOUT LOVING" (UK) 3) "KENZABURO OE'S LONG ROAD TO FATHERHOOD" (Japan)	(7)	03:36	0:16:14		
b. Winner Acceptance MUSIC: Winner Playon (ATPB)	(9)	01:00	0:17:14		

Figure 7.1   The final rundown, or routine, for the *23rd International Emmy Awards* program, produced by Joe Cates. Reproduced by permission of Joe Cates.

77th Annual Academy Awards
SHORT RUNDOWN

LIVE: Sunday, February 27, 2004
LOC: Kodak Theatre
Los Angeles, CA

IT#		PG	SEG	CUM	
	ACT 1				
	START TIME			5:29:55	
1.	VTPB: SHOW TITLE (MOS) (Announcer VO-Live) MUSIC: UNDERSCORE (LIVE)	(1)	0:25	5:30:20	
2	VTPB: OPENING COMMERCIAL BILLBOARDS (SOT) (Announcer VO-SOT) VTPB: MATTE: SHOW TITLE (MOS-KEYABLE LIVE SHOT) MUSIC: UNDERSCORE (LIVE-CONT'D)	(2)	**0:28**	5:30:48	
3.	VTPB: OPENING FILM (SOT) (3:13)	(3)	**3:13**	5:34:01	
4.	INTRO CHRIS ROCK (Announcer VO-Live) MUSIC: TYMP ROLL (LIVE) MUSIC: PLAYON (LIVE)	(4)	0:40	5:34:41	
5.	CHRIS ROCK MONOLOGUE/ INTRO PRESENTER (Chris Rock) LOC: MUSIC: PLAYON (LIVE)	(5)	10:00	5:44:41	

Figure 7.2 The final rundown from the *77th Annual Academy Awards,* produced by Gilbert Cates. You can see that it is very similar to the *23rd International Emmy Awards* rundown. Reproduced by permission of Gilbert Cates.

ROUTINE CONSIDERATIONS

Once we've got our talent booked, we'll want to know how they'll appear in our program. We need a routine because it may help us get a broad picture of the program and address potential problems before they occur. A typical routine for the acts planned for our production might look like the one on page 157. Note that the location for the acts isn't indicated, in this routine since the only location that's used is the stage.

Variety America—Date—Program

#	Description & Location	Run Time	Cumulative Time
1.	Tease—outside music hall with annc. & house music	:30	
2.	Titles & Billing—"Show Business" Playback & annc.	1:00	1:30
3.	Commercial break	2:00	3:30
4.	Intro show outside auditorium—audio from BIG BAND	1:00	4:30
5.	BIG BAND		
	5a. "Hot Time in Old Town Tonight"—with vocalist	3:00	7:30
	5b. "Blue Skies"—with vocalist & choir	3:30	11:00
6.	Intro ACOUSTIC STAR from audience	:30	11:30
7.	ACOUSTIC STAR sings: wi. Guitar in front of curtain		
	7a. "Tears in Heaven"	4:30	16:00
	7b. "Rollin & Tumblin"	4:00	20:00
8.	Surprise guest = LIVING LEGEND/ACOUSTIC STAR talk	1:00	21:00
	"Here Comes the Sun" duet with house orch.	4:30	25:30
9.	Insert file—RETIRED STARS segment with annc.	1:00	26:30
10.	Commercial break	2:00	28:30
11.	Intro STRING QUARTET annc. vo audience shots	:30	29:00
12.	STRING QUARTET—Beethoven quartet	9:00	38:00
13.	Insert file—RETIRED STARS segment 2 with annc.	2:00	40:00
14.	Intro BROADWAY STAR—annc vo audience shots	:15	40:15
	14a. "As Time Goes By"—lip-sync	2:15	42:30
	14b. "Another 100 People"—track & chroma wall	3:00	45:30
15.	Intro JAZZ FAMILY—annc vo audience shots	:15	45:45
	15a. "Lullaby of Birdland"	3:30	49:15
	15b. "Night in Tunisia	3:45	53:00
16.	Jam session with BIG BAND behind "Saints Go Marching In"	4:00	57:00
17.	Credits over "Saints"	1:00	58:00

Although this is an imaginary program, the following considerations that prompt this routine are very real.

#	Description & Location	Run Time	Cumulative Time
1.	Tease—outside music hall with annc. & house music	:30	

The tease invites the home audience, many of whom use these first seconds to "channel surf," to watch the program. It sets up the content of the program, and if it's exciting enough, it provides the best chance to capture and hold the viewers.

#	Description & Location	Run Time	Cumulative Time
2.	Titles & Billing—"Show Business" Slug & annc.	1:00	1:30

This is similar, except whereas the tease gave a taste of what is to be on the program, this lets the audience know more specifically who's on the program. It also fulfills credit/billing agreements. It's important that the credits be attractive, too, since we still want to hold the audience.

#	Description & Location	Run Time	Cumulative Time
3.	Commercial Break	2:00	3:30

This part of the routine mimics the routine for a music special I directed in Nashville. Having a commercial so soon in the program might be considered dangerous because that means it will be 3 minutes and 30 seconds into the program before the show begins. This may have been part of a contractual obligation to a sponsor. Ideally the tease and credits will have been strong enough to keep the audience watching the program.

#	Description & Location	Run Time	Cumulative Time
4.	Intro show outside auditorium—audio from BIG BAND	1:00	4:30

If the home audience stays through the first commercial, they'll probably stay to see at least a portion of the opening number. Since there's been a commercial, we may also attract latecomers who were still surfing. Therefore, this becomes an opportunity to reintroduce the show as well as the first act.

#	Description & Location	Run Time	Cumulative Time
5.	BIG BAND		
5a.	"Hot Time in Old Town Tonight"—with vocalist	3:00	7:30
5b.	"Blue Skies"—with vocalist & choir	3:30	11:00

The rule of thumb regarding productions is that you start with a big, bright, lively "up" number, perhaps the second-best act of the show, and end the program with the best of the show to "keep 'em coming back." In any event, in our program, the first act is a BIG BAND and should make for an exciting opening. On the production side, it's efficient to have had the time to preset the orchestra, since that's going to be one of the most complicated audio and stage setups. In this routine let's assume that the band is preset on stage and that the vocalist will walk out to a microphone in front of the orchestra when it's time to sing. The audio department would probably like the vocalist to work from the side of the orchestra so the singer would be off the axis of the orchestra. (A singer in front of an orchestra is "on the same axis" as the orchestra. If the orchestra is to the side of or in front of the singer, the singer is "off the axis" of the orchestra.) The best way to observe a live mix between vocalists and an orchestra is to watch a program like the late-night variety programs on CBS and NBC. When singers are featured, they face the audience, and their microphones are off-axis to the house orchestra. However, it usually doesn't happen that way in concert-style productions. We will not be able to arrange this for our imaginary situation, so a microphone with a very narrow live spot is required. We want to keep the sound of the orchestra out of the microphone of the singer. For the second number, I'm going to assume that a curtain at the back of the stage opens to reveal the chorus in place behind the orchestra. I would want them to "just appear" rather than walk into place. A walk-on might become an enormous stage wait, and the home audience might just decide to surf. If the choir can't be in place behind the orchestra, I'd suggest they work from one of the sides. The key point is to have the choir in place and miced and then revealed for the second number so we can get on with the show as quickly as possible. If all of that is impossible, we'd want to dramatize their entrance and incorporate it into the act. Perhaps they could arrive from the back of the house, singing or clapping, while the orchestra played. Audio would need to be consulted for any such plan so the chorus can be heard as they make their entrance. The chances are that audience mics would have been hung for applause, and they would be put to use here. Since there would be singing as well as applause, the audio team might use different "audience mics" than they normally would.

6.	Intro ACOUSTIC STAR from audience	:30	11:30

Once the band is finished, they have to get off the stage. This short introduction allows the curtain to close so the orchestra and choir can exit. Simultaneously, the crew can put the simple audio setup in place for the next act.

7.	ACOUSTIC STAR sings with acoustic guitar in front of curtain		
	7a. "Tears in Heaven"	4:30	16:00
	7b. "Rollin & Tumblin"	4:00	20:00

This setup probably requires no more than two mics: one for vocals and one for the guitar. The problem is that it's a quiet number. The members of the orchestra have to leave the stage behind the curtain during that quiet number. If the curtain has good sound-absorbing characteristics, we'll be able to continue with the production. If not, we'll have to wait for everyone to clear the stage before we begin the next number. That will require another edit.

8.	Surprise guest = LIVING LEGEND/ACOUSTIC STAR talk "Here Comes the Sun" Duet with House Orch.	1:00	21:00

Having a surprise guest is exciting. The staffs of both artists would need to be consulted to see if it would be feasible to make it a real surprise. It would be unusual, however, to find a manager who would agree to place an artist on the air in a totally unrehearsed situation. It's more likely that we'd have a rehearsal in which the two artists, who are probably old friends, would get a chance to rehearse the number before presenting it to the world.

9.	RETIRED STARs segment 2 with annc.	1:00	26:30

In this segment I'm going to assume that we talk to a "Retired Star." We'll see some stock black-and-white footage of an appearance made years ago and perhaps some recent footage of a performance if it's available, or an audio recording over stock video footage if it's not. The material would have been edited, transferred to a server, and possibly played back to the audience. Placing it in this spot in the program affords us a break that enables the crew to clear the orchestra for item 15, the JAZZ FAMILY, which is the next time the large area will be needed. Although it isn't indicated, I'd end this segment with a return to the audience applauding and then dissolve to a kind of "standby" picture— perhaps an exterior shot with the program title supered.

10.	Commercial break	2:00	28:30

It's best to hold the standby picture through the commercial break. Although the network might sell all the time in the breaks, the standby could be used as protection should there be some failure in the commercial playback. Additionally, the standby might be used as a still frame for program identification.

11.	Intro STRING QUARTET— Annc. VO Audience shots	:30	29:00

The implication of "Annc. VO Audience shots" is that we will come to a cover shot at the end of each performance. The announcer will introduce the next act—in this case the STRING QUARTET, with a voice over some video. It's the director's job to invent the video to help with the segue from item to item. One approach to the return from the commercial break is to create a montage of material generic to the production—upcoming acts, for example— and insert that during the editing session. Another approach is to start outside with an exterior shot of the theater and lose the supered name of the program (which had been part of the commercial break standby), and then slowly zoom in to the front of the theater and dissolve to a wide shot from the back of the house. That camera might then slowly zoom in, and as the announcer finishes the introduction, the music is cued to begin. The need to create material for this kind of moment often crops up in a production, and it's part of the director's job to cover such unscripted production demands.

12.	STRING QUARTET— Beethoven Quartet	9:00	38:00

This segment ends on applause. Following the quartet, we would play back the RETIRED STARS material to the floor and give ourselves the two-minute running time to clear the STRING QUARTET, with their music and mics.

13.	RETIRED STARS segment 2 with Annc.	2:00	40:00

If the playback of this segment were unavailable or not long enough to cover the scene change, we would take the time to make the change on stage and then proceed with the show, realizing that, once again, we had built in an edit.

14.	Intro BROADWAY STAR— Annc. VO Audience Shots	:15	40:15
14a.	"As Time Goes By"— LIP-SYNC	2:15	42:30

This segment features one performer standing in front of a curtain. In the second number, a chroma wall is used to key in backgrounds. It should be simple to shoot. The first song is a slow ballad. Too much cutting or moving around might distract from the song itself. In fact, the song could easily be played in a simple spotlight and require only one prop mic. We might have THE BROADWAY STAR enter from stage right or left and walk to the preset microphone. That would give us cover for the musical introduction and allow the audience to applaud.

14b.	"Another 100 People"— TRACK & Chroma Wall	3:00	45:30

The second song, another Broadway musical classic, is faster than the first, and because it's preceded by such a simple number, it demands a different approach. Whatever change in mood or setting occurs has to happen during the applause. Audiences are fascinated with set changes, so we may want to reveal how the effect is achieved. In any event, it has to happen quickly and offer a totally different look. I've chosen a chroma-key wall that flies in. It's an inexpensive way of achieving a "look" (in fact, chroma-key may now seem dated). I would hope that in this case it's

appropriate for the song, which comes from a Broadway play of the 1970s. It's really just another tool in the director's repertoire. Technically speaking, it's easy to achieve, since the chroma lighting can be preset and needs only to be turned on for the number.

15.	Intro JAZZ FAMILY—Annc. VO Audience shots	:15	45:45

The JAZZ FAMILY will be improvising on the songs they are slated to perform. Unlike the first "Band," this group ad-libs around a theme. It's important for the director/producer to understand the structure of the two pieces and know how each number will begin. I once shot a production with vocalist Roberta Flack. In rehearsal, she started with a four-bar piano intro. Somewhere between the last rehearsal and the recording, the band decided that it would sound better if the bass rather than the piano performed the four-bar intro. When we went on the air, live, I spent two bars shooting a close-up of Ms. Flack's hands before realizing what had happened. I slowly (though in a panic) dissolved through to the bass player—who was finished by the time the dissolve was over. It taught me to tell the musicians of my plans. With that experience in mind, I would ask the JAZZ FAMILY about the order in which they intended to take solos and then tell them about the way I intended to shoot them.

15b.	"Another 100 People"— TRACK & Chroma Wall	3:30	49:15
15b.	"Night in Tunisia"	3:45	53:00

At the end of "Night in Tunisia," we'd cut to the audience for applause and then have the JAZZ FAMILY start "When the Saints Go Marching In." Part of the preproduction for this program would have been a call to everyone who might be playing to make sure that this number would be acceptable. If someone didn't want to play this song, we'd move on to something else, possibly suggested by the orchestra. There are a few jazz standards that are really from the classical repertoire and for which music rights are not a consideration; one of Rachmaninoff's themes, for example, became immortalized in the jazz repertoire as the song "You Can't Go Home Again." One of the bonuses of including this jam session is that it allows the timing of the show to be more flexible. If there's a lot of time, this number could run for as long as 10 minutes; if there's little time, it can run for only 3 or even 2 minutes. It would be smart to overshoot this number and plan on editing it if it really "took off" after we were supposed to be finished.

16.	Jam Session with BIG BAND behind "Saints Go Marching In"	4:00	57:00

It's important to plan the entrances of the other artists, who need microphones. We'll have to arrange the order in which solos are taken and find some way to include the usually seated STRING QUARTET.

17.	Credits over "Saints"	1:00	58:00

I would hesitate to add credits while taping this live-to-tape, because credits offer an easy way to shorten or lengthen a production. If you record the credits live, you're stuck with whatever time they take during the recording. In fact, this last number was designed to be flexible, so it would be best to edit the credits in postproduction. At the very least, I'd retain an isolated feed of the last number, without credits, so changes could be made later if necessary.

PREPRODUCTION—THE REHEARSAL

Most television programs that feature variety entertainment, including programs like *The Tonight Show*, rehearse even well-established performers for appearances. The performers want to get the feel of the house band, and the band wants to run through the material to avoid any surprises. Camera operators and the director also like to know what's going to happen before they record. On a nightly program, which is being billed for studio costs all the time, rehearsals are usually done on the set. Station or network staff may be required to use the studio's rehearsal studio, even if it billed out at more than a rental facility might cost. Production companies usually hold rehearsals in a rented space because it's the least expensive way to work. For now, let's imagine that instead of this being a station- or network-produced program, we are packaging the program ourselves. This means that we're paid a stipulated sum to produce the program; we can spend whatever we like, wherever we like, as long as we produce the program at the total agreed-upon cost.

PREPRODUCTION—REHEARSAL HALL

General Rehearsal Guidelines

The director/producer must accomplish some very specific goals at the rehearsal studio. Later we'll discuss the rehearsal goals on the studio floor.

When I began to work as a director of musical productions, I would rush to find a shooting plan. I was terrified of not having an idea, so I'd impose something—anything—on the performance as long as I had something tangible to consider as a plan. After a while, I realized that the way to get an idea was to do nothing but listen and enjoy the first impression of the artist. Once I had an idea of what the music was about or what the mood of the piece was or maybe found some key part of the lyric, it would be easier to get an idea, and a plan would follow. Therefore, a primary goal of the first rehearsal is for the director *to just listen* and see if the rehearsal performance prompts an approach.

The rehearsal also involves other, more tangible goals. It's essential to be prepared to answer the questions that will inevitably come up at a production meeting prior to the recording. Various members of the television crew need detailed information about the performers. Bringing key members of your crew to these rehearsals can make the production go more smoothly, but unfortunately, that's a luxury, and it seldom happens. If key crew members can't attend these rehearsals, the director/producer is responsible for accurately conveying information and decisions to those who need to know. It's wise to check with the various crew heads to find out what they'd like to know. You will surely need to bring information back to the scene designer and the heads of lighting and audio. Of particular importance in any music program is the audio chief. Generally speaking, you must bring back the following things from your rehearsals:

1. A quarter-inch ground plan—including where musicians and their instruments and speakers are placed
2. A list of who's playing (or the name of the group/act) and the music or songs they are playing
3. A list of any special lighting or prop requirements

Quarter-Inch Ground Plan

A reasonable approximation is acceptable at this stage of the production, but indications of relative sizes will help everyone. The set designer and lighting designer need to create settings for the groups. The set designer and the audio chief need to know how many performers will be on stage and the placement of their instruments and electronic gear. They need to know the relationship of amplifiers and speakers to instruments and where the musicians are in relationship to one another—for example, drums in the back, piano at the far left, and so on. Are there vocalists or backup vocalists? If so, where are they placed in relationship to the orchestra? The set may be nothing more than a few platforms and some hanging units—posters suspended from fishing line or simple slashes of light on the cyc, the large white curtain the studio uses as a neutral background. In any event, the designers need to know how many hanging units or slashes of light there will be and how many stock or constructed platforms are needed. Knowing where the drummer sits and the size of the drum set helps determine the size of the carpet that should be provided for the drums (the drums usually need a carpet so the bass drum doesn't slip while it's being played). If there are background vocalists, it is essential to know the spatial relationship they require to the lead singer or singers. The lighting and set designers will also need to know if the musicians move around a lot and, if so, where. Justin Timberlake would probably move around the stage a lot, but an opera singer like Placido Domingo wouldn't. The quarter-inch ground plan also helps the audio crew. They need to know how many mics are needed and who gets them. They also need to plot the cable runs for the various mic positions. There are two schools of thought about how to mic musical performances. One suggests that one or two mics should be placed out near the audience to record the performance as it is heard. This approach is particularly prevalent in classical music coverage. More traditionally, for popular music and jazz, several mics are used to isolate each instrument or groups of instruments. Various kinds of microphones and pickup units are placed on or near the instruments or amplifiers. In response to the need for greater freedom of movement on stage, RF mics (radio frequency—battery-powered and wireless) have become a major part of music sound coverage.

The audio department will be called upon to fulfill tasks in at least four separate areas:

1. *Program audio:* The audio department supplies the audio that the audience at home hears. This may be a direct feed or, if the program is to be played at a later date, a feed that goes to a time-coded multiple-track recorder or, more probably, multiple tracks on a computer server that will be remixed and edited later.

2. *House audio:* If a studio audience is present, the audio department will be supplying a "house mix," in which the vocal mics will be amplified so they can be heard over the band.

3. *Musician foldback:* The audio department will be supplying "foldback" to the musicians. The foldback sound is an amplified version of the singer's mic. Typically, drummers can't hear the words of the song over the sound of the drums, so they wear headphones or have special speakers to amplify the singer's voice for them. The other musicians also need foldback. The foldback speakers at a concert are usually in front of the band, facing away from the audience.

4. *Intercom:* The audio crew needs to supply an intercom system that allows for communication among the various members of the crew and the director. Music productions can make unusual demands on this system. Sometimes the music is so loud that the camera crew can't hear instructions. However, some of the intercom systems and headsets are sufficiently isolated from the performance and amplified enough to allow the control room commands to be audible over the music.

Sometimes—especially when you are dealing with large groups—creating the quarter-inch ground plan can seem overwhelming. It's easiest to make a quarter-inch plan if you start by pretending there are no musicians or instruments. Start with the bare outline of the area, and then fill it up as if you were constructing the band. Start with the horn section, the violins, or anywhere you like. At some time, you'll fill in the rhythm section. Describe the kind of drums that are to be used. Is it a simple setup, with one bass drum, a snare, and a tom-tom with some cymbals, or does the group use a more elaborate setup? Are there conga players or tympani? If you don't know which drum is which (I often don't), ask the drummer to draw you a plan of the drum set he intends to use. Ask him to be specific about the names of the drums (i.e., high-hat, timbali, etc., not the brand names), since this information may be significant to the audio department. Keyboards are another area that can get very elaborate. If they are, be sure to let audio and lighting know what to expect.

If there is more than one percussionist, indicate where each is located in relation to the others. Some groups use electric basses, while others use acoustic basses; a different kind of mic setup will be needed for these two instrument types. Indicate which kind of bass is used and where the bass player is in relation to the drummer. Be very wary of changing the relationship of the musicians to one another just for the sake of the cameras. Musicians become accustomed to finding one another in a particular spot on the stage. Moving them around to get good shots can have a negative effect on their performances.

Some keyboard musicians play a number of keyboards, all of which must be miked. If they also sing at those keyboards, they'll need a microphone at each singing location as well. This is critical information for the audio crew.

Electric guitars and electric basses are miked at the appropriate amplifier. If the musicians also take vocal leads, their preferences must be noted. Sometimes a standing mic will do, but at other times, an RF mic must be supplied. If the guitar is acoustic, it will need a microphone—either a stand mic or a pickup taped to the sound board. Horn sections may share a few mics, although the placement of microphones for saxophones is obviously different from what it is for trumpets. A saxophone mic needs to point down into the bell of the instrument, but a trumpet mic points straight at the bell of the trumpet. The audio crew needs to know the makeup of the horn section. If there is a full orchestra with a string and woodwind section, that too should be noted on a quarter-inch ground plan.

List of Who's Playing and What They're Playing

Sometimes you may find that members of the crew are familiar with an act or a composition that you don't know very well. Discussing the performers and their performances with the crew chiefs can bring out unexpected and creative input, but it is best to consult with just a few trusted individuals, since several different opinions and a lot of conflicting advice can bring the production to a standstill.

List of Any Special Lighting or Prop Requirements

The lighting designer must not only know the details of the ground plan but know which instruments or singers get special lighting and in what areas they will be performing. It may be that the act can go anywhere, including into the audience, and the viewer must be able to see it *all*. You may then discover that there aren't sufficient lights to cover

that possibility, in which case the act needs to be told to limit audience movement to the first five rows or just the center section. It's better to find out about such problems while there is still time to do something about them. If an act has any special prop requirements, it's good to find out about them when you still have sufficient time to make whatever accommodation is necessary.

Specific Rehearsal Guidelines

The general rehearsal studio goals are the same for all acts. You need to get a quarter-inch ground plan of the space they need, a list of the performers and what they're performing, and any special lighting or prop requirements. However, the specific rehearsal goals for each performer will vary. Our imaginary magazine program spells out the specific goals for each kind of act. (A description of the Nashville program production schedule appears later in this chapter.) Some performers can be seen before the Nashville program rehearsals. First, the director/producer may have a chance to see the performers at local venues, which is a good opportunity to develop a shooting plan. If that is the case, the first rehearsal might be a kind of test to make sure that the plan developed at the local performance holds up in the rehearsal studio.

Let's assume that we'll be able to have an initial rehearsal of the BIG BAND and the STRING QUARTET in New York prior to going to Nashville. The BROADWAY STAR is in town, and we might meet with him, but since he's simply going to stand in place and sing a familiar song, there's very little we can rehearse. He does, however, appear later in a chroma-key production number, which requires a background with shots of New York and of him walking in the theater district. We'll be shooting that with him during the preproduction period. The work for that is very much like what would be done if this were to be a single-camera music video, except fewer shots are required and the shots will probably be more traditional.

Although the members of the JAZZ FAMILY won't all be here until the Monday of shoot week, we can meet with one of them and establish a personal relationship. At the very least we'd want to call to find out what instruments they will be playing, which instrument will stand where, and information about the drum set. Additionally, we'd want to know what music they intend to play so whoever is handling the legal affairs for this production can clear the music with Broadcast Music

Incorporated (BMI) or the American Society of Composers Authors and Publishers (ASCAP). We'd also be able to arrange a comfortable schedule that's compatible with their travel and rehearsal needs.

The LIVING LEGEND and the ACOUSTIC STAR fly in at the same time. Questions about their arrival, hotels, and so forth, as well as about what they'll be singing, would have been arranged by phone, with a follow-up confirmation fax or e-mail. The BIG BAND will need a large studio. They'll probably need to rehearse no more than three hours, but they may have a four-hour minimum call, which would have been dictated by union contract. The STRING QUARTET will be able to rehearse another day but at a smaller studio. Music rehearsals are often done in the afternoon, since so many of the musicians will have worked late the night before.

Thirty to 60 minutes are generally required to set up prior to a BIG BAND's arrival at a rehearsal. During this time, chairs will be set out, and the musicians' parts will be placed on the appropriate chairs or music stands. The drummer's rug will be set in place. In addition to the music and leader, there will be someone in charge of maintaining the scores for the various instruments. There may also be someone to write score and copy parts. If these are union studio musicians, you can expect them to be punctual; they should be seated to begin rehearsals exactly on time.

Before the rehearsal, the director/producer receives and reviews a list of the players and the instruments they play. Rights to the BIG BAND's music should also have been negotiated prior to the rehearsal; rehearsing an orchestra with music that is not cleared for your broadcast can be a very expensive mistake. At the rehearsal, the director/producer will draw the rough quarter-inch ground plan showing each instrument's location. It's wise to get at least two copies of the conductor's score—even if you can't read music. Later, you can find someone who will read the score, and you can mark it as outlined in Chapter 6. It's a good idea to get two or more copies because a lot of tentative comments are marked on the first score, which then becomes too messy to read; the second copy affords a chance to make a clean version.

After the rehearsal is over, when you've decided what you're going to shoot, you'll need to produce a shooting score with shot sheets for your camera operators so they know each of their shots. It's possible to "wing it" or ad-lib each performance or, film style, to shoot a great deal of coverage and then create the program in an edit suite. Given the

opportunity to formulate a plan, however, the expectations are that the director's work will be more polished than it would be without one. Without a plan, all you can do is to "go with the flow," which is basically a reactive process: first the music happens, then you react. Unfortunately, that's too late. The alternative is to get to the right shot an instant before it's needed. That requires a shooting script or a very thorough knowledge of the music.

It's enormously helpful to have an audio recording—of any quality—of the rehearsal. Later, this recording can be used in conjunction with the score to create a shooting script. It's sometimes helpful to play the recording at a production meeting for crew chiefs and other participants so they can become acquainted with the program's content.

In order to get the audio recording, explain to the conductor at the beginning of the rehearsal that once the music or score is finalized, you'd like to be able to set it for cameras, which will require one clean play-through. A play-through for you becomes part of the rehearsal procedure.

As the band begins to play, it's wise to resist the immediate tendency to begin devising a shooting scheme for each piece. Instead, just listen, and you will find that ideas just come to you. Mull over a few of the ideas, and take the time to be clear about who takes solos and when.

This part of the rehearsal is really for the band. They're coordinating the material they're going to play on the program. There'll be a lot of stopping and starting as various parts are worked out. Use that time to get a feel for the piece. Even if you know the piece well, listen to it as if you were coming to it for the first time. Relax. Let yourself get into the mood of the piece. Then take some time to think about how you'd like to see it. Once you've allowed yourself the time to get a feel for the piece, you can start constructing a shooting plan. Assume for a moment that the music will begin with the entire band playing a statement of the melody line; then the vocalist will take a lead, followed by various instruments—the sax, the piano, a trumpet. You need to know who takes the lead and when. What camera can you use to get the best shot of the lead musician or vocalist? If you have the time and there are enough rehearsals, physically stand where each shot will be coming from and imagine what it will look like. Mark it in the score if you can. If you have a lot of time at your disposal, stand at the places you *don't* expect to be shooting from and see what you're missing. You may be tempted to change your mind and your shooting script. Do the same thing with the second number they are going to play.

During the last part of the rehearsal, work on the last number on the program—in this case, "When the Saints Go Marching In." During taping, the JAZZ FAMILY will be on stage, and members of the BIG BAND will have to join them. This rehearsal is a good time to work out how the BIG BAND members will enter the stage. Give the musicians a break. Move the chairs around and set the stage for what you imagine the last act's setup will be. Have a plan ready for the BIG BAND's entrance before the rehearsal, and when the break is over, rehearse their entrance. This is one of the times it would be helpful to have the audio chief with you. If you can't, make sure you've discussed your plans before the rehearsal. At worst, know where to reach the audio chief or engineer-in-charge so you can, if necessary, call him or her from the rehearsal studio.

At the end of the rehearsal, go over the next stages in the production. Outline the schedule and make sure everyone understands where to meet and when. Have printed agendas for the members of the bands. Include all the important phone numbers and addresses, as well as dates and times. That allows the group to make plans around your rehearsal and shooting schedule. If the agenda is kept handy, it serves as a written reminder to each of them of where they are to be, when they should be there, and whom to call if there is a problem.

If you don't read music, you can arrange to meet with the arranger or someone who knows music to go over the score. When you play the recording you've made at the rehearsal and have the score, it's possible to mark the score exactly as you would a script. It allows you to know how much time you have to get a camera from one shot to the next. If you can arrange to have someone at the program's recording who can read the score, he or she can preset the shots you've designed at the moment before you need to "take" the shot. If you have to work alone, then you can still use the score and audio rehearsal track by using a stopwatch. The time for each shot won't be exact, but the timing usually remains remarkably close, and the marked score lets you know which shot comes when. Figure 7.3 shows an example of a marked score. Figure 7.4 is an example of a marked script for a musical production. Note how similar it is to the scripts marked for dramatic productions.

There are many opinions about how to shoot classical music. The most prevalent is the one in which the director strives to explain the music

visually. Directing this way forces the director/producer to remain true to the composer's structure. It's as if you were saying, "Look, the first violin states the theme, then the cello answers, then both the second violin and viola respond, and then they all join in. Now look, here's the first violin in conversation with the viola." If you can get the shots that will make that clear, you're helping the audience to understand the nature of the music, and usually that makes listening to the music more enjoyable.

It's certainly possible to approach the music in a less musically structured way. You might want to evoke a mood rather than deal with the structure of the piece. For example, I once shot the Juilliard String Quartet and dwelled on the shadows of the musicians as a device to get from one shot to the next. Even so, it's useful to have a shooting plan that can be read from the score, since you can then be prepared for the mood changes you want to emphasize.

Prior to meeting with the STRING QUARTET, find out what they expect to play, and get a copy of the score and a recording of the piece. Obviously, it would be good to hear the quartet's rendition, but almost anyone's performance will be useful. Listen to the music, and analyze it if you can—either alone or with a musicologist. There are only four seated musicians, and something is sure to happen among the instruments. How will you make those relationships visible? What camera angles and what devices will you use? How can you prepare before the first rehearsal?

During the rehearsal the players will stop and talk among themselves, analyzing parts of what they're playing. Some of what they're saying may give you insights that can become part of your production. Even if you already have a plan for shooting, there's still time to be flexible. Before the players leave, it is a good idea to make a recording of the rehearsal as a guide for your own homework. The rehearsal with the STRING QUARTET will probably not take longer than two hours, but you may pay for more if there is a longer minimum call.

The next element of our program, the BROADWAY STAR, performs to a music track. The procedures used here are the same as what would be used for any artist singing any material to track. Music delivery to singers is done in one of the following ways:

1. *Live:* They sing with no musical background or with anything from a single instrument to a full orchestra as a musical background.
2. *Live to track:* They actually sing, but the background music comes from a prerecorded mixed sound track. Often stars with well-known

Figure 7.3 A marked score from Dr. Jeff Benedict's "Castle Creek Shuffle." Note that bars are marked at the top of the score. Shots are indicated where they happen and are noted in the manner of a drama. Reproduced by permission of Dr. Jeff Benedict.

""Academy of Television Hall of Fame"   * * **REVISED**   as of 11/5/02 10:18 PM

(22)   45.

INTRO ALEC
BALDWIN/PLAYON
(Cont'd)

*   CHRISTINA

CAN YOU IMAGINE

HOW MUCH WE MISS YOU

THE MORE I SEE YOU

AS YEARS GO BY   38

YOU KNOW THE ONLY ONE FOR ME

CAN ONLY BE YOU   39

*   JOHN HOLLEY

OUR ARMS WON'T FREE YOU   40

*   CHRISTINA & JOHN

AND OUR HEARTS WON'T TRY   41

MUSIC CONTINUES

ANNOUNCER VO-LIVE

Ladies and gentlemen, to induct honoree John
Frankenheimer, please welcome Alec Baldwin.   43

(INTO: ALEC BALDWIN TALK/INTRO ANGELA LANSBURY)

Figure 7.4   A marked script of musical material from a network production. Script courtesy of Steve Binder.

hits prefer to appear on television singing to the tracks of their hit songs rather than try to have house orchestras attempt to replicate the intricate mix of well-known recordings.

3. *Lip-sync:* They sing aloud as if they were recording that audio. However, the audio comes from the prerecorded mixed track of both the instrumental music and their voices. They do not just move their lips. I have had to work with novice performers who were unwilling to actually sing out loud during a lip-sync performance. When that happens, the body doesn't look right; it lacks the physical reality caused by the kind of breathing that's necessary to sing. The energy required in holding notes is missing, and often the phrasing of the breathing doesn't match what's being heard. Singers are apt to miss entrances. It's like watching a bad actor carry an empty suitcases on stage. The suitcases are supposed to be full and heavy, but since they're really empty, the actor handles the task with no strain, and it looks—and is—false.

Our program contains examples of all three of these styles. In the BIG BAND number, there is a live vocalist and a live choir singing with the musicians. The BROADWAY STAR's first number is a lip-sync production from a recent album, and his last song is sung to track.

RECORDING STEPS

In recording the chroma-key piece that is being done to track, it would be wise to have as much editing flexibility as possible. Therefore, each element—both video and audio—will be recorded separately as well as in a mix. Here's how you create the audio and video to the chroma-key number.

Audio

1. Get a copy of the mixed sound track without the vocal track. In our example, the BROADWAY STAR's record company will provide this.
2. Lay that track onto a betasp, a one-inch videotape, or a digital track on a computer, depending on what playback will be available. The video background that we'll be shooting will be edited onto that same tape or file. Each shot will then be exactly in place because it will have been edited in according to the music. That will become the playback source.
3. During the Nashville program production, the audio portion of that tape or file will serve as the playback source and will be fed to the auditorium. The BROADWAY STAR and the audience will hear the music, and the star will sing to it.
4. The audio engineers will record and mix the BROADWAY STAR's live audio track with the track from the playback source.
5. Simultaneously, the audio engineers will also record the output from the BROADWAY STAR's microphone on a separate track. We'll retain all the elements so we can remix at a later date.

Video

1. The camera or cameras shooting the BROADWAY STAR will have their output recorded as isolated feeds. A "feed" is the transmission from one source to another. The source can be audio, video, or both. For example, the output of a singer's mic is fed to an audio switcher. There it is mixed with the feed of a live or taped orchestra. That mixed feed is then fed to the program. Similarly, a live news remote—which may be just audio or both audio and video—is handled as a feed from the location. It is then fed to air, where the audience sees it. Sometimes, the output of every camera in a shoot is recorded to isolated tracks, tape decks or servers as well as to the switcher. In this way, any shot can be used in postproduction even in a program that is switched live.
2. The mixed feed will be recorded on a second deck or track. The mixed video consists of the cameras recording the BROADWAY STAR and the output of the playback, which has the prerecorded video scenes from around New York. That's the same tape or file that is being used to supply the audio playback to the theater and the performer. At the end of it all, we'll have all the elements, both isolated and mixed, which include:
   a. The original music track
   b. The production voice track
   c. The original footage of New York scenes, both edited and unedited
   d. The original footage of the BROADWAY STAR in front of a chroma blue wall

Labeling these elements—and in fact all the elements of every shoot—is vital. That's particularly true where an editing facility is charging by the hour. Spending a half-hour looking at tapes or drives to decide what's on a poorly labeled box is an expensive waste of time and money.

Before shooting in Nashville, the following elements must be prepared:

- The New York chroma-key backgrounds for the BROADWAY STAR's second number
- Some stock elements for the RETIRED STARs

The work on these elements, which is done ahead of time, is similar to the preparation and production required for any single-camera location music video. Because this is a production slated for network viewing, we would almost certainly have to come up with a plan of what we want to do and when and where we want to do it. Under less demanding circumstances it might be possible to just go out and use nothing but "grab shots," but those usually look like grab shots—there is almost always something slightly wrong with the pictures. A specific plan, even a poor one, has the advantage of giving you something from which you can deviate. The work required to design a plan often helps to suggest creative ideas and solutions that might never have occurred without that effort. Even a plan that calls for nothing but grab shots will still require plans for where to go with the crew and gear.

Whatever way you shoot, you'll have to arrange a shooting schedule and get a crew, permits, and permissions. Apart from the "strictness" about permits, the tasks of arranging a schedule, finding a crew, creating an edit log, and so on are necessary for any production anywhere.

If this were a music video, we'd use many more shots than we will here. In this example, the video is intended to be a background, not the kind of material that would be shot for MTV or VH1. In a music video, the visuals are often given the same weight as the performer. Also, the conventions for music videos usually require many more cuts or dissolves than are used in this kind of concert format.

For our purposes, we'll use the city and create a background that gives a sense of New York from morning to night. The song lasts three minutes, so how many shots do we need? Because of the nature of the performer and the material that will be sung, we want the backgrounds to remain a background element. A lot of quick shots might be distracting, but if we take too long between background changes, the sense of montage will not be effective. A change every 15 seconds is probably appropriate for our purposes, and it is certainly enough to make the point for this text. That means 12 shots are required to cover the three minutes of singing. We'll also need 4 additional shots, which will be used full frame to cover those places where the music plays but the BROADWAY STAR is not singing.

Shot List

BROADWAY STAR Location Production

1. Dawn over the East River. East 42nd St. & East River Drive. (Note: This is done because the sun rises in the east, and this is the best shot of it. It should be a stop-motion picture, with a frame every other second. Since there are 30 frames a second, it takes 1 minute to shoot a second's worth of material, and 15 minutes to shoot 15 seconds' worth of material. That's about the duration of a sunrise. Alternatively, one could simply shoot for an hour, from darkness to light and then achieve the effect in postproduction. I'd prefer to do that, since I could then choose the best shots of the light as it occurred. This, however, is not the most cost-effective way of working.)

2. People coming out of Grand Central Station—42nd St. & Park Ave.

3. People coming out of the Port Authority Bus Station—42nd St. & 8th Ave.

4. People arriving at the docks of the Princess Line—57th St. & 12th Ave.

5. Scurrying at Wall Street (perhaps stock black-and-white 1940s footage?).

6. Dutch angle of signs from immigration: "Customs," "Baggage," and so on—57th St. & 12th Ave. (A "Dutch angle" is a shot that purposely distorts the horizontal attitude of the screen. The camera is angled at anything but parallel to the horizon. Batman movies and other comic books or graphic novels are classic examples of the use of Dutch angles, particularly at frames with words like "Pow!" and "Arghhh!")

7. Follow a hand truck in the Garment Center—36th St. & 8th Ave.

8. Long Island Expressway at rush hour—34th St. & 1st Ave.

9. Subway station interior as people line up for Metrocards—34th St. & 7th Ave.

10. Hot dog vendors returning carts? (Note: Talent releases would be needed from the vendors if we use them. If that were not feasible, we'd have to hire extras to "return the carts.")

11. Baby sleeping in mother's arms (setup?).

12. Night over the Statue of Liberty (stock footage).

13. BROADWAY STAR—walk-by in the theater section.

14. BROADWAY STAR—he arrives at the theater.

15. BROADWAY STAR—his name on the dressing room door, and he enters the room.

16. Close-up of makeup being put on the BROADWAY STAR's face. Push through to his image in the mirror and go out of focus.

17. Grab shots. This schedule allows time for "grab shots," which are shots that seem appealing but are unplanned. It would be wise to get additional night shots that might be included in the sequence dedicated to a night in the city. Typical grab shots would include shots of

New York nightlife, Times Square, the theater district, and so on. This section is now covered by shots of the Statue of Liberty at night. The additional grab shots would be used to augment this sequence or as a cover if the stock footage proves unusable. The grab shots are a kind of insurance policy that there will be something to run for that night sequence. Releases will have to be obtained if the grab shots include anyone who might be recognized.

Location Shooting Schedule

Once the shots are set, a location shooting schedule needs to be made up. This schedule calls for shots at both dawn and dusk. The times allocated on the following schedule represent a realistic attempt at a tight schedule. Although it might be possible to get everything done in one day, there would probably be extensive overtime involved, so shooting over a period of two days is a better plan. Besides, when shoot days go on for too long, everything takes longer than it would have if everyone wasn't so tired. A shot that might take a half-hour to set up at the start of the day takes a full hour at the end of the day. Decisions aren't as sharp. Second-rate material is accepted and then hated later in the edit room. Like all production schedules, this production schedule contains the following:

1. Production name and phone number for the production company
2. Location schedule, including shots to be made
3. Names of crew members
4. Crew members' jobs
5. Phone numbers for the crew, and e-mail addresses

A separate location schedule contains the names and numbers of all location contacts, such as our contact at the United Nations Plaza, and the chief of security there for shot #1. Similarly, we would want to have the contact information at Grand Central Station, including the name and number of the security chief there, for shot #2—and so on.

Production name—contact phone number

Location schedule—day 1 (with day and date)— shooting shots 1, 2, 3, 7, 9, and 11

Names of crew members, their crew assignments, and phone numbers

• 4:30–5:00 a.m.	Set up at UN Plaza for shot #1 Dawn over East River (East 46th St.)
• 5:00–6:00 a.m.	Record shot #1
• 6:00–7:00 a.m.	Wrap & travel to Grand Central Station (East 42nd St.)
• 7:00–8:00 a.m.	Record commuters arriving at Grand Central Station— shot #2
• 8:00–8:30 a.m.	Downstairs for shot of people in line at subway
• 8:30–9:00 a.m.	Record line for subway tokens—shot #9 (extras or signed releases and city permits)
• 9:00–9:30 a.m.	Wrap & travel to bus station (West 42nd St.)
• 9:30–10:00 a.m.	Record bus station—shot #3
• 10:00–10:30 a.m.	Wrap
• 10:30–11:30 a.m.	Lunch (it's been six hours since the call)
• 11:30–12:00 noon	Travel & set up Garment Center for hand truck (West 35th St.)
• 12:00–12:30 p.m.	Record hand truck shot— shot #7
• 12:30–1:30 p.m.	Set up on West 35th St. area—baby sleeping— shot #11. Baby & mother to arrive for shot at 12:00. Makeup and nurse may be required.
• 1:30–2:00 p.m.	Record baby sleeping— shot #11
• 2:00–2:30 p.m.	Wrap and travel home

This schedule means we will have shot six setups on the first day and nine on the second. That's considered a very full schedule, particularly since there is travel and packing time at each location. This could be considered a 12-hour day if the crew included time to pick up and return equipment.

Day two would be arranged to get night shots, so it would start later. These later shots are of hot dog vendors returning carts and to get a "late" feeling for shots of night life related to the BROADWAY STAR. We want to quit at 8:30 p.m. Ten hours before 8:30 p.m. becomes the start of our shoot day, so we'll begin at 10:30 in the morning.

Production name—contact phone number

Location schedule—day 2 (with day and date) shooting shots 4, 6, 8, 10, 13, 14, 15, 16, and 17

Names of crew members, their crew assignments,
   and phone numbers

• 10:30–11:00 a.m.	Travel to the docks of the Princess Line for shots #4 & #6
• 11:00–12:00 noon	Princess Line arrivals (or gangplank being lowered), which will have to be cleared with the Princess Line. The montage shots for #6 are "pickup" shots taken from signs at any arrival dock.
• 12:00–12:30 p.m.	Travel to Theater District
• 12:30–2:30 p.m.	Shots #13–16, with BROADWAY STAR. These are all shots in and around the theater in which he is appearing.
• 2:30–3:30 p.m.	Lunch
• 3:30–4:00 p.m.	Shot #10—travel to hot dog vendor garage and video hot dog stands returning to and leaving for the garage (releases required)
• 4:00–4:30 p.m.	Record 10—hot dogs
• 4:30–5:00 p.m.	Travel to Long Island Expressway
• 5:00–6:00 p.m.	Record 8—Long Island Expressway
• 6:00–8:00 p.m.	Shot #17—night life, Times Square, and Theater District
• 8:00–8:30 p.m.	Wrap and travel home

Before signing off on this schedule, it would be prudent to make sure that the shots of crowds could be done without using American Federation of Radio and Television Artists (AFTRA) talent. Permission to shoot at public locations such as Grand Central Station and the New York Subway System would also be mandatory. Problems in this area might require a third day of shooting. Additional costs would also be incurred if AFTRA talent and rental locations were required.

Arrangements for this shoot require renting a camera package and hiring at least one camera operator. Additionally, the crew might need to include a grip/lighting person but no audio tech. This can be done in several ways. If this were a network program, a top-rated crew would be used—either a staff crew from the network, which is highly unlikely in today's market, or a freelance crew. They'd either have their own equipment or would rent it from a reliable and often-used source. Crews want to know the

peculiarities of any gear they use, so even if the production company could get a better price for rented gear, it would still make sense to let the crew negotiate their own equipment or let them use their own gear and pay standard rental fees for it. The first day can be shot without any lights, although it would be useful (almost mandatory) to have a stagehand/grip to work with screens and reflectors and to work with the operator on shots like #7, the hand truck in the garment center. The second day, on which we shoot in a dressing room, some small portable lighting units would be required. The camera operator or location lighting director would decide what's needed after a location survey. On a low-budget production, there would be no survey, and we'd simply bring along a light kit or two. With so many formats available, the choice of recording media would depend on prior arrangements with the Nashville production company.

A location manager might be hired for a week, including two and half days of prep, the shoot days, and a half-day of wrap for this seemingly simple shoot. If you didn't have a crew in mind, the location manager would be able to make suggestions and arrange for you to see some freelancers' reels. The location manager would also arrange for transportation and would know the local rules. Before the shoot, that person is responsible for obtaining all of the necessary permits and permissions, including the specialized permits required when working with children or the baby appearing in shot #11. The location manager would coordinate the necessary legal matters with the legal staff working on the production. Obtaining the permits would require sufficient lead time for those tasks to be accomplished, which would add to the amount of time the location manager was on our payroll.

Let's assume the shoot and the edit go well. The director/producer's work for the edit session is similar to the preparation for making a short documentary (discussed in Chapter 10). We'd need to leave the edit session with a full background piece for the BROADWAY STAR. We might also want to take care of the RETIRED STAR segments during the preproduction edit. This means we should visit a stock-footage house prior to that edit session.

STOCK SHOTS

There are stock libraries for both audio and video material. Our production needs a few different kinds of stock material. The RETIRED STAR segments require portions of tape that are now part of a stock library. Stock footage is also needed for shot #5 of people scurrying in the Wall Street area. A third stock piece comes from one of the RETIRED STARS, who has a film copy of one of his or her old performances. We'll also use stock music underneath the interview portion of the production.

Music Stock Libraries

Music stock libraries, which are often referred to as production music libraries, license materials for use in various media. Once a fee is paid, the music or footage is cleared and can be used for air or for other agreed-upon release. Without a license, the network or station (and then the producer) can be sued for copyright infringement. Judgments in the area of $10,000 and more are usual in such instances. Music libraries and stock footage companies charge by the amount of material used and the breadth of the expected distribution. For example, background music for a 30-second commercial running in a small local market for a 13-week run will cost less than the same music for a full-network 30-second commercial with no time limit.

Music libraries usually charge a modest listening fee, as well as a licensing fee, which allows the music to be used under carefully stipulated terms. The listening fee pays for some of the library's overhead and for the librarian's time. Librarians know the music cues and can help find a piece quickly. The licensing fee is payment to the owner of the material for its use. It may also include compensation for the licensing agent, as well as composers' fees, artists' fees, arrangements, and property searches. It releases the material to the buyer under the stipulated terms of the release or licensing agreement—13 weeks in a local market, for example. It usually also pays for delivery of the material in a manner suitable for network production. Audio material will be delivered either on quarter-inch audiotape, tails out, or on a CD or DAT cartridge. It some cases it may be sent as a file, computer to computer.

Video Stock Libraries

Video stock libraries will often forgo a "viewing fee" and simply let you scan through selected files or window dub viewing tapes. The cost of use is based on the amount of footage used and the markets in which

the footage is aired. They deliver the selected footage in whatever format you require for broadcast—tape, film, or file. Different libraries will have different price structures for the use of material, but the cost is seldom less than $50 per second. More typically, rates range from $75 to $100 per second. Depending on the stock library and the rarity of the footage, network commercial usage starts at approximately $2,000 for the first cut and $300 per second thereafter. If you could create a commercial from just this stock footage, the total cost for the footage would be $11,000 for a 30-second spot. That would be considered very cheap for a network commercial!

Nonlibrary Material

If we want to use the film clip that the RETIRED STAR has of a past performance, we must first acquire the rights to it. At the stock library we bought all rights for our usage and an airworthy copy of the material. In this case we will be responsible for obtaining all the permissions and assuring rights for broadcast, as well as preparing the material for insertion into the program. If it is on film, it will have to be transferred to tape or a file. If it is on tape, we may need to adapt it to our requirements. A VHS tape, for example, would need to be transferred to a more professional format. We would have to locate all the people and entities who might make claims to the material and acquire the rights from them. Sometimes materials simply can't be used because it's too hard to get the rights. Occasionally, producers decide to take risks and air the footage without getting the total rights. Each usage of "stock" material creates its own problems and solutions.

I once produced a tap dancing program for which I was able to acquire the rights for almost everything except a public relations black-and-white still from the 1930s. The legal affairs office at the network held up final acceptance of the program until I got a letter from the film studio assuring me that they wouldn't sue if the still was used. We were all concerned that the studio didn't have all the rights. A claim might have been made by the photographer or someone appearing in the still. In the 1930s, when that publicity shot had been made, rights for subsequent use may not have been granted, and they might not even have existed. Although the chances of a lawsuit were slim, it was definitely a possibility, and I was glad when the network finally took a chance and ran the program including that 1930 photograph. Happily, no suit was ever filed.

BASIC SHOOTING CONCEPTS

By now we have rehearsed all of the material we can. We've shot the single-camera material that will be inserted into the program. Now, before we sit down in the booth to start shooting the production, we know we have a few basic ideas we can use. As we go over the numbers we'll be called on to shoot, there are a few "classic" concepts that we might think about. These keep cropping up in televised musical productions and, in fact, serve as a kind of fallback position in any format that is not totally linear. The significant idea is that the video portion of any production consists of just two elements: the shot itself and the way in which you get from shot to shot—montage.

Take a moment to think about shooting just one person. Think of a chest shot of a singer against a black background (see shot #1).

Shot #1

The singer can be anywhere in the frame, and facing any direction. We usually think of the singer head on to the camera and seen from camera 2's position. However, if the singer was looking left to right, then her head would probably be shot so it was on the left side of the frame as in shot #2.

Shot #2

The singer could also be shot in profile from camera 1's position (shot #3).

Shot #3

On the other hand, if the singer looked right to left, the opposite would be true, and she would be placed on the right side of the frame, perhaps in a profile from camera 3 as in shot #4.

Shot #4

But what if that's changed? What if the head is seen from camera 2 and placed at the very bottom of the frame, with the top two-thirds of the frame as head room? (See shot #5.)

Shot #5

What if it's a profile? How would a profile from camera 1 and camera 3 differ? (See shot #6.)

Shot #6

How does it "feel" if there is no "nose" room and the face in profile is pressed close to the frame as in shot #7? Doesn't that create an unusual sense of tension? What other framings are possible?

Shot #7

Instead of just dealing with a chest shot, expand the idea. Include a head-to-toe shot (shot #8).

Shot #8

As the figure is placed in different parts of the frame . . .

Shot #9

facing in different directions . . .

Shot #10

seen from different camera positions, different kinds of tensions are evoked (see shots #9–11).

Shot #11

All of that is simply "the shot."

How do you get from one shot to the next? What is the montage? In its simplest form one can cut or "take" from shot to shot. A change from shot to shot can offer more possibilities with a dissolve. The dissolve can be either short, long, very short, very long, or very very long, and so on.

Finally, one can wipe. There are many kinds of wipes, and with computer switchers the wipes can fly in, sprinkle in, or zoom in and take on whatever shape one can imagine. Pictures regularly fly in or out, appearing to be the turning pages of a book. They explode in or out like the bursting of a star. With the advent of digital switching, all of the pixels that make up a picture can be programmed to appear or disappear at the push of a button, and the duration of the move can be totally controlled and repeated.

All of the preceding concern shots that are static. But shots are not static; they move. The performer moves, the cameras move, and the lenses move. We move by panning and zooming and changing focus. Each of those movements can be manipulated into the change from shot to shot. Imagine the following. We start with a singer in a shoulder shot on camera 3 against a black cyc. Camera 3 has taken a center position near camera 2. Slowly, camera 3 zooms out. As the shot continues to widen to a head-to-toe shot, the operator puts the figure, still looking directly at us, on the right side of the frame. (It'll look like shot #12 before the figure is panned over to the right.) Now, very slowly, we dissolve on a profile shot of the same singer looking from left to right, as seen by camera 2 (shot #13). Its time on the screen is handled as it was in the first picture.

Later, it too widens. But for a while the two pictures remain on screen, each sharing 50 percent of the video, against a black background. On the left is the profile of the singer appearing to look at the head-to-toe image of the singer, and on the right is the singer (Figures 7.5 and 7.6). Later the head-to-toe shot on the right is faded out as the camera operator with the profile shot widens out to a head-to-toe shot.

Now, very slowly, we dissolve on a profile shot of the same singer, now looking from right to left, appearing to be looking at the head-to-toe shot of herself. We continue with our moves as we did with the other two shots.

In a different version of the same setup, each shot is started out of focus and racks into focus as the camera widens.

Shot #12

Shot #13

The shots can be dissolved away as the leaving shot pans off the screen and the incoming shot pans onto the screen. The shots can be right/left wiped in as static shots that then move or as moving shots. The trick is to visualize ahead of time what is possible in terms of the shots and then see if you can find a unique but appropriate way to get from shot to shot.

Another way is to mentally divide the screen into quadrants and see where the singer's head appears. Divide the screen into nine boxes and see what that offers. If you mark the camera's viewfinders with a grease pencil, you can have the camera operators place the heads of the singer in different parts of the marked-off frame. There are other ways to manipulate the images. I used to put elements in front of the lens to achieve different effects. Black or white veils from a millinery supply store softened the image. Once I placed Saran Wrap™ on the lens shade and put Vaseline® on the outside to duplicate a "Hartley" lens. That looked best against a light background.

To stir your imagination about shooting musical numbers, you might visit sources such as novelty stores, which are an inexpensive source of cheap lenses and sometimes trick mirrors that break up pictures in ways that are interesting. Looking through books such as *The Technique of Special Effects in Television*, by Bernard Wilkie, helped to stir my imagination as to what was possible. In fact, if you Google the words *special effects*, you'll discover more than 70 million possible websites. If you include the word *books* (i.e., *special effects books*), it will limit the results to just a bit more than 50 million possible sites. Comic books and graphic novels are another source of inspiration for conceiving unique shooting plans.

Figure 7.6 This is what the shot looks like on the air as a super (midway through a dissolve).

THE PRODUCTION

Television Studio Rehearsal and Production

Assuming we have taken care of most of the legal and logistical affairs at our home office and have edited all our preproduction material, we are ready to go to Nashville and start working there. The Nashville program rehearsal schedule might look like this:

Variety America— rehearsal schedule:

Mon. (date)
GRAND OLE OPRY
* 8 a.m.—12.00 noon
  Set & light
* 12.00 p.m.—1 p.m.
  Lunch
* 1—6 p.m.
  Continue set & light

REHEARSAL STUDIO
* 1:30—5:30 p.m.
  ORCHESTRA READING
  COLUMBIA RECORDING/STUDIO B
  123 Music Square East
  Nashville, TN
  615-765-4321

Figure 7.5 This is what shots #12 and #13 look like in the control room. The monitors in the control room show all the shots that make up the supered image.

Tues. (date)

- 8:00–9:00 a.m.
  Setup & ESU (engineering setup)
- 9:00–10:00 a.m.
  BROADWAY STAR—lip-sync
- 10:00–11:00 a.m.
  Set & balance STRING QUARTET
- 11:00–11:30 a.m.
  Rehearse STRING QUARTET
- 11:30–12:30 p.m.
  Set & balance BIG BAND
- 12:30–1:00 p.m.
  Rehearse BIG BAND
- 1:00–2:00 p.m.
  Lunch (Note: During lunch, take a half-hour to record outside with RETIRED STARS. This half-hour recording will mean juggling the lunch schedule with one camera operator if a one-hour lunch is mandatory. If the contract allows us either to buy the half-hour with overtime or to simply call that camera operator back a half-hour later, that's the simplest solution. The stage crew will also strike the BIG BAND chairs and set up for the JAZZ FAMILY.)
- 2:00–2:30 p.m.
  Set & rehearse ACOUSTIC STAR
- 2:30–3:00 p.m.
  Set & balance house orchestra
- 3:00–3:30 p.m.
  Rehearse music cues and ACOUSTIC STAR/ LIVING LEGEND duo
- 3:30–4:30 p.m.
  Set & balance JAZZ FAMILY
- 4:30–5:00 p.m.
  JAZZ FAMILY rehearsal
- 5:00–6:00 p.m.
  Jam session rehearsal
- 6:00–7:00 p.m.
  Dinner (Note: Dinner could happen between 6:30 and 7:30 if the extra half-hour is needed.)
- 7:00–7:30 p.m.
  Audience in
- 7:30–9:30 p.m.
  Record

By rehearsal time, if not earlier, the functions of the director and the producer need to have been separated. The director needs to concentrate on shooting the production, and a producer needs to address the contractual elements, personnel problems, and all the arrangements necessary to move the

production forward. Even in a production mounted on a smaller scale, it is still wise to have someone take over the producer's function and let the director concentrate on directing.

Before leaving for Nashville, we would have accomplished the following:

1. Contacted the talent or their agents, and viewed their performance or rehearsed with them
2. Had the preproduction meetings
3. Secured all hotel rooms and transportation
4. Made all arrangements for the set
5. Made all arrangements for the house orchestra and arrangements for all music
6. Secured the production's studio and crew, as well as all the gear needed
7. Arranged for an audience
8. Arranged for catering
9. Forwarded edited material to the Nashville facility so it could be checked out and approved by Nashville engineering. If there were any technical problems with the piece, we would want to know about it while there was still time to do something about it.

Several trips to the location are usually required to prepare and confirm all of these arrangements. On the week before production we might arrive on Wednesday or Thursday before our Monday orchestra rehearsal to take care of any last-minute arrangements. Our major tasks at that time are to confirm, in person, all that had been agreed to earlier and any last-minute items, including the following:

1. Legal affairs, including rights for all music as well as all contracts
2. Coordination with our location production manager—someone who knows local talent, crews, and equipment
3. Preparation of routines, rehearsal schedules, scripts, and office services

Let's assume we've rented the Grand Ole Opry for our production. We've phoned, e-mailed, and faxed one another about what each organization will supply, and, fortunately, many of our needs have been taken care of by them. If this was going to be an outdoor concert at a local park, our needs and concerns would be very similar. In fact, even if elements of the production were taking place as part of a college or high school production, the preproduction concerns and rehearsal agenda would be very similar to those of a network production. No matter where you're working, you're going to have to let the right departments—music, stage design, lighting design, engineering, stage crew—know who's singing what, what mics are needed, where the singers are standing in relation to each other and to the set, when they appear in the program, and many other similar details.

Starting Monday morning, the set will begin to go up on the stage, and we should be there to answer any questions that might arise. The set designer, the lighting designer, and the unit production manager will also be there. The director probably goes to the afternoon house-orchestra rehearsal to see, hear, and, if possible, record (this is a rehearsal-only track for the director's use) the following:

1. The opening number
2. Background music under the introduction to each segment
3. "Here Comes the Sun," with the ACOUSTIC STAR and the LIVING LEGEND
4. "Saints," in the jam session

In reality, we probably would not have a house orchestra, but instead, we would ask the first act, the BIG BAND, to play "There's No Business Like Show Business" to serve as stock music for the intros. The LIVING LEGEND would have to sing without an orchestral background, which is entirely appropriate for his music. However, for the purposes of this chapter, I've included a house orchestra. They sit in front of the stage in the orchestra pit, or they might be placed on a side of the studio and never be seen. Not showing the orchestra saves paying them for an on-camera appearance and probably saves an hour in "dressing" the orchestra area. A dressed orchestra area is clear of all the musicians' jackets, coffee cups, and instrument cases. Messy microphone wires have to be "dressed" so the floor is neat.

As a director/producer I would have heard at least a piano version of the original material prior to the Monday orchestra rehearsal. I'd also want to attend the rehearsal with the ACOUSTIC STAR and the LIVING LEGEND. This is to allay any concerns they might have and to get a feel for the way they work together. This rehearsal is conducted in the same way as the ones we had earlier in the rehearsal studio, but since the performers stay in place, there is no need for a ground plan. That night we'd confirm

that our talent had checked into their hotels in Nashville. We would also take care of any last-minute problems, which can range from sick talent and snow or other weather delays to ego, artistic temperament, or negotiating ploys by talent and their representatives.

As of Tuesday, our rehearsal will be oriented to the studio production. The set and lighting crews will need to work with the actual production to work out the details of their plans. Audio will have notes about how things have to be miked and will have cables and microphones ready for the performers. They may have even been in phone contact to make sure that preferred mics are being used.

When we leave the facility, the crew we've been working with will start working with the next production that has rented the facility. Our production is very important to us, but it's just another production to the crew. Our anxieties are not theirs. A professional approach will be expected—ultimately demanded—and appreciated.

Camera Placement

The key to camera placement has to do with the wide shot. Close-ups take care of themselves. A head shot and a profile shot will be considerably different depending on the direction from which they come, but they are apt to be okay no matter what's happening in the background. The important shot to get right is the wide shot. Keeping that in mind, the director will arrange the layout of cameras, reading from house left to right. The placement of cameras will differ with different directors. However, some fundamental camera positions seem inevitable. I have numbered the cameras, left to right, as they would be most typically numbered. If there were just three cameras, they would most likely be set out left to right, with camera 1 on stage at audience left, camera 2 wide in the middle, and camera 3 on audience right, either on the stage or on a platform at stage height. Because this is a major production, I am assuming that we have more than three cameras.

Cameras 1 and 2
Cameras 1 and 2 are in the camera-left position. The camera-left position may be the most critical because, since most bass and guitar players are right-handed, cameras 1 and 2 are in position to get the most direct shots of the guitarists' and bass

player's hands. Camera 2 is on stage, mounted on a pedestal with wheels. Camera 1 is on stage but is handheld. It's important to have a steady shot on one of the cameras, while the handheld can get odd (Dutch) angles. The handheld camera is also useful for getting reverse shots past the performers into the audience. It's easiest to set up this camera for reverse shots while camera 2 is on line, shooting toward the right side of the stage. That way the handheld camera is less likely to walk through a shot that's on the air.

Cameras 3 and 4

Cameras 3 and 4 are in the middle. Having two cameras with head-on shots allows the director to cut or dissolve from a head-on full-face shot to a head-on head-to-toe shot. The chances are that one of the cameras will be on a jib arm, mounted on a crane, with room to move forward or backward on an attached ramp to the stage. That way it can move in and out, as well as arc left and right, high and low. The other head-on camera might be on a tripod. In some typical configurations, the camera mounted on a jib travels on a ramp in front of the stage and can move right to left rather than forward and backward. When working with a low-budget production, it's sometimes useful to put a camera in the lap of someone in a wheelchair and let that person get the shots that a crane might get. The shots won't be as smooth, but it's an attractive alternative.

Camera 5

Camera 5 is placed at the camera-right position on stage. It gets head-on close-ups of the first two violins in the STRING QUARTET and is available for matching profiles to camera 2's shots. Shooting a profile from camera 2 shows a face looking from left to right; camera 5 sees the same profile right to left. Going from camera 2 to camera 5 would essentially jump cut, or "jump dissolve," but it might be more interesting that way.

Camera 6

Camera 6 is in the balcony. It would be best if it had the capability to move left and right as well as zoom in and out, but that requires tracks, a prepared floor, or a jib arm for the camera—all expensive options. I might want to use it for the end or the beginning of each act. It can also be useful in getting close-ups of the audience.

Camera 7

Camera 7 is a handheld-type camera that can be "quick-mounted" on a tripod or pedestal in the back of the auditorium. The quick mount allows the camera to be removed from the tripod and used as a handheld camera. It can be used for the audience shots and for interviews with the RETIRED STARS.

It would be entirely possible to shoot this production with only two or three cameras, and for a long time that's how network productions were done. It's still how many local variety programs and university programs are shot.

At the networks, Marty Callner directed *NSYNC* live from Madison Square Garden for HBO using 31 cameras. Roger Goodman shot *ABC 2000* with an astonishing array of hardware. This millennium special included work from 60 countries, utilizing more than 500 cameras, 32 switchers, and 4 control rooms. No matter how many sources were used, the results had to look good just one screen at a time.

Production Rehearsal

As in the preproduction rehearsals, the function of the rehearsal should be determined before the rehearsal begins. Earlier we needed to get some ideas about how to shoot the acts and some specific information for audio, sets, and lighting. Now, once again, the question is, what do I want to accomplish with this rehearsal? In a music program at least three things need to be accomplished:

1. Have everyone listen to the music and agree on what will be on the program, when it will appear in the program, and where it is to be shot on the stage.
2. Work out a shooting plan for all the performers.
3. "Semifinalize" the shooting plan. The director is almost always open, up to the last minute, to additions or changes that will enhance the project. There are, however, times where it is simply too late to make any changes. Should a change of plans occur when an act is recording, the director might say something like "Adding shots: take 3, . . . take 2, . . . take 1, . . . back to script, . . . take 3 shot #99, . . ." and so on, which would bring everyone back to the plan.

The schedule has been set up to accomplish what's needed for the director and to accommodate the talent's and crew's needs. Because it's an easy audio setup, we start with the BROADWAY STAR. Starting this way allows an audio-assist (part of the audio crew) extra time to set up the larger numbers, such as the BIG BAND and the house orchestra. The BROADWAY STAR requires only one person on the audio board. An audio-assist might be setting up cable behind the curtain while the rehearsal is going on.

9:00—10:00: BROADWAY STAR—single performer to tracks

From 9:00 to 10:00 a.m. we are working with the BROADWAY STAR in front of the curtain. He needs to know how he'll be introduced and how he gets on stage. He also has to meet with the stage manager to get his dressing room assignment and learn who will be the liaison to the control room. Although there are no special arrangements that need to be made, this would be the time for the stage manager and the director to discuss any signals that the star needs to know. This arrangement is similar to the way one would handle a guest on a demonstration program.

The BROADWAY STAR lip-syncs the first numbers. We'll have to set our shots and arrange "camera business" to cover whatever parts of the song have no vocals. Most songs seem to start with a music introduction before the singer begins. The director will need to create something to cover that "music-only" part of the song. Perhaps we start out of focus and come to focus as the first bars are played prior to the first notes that are sung. We might start out very wide and zoom in to a close-up just as the artist is about to sing. One danger in this approach is that if the artist is seen in a clear close-up before he or she starts to sing, the audience gets to see the artist in an unflattering position, vamping—doing nothing but waiting for the intro to be finished. A close-up of this waiting may be very unflattering to the artist and uncomfortable for the audience. It also misses the opportunity to create an interesting visual frame around the performance.

We'll presume that the song is sung in a spotlight against the curtain at the edge of the stage and that there is black all around. The agenda for this part of the rehearsal is to help establish the audio level required for playback to the floor and to let the singer get the feel of the lighting. Also, the crew will get a sense of the tempo of the song and learn how camera,

light, and crew moves have to be made. Because it's being shot against black, we know we'll handle it with one of the standard shooting patterns described earlier in this chapter. We'll rehearse whatever choice we've made to see how it looks.

By now, the director will have decided on a device to get to the second number. Since the second number is a chroma-key piece, the BROADWAY STAR either moves to a chroma wall or stands in place as the wall is let in from the grid above. The video cover between songs might be of the audience's hands clapping, which covers the transition and prevents the home audience from seeing the move. If you wanted the home audience to see the set change, you might use a wide shot of the chroma wall as it was coming into view.

Whatever device is chosen, there will need to be a light change, and a mark will have to be established for both the wall and the position of the BROADWAY STAR so the chroma-key effect can be optimized. Let's assume that the BROADWAY STAR walks to the chroma wall during applause and that we dissolve from clapping hands to the first shots on our preproduced New York background. This time the BROADWAY STAR is singing to track; the instrumental part of the audio comes from the playback. His voice will be recorded from a handheld mic.

To achieve this scene shift, we rehearse the change. First, the chroma blue or green wall is brought in and set, and the set is marked. Then the talent is set in place and marked. (These floor markings will be made using a stand-in performer or our stage manager wearing a headset.) We want to be sure that there is sufficient separation from the wall so the light on the BROADWAY STAR doesn't spill onto the chroma wall, which needs its own even wash of light. Depending on the hair color, we might include a blue or green gelled backlight on our talent to add to the separation for the key effect.

Once the marks are established, we would bring in the BROADWAY STAR so we can see what adjustments need to be made to accommodate his clothing and coloring. We want to make sure that the audio level from the playback is appropriate and that the mix from the live mic works with the playback audio. Once all the pieces of the "cross-over" have been rehearsed, we rehearse the song. It sometimes feels silly to rehearse a simple effect like the crossover from the lip-sync number to the "to-track" number, but it's never as easy as it looks. Practically speaking, a lot of people will be involved with this, and they all need to be focused on the event at the same time. The stage crew needs to lower the wall, the lighting crew needs to make the lighting change, the BROADWAY STAR has to move to his second position, and playback has to begin the playback on cue.

Once the crossover has been rehearsed, the "to-track" number will be rehearsed. We probably need to adjust the images in the camera frame so the apparent size of the BROADWAY STAR looks good when keyed to the prerecorded and edited footage. This would be helped by feeding the video mix of the playback and the live output into the camera viewfinder. If that feature was not a part of the camera's capabilities, one might use a grease pencil on the camera operator's viewfinder and arrange to place a monitor nearby.

10:00–11:30: STRING QUARTET
set/balance/and rehearse small orchestra
From 10:00 to 11:00 the STRING QUARTET sets up. This, too, probably requires a simple audio setup. It might be done with just one mic, although there are some audio engineers who would want to use four or more mics. In any event, the schedule allows an hour and a half to set up, balance, and rehearse the group. It's a more demanding setup than the one for the BROADWAY STAR because of the critical nature of the audio balance. Everyone in the production, including stagehands who may be setting up for the band, must stop so there is silence and audio can get a clean sound check from the instruments. The hour-and-a-half rehearsal time allotted to the STRING QUARTET is probably barely enough. As a director I would want to plan to shoot the STRING QUARTET so the audience had an idea about the structure of the music or became involved in the interplay between the musicians.

It would be unusual to find a television crew that was familiar with Beethoven string quartets. Even the crew at Lincoln Center in New York might need a refresher course. Our crew will need time to get used to working with the STRING QUARTET. In this case I would have explained to the STRING QUARTET that at least three run-throughs of the music will be necessary so the following can be accomplished:

1. Audio gets a chance to hear the entire piece, and the director gets a chance to call the prearranged shots.
2. Everyone gets a chance to make corrections.

3. Everyone gets a chance to feel comfortable with the corrections.

Since the running time of the STRING QUARTET is 9 minutes, three run-throughs will take at least 30 minutes. That leaves 60 minutes to set up the act, take the required 5-minute break, and talk through any changes. All of the hour-and-a-half rehearsal schedule will probably be needed.

During the actual running of the program, there is a two-minute commercial before the STRING QUARTET begins to play, and the preceding act will have been an easy setup, so we may be able to record the STRING QUARTET as if this were a live program.

11:00–1:00: BIG BAND and choir
By the time we get to rehearse the BIG BAND, there has been sufficient time to set mics, cables, and chairs. Since we rehearsed with them earlier, we would have created a marked score and shot sheets that implement our working plan for the BIG BAND's numbers. The function of this rehearsal is to acquaint the crew with the music and our plan and to make any necessary changes to make the plan work. A possible rehearsal sequence might be similar to what's in place for the STRING QUARTET:

1. With the camera crew on the floor wearing headsets, the band plays through the first number while we call the shots on headphones. Audio gets to hear the whole number.
2. The camera crew gets on camera, and the number is played again as the camera crew works out the shots. The director and production assistant note any mistakes or changes they wish to make. Unless there is a real disaster, the musicians are not interrupted. Any changes or corrections are passed on to the crew after the number is completed. A pencil tic mark on the score is usually sufficient to remind the director about anything that happened that needs attention.
3. A last run-through of the number is done to proof changes and corrections. The entrance of the chorus is rehearsed, and if it goes smoothly, the next song the group does is rehearsed in the same way. The last thing to be worked on is the ad-libbed "Saints" number at the end of the program. That is scheduled for 5:00 p.m., after the JAZZ FAMILY rehearsal. The closing

"Saints" number uses the stage and audio setup used by the JAZZ FAMILY. Those members of the BIG BAND who appear in the number are reminded of the 5:00 p.m. rehearsal.

1:00–2:00: Lunch

During lunch the director/producer will be working with a single camera crew, taping the responses for the RETIRED STARS' piece. These two responses should be short, since the entire segment is short. We need to know the questions we are going to be asking the RETIRED STARS and what responses are required. There would have been some preliminary discussions with them, and a very loose script or outline of the pieces would have been made to use as a guide through the taping. Essentially, this portion of the program is like producing a minidocumentary.

2:00–2:30: ACOUSTIC STAR

The ACOUSTIC STAR sits on a stool in front of the curtain, plays the guitar, and sings. Two mics are needed—one for voice and one for the guitar. The words to the songs and the style of shooting would have been determined before the rehearsal. As with the BIG BAND's rehearsal, the purpose is to let the crew see the numbers and to acquaint them with the shooting plan. It's also an opportunity to make any needed changes.

2:30–3:30: House band and ACOUSTIC STAR/LIVING LEGEND duet

This hour has been set aside to balance and rehearse the house orchestra. The orchestra will have to rehearse the opening and closing. They will have music to cover acts getting on and off stage, and they will have special music to get us into a station break and then back into the show after a station break. The most important "act" element to be balanced is the number with the ACOUSTIC STAR and the LIVING LEGEND. From 2:00 until 2:30, we were able to rehearse the ACOUSTIC STAR's solo number. Since the duet between the ACOUSTIC STAR and the LIVING LEGEND is scored with an orchestra, we will first have to balance the orchestra. The ACOUSTIC STAR and the LIVING LEGEND will have to wait for that balance. However, the house musicians and the crew will have worked together in Nashville before, so the setup can be accomplished fairly quickly. This is one of the advantages of working within an established venue. The music background used with the

ACOUSTIC STAR and the LIVING LEGEND was rehearsed the previous day, so this balance should be easy and quick. When the LIVING LEGEND appears, audio may need to find a way to add another set of mics to the ones that the ACOUSTIC STAR is using. The applause for the last number should be adequate to cover someone coming on stage and placing the mics, or the two performers can share one set of mics. That decision lies in the hands of the audio department. Our job is to arrange a suitable video entrance for the LIVING LEGEND.

3:30–5:00: JAZZ FAMILY—jazz small group

From 3:30 to 5:00 p.m. we rehearse the JAZZ FAMILY. Essentially, this is a small jazz group. Our rehearsal procedure for them would be the same if they were anything from a trio to an octet. As is the case with all the acts, they'll need to know how to get on and off stage during the performance. In this case, we've arranged for them to be preset backstage so when the curtain is opened, it reveals them, and they play until the program is over. Most often jazz starts by stating a melody and then improvising on it. Usually the improvisation features one instrument at a time and four bars from each, followed sometimes by two bars each. At the end of the piece there is a return to a statement of the melody. The director can function best—that is, taking the right camera at the right place at the right time—by being aware of the order of the solos. If the musicians understand the director's needs, they are often willing to preplan their solos. If not, they can still help by predetermining which two or three instruments will take the first solo. If they are unable to commit to an order prior to the recording, you have to stay with a wide shot or a close-up of the leader until a soloist emerges.

You will need to improvise the shooting of this number, and the rehearsal for this group should accomplish three things:

1. As in the rehearsal of the BIG BAND, which took place in a studio, the JAZZ FAMILY rehearsal is a time to listen to the mood of the music and let that help stimulate a plan for shooting. This means you may ask the group to give you an idea of the music before you see them on camera. Of course, one is sometimes called on to shoot without being able to formulate a plan, but since this is a rehearsal for the director, too, planning is in order. The

tempo and the interplay between the players will help generate your plan. These elements may determine what you ask from your lighting director, and they may affect whether the piece is shot with all cuts or all dissolves or, for that matter, all wipes or some other such combination.

2. Audio gets to work out a balance.
3. The director and camera crew get to find out what shots exist and also have a chance to work out a few plans of coverage. The best way to do that is systematically. First, set the lighting that will be used. Ask the players to stand or sit in position as if they were playing, unless they feel more comfortable actually playing. Turn off the audio in the control room so you are not tempted to react to the music. Use the time to see what each camera's wide shot looks like. Then see what kinds of combinations exist from each camera position. Start with camera 1. Look at every possible close-up available to that camera.
   a. Close-up. The close-up starts with the face of a player and then close-ups of the hands of the player.
   b. Pan to the next player. Get a close-up of the face. Close-up hands, and so on.
   c. Then ask camera 1 to widen out. Note the pictures that happen along the way.
   d. What does camera 1 see from a far left position?
   e. How does it look from a high position at the left, then a low position left?
   f. How does it look trucking or panning to a right position?
   g. How does it look from a high position at the right, then low position right?

Learn what the potential shots are for each camera. If you can visualize each camera's shots in advance, so much the better. The objective is to know what the options are and then formulate a plan for shooting.

A typical plan for shooting might be to dissolve or cut from a wide shot to a cross two-shot and then zoom to one of the players in that shot. I might limit the montage so nothing but dissolves was used to get from shot to shot. Perhaps heavy blue backlights might be used if it was a slow number and if lighting could accommodate that plan. The last number in the program, "When the Saints Go Marching In," is ad-libbed; all the talent in the program join in. It would probably be best for audio if all the solos were taken at the microphones used by the JAZZ FAMILY. If additional mics needed to be added, that could be accomplished during the applause, or they could have been prehung and "let in" from the grid or simply left in place during the setup for the JAZZ FAMILY.

In order to shoot the lead musician or vocalist during the ad-libbed portion of the taping, I've found a trick that seems to work well. You can usually get your video coverage by assigning one or two mics as the vocal mics. Make sure the vocalists know about the assignment, and then keep a camera on those mics. The lead singer is sure to use one, and as soon as he or she starts to sing, you can call for the shot. This can be a very effective device when shooting rock concerts.

We want to arrange for the artists to come on stage in a predetermined manner. The BROADWAY STAR might come in after the first eight bars of music, sing eight bars, and introduce the ACOUSTIC STAR. After the ACOUSTIC STAR sings, the LIVING LEGEND sings. Finally, the cast on stage waves to the members of the BIG BAND to join in. The players then have to determine who will play lead, and we cover the mics as if it were a rock concert and we didn't know who was going to sing next.

If the members of the STRING QUARTET are willing to join in, we have to arrange some special break for them. The details might be arranged at the 5:00 p.m. rehearsal, although the group's willingness to appear would have been discussed earlier.

Editing

The next step in the production—editing—should be mechanical by this time. Our "booth PA" would have maintained a time-code log of the production. Each act is shot in sequence. It's not necessary to do that, but it may be easier for editing. If there had been any mistakes during production, we would have reshot. As the cost of the actual recording has gone down, the output of each camera would have been recorded so that in most cases corrections in the switched numbers could be made without any reshooting.

All openings and closings of numbers are open ended. Also, there are lots of wild shots of the audience applauding. (While we hope we have been able to get shots of the audience applauding wildly throughout the program, we may not have enough footage, so in this case "wild" means that the shots are done separately from any of the performances.) These wild shots, which are unrelated to any specific performance, may be inserted in the program at any time as a part of any number. During the shooting, the lighting director might bring up the house lights and any specials that had been rigged for the shot. The applause signs would blink, and the stage managers would encourage the audience to whoop it up. Some typical wild shots are close-ups of applauding hands, two or three people in the audience applauding, or a trucking shot down the aisle. Another set of such wild cover shots would be wide shots looking at the audience from the stage. This requires masking the cameras that were on stage for the performers during the actual shooting. Essentially, it's the point of view of the performers after they are finished. The audience and applause shots are used as a pad in the editing process. Fades to black are also done in editing. The show is planned with a final number that can run either short or long to make timing easier.

By the time we are through with this program, we will have worked with music in most styles and found an agenda for working with each kind of number:

1. Single-camera (for the chroma-key)
2. Multiple-camera
3. Stock footage
4. Vocals that are:
   a. Lip-synced
   b. Sung to track
   c. Live to orchestra, with and without amplification
   d. Live and acoustic
5. Music that is:
   a. Scored and contemporary
   b. Scored and classical
   c. Jazz, based on a theme

REVIEW

- Work in musical production for television can be categorized by three different criteria:
  1. Type of material: improvised or scored
  2. Type of performance: live or edited
  3. Type of production: single-camera or multiple-camera
- In preproduction the producer/director must:
  1. Get the talent, recognizing that there will be last-minute additions and deletions

2. Create a *routine* for the program
3. Create a *rehearsal schedule* for the program
4. Create a *shooting schedule* for the program
5. Rehearse
6. Prerecord

- A rule of thumb regarding musical productions is that you start with a big, bright, "up" number, perhaps your second-best act of the show, and end your program with the best of the show to "keep 'em coming back." The same "rule" is often used in programming other formats.
- When singers are featured, they should be blocked so they face the audience and their microphones are off-axis to the house orchestra whenever possible.
- First off-set rehearsals for musical productions have very specific goals:
  1. Create a quarter-inch ground plan for use by:
     a. The set designer, who creates the setting used by all elements of the program
     b. The lighting designer, who lights all the settings and acts
     c. The audio crew, who needs to know where to place mics and speakers. The audio crew will also need to supply:
        (1) an audio mix to the program feed (either live, tape, or multitrack file)
        (2) an audio mix to studio audience
        (3) a voice-only "foldback" to the musicians
        (4) an intercom
  2. Obtain a copy of the score to create a shooting script.
  3. Record your own copy of the music as played in rehearsal to coordinate the shooting script.
  4. Be sure that the talent is aware of the schedule before they leave the first rehearsal.
- In shooting classical music, it is generally accepted that the director's job is to explain the music visually. Sometimes, however, the director uses the video to enhance a mood or make a statement about the music.
- Vocalists can be accompanied in any one of three ways:
  1. Live
  2. Live to track
  3. Lip-sync (Lip-sync performances must be handled as if the singer were really singing. In order to make it look real, it's essential

that the singer really "sings out" along with the recorded sound.)

- In a "music video," the visuals are often given the same weight as the performer. Also, the conventions for music videos usually require many more cuts or dissolves than are usually used in a concert-type format.
- Stock material, audio or video, usually requires a licensing fee, which is linked to the amount of material and the scope of its broadcast use. Companies that supply such material often charge relatively low search fees.
- Shooting plan: the two basic elements of a shooting plan revolve around the shot and the way one gets from shot to shot (montage).
- Prior to beginning camera rehearsal, the following must be accomplished:
    1. Talent contacted and viewed or rehearsed if possible
    2. Preproduction meetings: completed
    3. Routines: prepared
    4. Schedules prepared: rehearsal and production—possibly editing
    5. Scripts: written and copies prepared
    6. Hotel rooms and transportation: secured (if applicable)
    7. Office staff: all arrangements made (sometimes this is simply a laptop with Internet access and a portable printer)
    8. Set/sets: all arrangements made for completion, delivery, and setup
    9. Studio, crew, and all gear: secured
    10. Music: house orchestra and arrangements for all music confirmed
    11. Audience: secured
    12. Catering: arranged
    13. Preedited material: forwarded to the production facility for playback
    14. Legal affairs, including rights for all music as well as all contracts: in place
- Prior to production the following departments must be alerted to what the production's needs will be:
    1. Music
    2. Stage design
    3. Lighting design
    4. Engineering
    5. Stage crew
    6. Location crew
- The director visits the set as it's going up and the orchestra sees it while they are rehearsing to note any problems while there is still time to make small changes.
- The camera-left cameras get the best shots of right-handed guitarists' and bass players' hands. The key to placing the cameras lies in the consideration of the wide shot.
- The function of the rehearsal should be determined before the rehearsal begins. The question to ask is, what do I want to accomplish with this rehearsal? In a music program, at least three things need to be accomplished:
    1. Everyone hears the music.
    2. A shooting plan is worked out.
    3. The shooting plan is finalized.

chapter eight

Commercials and Public Service Announcements

SIMILARITIES AND DIFFERENCES

Television commercials are television messages designed to sell a product, service, or an idea. A *public service announcement*, or PSA (*public service bulletin* [PSB] in the United Kingdom), is similar to a commercial but is produced for a socially relevant cause or a nonprofit organization. PSAs are usually dedicated to improving or serving organizations involved in education, health, welfare, safety, and so on. In the United States, commercial television stations are required by federal communications law to provide service to the community, and airing PSAs is considered a form of community service. Stations usually use their inventory of unpurchased air time to run PSAs. There is no charge to the nonprofit organization, but the PSAs are most often scheduled to run during non–prime time periods.

PSAs have the same running time as commercials—usually 30 seconds—but they can be :10, :15, :60, or longer. They run adjacent to commercials or in commercial time slots. Like commercials, they are expected to motivate some action, such as "Get a checkup!" or "Visit your local library!" or to change behavior, such as "Stop smoking!" or "Eat smart!" The message must be timely, accurate, and relevant to the community. Restraints on the message regarding political, religious, and controversial material may exist to protect the station from involvement in issues that demand rebuttals, counter-rebuttals, and possible litigation.

The production of a PSA is handled as if it were a commercial. PSAs may seem easy to make, because, like commercials, they're short and thus appear to be made with minimal effort. That's a common misconception. If a PSA is to get significant air time, it must be perceived by the stations as being worthy of being aired. This is of particular concern to stations because although PSAs are often aired late at night, they are nevertheless aired between expensive and carefully produced commercial messages. Stations want commercial breaks, even those with PSAs, to look good and not "turn off" viewers. That means the PSAs have to look as good as commercials.

The cost of producing a commercial can run into hundreds of thousands of dollars if it's to look exactly right. Even then, the cost of production is just the beginning. No matter how extravagant the commercial production budget, the cost of running the commercial is much greater. With that kind of investment, commercial production is expected to be flawless. Anything less might in some way mar the sponsor's image, and it would do so at tremendous cost in both production and air time. The viewer cannot help but compare the PSA with the commercial that he or she just watched. A shoddy PSA might reflect on the commercials surrounding it when they are aired. Stations and sponsors want PSAs to be at least a close second in production values if they are to be considered for airing. Then, too, if they seem to be created with less care than the commercials that surround them, they do not help the organizations or causes for which they were created.

The networks and many independent stations provide guidelines for PSA production. The guidelines can usually be obtained by calling the local station and speaking with anyone in community affairs or with a public service coordinator. At smaller stations, the news director may be the appropriate contact.

It's sensible to request a copy of these so your PSAs comply. Otherwise, you may spend a lot of time preparing messages that go unseen. Often a station will suggest that a storyboard be submitted for approval. It's sensible to do this rather than spend money for a production that may be found to be unsuitable for broadcast.

Guidelines will also spell out requirements for the technical requirements of the spot. At one time stations required color bars, tone, slates, and so on at the start of each spot, but the move to digital media has changed that for most stations. The appropriate format for slating and delivery of the PSA or spots should be ascertained on a station by station basis. The slate, or some form of identification, is essential to assure the station that it's running the right spot. The commercial or PSA information includes the following:

1. The name of the client or agency responsible for the spot—so they can be notified in case there is a problem with the content of the spot.
2. The name of the spot—which serves as a check with the broadcast coordinator's log.
3. The producing company—because it, along with the client or agency, may be notified if there is some technical difficulty with the spot.
4. The total running time (TRT)—to confirm length (e.g., the first spot runs one minute; the next, which the station is running, is a :30; and it's followed by a :10).
5. The production or editing date—to determine timeliness and version.
6. Some kind of reference code—for ease of handling and for a double-check with the daily log.

The guidelines may specify that commercials usually run for 30 seconds but have only 28 seconds of copy to allow for a fade-up and fade-out.

The guidelines would also indicate the appropriate duration for phone numbers (5 to 10 seconds), safe copy area, and so on. Questions about using celebrities, politicians, and other spokespersons are also covered in most stations' guidelines, as are requirements for proof of nonprofit status.

In some ways PSAs are a wonderful way to study television production. Like longer forms, they can be studied in terms of preproduction, production, and postproduction. They require a limited amount of time but demand a great deal of focus. If properly conceived, they are short enough to be able to be produced well.

PREPRODUCTION

The preproduction for shooting PSAs starts with discussions that lead to several concepts. These are then whittled down to one central working idea. From that a script evolves. In most television formats, the director has nothing to do with the creation of the script. In fact, the director of professional commercials seldom writes or "creates" the commercial. The director is often absent from the editing process. The creation of the idea, script, and storyboards (which present the script in a kind of comic book format) is done by an advertising agency. Both the preproduction and postproduction are done by the agency producer in conjunction with the commercial producer and sometimes the client.

Before being produced, a commercial message or PSA is studied thoroughly. First, the target audience and the goals of the commercial or PSA must be analyzed. The message's language and presentation must be checked, reanalyzed, and rechecked. The production company hired to carry out the production will be considered and reconsidered. The talent and the director, as well as the crew and the postproduction facility to be used, are very carefully scrutinized. Every step along the way is thought out, evaluated, challenged, and then finally accepted and executed. Along the way, some of the best writers, producers, directors, and crews may work on the project.

In smaller markets, a service organization may work directly with a station, college, or university to produce a PSA. In larger markets an agency is asked, or offers, to work for specific organizations that wish to have PSAs or other media prepared and placed. Usually, the agencies or the local station handle PSA assignments with the same personnel and in the same way they handle any client. This occurs for four good reasons:

- To many in the industry, making a PSA is an opportunity to "give back" to the community.
- The quality of the campaign and production will help define the agency and the production company in the creative community, and therefore the work is taken very seriously. No agency or production company wants to be seen as doing shoddy or poor work.
- It is often a way in which an agency or a station that is limited in what it does for clients by working in some single area—retail sales, for

example—can "stretch its wings." Work on a PSA project might create opportunities that would be impossible with the agency's or station's current clients.

- Other clients may appreciate well-made PSAs and ask the station or agency to produce some for causes that are important to them. This becomes a form of professional networking.

Not all agencies or stations, and not all students, will handle all PSAs in the same way. Some consider making a PSA an odious chore that they are compelled to perform for a demanding client, boss, teacher, or "image." However, in order to produce any commercial or PSA, the following steps must be taken:

1. Meetings are scheduled with the public service organization, and the nonprofit organization's goals are discussed.

2. Executives, account executives, or project leaders meet with a creative team. (This may simply mean "Self, what do I do now?")

3. The creative team provides ideas, which are then analyzed—sometimes with the client, sometimes just in-house, and sometimes all alone. Storyboards or scripts are created (Figure 8.1).

4. The client chooses a campaign.

5. The process to production continues through preproduction, production, and postproduction.

The in-house cost of the project is handled as a charitable contribution. Production costs are handled the same way whenever possible. For example, a production company may have to pay the crew but will not mark up the production costs.

Student-produced PSAs are at a disadvantage: their casts and crews, like the students themselves, are learning the craft. Few writing classes emphasize

Figure 8.1 This storyboard is typical of those from the MJA agency. The work of other agencies may look different. Some storyboards use clip art, some use drawings, and some use simple stick figures. Used by permission from MJA, New York/San Francisco.

writing television commercials or PSAs, which are very specific forms. Production classes that attempt to produce PSAs may be plagued with hidden script or production problems, as well as hardware and budgetary limitations. Furthermore, while a professional cast and crew might be able to help a neophyte director, such help is scarce for the student director. The best guidance for anyone who wants to direct and produce successful PSAs is to recognize and work within whatever limitations exist for them and to emulate the steps taken in professional commercial production as much as possible.

Usually projects go wrong when they start with a point of view that's geared to production instead of beginning with an idea: "Let's go down to the beach or over to the poor section of town. We can shoot a lot of garbage, graffiti, flotsam, and jetsam and put a tag on it that says something like 'It's our home. Let's keep it clean!'" Although it's a nice sentiment, and it might actually make a good visual PSA, it's been seen too often. It doesn't have the spark of an original idea, no matter how well you shoot the garbage, graffiti, flotsam, and jetsam (or what have you).

Professionals start with conferences with their clients because they know that the idea for the commercial must come out of the client's needs. Stating those needs in one clear sentence is often the key to making the commercial work. The sentence may be "Drinking [the client's soda] makes you feel wonderful." That sentence will be discussed for its possibilities. What exactly does "feel wonderful" mean? How can we illustrate feeling wonderful? Is there sufficient material in our daily life to show how the client's soda goes with feeling wonderful? Should the pitch be to someone who isn't having a wonderful time and whose whole day becomes wonderful because of the client's soda? Those questions and the discussions surrounding them, and many more, inevitably lead to some ideas of how to "sell" the idea that drinking the client's soda will make a person feel wonderful. Many approaches will be tried, although only a few may be presented to the client. Each, however, will contain just that one idea. In this case that one idea is "Drinking [the client's soda] makes you feel wonderful."

Arriving at that one statement is sometimes easier for a commercial than for a PSA because the commercial's goals are so apparent. Manufacturing clients want the public to buy their products—anywhere. They want us to buy and drink Coke®, to buy and drive a Ford®, or to use Dawn®

dishwashing liquid. Retail clients want the public to buy the Coke, Ford, or Dawn from their particular restaurant, dealership, or grocery store. Knowing the ground rules and what results are anticipated changes the nature of what is said to the public; with a PSA, the real message may not be as apparent.

The wording of the PSA's message is very important because it affects what we shoot. Consider the two statements "Don't litter" and "Keep our city clean." Either could be used for a campaign—neither is right or wrong, better or worse. As a director/producer you might prefer one to the other. "Keep our city clean" is more positive and suggests more action to me, but if the client prefers "Don't litter," that's the way it's apt to get made. With a PSA, unlike the case with a commercial, the director/producer may voice creative suggestions. The director/producer of commercials usually doesn't have much input about which approach is taken, even though the choice might have a profound effect on the work that's produced. As a director/producer I've often wished for a better script and sometimes have been able to make suggestions. Most of the time the storyboards with the script and all the shots laid out have been approved, and the job of the director/producer is to make the approved boards work. Sometimes, but rarely, that does include rewriting the spot. At some time—eventually—the agency or the station and the client agree on the desired action and the message. At an agency, a creative director working with the account executives, copy editors, and art directors creates a plan or campaign that may include other media as well as television commercials to achieve their goals. At a station, the same task may be accomplished by a director/producer working alone.

Lots of books about advertising, creating campaigns, writing copy, and so on are available. They attempt to give the reader tools to find the right approach and the right questions to ask, but the process is a creative one, and no single answer will work for everything or everyone. The key may be in asking good questions and then in holding one's creative values to high standards. Although this book is about production, the idea and script will have a profound influence on the effect of the commercial or PSA. All commercials tend to fall into well-defined types. Many authors have listed the prevalent commercial types. In his book *Ogilvy on Advertising*, David Ogilvy lists some specific categories in which successful television ads tend to fall. These are some of my favorites:

1. *Characters:* Zeke and Eb, two old codgers you'll never forget, along with the product with which they are associated (this can even be an animal ... or animated!).
2. *Comedy:* The danger here is that the audience will remember the joke, not the product.
3. *Demonstrations:* An "infomercial" is a long demonstration. Commercials for Dentsu Knives and Krazy Glue® are short ones.
4. *Problem solving:* How do you serve the unexpected guests who arrive ten minutes after you get home? Easy—just use the client's product.
5. *Reasons:* Here are three good reasons why you should use the client's product. This approach is self-explanatory.
6. *Slice of life:* These may feel trite, but they do work. Often two actors argue over the merits of a product, and one is finally convinced. Sometimes there's simply a question, such as "Oh, Madge, how do you get your dishes so clean?" or a statement, such as "Bob, I can't tell you how much trouble I used to have getting a great shine on my car, but that's all changed now. . . ." In some ways this may be considered a variation on problem solving.
7. *Talking heads:* A pitchman (someone dressed as a doctor or a mechanic, a group of women around a table) tells the audience how wonderful the product is.
8. *Testimonials:* Hidden-camera technique, as well as stars and personalities. The danger of using stars is that the audience remembers the star but not the product!

There are more, but these are the most frequently seen.

Once the agency, station, or project leader has come up with a campaign and the commercials to tell the story, they present the client with their plan. This presentation may include mockups of the campaign, including magazine layouts, radio scripts, and television storyboards. The storyboards are usually 4, 8, or 16 panels; sometimes more are needed or, as in Figure 8.1, fewer. Sometimes they're like children's books, with tabs to pull, flaps to lift, and so on. These storyboards are usually an artist's representation of the proposed commercial. They are either freehand sketches or can be created from any of a number of computer programs. Sometimes they are simple stick drawings. Each panel is numbered and represents an edit point or indicates a montage sequence. Under each panel is the copy or audio that will go with that panel. Once the client agrees to the storyboard, it's put into the production process. At an agency, the "job" is put in the hands of an agency producer, who sends it out for bids. Sometimes a favorite production company is asked how much the spot or spots would cost. Sometimes a formal presentation takes place in which a number of production companies are invited to bid on a job. Their bids are based on the storyboards or presentations that are often made to all the bidding companies at a single meeting. Most of the time a limited number of companies, perhaps three or four, with whom the agency is familiar will be asked to bid on producing a specific set of storyboards. They may be asked to price it out, with and without editing, or to bid the job digitally as well as on film. The production companies that are asked to bid would probably include an established company whose work is well known but expensive; a second production company whose work is known but may be slightly less expensive; and a new company that is trying to make a name for itself. New companies are offered the opportunity to bid when their work is seen and admired. Sometimes samples of their work will have been presented by an agent or other representative of the director/producer.

The chain of command is more direct at a station or at a university. Once the green light is given, the director/producer or project leader gathers the crew and gear needed to make the PSA. It's then scheduled and done. Many of the questions to be answered, however, will be the same as those answered by an advertising agency and production company. The questions start with a production breakdown. A production breakdown is needed not only to create a bid but also to create the work plan for the job. Even if there were no money involved, the same questions would have to be asked:

1. What are the casting requirements?
2. When is the cast needed?
3. Where will the shoot take place?
4. How much time will be needed to shoot it?

The answers to these and other questions are just as relevant for a PSA being produced by the most prestigious production company as for a student television production at a high school.

COST ANALYSIS

All the companies that are asked to bid analyze the storyboards and submit their bids. Both the agency and the production company will want to know the cost of making the spots. This will depend on factors like these:

1. How long will it take to shoot the spots?
2. How large a crew will be needed?
3. What is the specific gear that will be needed?
4. What specific locations, props, or sets will be needed?
5. What talent will be used? For how long? At what cost? And so on.
6. Are there any rights issues that need to be factored in?

Not all of the production companies will see the same boards in the same way. One company may interpret a panel showing a couple at an airline counter in Paris as requiring a trip to Paris for the cast and crew. Another company might want to shoot at an airline terminal in the United States with some Parisian posters. Another plan might call for the scene to be shot at a constructed set on a sound stage. How the shoot is broken down will affect the look of the commercial and its cost. In selecting the production company, the advertising agency and client will weigh the choices that were presented to them. The lowest bid will not always be the winner.

For the production company, the process of considering the production's needs starts with numbering each panel on the storyboard and giving a specific number and letter, if needed, to each shot. Thus, panels might be numbered 1, 2, 3a, 3b, 3c, 4, 5, 6, and so on. In our imaginary case with the panel at the Parisian airline counter, shot #3 may require a very long zoom, which would be represented on the storyboards with three panels lettered a, b, and c.

Breaking the storyboard down into separate shots makes it easier to consider each element of the production. Many helpful websites are available for commercial producers. In fact, Googling "TV commercial production forms" yields over 2 million sites. The Association of Commercial Producers (AICP), aicp.com, offers its members a standard breakdown form and a number of excellent checklists for commercial production. Other websites also offer examples and forms for production analysis.

An example of the kind of budgeting template that is available is Figure 3.1a from Gorilla. Cost analysis is based on a number of considerations:

1. *The cast:* Are stars or personalities involved? If so, do they need special and costly handling, such as a limousine, personal assistants, personal makeup, hair stylists, and so on? Who pays for this? Are there many people in the spot? Is the commercial to shot under the jurisdiction of the Screen Actors Guild (SAG, for film) or of the American Federation of Television and Radio Artists (AFTRA, for digital, tape or live work)?
2. *The crew:* How many crew members are required, and how long will they be needed? Who is available? You may not need a gardener for a men's clothing commercial, but you probably will need extra costume hands. The costume "A team" may cost $500 a day, the "B team" $250, and you might get a production assistant (PA) for $75.00 day . . . or less. Whom do you select?

There is a tradeoff in using inexperienced help. More expensive personnel may know more about the job and be able to get it done faster, or they may have greater skill. Their sense of studio discipline is also significant to the production. For example, an accidental coffee spill on a costume may create a severe setback to a commercial's production schedule. The $75 PA is more apt to have brought a coffee cup into the room than the others (not all PAs and not all the time). Drinking coffee from a cardboard cup seems like such a harmless thing to do in a costume room or, for that matter, a control room, but experienced hands are very careful about where they drink and leave coffee. The person making out the budget will have to assign a monetary value to that experience and hope that when the bid is being considered, the agency appreciates the distinction. Recognition of the value of an experienced crew is one of the reasons why the cheapest bid isn't always the one that gets the job.

---

3. *Gear:* What kind and how much is needed?
4. *Time:* How much preproduction will be required? Locations need to be scouted, arrangements made, and props acquired or rented. How many preproduction days will be needed, and how many people at what price

will be required at that stage of the process? How many production days will be needed? Is the production house bidding for postproduction as well? If so, how many postproduction days? What's included in the postproduction? Digital graphics? Film transfer? And so on.

5. *Operational expenses:* Rights and clearances, rentals, insurance, benefits, office space, and similar issues should be covered.

SPECIALIZED GEAR

The production of commercials has resulted in the design of some specialized tools and pieces of gear.

Sweep Table

As discussed in Chapter 2 on facilities, a *sweep table* (Figures 8.2 and 8.3) is a long table on which a product is placed. The table is covered with a long roll of paper or fabric, or with a Lucite plastic top, which sweeps up from the surface to the top of the camera's frame. It appears as if the product is floating in a field that has no end. Cans of tomato sauce, boxes of toothpaste, and all types of boxed and canned goods are photographed on sweep tables in consumer goods commercials.

Figure 8.2 This sweep table, made of seamless paper on a table, is set up for a single-camera shot. The food is the product and will be shot so there is room for a price to be inserted.

Figure 8.3 The food, as shot.

Light Tent

A *light tent* is a paper or fabric "tent" into which a product is inserted, sometimes on a table made of frosted glass. It has a hole in the fabric through which the camera lens is inserted. The product may then be lit from the bottom, the top, or from all around, and no reflections or sources of light are visible, so the product seems to glow from within.

Image Motion Control

In the 1970s, advertisements began to appear in television trade magazines for a device called a *shot-box*. This device allowed a camera operator to "program" and then repeat a move. For example, a zoom-out could start off slowly and then pull back with increasing speed to a selected framing. The camera operator "recorded" the move, and the shot-box would repeat it, or it could be adjusted in a number of ways that would refine the shot. Once set, the camera operator was able to play back that move as many times as needed. Later, in the edit bay, type or animation might be added to the correctly repositioned product.

Since that original shot-box, many improvements have been made. The *image motion camera* (IMC), which is a camera mounted on a kind of animation stand (Figure 8.4), is one example. This camera, which can shoot everything from macro to micro photography, is mounted on an arm extended over poles over a table. The mount affords programmable movement in all directions. The camera

Figure 8.4 An image motion control camera at Realtime Video in San Francisco.

Figure 8.5 The controller for the camera in Figure 8.4.

can be moved up and down on the poles and can pan and tilt over the entire area of the table. The table can move in any direction and is lighted either from the top or the bottom. Additionally, the lens can be programmed to rack focus and zoom at whatever timing and to whatever degree is desired. All moves are computer controlled (Figure 8.5).

I once used an IMC to record a scene that existed on a slide. I started with an image that filled the screen using 75 percent of the slide and then panned and zoomed down to an image that was 50 percent of the slide's total area—all in less than three seconds. In fact, I made the same move at a number of different timings to see which would work best with the rest of the commercial. All the moves were totally accurate. Once the shot was

programmed, which took less than half an hour, it took less than five minutes to record. The same results might now be made in postproduction.

Animation

With computers as accessible as they are today, and with their capabilities increasing so quickly, great advances are being made in the area of animation and motion graphics. Of course, huge computers are working in 3-D animation and in real-time constructions in a way that would have been impossible in an earlier age. But the truly significant news is the availability of programs and hardware for low-budget productions. It's becoming increasingly more possible for commercials, PSAs, and "shorts" to be considered for production at facilities in which the work is done entirely by a small number of personally involved producers and directors. Student programs in animation have grown so quickly that student animation awards are now a part of many student festivals, including the Academy of Television Arts and Sciences Student Awards. With this availability, and with encouragement, a growing number of PSAs are being created using animation.

PRODUCTION

Once the approach and gear have been determined, the procedure for analyzing the production elements of the boards remains the same, whether it's one spokesperson on camera in front of a cyc or 50 couples swimming through the dancing fountains of Rome. The analysis breaks the commercial down into the time needed and the real costs of all the elements that make up the commercial. That real-cost estimate is what the production company uses as the basis for its bid. It's what the director/producer knows will be needed to make the production happen. In an agency-driven production, that bid will be determined by a formula. The bid might be the actual cost of the spot or spots plus 20 percent, with a 10 or 15 percent contingency fee. The agency might simply double the real costs and assume all contingency fees, or it might work with some other formula. At the same time the production company will want to arrange a schedule for payment for its work. A standard arrangement for companies that complete the entire project, including editing, has been one-third at the start of the job, one-third when the principle photography is done, and one-third when the job is completed. When comparing the bids, the agency will keep in mind not only the cost issues but also the production company's approach to the job.

After the client and agency have agreed on the boards and the preproduction stage is completed, the shooting begins. Of course, changes will occur after this, but once the final go-ahead has been given, the production begins based on the agreement. Costs for any changes will have to be negotiated. Commercials and PSAs are usually shot film-style, using a single camera. But whether the project is a single- or multiple-camera, a full-blown agency shoot or a student production, shooting begins only when:

1. The facility or location is ready—the set is in place, the location has been prepared, and permits are in place.
2. All personnel—client, agency, cast, crew, security, and so on—have their calls and have been confirmed in a timely manner.
3. All rentals are set, including cameras, mikes, lights, props, vehicles, locations, costumes, gaffer supplies, special effects items, intercoms, and portable toilets.
4. All legal work is done—contracts are signed and in place, as are all insurance and union clearances.
5. Rights (if any are needed) have been secured for music, lyrics, poetry, and anything else requiring permission.

SHOOTING

For our example we will assume that the shoot is being done in single-camera format. If it were to be done in multiple-camera format, there would be a number of obvious differences. There would be more cameras, and the production would usually be completed 30 seconds after it began. However, the preparatory steps for both types of shoots are very similar. Planning and getting ready are crucial. One of the most perceptive statements I ever heard from a student was his realization that the shoot was mostly proof of the preparation.

The advice for shooting a small-location documentary is the same as it is for shooting PSAs on location. The significant difference is that in a documentary one is a journalist, capturing what happens—artfully, everyone hopes. In a commercial,

however, everything must be perfect. In a sense, money is not the issue; getting the shot exactly as planned is. There are no excuses for anything less. This means that more time must be spent on each shot, and more backups must always be at hand. Perhaps there is little likelihood that a very wide-angle lens will be necessary, but just in case, it's good planning to have one standing by. Some new opportunity might reveal itself on location. "Just in case," however, can get very expensive.

Shot Procedure

One significant difference between a commercial and other types of formats is the care given to each shot. The shot procedure is as follows:

1. First, get a starting position—a tentative first mark—and mark it as "#1." You can use a piece of gaffer tape and a pental for the marks. Set up the camera at that location.
2. Look through the viewfinder or at a monitor and make sure the setting is right. Some things don't photograph well, whereas others that might seem to have no potential look great. The lens does make a difference. Look at the screen as if it were an abstract painting. Look at it from side to side and top to bottom. Look at the lines created by whatever it is you're shooting. Is it a pleasant composition? Is the light falling well? Where will additional lights go? Are there distracting shadows? Is there *anything* that is distracting? If there is, fix it, and fix it immediately. If for some reason you can't fix it immediately, take the time to make a note and find someone else to fix it. Problems relegated to memory usually fly away as soon as the next disaster presents itself.
3. It's hard to imagine how the setting will look until it's fully set up, but there's usually a three-hour savings if you can visualize the look of the set before everything is in place and tweaked.

One of the production companies with which I've worked kept a list of client nightmares. High on the list was the statement "Well, could you light it first and then let me see it, because I can't tell if it looks okay yet?" Of course, the client was right, but if the client doesn't like the way it looks after all the work has been done, the alternative will probably be to start all over from the beginning,

Figure 8.6 Floor marks for a camera mounted on a dolly on tracks.

Figure 8.8 A piece of gaffer tape or a grease pencil is used on the pedestal to mark the height of the camera.

which is not only very costly but very disheartening. It's also hard to anticipate when drawing up a budget to present in the bidding process.

Now you've seen the opening frame to the shot and approved it and had the agency and the client approve it. Your opening mark is good, and you don't want to lose it. Mark and thoroughly check *all* the marks.

1. Mark the floor (Figure 8.6).
2. Mark the pedestal position (Figures 8.7 and 8.8).
3. Mark the focus (Figure 8.9).
4. Mark the pan and tilt positions (Figure 8.10).
5. Mark the viewfinder (use a grease pencil).

6. Mark the monitor (Figure 8.11). Use a grease pencil to outline the key position of elements in the frame. Grease pencil marks on the monitor will help the camera operator, the director, the producer, the agency, and the client stay aware of what might be unusual framing if it were not for the addition of graphics that will happen in postproduction.

Those are the starting marks. Now move to whatever is the second position of the shot, then the third, and continuing all the way to the last. Get approval for each section. If there is a stop along the way, mark and label each section in the same way. If there are more sections to the shot, mark them; if there are fewer, so much the better.

Figure 8.7 Marks for a single-camera shoot. The crane is a Chapman Crane, with color-coded marks. As the crane is raised, the marks line up.

Figure 8.9 A mark on the focus knob helps find focus quickly.

Figure 8.10 The opening marks for pan and tilt can be set.

When you move from the first position to the second, you should notice if something in the shot, such as a branch or a prop, has to be moved. That may affect your first position. Go back and make sure that the fix for the second position hasn't hurt the look of the first position. If it has, fix it. Continue in this manner until you've come to the final position and marked it. The final mark will be important, even if the in-between marks aren't critical.

Presumably, Lighting has been watching the moves and now needs time to set the lights for the specific marks. When Lighting and Set Decoration are ready, walk through the shot very slowly. Think

Figure 8.11 The monitor is marked to indicate the graphics that will be added in postproduction.

slow motion. Use the talent, if possible, but if not, use stand-ins. Look at the framing top to bottom and side to side all along the way. Check the set props and the lighting, making sure that they work in every marked position and in all the stops along the way. Lighting and Set Decoration or Art Direction should be looking at the shots with you. They'll need to make notes at each point in the shot and make appropriate changes.

It will take time to accomplish all the marks and tweaking that this style of work demands. That time costs money while the crew works on the shot. A different and more critical element is the time the shot itself takes. That is the next thing you'll need to test. Once everything is in place, run the shot at "take" speed, and make sure it can be done well. If not, adjustments will have to be made. Once everyone has had the opportunity to make his or her fixes, it's time to actually try to make the shot. Often the director or producer will have to set a time limit on how long the "fixes" can go on. Even though some members of the crew are never really satisfied with the way a shot looks, almost everyone will accept a reasonable cutoff time. I once worked with a stagehand who had on a T-shirt that said, "It's not the time it takes to take the takes that takes the time. It's the time it takes to set up the takes that takes the time it takes."

Some director/producers like to use the playback mode on commercial shoots so once the shot or take is done, everyone can see it and can be specific about corrections that have to be made. In episodic dramas, production companies often avoid the playback option, fearing that too many viewers will voice too many opinions, which will prolong the process and add unacceptable cost to the project.

Multiple-Camera Shoots

Most commercials are shot with a single camera and then edited. Some commercial productions simply cannot be done in a "one-take" multiple-camera format. Some things just don't happen on cue. How, for example, do you get popcorn to pop on cue, or a child to giggle, or a cat to wake up and cross to a bowl in 3.5 seconds? There is no question that such commercials absolutely demand single-camera production. Other considerations, such as lighting or the number of shots, are equally relevant and require a production using single-camera techniques.

However, some commercials still are shot using multiple cameras. Sometimes two or three cameras are used to "catch a moment": a pie in the face, a high-risk stunt, and so on. These shots are handled as if they were to be integrated into a single-camera production. The other use for multiple-camera commercials is usually for low-budget, syndicated, or local station productions, in which the entire production, or a significant part of the production, is shot at one time and often switched as it is happening. Shooting with multiple cameras means one has to work around some restrictions. Usually, there can be no light stands on the floor. Every element has to occur on cue within a very clearly defined time frame. It also offers some bonuses: real reactions can be recorded from multiple angles, and a finished commercial can get on the air quickly. Whatever the number of cameras used, many of the production elements will remain the same through all the stages of preproduction, production, and postproduction.

Keeping a log during production, the associate director/stage manager or production assistant makes careful note of the take and the time code of each shot. With or without time code, it's wise to use consecutive take numbers in which there are no duplicates. Using consecutive slates throughout the shoot is helpful because there can only be one of each take in the entire shoot. Even if you have hundreds of slate numbers, you'll never mistake "Scene Two, Take One" with "Scene One, Take Two." (This important practice is explained further in Chapter 10.)

The log with take numbers or the time code for a commercial/PSA shoot is different from the log for the final production. The shoot log should always contain:

1. Production name, client, agency, and producer
2. Reel or hard drive number
3. Date or dates of production
4. Name of the person writing the log
5. Notes and comments about each take written down as the production is shooting
6. Name of the segments or shot numbers, with take number, time codes, or both, if possible

The container or digital drive should have all the log information and labels indicating whether the contents are original footage, submaster, edited master, dubbing master, or a dub. Additional notes may be added at the end of each production day.

These notes will be used in the postproduction process.

Extra Shots and Wrapping Up

During production, certain shots that were not indicated on the storyboards may seem like a good idea. When these shots do seem appropriate, it's sensible to take the time to shoot them. Often a spontaneous shot works out very well, but you can't let the process get out of hand. If there's an unlimited budget and unlimited editing time (something I have never experienced), then shoot it all. If there are time and budgetary constraints, you have to consider those constraints as well. There is no rule for how far to stray from the boards, but it certainly is done, and some of the best work comes from shots that happened on the spur of the moment. You may also find that a lot of unnecessary work is done in order to get high-quality footage for a producer's, agency's, or crew member's personal reel.

Whether it's a single-camera or multiple-camera shoot, it's a good idea to go over notes immediately after the shoot has ended. During the wrap, while the bulk of the crew puts away cables, cameras, and lights, and wraps various other parts of the gear, the director/producer, the agency, and the client should discuss the selected takes. They may wish to view them with everyone's notes and anyone who can be of assistance, such as the AD or PA. There will be time to look at the material later, but those first comments are often very telling. Some minor mistake that might go unnoticed later may be discussed initially and then forgotten, so it's best to be as specific as possible and write down everything while the day's shoot is still fresh.

POSTPRODUCTION

Before the edit session, the producer and agency will meet and discuss the edit again. Current editing procedures require that either during the recording or soon afterward, the Society of Motion Picture Television Engineers (SMPTE) time code must be recorded onto the master as a digital frame of reference that can be addressed by a computer. SMPTE code breaks time into hours, minutes, seconds, and frames. There are 30 frames per second. Normally, the code doesn't appear as video, although once it is there, it can be made to appear on the screen as an editing tool. Once the material is transferred to a digital format DVD, copies can be made or the files can be transferred in whatever way is easiest to access, including e-mail. These copies contain the original audio and video as well as a visual readout of the time code.

In the most economical of situations, the dub, file or tape, allows the director, producer, agency, and client to have a common reference when they discuss a take they like. They will refer to the selected takes by time-code address. Often the notes made while this is being done serve to create a preliminary paper edit of the program or commercial. This paper edit is called an edit decision list, or EDL.

Although editing hardware and software are constantly being upgraded and changed, the primary tool for cutting commercials offline is the Avid system, which is available in several configurations that can be customized for particular projects. Other, similar systems that are DOS or Windows based and Mac based are also available. Final Cut Pro® and other programs have changed the nature of the hardware/software configurations for commercial and PSA editing. They all allow for instantaneous random access of digitally stored information. They all work with a time line. With these tools, the director/producer can see the commercial (or the program, for that matter) cut in a number of different ways. A scene or shot can be extended, deleted, dissolved, or cut to create a number of variations of the same spot. In some systems, once a version is agreed on, a decision list is generated and used to create the master at an online session. Today, however, the material created in low resolution is simply reconstituted in high resolution on the same system that was used for the edit session. As storage systems have become more affordable and accessible, the material is worked on in high resolution from the very beginning and is then released for file transfer and transmission. Some edit sessions can cost as much as $600 an hour. They allow for the manipulation of many layers in real time at high resolution with the accuracy inherent to digital media.

When completed, the project may be dubbed for various markets and shipped or transmitted to the stations. PSAs are handled in the same way as commercials, but they are usually shipped with explanatory press releases.

REVIEW

- Public service announcements (PSAs) and commercials are similar in length and require production values that are similar.
- PSAs and commercials are also similar in that they attempt to motivate the public to a course of action.
- The commercial/PSA slate, which identifies the spot, and assures the station it is running the right spot, contains:
  1. The name of the spot
  2. The producing company
  3. The total running time (TRT)
  4. The production or editing date
  5. Some kind of reference code
  6. Additionally, if the spot exists on tape, there is usually a video and audio countdown.
- There are four reasons why agencies and production personnel work on PSAs:
  1. To many in the industry, making a PSA is an opportunity to "give back" to the community.
  2. The quality of the campaign and production will help define the agency and the production company in the creative community.
  3. It is often a way for an agency or a station that is limited to clients in one area—retail sales, for example—to "stretch its wings."
  4. Another client may appreciate well-made PSAs and ask the station or agency to produce one for a cause that is important to it.
- The wording of the PSA's message is very important because it affects what we shoot.
- Storyboards for commercials are usually 4, 8, or 16 panels. They indicate how the commercial or PSA should look. Under each panel is the copy or audio that will go with that panel. Each panel is numbered to assist in production breakdown.
- No matter who makes the commercial or PSA, or where, the following questions must be answered:
  1. What are the casting requirements?
  2. When is the cast needed?
  3. Where will the shoot take place?
  4. How much time will be needed to shoot this?

- Cost analysis of the production will have to answer these questions:
  1. How long will it take to shoot the spots?
  2. How large a crew will be needed?
  3. What gear will be needed?
  4. What locations, props, or sets will be needed?
  5. What talent will be used? For how long?
- Some typical but specialized gear used in shooting commercials include the following:
  1. A sweep table
  2. A light tent
  3. An image motion camera
- Shooting begins only when:
  1. The facility or location is ready—the set is in place, the location has been prepared, and permits are in place.
  2. All personnel—client, agency, cast, crew, security, and so on—have their calls and have been confirmed in a timely manner.
  3. All rentals are set, including cameras, mics, lights, props, vehicles, locations, costumes, gaffer supplies, special effects items, intercoms, and portable toilets.
  4. All legal work is done—contracts are signed and in place, as are all insurance and union clearances.
  5. Rights (if any are needed) have been secured for music, lyrics, poetry, and anything else requiring permission.
- Shot procedure—for starting marks:
  1. First, get a starting position—a tentative first mark. Get it approved.
  2. Mark it and label it "one."
  3. Mark the floor.
  4. Mark the pedestal position.
  5. Mark the focus.
  6. Mark the pan and tilt positions.
  7. Mark the viewfinder.
  8. Mark the monitor.
- Mark every stop along the way in the same manner.
- Stop and fix every problem as it comes up.
- During production, the associate director/stage manager or production assistant makes careful note of the take and the time code of each shot.
- The log with the time code for a commercial/PSA shoot is different from the slate. It should always contain the following:
  1. Production name, client, agency, and producer
  2. Reel or hard drive
  3. Date or dates of production
  4. Name of the person writing the log
  5. Name of the segments or shot numbers, with time code if possible
  6. Notes and comments about each take
- The container should have all the log information, as well as labels indicating whether the recording is original footage, submaster, edited master, dubbing master, or a dub.
- Go over editing notes immediately after the shoot while the circumstances surrounding the notes are still fresh in your mind. Add any additional notes.
- In the postproduction session, the material is digitized if it was shot on film. The producer and the client then view the material and edit it using a wide range of production hardware and software. The material is then dubbed and shipped to stations or is transmitted to stations in a digital format.

chapter nine

News

To understand the basics of directing and producing news programs, it's important to be familiar with what is known in television production as the "wraparound" format. In the wraparound format, someone leads in to and out of story packages. On a news broadcast, the story packages contain the news. Reporters and newscasters lead in to and out of the stories; their comments give them added dimension. Often their taste and judgment are accepted as representing the station's point of view to the community. On other wraparound programs, such as *20/20*, *60 Minutes*, or most of the musical portions of MTV, the hosts, narrators, commentators, or even salespersons may have similar program functions, but their messages are not as timely, and they are usually not considered to represent the station's viewpoint.

NEWS PROGRAM CHARACTERISTICS

If most of the stories presented are current, then the program is a news program. If the story is an ongoing one, then it still may be a part of a news program, but it is more likely to be part of a news magazine program. This distinction follows the common printed forms: the newspaper and the news magazine. Chapter 10, "Documentaries and Reality Programming," addresses news magazine material and covers the simplest kind of wraparound programs as well as the production of short documentary packages. Work on a news program is unlike work on a magazine program because the content is different. That changes things in a number of ways:

1. The news has to be immediately responsive to events. Magazines can take more time to choose their subjects and can also spend more time in research and production.

2. News programs tend to use more high-tech equipment in presenting material. They must deal with daily deadlines. They often need to explain material that may be unfamiliar yet is critical to the audience's understanding. That puts unique technical demands on television news production. It creates a need for fast editing techniques. It demands rapid and specialized graphic techniques and fast research and answers. For example, it would not be considered unusual for a news operation to need a relief map of the Middle East or Bosnia-Herzegovina within an hour or less. The news team must be able to gather obscure facts quickly; for example, during a presidential election, a reporter might have an immediate and sudden need to know obscure facts, such as the number of times a presidential candidate lost the electoral votes in his home state, or facts about a candidate's education, etc.

3. Television news usually runs at a faster pace than does a television magazine program, and the stories tend to be shorter.

In addition to the outward distinction between news and magazine programs, a further distinction must be made in news programs in general. News operations function on a number of different levels. There's the kind of big-city newsroom that one finds in the top-10 markets. There may be a somewhat less high-tech approach in some of the remaining top-90 markets. The news in even smaller markets—and there are many of them—is geared toward different needs. Farm news, for example, is important in regions with a lot of farming. Smaller markets also work within different parameters, not the least important of which is an operating budget.

This does not necessarily result in less concern for journalism or production, but it's apt to mean less-expensive hardware and fewer operational personnel to run it. Some years ago, while directing the news at WNET, the public broadcast station in New York, we found ourselves using chalkboards to post election results during our local news broadcast. It wasn't very high tech, but the audience got the message, and the press thought it was inventive.

There are some very special characteristics of working on a news program. The directing and producing functions in the news operation differ from most other formats in that in news they are almost always separate: the people who direct the news usually do not produce the program. In smaller markets, the news operation may indeed be a "one-person show," but world news and major national stories will be lead-ins and lead-outs for syndicated packages or satellite feeds. Almost all of the people involved with news broadcasting assume that they are on call 24 hours a day, and when an emergency happens, they *expect* to be called and asked to pitch in.

PREPRODUCTION

The Director

There is an important distinction between the person who directs the news and the "news director." The news director is the executive in charge of news for the station. On the executive level this position is probably on par with the program director. The director of the news is responsible for the actual hands-on work of putting the broadcast on the air. The director of the news usually directs the wraparounds that are the day-to-day format for the station's broadcasts. Occasionally, the individuals who direct the news direct inserts, and sometimes they are called on to direct entire live events that are happening locally. When that happens, they are no longer directing, properly speaking, a news broadcast, but are instead directing a live-transmission special. There are some ramifications to that. A "special" could be anything from a planned local town hall meeting to the coverage of a disaster at a local site. It usually has longer segments, different pacing, and sometimes different crews than the usual news broadcast. Depending on the nature of the special, there may be hazards or long, unrelieved stretches. There may also be contractual differences between directing the regular news and a special broadcast. Chapter 11, "Multiple-Camera Remotes," explores the role of the director and producer in various locations and remote situations.

Directors of the news seem to have certain characteristics that are imperative for doing the job well. A key attribute is that in times of the inevitable control room crisis, they are creative and flexible and generally are prepared with a fallback position, . . . *and* they remain calm. The actual job of directing the news is very straightforward and is essentially the same everywhere. There are many stations in the world, with many versions of the news—including morning news, noon news, evening news, and late-night news. Someone directs each of those broadcasts. Inevitably, everywhere, things go wrong. It's usually because of a suddenly apparent fault in the program's organization or faulty communication among coworkers caused by inexperience, carelessness, ineptitude, or perhaps an engineering or mechanical problem. The cause is important only insofar as identifying it can reduce the chances of it happening again. The director must resolve the problem on the air as it occurs. The director's calm and steady hand—and fallback positions—is important during the times when other production staff may be frantic and stressed.

Wherever news production occurs, the director must orchestrate two parts of a typical news broadcast: the curtains, which are the introduction to the package and the exit from the package, and the package itself, which is a feed from some other source—live, tape, film, or server.

The routine for news programs is almost always done by formula:

- There's a standard opening that may be on tape, film, or server, or it may be a wide shot of the studio showing the anchors walking in. It may be a combination of live talent and graphics or a prerecorded package or animated graphic playback, but it's standard, and it's usually put on the air by the director.
- The opening is followed by a commercial or by the anchor, who introduces, or "teases," the first story. In a complicated production, the anchor's introduction may call for a number of elements—such as a lower-third super of the anchor's name, a chroma-keyed graphic or a wiped icon in a box behind the anchor's head, digital video wipes, or other graphic devices intended to enhance the presentation. Essentially, however, the anchor is simply introducing the first playback or live feed in the program.

A *lower-third super* is information, usually in the form of type, that is "supered" (superimposed) over another source of video. (Actually, "keyed" would be the correct term to use, since one can see through a super but not a key. However, "super" is most commonly used.) The lower-third super gives information about the video—usually a person's name and some identifier—for example, "Dr. John Smith, Professor, State University." Simple locators might be "File Footage," "Live," or "Recorded Earlier." One of television's most thrilling lower-third super locators was "Live from the Moon." *Chroma-key* is a special-effects key that uses color (usually blue or green) to insert one video source into another. (When Walter Cronkite was an anchor at CBS News, they used green as a chroma source because Cronkite had very blue eyes. If they had used blue as the key color, a portion of all the material intended for the key would have appeared in Cronkite's eyes.) Chroma-key is most often associated with meteorologists, who stand in front of the colored screen, with the weather map "keyed" onto the screen. Chroma-key is sometimes used to present news segments as well. At other times, however, a *wipe,* which is a device that places two or more picture sources on the screen at the same time, is used instead of a key source. The traditional film-composite picture usually has one picture on the left and one on the right. Wipes were popular devices for showing phone calls in motion pictures in the 1930s. With the advent of digital video and switchers, more elaborate wipes have been developed that provide many more ways to wipe material in and out. One picture can appear to push another off the screen. New video can appear as a page that gets turned over or that sweeps on screen and grows to take over the entire picture. A small box behind the newscaster's head can be used to show icons or actual pictures of falling rain or a tornado or graphics of a gun, flames, and so forth.

- The package, which may be an edited tape, a feed from a digital server, or a live feed, is aired. While that's happening, graphics or supers may have to be added. During the airing of the package, the director may have to integrate additional live feeds, superimpose more graphic material, mix audio feeds, and generally orchestrate numerous elements. Essentially, as the tape/server/live package is put on the air, the director calls for the various elements that are to be added.

- At the end of the first package, the director returns to the anchor, who either introduces the next piece or leads to a commercial.

That's the way the production will continue for the rest of the program. Somewhere later in the program, the cameras leave the anchor or coanchors and may turn to the sports anchor, who introduces the sports packages, which require the same kind of integration as the news packages. The weather anchor relates to his or her own graphics and weather packages in the same way.

Changes in the planned order of the program are usually necessary. Sometimes it's a breaking news story. Then, too, new information may come in from the field, or a story that arrived late may still be in the edit bay when the program goes on the air. Sometimes segments are designed with packages of varying lengths to facilitate coping with time constraints. The producer may plan the program so it ends with a choice of three human-interest stories, with running times of :30, 1:00, and 1:30, respectively. Any or all can be run or deleted to make up time, depending on how much time is left in the last segment. The producer decides which of them will run while the show is on the air. The only caveat is that none of these stories can be promoted before the producer makes the decision. Ordinarily that means the selected piece gets teased only in the last break. Sometimes various lengths of credits are used as a pad for ending a program.

Through all of this, the director's function will remain constant: managing the mixing of the elements to make a cohesive production. At the networks and major stations, decisions about time are handled by the associate director and the producer.

Two tools that are significant to getting the program on the air are the rundown, or routine, and the script. As we examine the work of the producer, it will be easy to see how the routine and the script facilitate the jobs of not just the director but also a number of different departments as well.

The Producer

It has been said that news can be broken down into three areas: news gathering, news production, and news presentation. The producer is involved with all of these areas in a way that the director is not. Producers are actively involved in the choice of stories, the process of acquiring footage to make a news package, and the story order of the program. They also are responsible for the creation of the program routine and for the staff who write the scripts and create the graphics. Finally, they oversee the internal structure and the staff who keep the program on the air. In practice, the assignment editor makes decisions regarding stories to be covered, and reporters and crews to be assigned, without consulting the producer.

There are probably almost as many ways of producing news programs as there are stations, news broadcasts, staffs, and producers. Even at the same station, it's likely that the early-morning news will be produced by a different producer than the evening news. It will come as no surprise that stations with big budgets have different problems than stations with smaller budgets. There is no single model that will serve for all operations. In order to explain what the producer does, I've created an imaginary producer who works at a large, independent station in a metropolis. In fact, this imaginary producer is a combination of a number of producers with whom I've worked in New York, along with one in Beaumont, Texas, and some from the Los Angeles news community.

A look at a typical workday will provide some insight into the producer's role in the production of a news broadcast. This producer produces the 10 o'clock evening news at a large station, but producing at a smaller station requires the same basic skills. Whether it's a small or large station, it's the producer who has story authority and decides what stories get priority.

At larger stations, an assignment editor plays a critical role in gathering the news. Assignment editors are often the first to learn of stories. They monitor police and fire calls, CNN, and local and national wire services. Also, they are the contact for media reps, public relations offers, and stringers (freelancers). They put out briefs for an in-house daybook that prioritizes known events. They handle all e-mails and faxed materials relating to the stories. They assign reporters, crew trucks, and helicopters to cover the news, and they set up incoming and outgoing satellite feeds and book satellite time. They also assign PAs and interns to hunt down archival footage, to messenger tapes, and sometimes to assist reporters.

Regardless of the size of the station or audience, producers have to manage resources to get the best possible program on the air. They create the program rundown, oversee the creation of a script, and

manage the talent and staff. At smaller stations, they may also write the show themselves, arrange graphics, and prepare the program for air. They may even then direct the show and put the news on the air. (While the terms "rundown" and "routine" are often used interchangeably, producers tend to use "rundown," whereas technical staff tend to use "routine." The example rundown/routine appearing later in this chapter reflects these differing usages.) Producers at smaller stations do all the things that are done at a large station but are more limited in scope and in budget; they may have to shoot and edit the stories themselves.

The 10 o'clock evening news producer might officially start work at 1:00 in the afternoon. More likely the day begins at 7:00 or 8:00 A.M., away from the studio. Those early-morning hours will be spent reading the morning newspapers, logging on to Internet news sources, and watching the station's early-morning news program. That program either will have been recorded or have been seen live. Perhaps the producer will also record and shuttle through the competition's morning news program to see whether anything was missed and to see the way stories were presented by the competition. From the early-morning screenings, the producer knows what stories are available and what stories may be breaking.

At stations where there is complete integration of computer technology, the producer may log on to the station's system from home and explore any relevant digitally created media. The producer could research an internal daily log to discover what staff assignments have been made, whether anyone has called in sick, what stories are on the city's daily log, or ongoing editorial or graphic work. The mayor's public relations office often releases a daily log, or "daybook," that lists the day's events—stories that can be covered. Other organizations and businesses also submit items that they feel are newsworthy. In both large and small markets, notices may be kept on file and referred to regularly. These are events for which there may be some public relations background and events that are covered annually—a state fair, a high school graduation, and so on.

Typical daybook events might include the mayor's plan to give a speech at the Police Academy at 1:00 P.M. or the finals of a local baking, spelling, or college sports contest. At stations that aren't as fully integrated, the producer calls the station and tries to get the same information from an "overnight person"—an assignment editor, a production assistant, a secretary, the phone operator, or someone else on staff. At our imaginary independent local urban station, the producer calls the assignment editor to discuss which reporters have been assigned to which local stories. Throughout the day, the assignment editor will act as a liaison with reporters in the field and will coordinate the field activities with the 10 o'clock news evening producer and other producers who may be handling the noon and 6 o'clock news programs, as well as any breaking news story.

News services such as CNN and the Associated Press News Service are constantly updating feeds of national and international news. Depending on his or her access to these sources, the producer can begin to formulate a plan for including these news packages into the evening program. Many university and college stations subscribe to news services such as those offered by the Cable News Network (CNN), the American Broadcast Company (ABC), the Associated Press (AP), Dow Jones, and others to get the same kinds of stories and backup material that local stations and networks obtain.

Additionally, most large cities use "stringers" as a regular part of the production scheme. Video stringers are freelance video journalists who work predominantly in the evening hours, when station crews are slim or nonexistent. They cover events that they hear about by listening to police and fire department transmissions on radio scanners. They follow the calls to whatever they think will make a good story and then shoot it. They may follow the fire truck to a fire, shoot generic footage, and prepare story material suitable for insertion in any news broadcast in town. They make dubs of the pieces and deliver the footage to each station early enough to make the early news. The footage is sold on an as-used basis. In Los Angeles, footage shot by stringers is offered to a number of channels, including 2, 4, 5, 7, 9, 11, and 13. Currently, the rate for typical footage is $150 per story, so, for example, if all seven UHF stations use the fire, the freelance stringer would make $1,050. Major stories and exclusivity are subject to negotiation. UHF stations and news services are additional markets for these freelance video journalists.

More and more news programs are using amateur footage, which local TV crews call "Street Seens" or "Street Scenes." These average citizen journalists with digital cameras and cell phone cameras are often already on the scene when it would

be impossible to get a reporter there on time. This footage is particularly crucial in times of catastrophic occurrences such as tornadoes, hurricanes, and other similar events.

There are, however, dangers in using such footage. One of the most notable examples of nonprofessional usage occurred in Los Angeles, when an amateur cameraperson shot video of Los Angeles policemen beating Rodney King. Before that, there had been many other stories—fires, local events, human interest stories, and so on—in which amateurs had seen their footage gain local exposure. None achieved such a wide viewing audience. The use of the King footage took on added significance because of the national attention it received and because of the litigation that followed its unauthorized use. Since then, stations have become more careful about the legal aspects of using amateur footage. News directors are very concerned about the source of the stories they air; they need to be certain that the material aired is genuine and that the citizen journalist footage has not been staged and is unencumbered by any legal constraints.

The evening news producer will probably arrive at the station between noon and 1:00 P.M. and begin working on the show's routine. In a one-hour news broadcast, the producer will usually have to fill 24 to 26 minutes with news. Most stories run between 70 seconds and 2 minutes. The rest of the program will be filled with commercials, which run for a total of 14 to 16 minutes; sports news, which might typically run 3:30; weather, 3:00; a number of features such as "health and fitness," and "entertainment," which run 2:00 to 3:00 each; and time for comments about the stories, as well as 2 minutes total for the opening, the close, and throws to commercial breaks.

ROUTINES AND RUNDOWNS

Before there were computerized programs for creating news broadcasts, producers created a variety of in-house outline templates. The computer programs are based on the needs originally identified in the hard-copy versions, which are still used by some stations. The hard-copy version is significant in that it shows, in a very simple way, how a news program is put together. The template lets the producer fill in what's supposed to happen for every 15 seconds of the program. In a similar way, computerized programs achieve the same end. The final routine, computerized or not, must indicate the following:

1. *The date and time the routine was created.* This is to ensure that everyone is working from the most current version of the routine.
2. *The page number of the routine if a hard-copy script is being used.* When last-minute changes occur, pages may get out of place. It's best to have a point of departure so everyone can get into the same order—even if that order is out of the original order. Page numbers and segment letters help.
3. *A designation for the segment, such as A, B, C, or 100, 101, 102–200, 201, and so on.* Usually the segments are separated by commercials. This puts a priority on each segment of the news and allows the producer to move blocks of packages around while on the air. For example, a breaking news story about a hostage crisis might cause the original C segment, a story about a cat that saved a dog, to be deleted or moved down one notch to allow a live feed on the air.
4. *Who is introducing the segment.*
5. *Where the segment originates.* For example: Host on camera 1 with graphics, and playback from server with the name of piece.
6. *The rundown also indicates the duration of the segment.*

Several popular software programs are used in creating news broadcasts. These computer programs present a template for a routine and then create links for various functions, such as the script, tech routine, supers, and graphics. In fact, a Google search of "News Services" turned up over 50 million sources. Two of the most popular software programs for on-air broadcasting are iNEWS by Avid and the Associated Press Electronic News Production System, (AP-ENPS). The programs are frequently updated, and they now include programmable video sources. Stations and other users, such as universities, make arrangements with various services for access. Figures 9.1 and 9.2 are examples of routines from KCBS and KTLA in Los Angeles, respectively. Figure 9.3 is a screen shot from Avid iNEWS.

Between 1:30 and 2:30 P.M., the writers and other members of the late-news staff start arriving. The job of news gathering actually began earlier, when the program's reporters were given assignments and crews. Those reporters and crews may now be out covering the stories, or they may already have filed certain ones for earlier broadcasts. The writers and support staff will become involved in news production as they get their assignments for the 10 o'clock news. The writers will probably work on one or two stories and be responsible for introductions, the repackaging of stories that aired earlier, and "sound bites." Sound bites are segments from recorded events that are used without significant embellishment. They are excerpted segments, such as portions of speeches delivered by the president to Congress, or quotations that add dimension to stories.

The writers will also have to log the footage from the field. Field footage may be transmitted via microwave to the station and coordinated through the assignment editor. At smaller stations, it's brought in with the truck and prepared by the reporter, although transmission and editing from the field are becoming more common. At larger stations, the writers write their stories and edit them with a staff editor, having first reviewed the approach to the story with the producer. As they work, they may use footage shot by a station crew, freelancers, or AP-ENPS or a comparable program.

Clipedit is another program currently finding favor for constructing packages for the news. Depending on the arrangements made with other stations and news services, it allows the user to access and view footage from a variety of sources. The user can view the footage in a portion of a screen while the rest of the screen is used for writing copy. The piece, after being edited by the writer, can be sent via overnight air delivery to the station's server and loaded into the news program's lineup. The material will automatically be linked to the producer's rundown and also to any changes that are made in the rundown. Along the way, the producer will be able to log on to the work in progress and comment if necessary. During writing, identifiers are added into the script at the appropriate places. This includes what the on-air copy should say—for example, "Alan Jones, Professor of Economics, State University."

Once the story is cut and the timing is known, times indicating when to super graphics and how long to keep them on the screen may be indicated on the script. Additionally, the script indicates the in-cue and out-cue for each story, as well as the copy and notes for voice-overs from the anchor, takes to remote sites, and any other pertinent material.

[KCBS]SHOW.5PM.RUNDOWN 9/14/2005 16:42:55
0:27 under

Page	Talent	IF	Slug	EFX/GFX	PB	Tape	IN?	SS	SS/No.	Cutline	Cam/Notes	Backtime
												17:23:24
L01	LAUR		5-VO IRAQ/BUSH AT UN	KY	R	VO	Yes	PR	PROF	BATTLE	C1-PRKY/LD	17:23:24
L02	*		5-SOT IRAQ/BUSH AT UN		G	SOT	Yes					17:23:43
L03	LAUR		5-FCTZ BUSH ADDRESS	FCTZ				B	3500	BUSH A		17:23:53
												17:24:01
L04	PAUL		5-VO FLU FORECAST	KY	B	VO	Yes	A	3512	FLU LO	C3-KY/PM	17:24:01
												17:24:25
L05	PAUL		5-VO AUTISM CURE	KY	R	VO	NO!	A	3513	AUTISM	C3-KY/PM	17:24:25
												17:24:52
*L90	L/P		5-TEASE 3	2SHOT							C2-2SHOT	17:24:52
*L91	**LIVE	2	TZ3-**GILE LIVE TEASE**	RM 34		**LIVE					RM:34	17:25:27
*L92			TZ3-TEASE SLOT MACHIN		G	VO	NO!					17:25:27
*L93			TZ3-TEASE DR PHIL		B	VO	NO!				**Wipe/Chy+NXs	17:25:27
M0			BREAK 3	(3.05)								17:25:27
												17:28:12
*			5:30 PM SHOW									17:28:12
			BURIED OPEN (PROF:210 L	PROF/21	P/	PROF					Profile/SOT	17:28:12
M01	LAUR		5:30 COLD OPEN:SEA LION		R	TOPV	Yes					17:28:27
*												17:28:37
M02	L/P		5-2SHOT HELLO	2SHOT							C2-(2S), **Zoom i	17:28:37
												17:28:47
M03	PAUL		5-LEAD UNRULY SEA LION	KY				A	3509	SEA LIO	C3-KY/PM	17:28:47
			(MICHELE GILE)	DB				B	3510	SEA LIO	DB-C3/RM:34	17:29:01
*	*LV	2	5-UNRULY SEA LIONS	RM 34							RM:34	17:29:01
M04			5-UNRULY SEA LIONS PKG		G	PKG	Yes					17:29:16
*			5-UNRULY SEA LIONS PKG									
*	*LV	2	5-UNRULY SEA LIONS	RM 34							RM:34	17:30:46
												17:31:01
M05	PAUL		5-VO CHANGES ON COURT	KY	B	VO	Yes	A	2503	CHANG	C3-KY/PM	17:31:01
M06	PAUL		5-SOT ROBERTS EXCHAN		R	SOTV	NO!					17:31:13
												17:31:38
M07	LAUR		5-VO JUMBO JACKPOT	KY	G	VO	Yes	A	2514	JUMBO	C1-KY/LD	17:31:38
M08	LAUR		5-FC THE MEGA BREAKDO	FC				B	3508	JUMBO		17:32:03
												17:32:03
M09	L/P		5-LEAD DR PHIL PART 3	2-SHOT							C2-2SHOT	17:32:03
			(PAUL MAGERS)									17:32:13
M10	*		5-DR PHIL PART 3 PKG		B	PKG	Yes					17:32:13
*	*		5-DR PHIL PART 3 PKG									
M11	PAUL		5-FC TEASE TOMORROW	FCTZ				B	3514	DR. PHI		17:36:50
*												17:37:00
*M90	L/P		5-TEASE 4	2SHOT							C2-2SHOT	17:37:00
*M93	*JIM*		TZ4-SPORTS DREW		R	VO	Yes					17:37:30
N00			BREAK 4	(2.46)								17:37:30
												17:40:16
			5 QUICK REJOIN	PROF/00	P/	PROF						17:40:16
												17:40:21
N01	P/L		5-TOSS SPORTS	3SHOT							C1-(3S/LT)	17:40:21
*			(ADD SPORTS EARLY TICK									17:40:31
*	JHI		SPORTS									17:40:31
N02	JHI		ANGELS-MARINERS		R	VO-W	NO!				C3-CU/JH	17:43:31
N03			DODGERS PREP ROCKIES		G	VO-W	Yes					17:43:31
N04			EDWIN JACKSON SOUND`		B	SOT	Yes					17:43:31
N05	JHI		KINGS PRACTICE		R	VO-W	Yes				C3-CU/JH	17:43:31
N06			JEREMY ROENICK SOUND		G	SOT	Yes					17:43:31
N07	JHI		MAURICE DREW GRANDFA		B	VO-W	Yes				C3-CU/JH	17:43:31
N08			SOUND-DREW		R	SOT	Yes					17:43:31
												17:43:31
*			(TOSS BACK SPORTS)								C1-(3S/LT)	17:43:31

Figure 9.1   A producer's rundown from KCBS2 News Los Angeles. Reading from left to right, the columns show the following: *Page*—script page numbers are grouped by letters and numbers to indicate the story sequence; *Talent*—who's doing the story; *IF*—Inter-Frequency communication, the assignment of internal communication channels; *Slug*—what the item is about; *EFX/GFX*—effects or graphics; *PB*—playback source (Red, Green, Blue Server); *Tape*—how the package is delivered; *IN*—is the package ready?; *SS*—graphic assignment, indicating the holding position for the graphic to be used, its status (e.g., "missing"), and/or the artist; *SS/No.*—where the graphic to be used is stored; *Cutline*—has some relevant graphic issue such as "Today" or "File Tape"; *Cam-notes*—director's notes; *Backtime*—the ideal time for the item to be "on air." This form is linked to Copy, Prompter, and Graphics so program events can be quickly rearranged on the air. Reproduced with permission from KCBS News in Los Angeles.

10p News At Ten RD KTLA

9/21/2005

Page	Anchor1	KTLA Apr	Story Slug	Segment	Graphics	Source	Wtr	Est Duration	Actual	Back	Front	Tape #	Status
A1	====		SQUEEZEBACK	SOT			CMI		0:16	9:57:14 PM	9:59:49 PM	X	
A2	H/L		GOOD EVENING	2-SHOT				0:10	0:05	9:57:14 PM	9:59:49 PM		
A3	HAL		JET BLUE EMERGENCY LANDING (DLP)	VO	DLP	AERIALS	SAU	0:30	0:30	9:57:24 PM	9:59:59 PM	X	
A4	HAL		LIVE JET BLUE EMERGENCY LANDING	LIVE PKG	2BX	JIM NASH	SAU	2:30	0:08	9:57:54 PM	10:00:29 PM	X	
A4X	JIM			LIVE VO					0:00	10:00:24 PM	10:02:59 PM		
A5	LU		PASSENGERS	COPY	KEY**		ASI	0:15	0:13	10:00:24 PM	10:02:59 PM		
A6	LU		LIVE PASSENGERS	LIVE PKG	2BX	FRANK BUCKLEY	ASI	2:30	0:06	10:00:39 PM	10:03:14 PM	X	
A7	HAL		HURRICANE RITA	COPY	KEY**	APTN CNS RE 67WE	SHA	0:20	0:19	10:03:09 PM	10:05:44 PM	X	
A8	HAL		PKG HURRICANE RITA	MAP PKG	MAP	KHWB CUSTOM PKG	SHA	2:00	1:58	10:03:29 PM	10:06:04 PM	X	
A9	LU		HOUSTON EVACS	VO	KEY**	CNS RT 67WE	SHA	0:25	0:26	10:05:29 PM	10:08:04 PM	X	
A10	HAL		NEW ORLEANS RITA	COPY			POC	0:15	0:10	10:05:54 PM	10:08:29 PM	X	
A11	HAL		LIVE NEW ORLEANS RITA	LIVE PKG	MAP	GRANT RAMPY	POC	2:00	1:32	10:06:09 PM	10:08:44 PM	X	
A12	LU		KEY WEST AFTERMATH	VO		CNS RT 36WE AND NS KT 06WE	ASI	0:20	0:20	10:08:09 PM	10:10:44 PM	X	
A13	LU		SOT KEY WEST AFTERMATH	SOTVO	WIP	CNS RT 36WE AND NS KT 06WE	ASI	0:25	0:26	10:08:29 PM	10:11:04 PM	X	
A14	HAL		ECONOMIC IMPACT HURRICANE	VO	KEY**	CNS	ASI	0:25	0:29	10:08:54 PM	10:11:29 PM		
A15	HAL		GAS GOUGING INVESTIGATION	VO	KEY**	CNS	POC	0:20	0:21	10:09:19 PM	10:11:54 PM	X	
A16	HAL		SOT GAS GOUGING	SOTVO	WIP	CNS	POC	0:25	0:28	10:09:39 PM	10:12:14 PM	X	
A17	LU		TIMES FEDERAL EMERGENCY	COPY			SAU	0:15	0:12	10:10:04 PM	10:12:39 PM		

Figure 9.2 This rundown from KTLA is self-explanatory. Note the similarities and differences between the rundown used at KCBS and KTLA. Reprinted with permission of KTLA-TV.

Figure 9.3   A screen shot of the Avid iNEWS Newsroom Computer System (NRCS) showing the customizable user interface. It can be tailored with customizable toolbars, templates, workspace display modes, and macros. News teams can monitor news sources, preview videos, write stories, monitor local and remote station rundowns, and produce newscasts using iNEWS.

Another source of material for programs comes from video news releases (VNRs). Although VNRs are often simply public relations kits, they often contain material that is appropriate for the news. The news director makes the decision about which of these VNRs will run and which won't.

While the writers are working on their stories, the producer is screening footage from the field and from other sources, such as CNN or the Associated Press News Service. The services tend to cover national and international stories rather than specific local stories. They may also offer access to archived footage.

As the stories are viewed and the day's events begin to take final shape, the producer will be working with writers, reporters, and the assignment editor covering any breaking story. The producer may juggle segment priorities and change the running order of the routine. As this process is being done on a computerized system, the events ripple down. As blocks are changed, the time for each item's airing is recalculated automatically. This screen, which may be changed even while the program is on the air, will be accessed throughout the day and will be accessible in the control room for the director and associate director while the program is running. At the networks, that screen will serve as the director's script, and there will be no hard copy.

By 4 P.M. the graphics designer assigned to the 10 o'clock news will log on to the station's computer news program, iNEWS, AP-ENPS, or whatever they are using, and discuss graphics for the evening's production. Many of the graphics used in earlier editions of the news will be used again. As the graphic artist works on new pieces, a producer at a larger station has access to a monitor that displays the designer's work. If a particular project requires some discussion, the designer and the producer can do so by phone, both of them seeing the same display on their screens.

By 5:45 P.M. the preliminary rundown has been formulated. It will probably be changed a number of times. This will happen both before and as it actually goes on the air as new stories come in or as developing stories become more or less important. At 6 P.M. or at some regularly scheduled time, there's a news briefing for the writers, reporters, and staff, in which the producer lays out the elements of the production according to the most up-to-date routine. This is meant to be a kind of status

report to determine what needs to be done and who's doing it. At some stations, this briefing is a less regular event than at others.

Between 6:30, when the news briefing is done, and 9:00, the elements of the production are finished. By 9:00 the "final" routine is usually set. At most of the larger network-affiliated stations, the producers and directors work from either a computer screen or the prompter screen. Where printed copies are required, the distribution would be available to some or all of the following:

1. One for the anchor, who will keep it handy on the set and will open it to each item as it airs in case there is a problem with the prompter.
2. One for the director, who now has 45 minutes to mark the script and to make sure that the required elements are in place.
3. One for the associate director or program production assistant. They will be responsible for tracking the time elements of the program. Using either hard copy or a computer screen, as soon as a commercial break occurs, the producer will want to know how much time is left in the break and where they are in relationship to the "ideal" routine time. As the stories are aired, the AD or PA will alert the control room to time left in each piece—counting down from 10 or 5 seconds.
4. One for the producer.
5. One for the record.
6. One for protection and for special uses. At some stations, this copy is for simultaneous interpretation, in which either a separate audio channel or local radio news station airs the audio portion of the program in a language other than English.
7. One copy for the hearing-impaired version of the program. Some stations simultaneously run visual text for watchers who are hearing impaired.

At many stations the scripts are distributed in different colors to limit confusion as to which anchor is to read particular pages. KCBS in Los Angeles used the following script color code:

1. White for the anchor who is reading the story
2. Green for the anchor who is not reading that story
3. Pink for directors

4. Yellow for associate directors
5. Goldenrod for stage managers

PRODUCTION/PRESENTATION

The Producer—On Air

As the news goes on the air, the producer sits in the back of the booth, behind a computer terminal. The computer rundown and the copy links to each item are available, as are various news services. A call or phone line directly to the set and outside lines are at hand. The producer can see upcoming news packages, the teleprompter, the cameras, any live feeds, and everything else the director and technical director have in front of them. Usually the producer also has a feed of the competition's news. Some of the later stories may still have been in the process of being cut as the program went on the air. Copy may arrive and be inserted and distributed while the program is on the air. There may be news stories that need to be watched as the story evolves. The chances are that the first few items are "set," but what happens during the first commercial break may change the lineup of the program. The on-air producer makes decisions about what should be on the air and when, and then serves as the conduit for information essential to running the program.

When changes are made, a number of people have to take action to ensure that the program looks smooth. The computer terminal assists by instantly informing everyone of the changes: showing the new order for air, recomputing segment times, and providing the updated news copy. When hard copy is being used, several different areas have to be notified. The teleprompter has to change, or the anchor has to read from the script. The director needs to be given a script to be "marked" during 1:30 to 2 minutes of break—if there is a break. Graphics probably needs to change its sequence, and even if the sequence is changed, there may be a need for stored graphics, such as "Live," or for new graphics to be created for a fast-breaking story. The technical director has to be informed, particularly if there is a new and unexpected live or remote feed. Apart from that, the new segment, or change in segments, also requires new timings for other scheduled events in the program.

Even in a broadcast that contains no major stories, the program's lineup will probably change. That's because stories are being edited while on the air or because remote feeds are not yet set. Sometimes it's because planned live events don't happen in time for the program's routine: "The district attorney will be arriving any moment now, and we'll switch live to that as soon as it happens, but now back to the studio."

The Director

Once the news goes on the air, the director stays with the script and with the program's conventions, knowing that the packages may have to be juggled. What was once the B segment may go into the C slot. The director's focus, however, stays on what's "on air."

The director must trust that with each change of plans the producer and the producer's staff will deliver an updated script and all crucial information in time to effect the needed changes. Where a computer program is constantly updating material, the director must assume that everyone will react to the updates efficiently. Since problems do occur, and the director is responsible for making "air" look good, the director needs to have a sense of caution.

Usually the director's next concern is nothing more than the next event—the next thing that is to happen. It can be summed up in the phrase "We finish this story, I go back to the anchor, and then ... ?" If there is no answer to "and then ... ?" the better news directors use their fallback positions. As a last-ditch fallback, the director can have the anchor lead to a commercial break, which gives a minute and a half or two minutes to figure out what to do next. In the 1950s a director's slogan was "If troubles hover, go to cover. If it's real bad, Jack, take black."

Each news program has its own conventions that help in times of need. Often it's the simple idea that coming out of a story, the program always goes back to the anchor. If something unplanned is going to happen, the anchor is going to have to say something. Whatever the anchor says is what's happening next. Inevitably, the director will hear about the change very soon after the anchor gets the note. In fact, the director may hear the news first. Directing is a job where too much concern for what's happening at the end of the program can get in the way of what's happening *now*. The director needs to stay focused on the immediate issues and work the rest of the program as it evolves.

One of the nice—and at the same time terrible—things about doing a news program is that when it's over, it's finished. You make note of whatever went wrong, and you try to arrange things so the odds of that particular problem ever happening again are minimized, but there's nothing more you can do about the show that just aired. There's no postproduction for a live news broadcast.

REVIEW

- News is a wraparound format in which someone leads into and out of story packages.
- Unlike magazine format programs, such as *60 Minutes* or *20/20*, the news has to be immediately responsive to events.
- The news director is the executive in charge of news for the station. The director of the news puts the stories on the air.
- At larger stations an assignment editor plays a critical role in gathering the news by doing the following:

  Monitor police and fire calls, CNN, Pathfire, Newspath, and wire services

  Serve as contact for media reps, public relations offers, and stringers (freelancers)

  Issue briefs for an in-house daybook that prioritizes known events

  Handle all faxed material relating to stories

  Set up incoming and outgoing satellite feeds and book satellite time

  Assign reporters, crew trucks, and helicopters to cover the news, as well as PAs to hunt down archival footage, messenger tapes, and sometimes assist reporters
- The director's function remains constant throughout the news broadcast. The director manages the mixing of the elements to make a cohesive production.
- Two tools that are significant to getting the program on the air are the rundown, or routine, and the script.
- News can be broken down into three areas:
  1. News gathering
  2. News production
  3. News presentation

- It is the producer who has story authority and who decides what stories to cover.
- The producer creates the program rundown, oversees the creation of a script—or at smaller stations, writes it—arranges graphics, and prepares the program for air.
  1. A typical one-hour news broadcast breaks down to: 24:00 of news, in which the stories run 70 to 120 seconds.

     $\underline{15:00 \text{ of commercials}} =$
     39:00

     39:00 +
     $\underline{3:30 \text{ of sports}} =$
     42:30

     42:30 +
     $\underline{3:00 \text{ of weather}} =$
     45:30

     45:30 +
     $\underline{3:00 \text{ of feature one "Health & Fitness"}} =$
     48:30

     48:30 +
     $\underline{3:00 \text{ of feature two "Entertainment"}} =$
     51:30

     51:30 +
     $\underline{3:00 \text{ of feature three "Special of the Week"}} =$
     54:30

     54:30 +
     $\underline{3:30 \text{ of opening/close/throws to}}$
     $\underline{\text{commercials & chatter}} =$
     58:00
  2. The final routine, computerized or not, must indicate:
     a. The date and time the routine was created
     b. Page number of the routine
     c. A designation for the segment, such as A, B, C, and so on
     d. Who is introducing the segment
     e. Where the segment originates
     f. The duration of the segment
- Where scripts are made, six or seven copies of the script go to:
  1. The anchor
  2. The director
  3. The associate director or program production assistant
  4. The producer
  5. The record

6. Protection and for special uses
7. Hearing-impaired transmission while on the air
- When changes are made "on air," those who must be notified are:
  1. The director
  2. The AD/PA in charge of timings
  3. The technical director (although the director may be his information link)
  4. The prompter

5. Graphics
6. The crew involved in making the live remote, if they are the upcoming event
7. The field producer of the event
- While "on air," the director's focus is usually limited to no more than the next few events of the program. Once they are taken care of, the focus continues to the next few events, and so on.

chapter ten

Documentaries and Reality Programming

This chapter consists of two parts. The first part deals with some of the background and thinking that go into producing a documentary, including:

- The idea
- The format in which the idea is presented
- The trends that may have affected the choices of format and storyline

The section on documentaries also examines the preproduction, production, and postproduction aspects of documentary production. For the most part, the material in this chapter deals with single-camera production. Multiple-camera documentaries are covered in Chapter 11, "Multiple-Camera Remotes." The second part of this chapter deals with reality programming.

BACKGROUND

Documentaries are produced using either single-camera or multiple-camera techniques. In documentaries, the functions of the director and the producer are often blurred. How narrowly the word *documentary* may be used has been the subject of an ongoing debate. For example, in the United Kingdom the term *documentary* covers very specific factual programs. In the same way specific names would be more commonly used to describe formats such as "current affairs." Early film documentaries—ranging from *Drifters,* made by John Grierson in 1920, to the newsreels of the 1930s and 1940s—were all single-camera works. Multiple-camera film documentaries—from *Triumph of the Will,* produced in 1935 by Leni Riefenstahl, to Michael Wadleigh's

1970 production of *Woodstock*—are also considered to be among the outstanding documentaries of the century.

Since the 1950s, multiple-camera live television shoots, including space exploration, concerts, and court proceedings have become equally significant. The coverage of the O.J. Simpson trial, the Hill/Thomas proceedings, and court coverage that goes back to the Joseph McCarthy Senate hearings on un-American Activities are certainly major documentaries produced using multiple-camera television techniques. They constitute a significant part of the programming produced by the news and documentary arms of the television networks. Multiple-camera live documentary transmissions are also the daily fare of channels that are almost wholly dedicated to live transmissions. This includes programming such as various court channels and the daily productions of United Nations sessions. Often the two production styles, single-camera and multiple-camera, are joined, as is the case with Olympic coverage. It is becoming increasingly common to see prepared background pieces that were shot using single-camera techniques presented in the same multiple-camera documentary program as the event itself.

However, most of the material in this chapter relates to single-camera rather than multiple-camera production because most documentaries are shot that way. Whether single-camera or multiple-camera, three concerns are central to documentary production:

1. *The idea:* The idea or concept for the documentary and some of the current popular documentary formats, with emphasis on interview and coverage, as in *The Nightly News, 20/20, 60 Minutes,* and so on.

2. *Specific documentary formats* (which act as the containers for the idea), including the following:

   a. *Found footage:* Some examples of this are *City of Gold* by Colin Low, *Wolf Koenig by the Canadian Film Board,* or *The Civil War* by Ken Burns.

   b. *Expanded coverage:* This can be edited or unedited. With edited programs, an event is covered, and the material shot is put together in the editing room. This method is used for regularly scheduled local or network news programs. Examples of unedited programs are live court trials, some of the events at the Olympics, and parts of the Democratic and Republican Party Conventions.

   c. *Creation:* In these programs, a dynamic situation is created. Examples of this are *Scared Straight* by Arnold Shapiro, *Survivor,* or "reality" programs that place individuals in contrived, often stressful, situations.

   d. *Recreation:* Events are recreated using documentary techniques and styles to simulate reality. Examples of this are programs about searching for Bigfoot or *I Shouldn't Be Alive.*

   e. *Montage/Quick cuts:* The 1960 commercial for Jamaica which used 50 shots in 60 seconds or Hertz "Arizona Vacation": God is Dog spelled backward by Dan McLaughlin.

3. *Trends:* These are affected by innovations and inventions in hardware and software and by changes in conventions. These trends shape our approach to documentary television production.

The Idea

An idea is the first step in developing a story or documentary. Some ideas make for wonderful television documentaries, but others, although meaningful and exciting, belong in other formats, such as newspapers, magazines, articles, or books. The first hurdle is making sure the idea can work in that medium. A documentary about hot-air ballooning in Arizona offers more visually striking pictures than a discussion of the economic effects of the trade alliance between the United States and China. The latter may be more relevant to our economy and will influence our lives more directly, but it will probably be hard to develop stunning visuals that will make it exciting television fare. That is not to imply that the choice of topic has to be mundane (or, for that matter, that hot-air ballooning is necessarily mundane), but there is an obligation to the audience to produce material that is compelling television. It's essential for a director/producer to understand the audience and the medium and to deliver a program that gets and holds the viewers' interest.

Often the idea, or the approach to the idea, is the most significant choice that the director/producer can make. An example of this is an extremely sensitive and poignant documentary that won first place in a College Television Award contest run by the Academy of Television Arts and Sciences. The documentary, which was created by students at Columbia University's School of Journalism, explored victims of AIDS. Instead of presenting the topic in a conventional and predictable manner—such as a dialogue with AIDS patients, loved ones of AIDS patients, or professional caregivers—the producers chose to explore the topic of babies born to mothers who have AIDS. Any of the other approaches might have yielded excellent documentaries, but the choice these students made clearly had a great deal of potential. The documentary focused on the care given to the children, the volunteers who nurtured and loved these abandoned children, and the mothers themselves—mothers who were now physically unable to care for their children. The documentary avoided maudlin sentiment but instead questioned what society can do both with and for these victims of AIDS. Its approach was unique and gripping. The production was also very well shot and edited.

Another first-place winner in the Academy of Television Arts and Sciences student documentary competition was a woman who found the material for her documentary at home. She documented the life of her mother, who had achieved prominence as a triathlete and was killed when an automobile stuck her while she was training.

One of the best places to start looking for material for a documentary is one's own life. There are stories to be found at home or at work or through some special interest or hobby. Newspapers and magazines are also excellent sources for production ideas. In a university setting one can often locate worthy special interest groups or sponsored events that lend themselves to documentary production. Sometimes, however, the idea you must use is not your choice because a client or production company has particular demands. Sometimes the material is truly exciting, but often it is extremely limited and inherently boring. The client may even know it's a dry topic but still want the story to be told. In that case, the director's/producer's job is straightforward: create wonderful technical works with outstandingly creative technical input, exciting camera work, and brilliant sound and score to bring a refreshing solution to a dull product. We've all seen sales pitches, tourism films, and propaganda films that do this successfully.

If this is the situation with your project, all you can do is hope the production is:

Fun,

Educational,

Prestigious, or

Lucrative.

I believe it should be at least two of these.

Formats

Documentaries present material in a number of different ways. An interview with visual coverage is probably the most popular format. This is the kind of material that's often seen in news programs. However, other documentary production formats or styles do exist. An awareness of the production techniques for the formats presented earlier in this chapter—*found footage, expanded coverage, creation, recreation,* and *montage*—can be useful when considering the best way to present a subject.

Found Footage

The documentary *City of Gold* is an example of found footage. It was made by placing a collection of old photographic glass negatives on an animation stand. The camera then moved over their backlit, glowing images. Watching the film, one almost loses sight of the fact that these are stills. They had been part of a collection of 200 eight-by-ten glass negatives, largely the works of A. E. Haig of Dawson City. He had documented some of the day-to-day events in the lives of people who had been prospectors in the Yukon Gold Rush.

Sometimes—as was the case in *City of Gold*—no film or video is available, but other visual sources can be used. Photographic archives and audio archives, as well as paintings and woodcuts, symbolic objects, and memorabilia, have been employed by documentarians for some time. They are excellent sources of historical perspective for documentaries. Sometimes they can be more revealing than interviews or other traditional ways of covering an event.

An interesting approach to making a short documentary is to audiorecord what your subject has to say about something or someone they either love or hate. Edit the audio track and then videotape objects, photographs, or other relevant images to be placed over the audio track. This is essentially what was done for *City of Gold*. It's an approach that's often used in producing and directing documentaries for television.

Expanded Coverage

Expanded coverage can be edited or unedited. Edited coverage is usually done with a single-camera crew. Sometimes several single-camera crews cover the same event, a technique that was made famous by Leni Riefenstahl in *Triumph of the Will* and is today commonly used for concerts.

Edited coverage of an event was more often seen on film than on tape. All of that changed with the acceptance of digital media. One of the most popular documentary films of all time is Michael Wadleigh's *Woodstock*. Shot on film, using many cameras and camera positions, it documents some, although not all, of the performances of that historic concert. It strives to imbue the viewers with a sense of what it was like to be there. It was very successful in its theatrical film release and successful, too, as an audio record/cassette/CD and, at the time, eight-track. Because of its success, many concerts and events were filmed and then taped in the same way. Today the same events would probably be covered with digital media. The preparation for edited coverage is similar to the preparation demanded in single-camera musical production that was covered in Chapter 7, "Music."

Unedited coverage is associated with programs that are produced with a remote truck and have a number of cameras and other sources channeled through a switcher at a remote site. In a sense, a baseball game is a kind of documentary that one might consider to be free of editing, although some editing in done for every game. There is the cutting or editing that is done as the game progresses, such as a close-up of the pitcher that cuts to a three-shot of the batter, the catcher, and the umpire; there are the video effects such as playback or slow-motion playback, which is a kind of editing of the event. There are breakaways to "packages" about the players, and there are commercials. The game itself, however, is unedited. It starts with the first pitch in the first inning and is over when the game is done. The following types of documentaries are done in this way:

1. Sporting events and parades
2. Musical events
3. Courtroom events
4. National and international events
   a. Elections: conventions and actual elections
   b. Disasters: fires, hurricanes, bombings
   c. Scientific events: walk on the moon, space exploration

The preparation for events that can be anticipated is very much like the preparation one would make for a concert event. Essentially, the director/producer tries to arrange things so all the action can be covered and will look beautiful. The idea is to make it look as though everything that happens is going exactly as planned and that the camera and sound are exactly where they need to be all the time. Ideally, the event is covered so seamlessly and smoothly that one imagines that the producer and director were working from a script. That requires getting cameras and microphones, along with graphics, and all the personnel—including announcers, stage managers, and technical and "stage" crew—in place so they can be ready at exactly the right moment, no matter what happens. This is covered in greater detail in Chapter 11, "Multiple-Camera Remotes," on remote broadcasting.

Creation

Creation as a part of documentary television production stems from formats that create an event for us and then document it. *Meet the Press* and ABC's *Nightline* regularly bring together people with different and conflicting points of view. The ensuing exchanges of ideas are what make the programs. For years, Allen Funt's *Candid Camera* filmed ordinary people as they reacted to the unusual scenarios that Funt and his staff had dreamed up. In literature, one could go back to James Boswell's *Life of Samuel Johnson,* in which Boswell recounts the verbal fireworks overheard at parties given for literary giants of the day. Their humorous remarks are similar to what we hear on some of the more stimulating television talk shows.

The most dramatic use of the creation format is usually shot with several single cameras and then edited. It's a technique we now see used in some of the more popular "reality" programs, which will be discussed later in this chapter.

Recreation

William Shakespeare is hardly thought of as being a documentarian, yet many of his plays attempt to recreate moments of great historic note. So can we say he was writing "documentaries"? Robert Flaherty's documentary *Nanook of the North,* which was released in 1922, hurled both Flaherty and the documentary into world prominence. It made frequent use of the device of recreation. Flaherty followed Nanook, the Eskimo subject of his film, and asked him to catch a fish "the old way"—essentially to recreate what had been done in the past. Flaherty also asked Nanook to "perform" numerous other activities for the camera.

Recreation, then, is not new to documentaries, and it is a valid form of making them. As recreation becomes more popular, it is critical that viewers are informed that what they are watching is not a recording of the actual event. With the sophistication of modern techniques, it has become mandatory that a disclaimer be used when appropriate. This is a moral obligation as well as a legal imperative. Not being clear can lead to serious consequences.

One of the best-known cases revolves around an incident in which producers at NBC were covering a story about automotive safety. In order to prove a point, they rigged a small explosion in a truck. The explosion illustrated the point they wanted to make, but they didn't tell the viewers that the explosion had been fabricated. If the program had been a drama, nobody would have thought an actual explosion occurred, but this is not the case when it's a documentary. The manufacturer sued NBC, and the ensuing publicity was damaging to the credibility of the program and the network. The production skills and techniques needed for re-creating situations and characters from real life are the same as for producing drama.

Montage

Montage is the combining of different and separate pictures. Montage makes it possible to work with a specific idea by showing various images around a single subject. An early television commercial for the island of Jamaica used 50 pictures of different photogenic island scenes cut together to an "island music" sound track, all to entice the viewer to come to Jamaica. No words were spoken, but the idea that Jamaica was a wonderful tourist destination was powerfully conveyed by the juxtaposed images. Numerous other documentaries and portions of documentaries have been made this way. Similar-style shots and editing make up the bulk of many of the music videos we see, particularly on MTV or VH1. In documentaries, montage techniques have been used to show the passage of time. We see a montage of pictures—first baby pictures, then grade school, and then high school graduation pictures; the subject of the documentary has gone from 8 months old to 18 years old. In the 1940s, pictures of locomotives rushing down the tracks, interspersed with postcards from New York, St. Louis, Colorado Springs, and then Los Angeles compressed into just a few seconds a journey from coast to coast that would have taken days.

Techniques of montage have been major tools in educational, industrial, public relations, and sponsored documentaries and films. In the most stereotypical cases, educational films start with a montage of students studying, and industrial films start with a montage either of smokestacks or idyllic fields, depending on the point the documentary is trying to make.

PREPRODUCTION, PRODUCTION, AND POSTPRODUCTION

This part of the chapter deals with the requirements for short, single-camera documentary pieces that are five to ten minutes long. This kind of production is often the "roll-in" material for wraparound programs such as *60 Minutes* and *Access Hollywood*, or for shorter pieces for the nightly news.

While it is true that documentaries that are a half-hour or longer afford the director/producer the opportunity to go into depth and explore a topic, studying the longer forms creates some problems. The production plans for longer documentaries usually require significant amounts of time and money. Unlike the shorter forms, time is spent building a rapport between the documentarian and the subjects. A greater amount of time is spent in other aspects of preproduction and in production. Then more footage takes more time to log and edit, and all of that usually requires larger budgets.

For our purposes, examining shorter pieces has advantages. The shorter form is easier to work with because it takes less time to produce, shoot, and edit. Because of that, it costs less, too. On the plus side, many of the techniques studied in the short form are similar to those found in longer forms. Both short

and long pieces often rely on a production plan that calls for interviews and coverage (or "B-roll"). The local news on most stations is filled with interview and coverage pieces that typically run 90 to 120 seconds. Network programs like *20/20* and *60 Minutes* produce somewhat longer segments in the same way as industrial and corporate productions.

Once the idea is in place, we must begin to consider preproduction, production, and postproduction plans. Ultimately, preproduction is going to yield a large collection of lists:

1. Lists of people to interview
2. Lists of questions to ask
3. Lists of potential visuals and activities
4. Lists of crew members' names
   a. Their addresses
   b. Their cell phone numbers
   c. Their e-mail addresses
   d. Their availability
5. Lists of equipment needed
6. Lists of services needed, such as:
   a. Animation
   b. Graphics
   c. Music cues
   d. Sound effects
   e. Sound mix
7. Proposed time lines

Preproduction starts with the research needed to make those lists.

Framing the right questions to the right people may be the hardest job of all. The director/producer must make sufficient contacts *before* the interviews are shot to determine the following:

1. Which individuals should be interviewed and those who can be omitted.
2. What questions to ask. Perhaps the most significant thing about asking questions has to do with always asking questions that bring out thoughts, feelings, or ideas. The best questions are "What do you think about ... ?" "How do you feel about ... ?" "What's your opinion about ... ?" Questions that can be answered with a simple "yes" or "no" or with terse answers like a date or an address are usually useless in the editing room.
3. The order in which to ask the questions.
4. Under what circumstances each question should be asked. (Some questions are only asked if the preceding question suggests it. For instance, if the answer to the question "Can you describe

the accident?" is "No," obviously there is no point in then asking what it looked like.)

There are two schools of thought about the length of an interview. Some feel that even though you may need only a short amount of screen time, the interview should be able to go on for 30 or 40 minutes. Most producers simply don't have that kind of time. Even if they did, they might still try to get what they need faster, feeling that casting is everything ("Either we get what we need in the first seven minutes, or just forget it!"). It doesn't matter which style you choose. What does matter is that you arrive at the interview prepared.

Preparation for the interview necessitates a thoughtful look at what you want to say with the documentary and writing whatever that is as a statement. Writing the statement somehow acts as a commitment and is the proof to yourself that you aren't being "gentle" to yourself and hedging. It's too easy to use a little "fuzzy-think" in which "about" substitutes for "is." The writing also defines your goal with each of the interviews and commits your choice to that specific written statement. You're allowed to change your mind, but once you commit to your goals, you can prepare questions that result in the answers you want. Along the way you may discover that the answers you want don't reflect things as they are, and you may need to change your approach. To help me

stay honest with myself and to give myself a strong "fallback" position, I've developed the following template for both my own and my students' work.

Documentary Production Plan

1. A title for the piece (a sentence)
2. A paragraph explaining the reason for the particular choice
3. An editorial rundown or summary of the piece, as if it had been shot. This includes a list of shots and their duration. (For a two- to five-minute piece, this is usually a half- to full-page outline.) This is essentially a plan of the sequence of shots: where they occur, what happens in the shot, and the duration of each shot. Overshooting requires lots of logging time and searching. Undershooting leaves potential problems in coverage. The routine or rundown gives you an idea of how much you need to shoot for each segment of the production. The following example is part of a rundown for a piece about retail bait-and-switch tactics, titled "Bait & Switch." A store will advertise a product at a very low price, but when a customer tries to purchase it, he or she is convinced to "switch" to a more expensive product. The title of the piece is "Bait & Switch." It's intended to inform the viewer about the dangers of bait-and-switch tactics in retail merchandising.

RUNDOWN

#	Scene	Run Time	Cumulative Time
1.	EXT NIGHT: CU. Store sign with aspirin on sale displayed in the window. This shot widens to show us a car parking. A woman exits car & walks to the store.	:15	
2.	INT: Woman walks in store and gets shopping cart	:05	:20 (*:15 +:05 = :20*)[*]
3.	INT: Med shot as she starts down the aisle getting various products	:10	:30 (*:20 +:10 = :30*)[*]
4.	INT. CU Medicines—all aspirin is gone	:05	:35
5.	INT: Medium shot of woman at aspirin CU a. Her face from behind aspirin as she leans in MED b. She is looking for aspirin WIDE c. She sets off down the aisle	:15	:50

[*]This is just a part of what would be a longer and more complete rundown. The computations in italics are not used in the rundown. They are shown here only to explain how the cumulative running time is computed.

Now you know what shots are needed and approximately how long each shot will be.

4. A list of the clearances needed. A location release form can be found at Google under "location release forms." It would also be wise to identify who will be in charge of the location on the day of the shoot. You should expect the unexpected. For example, you might get approval to shoot at a local supermarket from the store manager, but when you arrive at the store the day of the shoot, you learn it's the manager's day off. Then you need to find out if anyone else at the store was informed about your shoot. Always get a phone number from the person who gave you permission, and make sure that person informed others in charge about any particular details— for example, you were given permission to change the window setting as long as you put it back the way it was or you are going to use some shopping carts for a dolly shot.

5. A list of the individuals who are going to be interviewed and the schedule for the interviews. This may be very helpful to your crew. Even if you're using family and friends, being specific with them helps them arrange their time and makes you appear organized and professional.

6. A shoot day time schedule. Include travel and setup times.

7. Crew lists with each person's:
   a. Name
   b. Job
   c. Phone number and e-mail address
   d. Time of meeting
   e. Place of meeting

8. Location survey and maps. A complete location survey assumes that the director, the cameraperson or lighting person, and the engineer-in-charge already surveyed the location, preferably under circumstances similar to those that will be encountered during the shoot. Someone will obtain or make note of:
   a. A quarter-inch plan. If the crew heads don't provide this, I do.
   b. Pictures of the location
   c. The source of power and the nature of the power available. The source might be a tie-in to a nearby food stand or simply the homeowner's 40-amp circuit box. Your power needs might be a certain number and location of grounded outlets or simply an extension cord. Power is needed by both the engineering crew, who are responsible for camera and sound, and the stage or IA/gaffer crew, who are responsible for the setting, lights, and effects. (IA is short for IATSE, the International Alliance of Theatrical Stage Employees.)
   d. The length of power runs needed
   e. Are generators needed? If so, how big?
   f. Issues relevant to bringing in gear, such as permits and site accessibility
   g. Special gear needed, such as tractors, snowmobiles, and so on
   h. Crew and cast parking facilities
   i. Food service availability or alternatives
   j. Availability and location of restrooms
   k. Additionally, it's essential to make note of background noises that might disturb the shoot. Notes regarding the position of the sun for outdoor locations are important. Will you be shooting in bright sun or in shade? During the day or at night?

9. Prior to shooting, you need all the narration and questions you intend to use. The narration and questions may change by the time you actually shoot and edit, but having a working model prior to the shoot establishes a point of departure. What has to be changed is very specific, and at the very least you have a fallback position. It certainly increases your confidence.

10. Prior to editing, you need a scene or shot log with numbered shots so you can double-check that you've shot everything that's supposed to be shot.

11. Finally, you need the revised narration prior to editing. The revised narration will stem from the shoot, the logging of the shots, and the decisions that the editing process will force upon you. For example, your original plan may have been to begin with narration over generic pictures, but now you've decided to start with a powerful and unexpected sync-sound statement from one of the participants. That decision will change your narration, and you will need to be clear about it and have it available as a source before you edit.

Shooting

At a rental facility, whether it's in downtown New York or Los Angeles or at Anywhere State University, it takes at least an hour to complete the transaction for obtaining equipment. You need to park, get to the camera, try it out, and make sure that everything is in working condition. Then you have to pack it up and get it out to the car or van before shooting. Most rental facilities have a special room in which equipment can be set up and tested fully before being checked out. The entire package, including tripod, camera, recorder, audio package, and lights, is set up and operated to make sure that everything is in working order. Ideally, a short test recording is viewed on a source other than the one used to make the recording. This is done to make sure that all the cables and connections are working and that the camera is indeed running as it should be. The shooting sequence is as follows:

1. Arrive at the location with enough time to set up, and be ready to shoot the first shot on your shot list. Include adequate time to deal with the unforeseeable glitches that are a part of all productions. Guests and talent shouldn't wait for production.

2. Make sure you've arranged a workable camera axis sequence. If the interviewer stands to the left of the camera, the person being interviewed will look from right to left when answering questions. Consider in which direction you want on-camera talent to look. People with opposing views might look better appearing to face each other. The side of the camera from which you ask questions will affect the direction in which on-camera talent looks.

3. If tape is being shot, it's wise to lay down bars and tone before you tape so there is a reference source. (Bars and tone and their function are explained in Chapter 3, "Who's Who." Briefly, they are electronically generated video and audio standards that become references when the recording is played back.)

4. Remember to white-balance. White-balance, which deals with color temperature, is a way of adjusting the camera circuits so the proper ratio of red, blue, and green is established to yield white. Usually this is nothing more than focusing the camera on a white card or shirt under the existing light and then pushing a "white-balance" button.

5. After the interview:
   a. Get a master shot.
   b. Get "nodders," which are reverse shots of the host listening (and sometimes nodding as if to say, "Hmm, yes, how fascinating").

c. Get a "B-roll," or coverage, which aids in editing and illuminates the specifics of the story. Coverage may be either insert shots or background information. Insert shots usually address specific things mentioned in an interview, such as "the map," the model of the new building, the weapon in question, and so forth. Coverage or B-roll material that is used as background— important for editing cutaways—usually consists of the person being interviewed engaged in some action that can be used as an introduction to the piece and for edits within the piece. Shoot the subject working in the office, factory, or kitchen. Also shoot various elements that may give the viewer an insight into who they are or what links them to the project. This will be shots of pictures on the desk, degrees or citations on the wall, the tools they use for the activity, and so on. Creativity in B-roll material is very important in making an interesting piece.

d. Get shots that establish room or location presence and at least 30 seconds of location audio tone.

Notes on Shooting Techniques

All footage should be shot from a tripod, unless there is a very good reason not to. Good reasons have to do with the integrity of the project. Shooting inside a disco might look best handheld, but an interview with the disco owner seated at his desk probably should be shot from a tripod. This will depend on style. "Shaky-cam" technique may be a style that's appropriate to adopt for your project, but it's been overused, and you should have a very good reason for shooting that way.

All shots should have a five- to ten-second head (before the shot begins) *and a five- to ten-second tail* (after it ends). While digital formats may not require head and tail for the equipment to get up to speed, heads and tails on shots are very useful when the time comes to edit the piece. The sudden discovery that a shot needs to be stretched is a normal part of the editing process, and it's nice to have the extra footage available.

If you're not logging time code, *use consecutive slates* throughout the shoot. For example, your takes might be scene one, take one, two, three, and four, and then a jump to scene nine, so the takes would continue—five, six, and seven. After that, you might shoot scene three, but the takes would continue with eight, nine, and so on. That way there'll be only one "take number one" in the entire shoot. Your slate numbers may well number into the hundreds, but you'll never mistake "scene two take one" with "scene one take two" (not to mention Roman numeral II with Arabic numeral 11).

Be very aware of your shooting ratio. A shooting ratio is the relationship of original footage to footage actually used for the project. Some stations and executive producers balk at anything greater than four or five to one. Shirley Clarke, who produced and directed a number of award-winning features and documentaries, including *Cool World, Portrait of Jason,* and *Skyscraper,* usually shot a great deal of footage to make her documentaries. She once told me that in one of her early forays into inexpensive video rather than expensive film, she had shot 60 hours of some subject. At the time it seemed terrific, but later the thought of logging and editing the material completely turned her off the project. The 60 hours of material, which would have taken a week and half to log, stayed in boxes somewhere, unviewed. Sometimes projects do demand shooting ratios that are much higher than usual. Hidden-camera productions, work with children or animals, and sometimes scenic productions may all require greater shooting ratios than would normally be expected. The key is to be aware of the consequences *before* you run out of patience and editing time.

Labels are essential. The easiest way to keep yourself honest about labels is to put the label on the tape or disc the minute it comes out of the box. You should label everything you shoot with the following information:

1. Your name
2. The date
3. Name of the production: *East Side Edition, 60 Minutes, Greensboro Journal*
4. Name of the segment: Dr. Anderson interview, tattoo parlor, B-roll
5. Whether it is original footage, graphic layoff, submaster, edited master, and so on

Also note that "release labels," those that are being sent out for viewing or air, would probably have different information. The name of the segment would be deleted, and a code number and the name of the production company would be added.

Nine Tips on Shooting Interviews

1. Questions that elicit a thoughtful response, that ask how the subject feels or what they think about something, are best in at least two significant ways:
   a. As the subject thinks about the question and becomes involved in the answer, the artificiality imposed by a camera and interviewer becomes less significant, and the response becomes more genuine and more apt to contain important material.
   b. The answer is of sufficient length and significance to offer a number of choices for editing.
2. When possible, place the subject of your interview in a visually interesting place. The corners of rooms are usually better looking than flat walls. Avoid placing the subject directly against the wall, since there can be no backlighting that way, and there is no separation. It tends to look very flat.
3. Subjects who are backlit tend to look better than those with no backlight, although excessive backlighting can put the subject into silhouette. Avoid placing the subject against a visually charged or overly busy background.
4. Avoid interviews in any area where there is intrusive background sound. If an interview is edited where there is no background noise, the audience will not be disturbed where each edit occurs. It will appear as if the person being interviewed took a breath and began a new thought. However, if there is music in the background, for example, each edit will be obvious because the music will be interrupted.
5. The technique of having subjects rephrase the questions in their answers, if they seem comfortable with it, will allow you to cut the interview with fewer reverse shots to the interviewer. For example:

   Your question: *What is your name?*

   Subject's answer: "My name is Bill Smith" (instead of just saying "Bill Smith").

6. When asking questions, start with a wide shot or a medium shot. That way, one of the early answers from your subject will allow you room for a lower-third identifying super early in the finished piece when you edit it together. The super provides information about the subject, such as Bill Smith—Editor, *Times/Journal.* After

the first question is answered, change the focal length of the lens or change the framing. For example, start with a waist shot for the first question. When that question is answered, go to a chest shot and then a shoulder shot. Then return to the first framing. Feel free to ask the subject to "wait a second" while you reframe. (Asking the interviewee to "wait a second" at an emotionally charged moment might be disastrous to the interview, and might stifle future moments with the person being interviewed.) However, reframing this way offers you the opportunity of intercutting the same interview without needing irrelevant cutaways to hide what would otherwise be a jump cut.

7. After the interview is over, shoot what the English call "nodders." Nodders are pictures of the person who is asking the question nodding his or her head as though acknowledging a point. It makes for good cutaway material.

8. Shoot lots of "coverage." Typically, it's footage of the building in which the interview took place, the subject walking to his or her office, and shots of the subject on the phone, playing with the kids, reading a file, and so on. Coverage is also shots or cutaways to things mentioned in the interview, such as a picture, an album cover, or a trophy. Shooting from a very high or very low position often yields unusual and exciting coverage. Relevant extreme close-ups are also valuable coverage material. Sometimes, depending on the format of the program, it's wise to start the coverage out of focus, rack into focus, hold the shot, and then rack out of focus. This allows you to use different parts of the shot to create different moods.

9. At the end of the interview and the end of the coverage, while still on location, record at least 30 seconds of the sound of the room or location in silence. This is "room tone." The apparent silence of each room is in fact a different sound. Often, as you edit, you will find that you need that tone. You can get less tone, or even find it as you edit, but it's easier to get and not have to search or extend when editing.

Viewing

You should plan on viewing all your footage and logging what you see, even if you don't plan to use all that you view. Information from the viewing will be useful in the edit session when you are shuttling through the recording or finding "selects" for editing. When you edit in a digital format, the log will simply speed up the whole process, since you'll know what you have and where to find it.

When using time code, log the time-code numbers with the scene description. The aim is to know where each shot is and the approximate duration of each scene or shot. After you've logged all the footage, edit on paper before editing on tape or on the computer.

Editing on paper means writing down the time code or reference and the scene name for all the sequences in the entire program in the order in which you'll use them in your program. This is done to help make decisions about how the program is to go together prior to beginning the actual editing process.

When producing field pieces, a transcript of the interviews is usually made from which the producer edits. Not all productions, however, are done that way. News often doesn't have the time, and some producers say they would rather learn the original footage by constant viewing. Viewing rather than reading a transcript saves the out-of-pocket transcription costs, but one spends a lot of time both viewing and in the editing session trying to find a particular spot. Invariably, a decision must be made late at night after you've searched for something you think you've seen. After a while, it becomes increasingly easier to justify a poor second choice. I have never met anyone who worked with a transcript who wanted to work any other way. Students often resist taking the time to do the transcribing themselves or spending the money to have a transcription made, but it is what's done in the industry because it saves time and money and makes for a better-looking production.

Along the way, you should give some thought to "pacing." Pacing relates to how ideas are put together. Pacing may refer to the construction of the piece, the sentence structure in your narration, or to other elements of the production. Those elements may include performance levels, and it may relate to the relationship of elements that are happy, then sad, or big, then little. It also refers to the tempo or speed of the different segments, as well as the tempo within the segments. The pacing results from the choices you make regarding the length of shots, the type of shots you choose, and how they go together. The pacing can enhance the feeling of the piece.

Here's an example of pacing. Assume you see a slow panning shot at an industrial area at dusk as workers leave a building. Suddenly, just for an instant, there is a quick shot of a man pouring gasoline at the base of a building. The picture cuts back to the slow pan as more people casually exit and leave the building, with a sudden cut to a close-up of a match being lit. Then the pan continues slowly as it did before.

The preceding scenario will probably create a feeling of tension. The audience will want to know about the arsonist. Changing the shots would change the tempo and weaken the sense of tension. If you make the shots of the arsonist last as long as the shots of the pan, much of the tension will be gone. If you use dissolves instead of cuts, the pacing would become more relaxed. If the pan seemed to scan the horizon frantically, an entirely different tempo and message would be given. We assume that someone knows there is an arsonist or some danger to be sought out. Each segment of a piece needs to be considered in terms of its tempo and how it will affect the pacing of the piece. One of the important questions you have to ask is, how can I best present the elements of my story so the pacing propels the story forward?

Editing

Even though it's television—a video medium—video always follows audio. Unless you're working with sync-sound, the video is usually inserted *after* the audio has been laid down. Narration should be laid down first, and then video should be inserted over the narration track. That way, it's easier to edit so the video times out to end when the narration ends. If you think about editing a music video, it's obviously easier to cut the video to the music than it is to put down pictures and try to make the music work to whatever's there. The same is true for most narration. Therefore, *lay down the audio portion of each voice-over segment first, and immediately after each individual audio segment is down, add the video to that segment.* Then go on to the next edit, whether it is sync-sound, picture only, or picture with music/audio.

Do not lay down picture first and think you can always add the narration later. It *might* work, but then you have to force the narration to fit the hole. It's a disaster in the making.

A traditional rule is, never edit in the middle of a camera or subject move without a good reason. It's like saying, "Hey, look over here at all this terrific stuff that's happening," only to cut away to something else before the audience gets to see what you're excited about. This "rule" is often broken, however, and you may find some stylistic justification for breaking it—for example, to indicate a frenetic style or to mimic the "look" sometimes used to indicate that something exciting is happening, even when there isn't.

Always assume that you forgot *something*. (Bring along the script for the audio portions. Bring along a list of the production's credits.) Expect the machinery to fail somewhere along the line. Expect the entire process to take longer than you thought it would, and book enough time for that to happen. Leave yourself enough time to work without being rushed. This is the streamlined version of a documentary production template.

Preproduction Package

I. Proposal: The name of this piece is:

I wish to show/prove/explain and the point is:

II. Editorial rundown: (Example)

#	Description & Location	Run Time	Cumulative Time
1. Pix of subject		:10	
2. Newspaper montage		:20	:30
3. TV montage		1:00	1:30
4. Intro first interview		:10	1:40
5. First interview		:30	2:10
6. And so on			

III. Necessary clearances

1. Name
Position/Relationship to piece
Address
Phone Numbers; E-mail Address

2. Name
Position/Relationship to piece
Address
Phone Numbers; E-mail Address
And so on.

IV.   Questions

(Note: You may, of course, use the following questions, but you will surely want to make up *your own* questions, which are relevant to *your* topic and *your* subjects. Design your questions so they provoke answers that require more than one word: "How do you feel about ... ?" "What do you think about ... ?"

    1.   Subject 1
        a.   How did you become involved with ... ?
        b.   What were some of the things that influenced you?
        c.   What are some of your regrets?
        And so on

    2.   Subject 2
        a.   What made you first realize ... ?
        b.   Do you ever regret ... ?
        c.   What do you think of the future for ... ?
        And so on.

V.   Crew

    1.   Position
        a.   Name:
        b.   Address:
        c.   Phone Numbers:
        d.   E-mail Address:

    2.   Position
        a.   Name:
        b.   Address:
        c.   Phone Numbers:
        d.   E-mail Address:
        And so on.

VI. Schedule

00:00 a.m.:	Meet at (location and phone number)
00:00–00:00:	Travel to location # 1 (Address/Contact/Phone number)
00:00–00:00:	Setup
00:00–00:00:	Record
00:00–00:00:	Wrap and travel to location # 2 (Address/Contact/Phone number)
And so on.	

VII. Narration

#	Audio	Video
1.	There they are. The subject of my piece.	1. Pictures of subject
2.	We keep hearing about them in the newspapers.	2. Newspaper montage
3.	. . . on the television programs	3. Two scenes from News
4.	. . . but here's [First Interviewer's Name]. He has a different point of view.	4. B-roll first interviewee
5.	First Interview (Answer to third question: "How do you feel about it?")	5. First Interview footage

At California State University in Los Angeles, the following form has been used to issue equipment. It requests the same information that a video rental facility would demand.

PERMISSION TO GET CAMERA, SHOOT, AND EDIT

I hope to shoot and need a field package from:

Date_____   Times_____

to

Date_____   Times_____

(WHERE SPECIAL EDITING FACILITIES ARE NEEDED)

I will need to edit from:

Date_____   Times_____

to

To Date_____   Times_____

• I understand that I am responsible for the equipment.
• I understand that others may be waiting for the equipment and so will pick it up and return it as scheduled.
• I will call the office (phone number 555-123-4567) if there are any changes in my schedule.
• I will inform the office of any problems I encountered with equipment. That way the problem can be fixed and the next user is not apt to encounter the same problem.

Student's Signature _____ Date_____

Student's Printed Name _____

Student's ID#_____ Student's Phone Number_____

Faculty Signature_____

A Production Log for a Montage

Production

I was once asked to make a film for the government tourist agency in what was then Yugoslavia. At that time, Yugoslavia encompassed what is now Serbia, Croatia, Bosnia, and some of the other states nearby. It was unique in some ways because it was a nonaligned country, with links both to the East (the Soviet Union and its allies) and the West (the United States and its allies). Typically, Americans had an image of the country that hurt its tourism efforts. The Yugoslavian Tourist Association wanted me to make the country seem inviting to visitors who didn't speak French, German, Serbo-Croatian, or any of its languages. I am including some of the notes for that production here because the method of organizing the work is similar to the methods I've encountered while working with various documentarians for National Educational Television, CBS or NBC, and many of my own projects, both large and small. They are intended as a guide for how to organize the material that is to be shot.

I had an idea about how to do my Yugoslavian project early in our discussion. The Tourist Association wanted to keep translations to a minimum, so I decided to break the film into short segments and use short introductions in English, which could be translated into whatever language was appropriate. I utilized local music extensively for the film's audio track. Essentially, it would be a kind of music video about Yugoslavia. I found Yugoslavian groups who were performing mostly Western-style rock and roll or jazz, and I created a montage of pictures that related to five areas I thought would be significant to tourists. Eventually, it was titled *Postcards from Yugoslavia*. The film started with a brief introduction, which led to material about:

1. Scenery
2. Food
3. Shopping
4. Sports
5. People

It concluded with a short good-bye.

In order to shoot the film, I made two trips throughout the country. The first trip was to do the research in order to design the film. The second trip was to shoot the film. On the first trip I made lists of shots to be used for each of the five areas I had decided to shoot.

The following is a part of the outline for that documentary. It starts with the list for the "scenic" part of the film. All the shots in the film were numbered so none would be missed. I, the Tourist Association, the crew, and editing all used the list. Items 1–6 were the opening shots:

Item 1 was my introduction in Los Angeles about vacationing in Yugoslavia.

Item 2 showed popular misconceptions about Yugoslavia: pictures of rubble, and so forth.

Items 3, 4, and 5 showed attractive pictures of what I had found instead.

Item 6 was my introduction to the five areas of Yugoslavia and a promise to be brief.

OUTLINE: [This list was later incorporated into the script.]

POSTCARDS: AREA #1: SCENIC SECTION

7. IVAN INTRO

8. Dawn Kotor (follow a boat)

9. Dawn Hotel Jugoslavia

10. Lipica Campfire

11. Dubrovnik (stop motion—city comes to life)

12. Waterfalls

13. Parks

14. Helicopter stock shots

15. Modern buildings

16. Zemun

17. Cattle

18. Fields

19. Field implements

20. Sunsets: Dubrovnik

21. Bled

22. Shipboard

23. Yachts[*]

24. Flowers[*]

25. Fountains[*]

25a. Lipica Campfire

(*Pickups done on a daily basis. Also in this sequence will be shots from other areas, such as children, art, food, and so on.)

If the script were approved, and it was, this list of shots would serve as a checklist for the shots we had to get for each sequence. Once my lists were shot, I knew I had at least the minimum required for each of the five areas. I anticipated finding more material along the way, and I did. After the lists were made, I created a tentative script that had to be approved by the Tourist Association. Here are the first few pages of the script formatted in an audio/video style used by the Association and typical of commercials.

AUDIO

Sound FX, Music, The City—Use

Yugo music FX

IVAN—On Camera

Hi, I'm Ivan Cury, and this is the city in which I live and work. This summer I'm going to vacation where smart Europeans go: Yugoslavia

IVAN—On Camera

Most Americans think Yugoslavia looks like this. They think it's a poor Communist country with sad peasants who are oppressed by their government.

VIDEO

1. Montage LA life—include UCLA, etc. Last pix = Hollywood sign & pull into reveal Ivan who says

2. Swishpan to Black & White train station. Ivan speaks and says:

3. Cut to Ivan at (a) beach, then (b) pool, then (c) Belgrade, and (d) Adriatic or wherever . . .

AUDIO	VIDEO
Ivan On Camera at locations:	
They don't know that it looks like this.	4. Cut to next image (b)
Or this.	5a. Cut to next image (c)
Or this.	5b. Cut to next image (d)
They don't realize that Yugoslavia is a nonaligned country. It's as free from Russia as it is from the United States.	6. Cut to Ivan Zagreb.
In this film I'd like to show you some of the things that have made me such an ardent fan of Yugoslavia. There's some local music I'd like you to hear, and I'd like you to see the place for yourself. I promise to keep my comments brief, and it'll only take a few minutes to watch—I hope you like it.	
In the first place, it's a beautiful country.	

The following is a partial schedule that was developed to get the shots that were needed. This schedule is arranged to get as many shots as possible while at each location. The numbers at the beginning of each entry indicate the shots we would be getting at each location. In the first entry, our location was my hotel room at the Hotel Jugoslavia. The shot, "#8," was dawn coming up over the river, and it would be shot from my room, Room 804. After that we would go to Kalimegdan, which is a park near the hotel. There, the listed shots, 12/24/38/102/95/113, would be used in various segments of the film. Some of the shots appear in the segment on scenery (PRETTY PARK, FOUNTAINS, and SCULPTURE) and some on the segment about people (CHILDREN, COUPLES WALKING), and the chess shots would be used in the SPORT segment.

BEOGRAD SHOOTING SCHEDULE as of August 29,

Tuesday 5:30 a.m. at Hotel Jugoslavia Rm. 804

8. Exterior from Hotel Jugoslavia DAWN

Shots # 12/24/38/102/95/113 Kalimegdan PRETTY PARK / FOUNTAINS / CHILDREN / COUPLES WALKING IN THE PARK / CHESS / SCULPTURE

MOVE TO:

26/40a./47/49/52/71-76/122 Terazjie Marsala Tita WOMEN IN STREETS / NEWSPAPERS / LEADED GLASS / CHILDREN'S STORE / RECORD STORE / STREET MEAL SIGNS / PIZZA / HAMBURGER / HOT DOG

sync-sound _____

BGRDSCH September 2,—Rev 3

	Wednesday 12:00 p.m. RTB—10:00
12:30–3:30	4/46/70 Interior Hotel Belgrade
	INTRO sync-sound DUTY FREE STORE / MEAL
4:00–5:00	2. Train station—INTRO sync-sound
5:00–6:00	122. Marsala Tita GOOD-BYE
6:00–7:00	Lunch
7:00–8:00	19. Moma's house SUNSET
8:00–10:00	25/28/34/68 Exterior Skadarlija
	Lunch & INTRO BP sync-sound and night crowds including WOMEN & MEN @ CAFES / POURING LIQUIDS

Once the footage had been shot and viewed, a tentative edit schedule and scenario for the use of the shots was created. In each case there was an attempt to work from some kind of inner logic. Many of the segments followed a typical day from dawn to sunset or followed a shopper from cashing an American Express check to being exhausted at the end of the day. The following edit notes were kept short and were used to help find particular shots.

EDIT September 19

SCENIC

Dawn to sunset: Shot at dawn (Kotor?) ... flower ...

church with clouds, flowers ... Bled ... Plitvice ... tiles ...

roofs ... mountain view ... clouds with moon ...

sunset ... a child's face ... sunset.

> Ivan Copy Skadarlija

BEAUTIFUL PEOPLE

Activities from dawn to dusk: Man in Zagreb bows to us,

workers coming to work ... butcher ... shepherdess ...

Jewish Service & Catholic Service ... children going to

school (?) ... Girl in "Club Hollywood" dancing ... Armenian

girl in shop ... Shepherd ... man with computer ... fast

montage of many faces and hands waving.

> Ivan Copy Sarajevo

SHOPPING

The manner of payment/the running to buy/the goods

bought: Money in market ... Amex shot ... feet in

Dubrovnik ... walk through Diocletian palace ... fast

montage: crystal, leather, copper, duty-free shop, dresses,

menswear, local items ... tired person Ivan Copy Ljubliana

FOOD

From the raw goods to the delivered product: Pigs, cows, fields

of wheat/corn. Bottling plant vegetables in market ... wide shot market ...

pouring liquid ... café ... café ... foods cooking ... café ... café and a goodnight

from the bartender (empty plates).

> Ivan Copy Plitvice

REALITY PROGRAMMING

The major difference between documentaries and reality programming seems to be about information and entertainment. Documentaries primarily aim to inform, but they can be entertaining. Reality programs aim to entertain, but they can be informative. In fact, "reality programming" is a programming, not a production concept. For the most part, reality programs are usually contests of one sort or another. The idea of their being "reality" comes from the fact that they all depend on spontaneous moments. That being said, some reality programs really are similar to documentaries in that they strive to document groups or individuals with the same focus that would be used in a documentary.

The history of reality television goes back to the 1948 debut of Allen Funt's *Candid Camera,* which was based on his successful 1947 radio show *Candid Microphone.* At the same time, talent shows such as *Ted Mack's Original Amateur Hour,* which was patterned on the 1930s *Major Bowes' Amateur Hour* and *Arthur Godfrey Talent Scouts,* went on the air. They were considered talent contests and were in fact very much like *America's Got Talent.*

In the 1950s, *Truth or Consequences* and *Beat the Clock* were considered game shows, but today they would fall under the category of reality programming. In the 1970s, Chuck Barris brought *The Dating Game* and *The Newlywed Game* to mainstream television. Essentially they were game shows, as was *The Gong Show,* which premiered in 1976. Talent was judged by three celebrity judges, very much like *American Idol,* but unlike *American Idol, The Gong Show* had no audience voting. Chuck Barris, of course, had a much different and less serious attitude toward the talent.

The program that could be considered the first true reality program was *An American Family,* which premiered on PBS in 1973. This program, which used more than 300 hours of footage to create 12 one-hour episodes, followed the everyday lives of the Loud family of Santa Barbara, California. It is a significant production and an early example of reality programming because of the way it was shot. It permitted the Loud family to just carry on their lives without any interference, and it attempted to remain unobtrusive—to merely report without comment. For the time in which it was produced, it used an enormous amount of footage and editing time. With the advent of inexpensive cameras and avid and final cut editing systems,

this kind of programming became much cheaper and easier to do. Now programs that follow subjects, such as *The Real Housewives of Orange County* and *New Jersey Wives,* are typical television fare.

The popularity of the genre cannot be denied. There's even a television channel devoted to it. As its popularity has increased, producers have begun to use many different production formats. If you were to look up a list of reality television programs on *Wikipedia,* you would find several that, although similar, fall into a variety of categories:

Documentary:	*An American Family, The Real Housewives of Orange County*
Historical recreation:	*MTV's 70's House, Colonial House*
Science:	*Mythbusters, Ghost Hunters*
Dating:	*Blind Date, The Bachelor*
Law enforcement/ military:	*COPS, Rescue 911*
Makeover:	*Extreme Makeover, Yard Crashers*
Lifestyle changes:	*The Biggest Loser, Supernanny*
Fantasies fulfilled:	*Three Wishes, Thrill of a Lifetime*
Docusoaps starring celebrities:	*This Is Your Life, The Osbournes*
Hidden camera:	*Candid Camera, TV's Bloopers & Practical Jokes*
Reality game shows/reality "playoffs":	*Beat the Clock, Truth or Consequences*
Talent searches:	*Original Amateur Hour, American Idol*
Spoofs:	*The Joe Schmo Show, My Big Fat Obnoxious Boss*

As a production format, reality programming requires, broadly speaking, the same kind of staffing that's required for most other formats. The key ingredient may be that the bulk of the material is spontaneous, but ultimately the material is scripted. We are led in and out of segments, scripted questions are asked, and situations are created that provoke unscripted responses. Different kinds of reality programs require different kinds of skills in the positions that are a part of every television production.

This book is primarily about directing and producing for television, but unlike other formats, the director's position in reality programming doesn't easily fall into any identifiable category. The directing skills associated with a reality program such as *American Idol* or *Dancing with the Stars* is different from those associated with programs such as *Survivor, Fear Factor,* or even *The Bachelor* or *The Biggest Loser.* Deciding what production criteria should be brought to evaluating the director's work on reality programs has been difficult for the Director's Guild of America and for various producers as well. Still, the format does exist and offers opportunities in direction and in production.

Now students may get involved in the production of "reality television" more easily than ever before. College game shows such as *GE College Bowl* and various local college quiz shows have been a staple at universities, colleges, and other schools for some time. With the availability of digital video, the possibility of students creating true reality television has been simplified. With low-cost cameras, flip cameras, and even cell phones, and with some of the easy-to-use and widely available editing programs, it's possible to create a true multiple-camera reality program without a studio and without spending a great deal of money.

Some of the ideas for programs revolve around recording the daily events in a classroom, a dorm room, a central gathering place, or a class seminar. The issue of personal privacy has to be addressed, but once that has been done, there is every possibility of creating a program from that material. It requires setting up a number of unobtrusive cameras and then recording and editing the ensuing events.

A more dynamic approach might be patterned after Arnold Shapiro, who produced *Scared Straight* and a number of other programs. He put disparate groups together and recorded the events that ensued. In *Scared Straight* we meet a group of teenagers who have been arrested for juvenile delinquency but seem to be arrogant about the crimes they have committed. They're sent to a prison where they are confronted by a group of inmates who tell them in harsh language what life

in prison is really like. The prisoners attempt to scare the teenagers straight—hence the title of the film. A number of cameras and microphones are there to document the confrontation, and the film is shot in a *cinema verité* style, in which the viewer is allowed to see all the film gear as well as the action.

Films and tapes in which confrontations occur have a long history. The preproduction focuses on finding the right place to bring the right people together and on finding the right questions to advance the action. The process is similar to the preparation for a simple interview. In a sense, although sparks are expected to fly, what's taking place is an interview between two or three groups. The major technical problem (assuming you have sufficient light) with these programs is audio. How do you get a microphone to the speaker when tempers are flaring or when the subject doesn't care about audio? Since hearing the participants is essential, the answer becomes a matter of "whatever works." The microphones on the cameras will probably "catch" everything that's said, but the rest of the sound—the scraping of chairs, other people in the room, people outside of the room—will all be caught along with whatever you want to hear.

The following are some ways to get workable audio:

- Put a microphone on everyone.
- Hide the microphones where the speakers can't help but speak into them.
- Have locations from which speakers talk, as in a town meeting.
- Have runners with microphones working the area in which the talk is happening.
- Have standby overhead mics (be cautious about this fallback position because omnidirectional overhead mics will pick up all the sound, including noise you don't want to hear when things are becoming heated).
- All of the above.

Cameras and cables have to be accounted for, but they can present the same kind of problems and challenges in either 180-degree or 360-degree shooting. A more significant choice has to be made regarding shooting in the round (360-degree shooting) or in a line (180-degree). Keeping all the action on one side of an imaginary 180-degree line helps inform the viewer of who is talking to whom and where they are on the set, but it may keep some of the participants somewhat out of contact with one another.

REVIEW

Background

- The three concerns one faces with a new project are:
  1. The idea
  2. The format that best presents the idea
  3. The trends that govern presentation
- When choosing a documentary subject, one should try to seek a topic that holds the promise of interesting visuals.
- Home, work, hobbies, interests, or newspapers or magazines are good places to find material for documentary production.
- Ideally, work on a project should be at least two of the following:
  1. Fun
  2. Educational
  3. Prestigious
  4. Lucrative
- Specific documentary formats include:
  1. Found Footage: *City of Gold* by Colin Low, *Wolf Koenig* by the Canadian Film Board, *Baseball* by Ken Burns
  2. Expanded coverage:
     a. Edited: *Cops*, portions of the evening news
     b. Unedited: The O.J. Simpson trial, some of the events at the Olympics, parts of the Democratic and Republican Party Conventions
  3. Creation: *Scared Straight*, by Arnold Shapiro, where the events of the documentary are created by the producer
  4. Recreation: *911, Unsolved Mysteries,* in which the events are recreated for the camera
  5. Montage/quick cuts: The 1960s television commercial for Jamaica or Hertz, or *God Is Dog Spelled Backward,* by Dan McLaughlin, MTV, and VH1
- Among the lists that will be generated in preproduction are:
  1. Lists of people to interview
  2. Lists of questions to ask, in what order to ask them, and under what circumstances.

Perhaps the most significant thing about asking questions has to do with always asking questions that try to find out:
   a. "What do you think about ... ?"
   b. "How do you feel about ... ?"
   c. "What's your opinion about ... ?"
   d. Questions that can be answered with "yes" or "no" or with short answers are useless in the editing room.
3. Lists of potential visuals and activities
4. Lists of crew members, their addresses, and their availabilities
5. Lists of equipment to order
6. Production time line

Production

- Production lists include location lists:
  1. The contacts:
     a. Their position or title
     b. Their phone number and e-mail address
     c. Where they can be reached when you are shooting
     d. Who will be in charge of the location when you are there and that person's phone number
  2. Persons to be interviewed
     a. Their names
     b. Their positions or titles
     c. Their phone numbers and e-mail addresses
     d. Scheduled time for the interview
  3. Crew list (which would *not* contain your list of questions):
     a. Name
     b. Title or position
     c. Phone number and e-mail address
     d. Time of meeting
     e. Place of meeting
  4. Location survey information, including:
     a. Full-day schedule
     b. Maps
     c. Quarter-inch plan (if possible)
     d. Photographs of the location
     e. Source of power
     f. List of gear
     g. Relevant documentation, including site permits and contacts, the locations of restrooms, and places to park.
- Standard procedure for checking out gear is to try everything at the rental facility before leaving. In the case of video gear, it is expected

that some footage will be run off and viewed at the facility using a different machine than was used for recording to ensure that the gear is in running order and in sync.

- A standard shooting sequence is:
  1. Arrive at the location with enough time to set up and ready to shoot the first shot on your shot list.
  2. Be sure you've arranged a workable camera-axis sequence.
  3. Lay down bars and tone before you tape.
  4. White-balance.
  5. Shoot.
- After the interview:
  1. Get a master shot.
  2. Get "nodders."
  3. Get a B-roll or coverage.

Tips

- Use shaky-cam techniques when appropriate and a tripod for all other times.
- Get sufficient head and tail to each shot.
- Log, using consecutive take numbers.
- Be aware of shooting ratios.
- Label everything with:
  1. Your name
  2. The date
  3. Name of the production: *East Side Edition, 60 Minutes, Greensboro Journal*
  4. Name of the segment: Dr. Anderson interview, tattoo parlor, B-roll
  5. Indicate whether it is original footage, graphic layoff, submaster, edited master, and so on
- Place the subject away from walls and away from busy backgrounds.
- Avoid background noise.
- Change the framing on the shot at the end of a response.
- Be sure to record "room tone."
- Extreme close-ups and high and low angles make for exciting coverage.

Postproduction

- Postproduction lists include:
  1. A shot log—log all material with a brief description of the footage and, if possible, a time code for each scene of the footage
  2. A paper edit—a list of where you will find each element of the production and the order in which it will be edited on to the master
  3. The narration
  4. Additional sound sources such as music or sound effects
  5. Checking the pacing of the production
  6. Audio before video

chapter eleven

Multiple-Camera Remotes

All of the formats in this book, except for this one, deal with the director's job in specific programming formats. Panel programs, musical productions, newscasts, and the other formats in this book make specific demands on the director and producer because of what the program is about. In this chapter we'll deal with the demands that stem from the director's working conditions—specifically working on location or at a "remote" site ... even if the remote site is right next door.

Remote sites are used because the locations offer unique possibilities. If it's a news event or a live documentary event—a space launch, for example—there is no choice. That's where the event is taking place, and that's where the production happens. If it's a concert or sporting event, the special qualities of the place command that site. Perhaps it's the largest coliseum in the area, and that's the only place big enough to accommodate the audience. Perhaps it's a sporting event, and it's the home team's stadium. The director/producer has to present that locale and the special qualities of that place to the audience as part of the event itself.

Being on location or at a "remote" helps you to understand how much you take for granted in a traditional control room. Once, while observing a production of *The Dukes of Hazzard*, I heard the director of photography tell the crew to begin setting up for the next shot. He said he'd shoot this one without any "gimmie's." "Gimmies?" I inquired. "What's a 'gimmie'?" He replied, "A gimmie is anything you want at the last minute ... you know, like 'Gimmie, a special lighting unit, or a flag, or a different lens' ... something you didn't count on but you'd like to have immediately." Control rooms and studios have lots of gimmies. Almost everything you need is right there, and if something comes up—some new request, some particular lens, or certain audio gear—you're usually close to a storage room or another studio or even a rental facility, where whatever it is that you need at the last minute can be found.

Only very large remote productions are equipped to supply a lot of last-minute gimmies. Even the biggest ones are usually more limited than most studio operations. Remote production requires detailed attention to the specific details of everything you're going to need *before* you get to the location.

The relationship of the truck to the site is also important. If it's possible to request a particular site for the truck, it's wise to choose one that is close to the event, particularly if it is the kind of event that allows for some rehearsal. Inevitably there will be times when the director will need to run to the performance area. After a while, "closer," which means less running, is better. That being said, one can make some basic assumptions.

THE BASICS

Since this is about multiple-camera location work, one can assume that the remote unit, no matter how small, has the following:

1. Two or more cameras
2. Some kind of video switcher
3. Microphones
4. An audio board
5. A sync generator if it's not built into the switcher
6. Assorted cables for:
   a. Video
   b. Audio
   c. Intercom
   d. Power
7. Mounts—at least tripods (on wheels or not)

8. An intercom system to the camera operators, audio, record/playback, and assignable areas
9. Video monitors for the director/producer, including:
   a. A camera monitor with the output of each camera
   b. A line monitor
   c. A preview monitor
   d. A return monitor (to ensure that what you think is going out really is going out!)
10. A system of audio monitors for production and a return feed for:
    a. Audio tech
    b. Director/producer
11. Recording devices and/or transmission capability
12. Clocks to monitor
    a. Tape or disk usage
    b. Production time
13. Chairs
14. Desk space
15. Lighting for the control area
16. Storage area for items in the control area, including:
    a. Tapes—hard drives
    b. Scripts
    c. Props
    d. Clothes
17. Probably: A graphics generator
18. Possibly: A pencil sharpener and a coatrack
19. If it's a truck—definitely: air conditioning (A sweater or jacket is often essential.)

Trucks

Trucks come in various sizes. Sometimes "the truck" is no more than a cart on wheels (Figure 11.1), and sometimes it's a van or a smaller truck (Figure 11.2). It may also be a massive unit—50 feet or more—or a series of units (Figure 11.3).

The largest configurations feature as many as five or more trucks that include generator trucks and units with separate control rooms, an external recording room with tape decks and servers, and vehicles to handle video and audio linkups away from the actual production team.

Most of the newer trucks record and play back onto servers. Major productions will also bring in grip trucks, honey wagons with toilet facilities, makeup rooms, costume maintenance, generators, and the like (Figures 11.4 and 11.5).

Figure 11.1 This cart on wheels has a switcher, an audio board, a graphic generator, and monitors for each camera, preview, line, and return feed.

"DIRECTING TOYS"

One of the joys of directing large-scale remotes is that they often offer the opportunity to use unusual devices. Orson Welles once said that working in Hollywood was like being a child again and getting a wonderful new toy. Remotes can offer much the same pleasure. Even with just three handheld cameras and a miniswitcher, it's possible to find ways to play. It's often helpful to imagine what could be done with an unlimited budget.

Once, for a college production with a very limited budget, it was discovered that very high and very low shots could be obtained by mounting a handheld camera on a broomstick that served as a sort of unipod. The camera operator was able to hold the camera high over his head or shoot upside down or at a Dutch angle with the camera on the ground.

A kaleidoscope effect that usually takes a very expensive switcher or is a postproduced effect was created, live, by taking an idea from one of those "toys" called a Talidescope. The Talidescope is nothing more than a hollow tube with two small mirrors set into a "V" along the inside of the tube. It has a viewing hole at one end and an opening to the surroundings at the other end. That effect was achieved with two full-length mirrors from Wal-Mart that were placed in a V-shaped jig in front of a monitor. The picture in the monitor could be controlled from the switcher. One of the three cameras was placed in front of the monitor with the mirrors, and as the output of the other cameras was switched into the monitor, a moving kaleidoscope effect was achieved.

Small Analog

High Definition   Serial Digital   Large Analog   Small Analog   Video Flypacks

For the more cost effective sports and the majority of our corporate events, we offer several smaller analog mobile video production units. Most are 28'-40' long and offer the following standard equipment:

VIDEO SWITCHING
GVG 250 or 300 switcher; 20-24 inputs; 2-3 M/Es,
DVEous or Abekas A51 DVE (1-2 Channels)
2 channel Abekas A42 Still Store

GRAPHICS
Chyron iNFiNiT! 060 processor, 250mb zip drive

CAMERAS, LENSES, SUPPORT
Up to 4 Ikegami HK-343 CCD Triax Studio cameras
Up to 3 Ikegami HL-43 CCD Triax Handheld cameras
Canon 45x and 33x studio lenses, Canon 14x-16x handheld lenses

VIDEO TAPE
Up to 5 Sony Beta SP VTRs, DNF slo-mo controllers
EVS LSM Digital Video Recorder available on some units
1 Panasonic VHS VTR

AUDIO
Soundcraft or Mackie Audio Console, 24 inputs
1 DigiCart, 1 CD Player, 4 chnls compressor/limiters
Microphones as needed

COMMUNICATIONS
RTS 6 channel intercom system
RTS 4 channel IFB system
1-2 Telos Links, 1-2 QKT phone couplers
4-8 line Phone system

OTHER
2-4 Frame Syncs, (1) light kit, (2) 13"& (3) 9" Outboard Monitors
4,000' Triax, 2,000' Coax, 1,500' DT12 Audio Mult
Power Requirements: Single Phase, 200 amps, 208 volts

Figure 11.2   While this truck from Total Production Services is considered a "small analog" truck, it can shoot in both analog and digital formats.

Crosscreek Television

Voyager 6

53' Expando Trailer

Video Production
3 deck (38'x 5' street side expando)
4 position mid deck
4 position back deck
Grass Valley Kalypso 4 ME with TRi Color display Serial Digital Switcher. Has 80 inputs 48 outputs, 6 internal DVE's, and Peripheral Buss Control. Gveious/ Dveious Dual Twin Serial Digital DVE

Graphics
Chyron INFiNiT! 060 processor, 128 meg memory, 601, Transform II, 9 Gig Hard Drive with external 2 gig Jazz, 250 ZIP and 230 Bernoulli. 2 keyboards
Duet LEX Dual Channel, CMIX effects, GPI/O card, 72GB HD, 72GB Clip Player, 2 GB Memory, CDRW drive, Duet Keyboard, 19" display monitor

Video Tape
4 Sony BVW-75 Beta SP VTR's
3 Sony DVW-500

1 Sony DVW-A500s
DNF ST-300 controllers.

1 EVS 4 Channel Video server
1 Fast Forward DDR w/ Lance controller
(Truck is wired for 14 machines)

Cameras/Lenses
6 Sony BVP 900's Studio Cameras Fujinon 70X and 66X lenses, 2X, Macro and Vector 70 Heads with Quickset Tripods.
3 Sony BVP 950 Handheld Cameras with Fujinon 19X with 2X lenses
3 Sachtler Tripods.
*Fuji 4.8 Wide Angle Lens, 1 Sony CA-905 Studio Build up kit for BVP 950. (Servo's available, Truck is wired for 16 cameras).

*Available on Request

Audio
Soundcraft Series 5 Audio Console 56 Dual input Mono, 4 Stereo inputs, 16 X Mix, 10 VCA Groups, 8 Groups, 8 mute groups, 12 Auxes. Mackie 1604 Portable Mixer, 1 Digi-Cart II (ZIP and 230 Bernoulli), 360 Systems Instant Replay Hard Disk Recorder, Mini Disc Player Recorder, Cassette Deck, CD Player, DAT,
8 channels DBX Compressor/Limiters, Tannoy and Hafler for Monitoring, ATI Audio Distribution.

Monitoring
2 Sony 20" (program/Preview)
1 Sony 13" TD Monitor
81 Ikegami B&W
6 Sony 14" Color
8 Sony 8" Color

Intercom/Communications
RTS Adam System, 72 X 72
Expandable to 136 X 136,
4 KP98-7 Key panels with expansion panels,
7 KP-32 Key panels,
1 Dual channel telephone IF,
12 powered channels of 2 wire intercom,
16 channels of IFB,
20 Dual channel belt packs,
5 single channel belt packs,
2 Telos Links,
2 Getner Hybrids,
4 Couplers.
12 CO Line Phone System.
2 Motorola UHF Base stations,
6 hand held radios.

System Equipment
PESA Jaguar Video Router 64x64
Video/Serial Digital 64x32 Stereo Audio, PESA Series V 48 X 80 Analog Router.
Grass Valley Terminal/ Distribution and A/D & D/A conversion.
16 DPS 470 A/D & D/A Frame Syncs

205-663-4411

CROSSCREEK
TELEVISION PRODUCTIONS

Dimensions/Power
208/240 Volts, 3 Phase, 200 Amps.
53' trailer (38'x 5' Street side expando)
13'6" height clear
8'6" wide clear (transport)

Audio

Production

Tape

Video

Figure 11.3 This truck from Crosscreek video is typical of the larger production trucks used for major events.

Figure 11.4 This truck is solely dedicated to the various cable, headsets, tripods, and miscellaneous engineering gear brought along to a major production.

Figure 11.5 These grip and lighting equipment carts are ready to be moved into place wherever they're needed.

JIBS AND CRANES

Most major remote performance events and many studio productions use jib arms and cranes. They make it possible to do graceful and exciting on-air moves. Several different kinds of jibs and cranes are available, however, and knowing what each will do and the crew or crews who know how to operate them is very important to the production.

Figure 11.6 This is a JimmyJib Lite with cable drive. It weighs 35 pounds and breaks down so it can fit into one portable case. Photo courtesy of JimmyJib.

The Jib

The jib is a boom arm set on a tripod or other stable support. The camera is mounted at one end of the boom. Counterweights and controls for maneuvering the camera are at the other end. In the case of a typical jib, such as the JimmyJib (Figure 11.6), the lens can get down as low as 6 to 10 inches from the ground (depending on the camera used), and then, with extensions, it has an 18-foot reach. The camera operator who usually works from the back end of the jib can pan, tilt, and/or move the arm either left and right or up and down. Other jib arms that are shorter or longer and have other kinds of characteristics for portability, stability, and personal preferences are available.

The Crane

Essentially, a crane is a large dolly with a jib arm. It is usually a four-wheeled cart with a jib arm that can be raised or lowered and swung or armed right or left. Sometimes the term "tongued" is used instead of "armed." At one end is the camera mounted on a pan and tilt head, and at the other end are counterweights. Sometimes the arm is mounted on an actual truck for shots that are almost exclusively used in films. (Figure 11.7 shows one type.) Other cranes such as the Chapman Zeus, the Nike, or the Chapman/Leonard Maverick are used primarily in studio productions, but they are sometimes used at remote sites. These, as well as others used in

Figure 11.7 A Chapman Gryo-camera car Super VI on the road. This was configured with a vibration isolator and a gyro stabilized head. As configured, it's the kind of mount that's most often used in film or single-camera productions. Photo courtesy of Chapman/Leonard Studio Equipment, Inc.

multiple-camera television productions, require a three- or four-person crew that consists of a camera operator, a crane driver, a boom (or arm) mover, and/or a cable person (usually).

The Technocrane, which has a telescoping arm, is typical of what is currently very popular (Figure 11.8). Others such as the Chapman/Leonard Hydrascope 15 or 30 are also capable of the same telescoping maneuvers. Telescoping eliminates a

Figure 11.8 A SuperTechno mounted on wheels. Operation would include a remote computer drive and an operator to swing the arm. Technocrane courtesy of Orion Technocrane.

problem that is inherent in older fixed-arm cranes, and it offers significant benefits.

The Problem

When a rigid crane arm swings from camera left to right, the camera stays exactly the same distance from the center of the crane throughout the arc. Imagine that you're shooting a rock concert. The pedestal of the crane is in the audience at center stage. You want to swing the crane from camera left in a horizontal line all the way over to camera right. Unfortunately, you'd probably hit the lead singer standing center stage because the length of the crane's arm is fixed. The distance to the left and right of the stage might be 30 feet in each direction from the center, but the distance to the center of the crane to the center of the stage might be just 15 feet.

The Solution

The arm of the Technocrane is a series of hollow square steel beams nested inside one another. They are capable of being extended and retracted from a remote position. This means that if we are shooting the same rock concert and wanted to swing the crane from the stage left position all the way over to the stage right position, the arm could be retracted as it swung toward center stage so as it passed the singer, the arm could be shortened to accommodate the shorter distance of the singer to the center. As the arm continued the move, past the singer, it would be extended so it could go all the way out to the other end of the stage.

The ability to extend and retract allows the director to create wonderful moving shots that are now part of the viewing audience's expectations. The Technocrane can be further enhanced with a remote head that is called a "Z-Head." It pans, tilts, and swings, but it also adds a "z-axis" that is controlled by a foot pedal, which allows for live "traveling" Dutch angles. (A traveling shot is one that is moving. It is panning or tilting, or both, as the shot is being done.) The Technocrane literature says, "We've pulled off some amazing traveling shots like moving under the lid of a grand piano or into a tiny cottage window."

The director's job in this kind of production is to find some new way or new time to use the gear and to find new ways to work with the crews that are available. One of the joys of such work is that the crews and the gear makers are constantly trying to do even better, and they often succeed.

In the next sections, we'll look at three major kinds of programming formats that are common to remote production and see how the demands of location work affect the director's and producer's choices. These are the remote multiple-camera formats we'll be examining:

1. Presentational material: concerts, plays, operas
2. Sports: not all sports, but theoretically all
3. News and documentary events: planned events like national conventions, elections, and swearing-in ceremonies, as well as those that are unplanned real-time events, such as breaking news or disasters

It is, of course, impossible to cover every possible remote or every situation that might occur on every location. In fact, the expression "The Devil is in the details" is particularly appropriate for any consideration of remote broadcast production. Each remote is different, and each has many details. This chapter can examine only the essentials.

It would be difficult to find a remote director or producer who didn't appreciate the absolute necessity of having a state-of-the-art remote unit with a knowledgeable crew on hand, but that is not what this book is about. While there is some material relevant to engineering, it is not about the details involved in the engineering of remotes. It is not about location concerns, such as hotel accommodations, or legal concerns, or even the arrangements for transmission and related technical considerations. It is about the director's and producer's actual broadcast production concerns, with the belief that the engineering staff will take care of their areas, no matter how difficult that may be. Engineering may have a particularly difficult task because of the nature of the venue, the needs of the production, and/or the limitations and opportunities presented by the production package. In all cases, the necessity of working under circumstances that are almost always demanding tends to bring together only those who are skilled in their jobs and are very responsible, positive, and supportive.

An examination of remote broadcasting must also consider two major differences that affect production. The first is the question of whether or not the production is really live. Productions such as the Oscars and the Emmys and other such productions are aired as they happen. Others, such as the Olympics, may be aired "as live" after the actual event has taken place in order to accommodate viewers in a different time zone. This kind of production has a different feel from those that are designed to be edited. If it's live, it happens. Then it's over, and there's no going back. When production stops are built in, events or songs may be repeated. Shots may be added later to cover mistakes or to fulfill specific needs. That ability to recreate a moment creates a different tension and gives a different feel to the production.

The second major difference is that some sports, such as baseball or football, happen every week during the season, and the crew that covers such events are part of a very short list of excellent engineers and technicians who have worked together and have worked out a course of action that covers most situations. Working on the same thing every week gives them very important insights and skills.

Documentary events and concerts happen infrequently. Therefore, a producer and crew may work together just four or five times a year or even less. Additionally, such events require that the "talent" and director/producer work in a more direct fashion than would be true for those who work on sporting events. For example, the producer of the *Academy Awards* broadcast has a closer relationship to the host of the program than the sports producer does to any of the pitchers on the team. The nature of the event creates a kind of dynamic that may affect the production.

TECH BOOKS

Perhaps the most significant working document that is a part of all of these remotes is the "Tech Book" (sometimes referred to as the "Production Book"), which lists all the relevant crew, gear, and recording or transmission requirements. Whenever possible, in every format, there is a production manager or technical producer who creates a Tech Book for the event. His or her job in creating the Tech Book is to try to cover all possible technical questions regarding the event. Only in the case of emergencies or natural disasters is this book omitted. Even then there is probably a standby Tech Book waiting to be used.

The Tech Book is usually 20 to 30 pages long and contains all the vital material that's important to the production. It answers questions about:

1. The venue: including all addresses, phone numbers, maps, and directions

2. The crew: positions, phone numbers, e-mail addresses
3. The equipment: what's included, how, when, and where it functions
4. Recording or transmission requirements
5. Rehearsal and recording schedule

Following is a template from an internationally broadcast entertainment special. The categories are the same as those found in sporting events and news and documentary events. The template has remained the same for many years, with changes in camera models, or other gear simply exchanged for whatever has passed out of use. Some of the material here isn't relevant for all remotes. A broadcast of a local high school game, for example, would probably not require international routing. The important thing is the material that is relevant.

Page 1: Lists location, overall schedule, names, titles, and phone numbers and extensions for all producers, director, and major production and generator trucks.

Page 2: Lists all domestic and international transmission data: routing, circuit, account numbers, start and end dates, and times.

Page 3: Lists all satellite transmissions and pertinent data.

Page 4: Lists all pre- and postshow transmission data.

Page 5: Page 1 of the equipment list: cameras (how many? what kind?), tripods (how many? what kind?), lenses (how many? what kind?), record decks (how many? what kind?), monitors (how many? what kind?), mics (how many? what kind?), spare batteries (how many? what kind?), and so on (Figure 11.9).

Page 6: Page 2 of the equipment list includes facilities for prompters, monitors, walkie systems, robo-cams, power plans, and utility production truck.

Page 7: Production schedule for first day: 6:30 A.M.–6:00 P.M.; setup crews.

Page 8: Production schedule for second day: 6:30 A.M.–6:00 P.M.; test systems.

Page 9: Production schedule for third day: 6:30 A.M.–7:00 P.M.; rehearsals.

Page 10: Production schedule for fourth day: 8:30 A.M.–midnight; rehearsal and live production.

Page 11: Continuation of schedule for live production day and strike.

Page 12: List of cameras, positions, lenses, supports, and accessories (sticks? robo-head? etc.); notes (moves during production, when and where, etc.).

Page 13: List of video monitors: placement, source, black-and-white/color, color correction if needed.

Page 14: List of video/audio feeds, including video format, audio feed description, formats.

Page 15: List of videotape machines, including function, location, video/audio routing.

Page 16: Continuation of record/playback machines.

Page 17: Continuation of record/playback machines.

Page 18: Mics and IFB (interruptible foldback—headsets for internal communication). Who gets what microphone? How is it designated? Where is it located? What kind is it? How long is it needed in each location? Who gets IFB? Where are the positions? What kind of IFB? How long is it needed in each position?

Page 19: Specific IFB routing lines 1–30. The number, user, type, headset, location, tied to, and notes.

Page 20: Specific IFB routing lines 31–60.

Page 21: Private line assignments. Channel, label, description, code for users—for example, director=DIR.

Page 22: Walkie assignments. Operator name, channel assignment, location, type, headset, links.

Page 23: Phone list, including line number, function (research coordinator, engineering, production), where placed, notes.

Page 24: Notes.

Page 25: Credential list.

Page 26: Cable management—kind of cable, from/to, length of run, notes.

Page 27: Map of venue with camera positions outlined.

2005 EMMY AWARDS - EQUIPMENT LIST

QTY	GAME CREEK VIDEO provides:
13	Sony HDC 1500 HHs
3	Osprey's w/ Build Up Kits for 21 x 7.8 Lens Fujinon or Cannon (for teleprompter cam)
2	Hard Cam Build Up's w/ Sticks for 72 x Lens Fujinon or Cannon (for teleprompter cam)
8	Tripods (Truck Compliment)
5	Canon 11 x 4.7 angle lens or equivalent
6	Canon 21 x 7.8 angle lens or equivalent
2	Canon 72 x Lenses w/ stabilizer, servo & manual zoom
2	HD EVS Machines 6 Ch w/ Monitoring.
1	HD EVS Machines 4 Ch w/ Monitoring
1	Spot Box
10	DVW A500's or DVW500 or equivalent (Please have shop backup standing by.)
1	DVW HD500's Record Decks or equivalent. (Please have shop backup standing by.)
2	DVD Player
1	VHS Deck
2	Miranda De-Embedders (sp?) for Deko Audio
3	KVM Extenders for Dekos
5	External Router Heads XY or 64 Button.
5	Throw Down Analog Video DA's
4	20" color monitors
9	13" color monitors
70	9" color monitors Refer to Video Monitor Tab, can substitute with 20" monitors using quad splits
4	AJA Converters (SDI to Component)
12	Throw Down Audio Monitors
2	Digicarts (1 w/ Zip drive)
6	Full KP Intercom Panels
3	Telos Link s or equivalent (AD Coord., Research Coord., Fashion Police Coord.)
1	Clear Comm. 2 – 4 Wire Adapter
45	25' Black XLR Cables
22	RE 50 Stick mics
3	Sony ECM 77 Lavalier Mics
22	Shure FP-23 Mic Pre-Amps
	Batteries for Mic to Line Amps
16	Hard Wire IFB Boxes
TBD	Lightweight headset (outside of production compliment)
13	(DT108?) Camera Head Sets
	BP325's Versacam Will Provide
	Cable Troughs - Truck Compliment (Generator Company is providing)
	Sleeving (for cables in case of rain) & tarps!
2	Cable Carts
1	DT12 Checker
	Rain bags for all Cams and Bags for DT12 and Triax Bells

Figure 11.9 A page from the Tech Book for an *Emmy Awards* program. While this year's program probably used different hardware, the template is significant because of the way it presents the material. Each year's show will simply update the previous year's Tech Book for the specific piece of gear and the quantity to be used.

PRESENTATION MATERIAL: CONCERTS, PLAYS, AND PRESENTATIONAL EVENTS

Every location and each type of presentation brings its own opportunities and challenges. For the director that means "How can I get the most out of this location?" A look at a few different kinds of musical and comedy stage presentations will demonstrate the differences that location work brings.

Stage

Award programs, telethons, amateur performances, comedy clubs, and the like usually take place at remote sites. In many ways they are similar to in-studio productions. There is usually a stage or performance area. There is talent, and the talent works from that defined stage area. However, there are differences.

The production is often more confined at a remote site than it is at a studio. The size of the venue is apt to be different from a studio. Acceptable camera positions can't be taken for granted. The cameras take up seating or table space. At major events, other organizations may be fighting for the same key shots or locations. The audience's line of sight is obstructed by the television cameras and crew. At a club, waiters have to be rerouted so that they don't cross in front of the cameras.

Remotes offer special challenges to the audio crew. There may be problems in arranging microphones for choruses and for the audience's response. A club's public address system and speakers contribute to the noise level created by waiters, customers, and cash registers and must be considered. Suppressing those sounds may require a change in the way the club operates. Cable position must always be considered, both for safety and for the sake of appearance. The production company should address any potential problem prior to arrival on location. A concern peculiar to remotes and not apt to be obvious is performers who unexpectedly leave the stage and work in the audience. It's useful to have a fallback position for such moments.

Let's look at an amateur night at a local comedy club. The problems would be similar to those incurred at a performance at a college dorm "rec room," YMCA, or similar location. In some ways, shooting this kind of an event is very simple for the director. There's the mic and, hopefully, on a raised stage there's the performer.

Minimum coverage consists of the following:

1. A camera dead center on the performer that is on a platform so it is raised over the heads of passing waiters, audience members walking to the restrooms, and so on. Because all the action is on the floor, unexpected crosses are taken for granted, and the director can just hope that the passing traffic doesn't either stop to chat or cross in front of the camera in the middle of a punch line. Essentially, this is the cover shot.
2. Another camera placed so it's set for reverse angles for when the audience laughs and applauds. It's also used to get profile shots of the performer. If the performer does go out into the audience, this camera will probably be used to cover that action.
3. If a third camera were present, the safest place for it would be near the center camera so it could have a different shot from the center camera's. This camera might be on a tripod or be handheld. With an isolated feed it's the "go-to" camera when something interferes with the center camera's cover shot.
4. In the best-case scenario, there is a handheld camera that can roam through the venue. This camera would be used to shoot either audience reaction or the performer if that seemed appropriate—for example, if the performer addressed the camera as it if were a person.

Light and Sound

The two most frequent problems, which are also those that plague most student productions, are light and sound. Light requires the following considerations:

- There must be sufficient light to see not only the performers but the audience as well, and to "carry" the performers if they go into the audience.
- For broadcast purposes the audience light levels may need to be controlled by the television crew. This is because the audience light level in club settings is usually very low. In fact, the audience is often in darkness. Sometimes the problem is resolved by painting the audience with gelled lights.

Sound requires these considerations:

- The sound level needs must be adjusted so the microphones exclude many of the usual ambient comedy club/nightclub sounds, such as orders being taken, cash registers or computers beeping, guests talking, and so on.
- Additional mics are needed to record audience reaction.
- Additional microphones may be needed if musicians are present.
- It may be wise to have the house PA system run by the television crew so the levels are consistent with what's needed for the broadcast.
- If the sound level from the performance is apt to be particularly loud, special headsets may be needed.

Whenever possible, it is prudent to record an isolated feed of a wide shot of the event, as well as a line cut of the same event, which may or may not include the wide shot. If all the cameras are isolated and there is a line cut as well, the entire event can be reedited and perhaps remixed in postproduction.

Popular Music: Rock and Roll, Country, and Jazz

Let's assume that we're going to shoot a special for one of the cable networks. The broadcast will come from a stadium, and it is material for which the director does not have a score. Some things will remain the same as when the production is shot in a studio. It's best to dedicate a camera, sometimes two, to the lead singer or performer. Guitarists and electric bass players tend to be right-handed, so a camera left position is usually a necessity.

One of the significant differences between directing remote and studio performances is the time frame. The remote may require a very long and large setup and simply one performance, as is the case for the opening ceremony to the Olympics. Also, two or more performances may be taped and edited into one broadcast performance. There may be days of rehearsal and one mostly rehearsed performance. Road tours may not offer the director "on-camera" rehearsal time, but there is often ample time to view the performance or single-camera tapes prior to actually shooting.

Unless it is a live-to-air performance, a great deal of the material will be reworked in postproduction.

The chances are that all the cameras and a line feed will be recorded. Portions of the audience will be specially lit, and members of the audience, especially photogenic members, will be placed strategically for shooting purposes.

The working relationship with the performers and their management team is subject to a number of considerations. DVD sales and the marketing possibilities of musical events, as well as the public relations value of the broadcast, bring both a very cooperative attitude and the potential for interference. It is at those times when outside sources hope to impose their vision on the production that a strong producer is most appreciated.

Preproduction

Since most performance remotes give a director just one chance to get it right, preproduction is very important. There certainly are times where a director is brought in to shoot an event without any preproduction work. Once I was flown in to shoot a three-day country music festival without ever seeing a ground plan, a routine, a list of the gear, the crew, or even a list of the performers. I learned later that it was a very successful program, but I felt like I was shooting a telethon, where "safe" was always a better choice than "creative."

Let's assume that the production group has been hired early in what is to be a national tour of a popular singing star. Usually the director would be familiar with the artist's work but would still want to contact the artist and road managers as early as possible. The director would want to see a number of performances and the actual venue where the concert was to be performed. It would be helpful if, as in the case of a studio production, the director arranged for a number of crew chiefs to see the performances and the venue.

Lighting Director

The road production has its own lighting director and crew. It's the job of the broadcast lighting director to work with the artist's lighting director to make sure that the needs of the television production are met. Most of the time the intention is to let the home audience get a sense of what the live concert is like, and that includes maintaining the integrity of the stage lighting. Usually, the lighting for the road show will remain intact and is adequate for broadcast purposes. It is likely, however, that the broadcast group will want to augment the stage lighting with additional units to light both the audience and the exterior of the venue itself.

Senior Audio

The road production has its own senior audio technician and crew. It's the job of the senior audio technician to work with the show's audio crew to ensure the broadcast feed and yet maintain the integrity of the artist's audio effects. There may be times when the broadcast takes a feed from the artist's audio output, so the feed to the television truck comes through a sound truck. The truck takes a separate feed to a multichannel recorder and then feeds the television truck either all the channels or a "mix" that is adequate for shooting but that will be enhanced at a later sweetening session. Audio, either show audio or broadcast audio, will need to work with the following:

- Program audio—mixed or unmixed.
- "Foldback" to the musicians, which amplifies the voice of the singer back to the musicians either through speakers or headsets.
- "House audio" (public address—PA) for the audience.
- Private intercom for cameras, the stage manager, lighting, and others related to the broadcast.
- The private intercom will need to be heard over the music and the roar of the crowd.
- And, finally, sometimes phone lines.

Television Location Manager

The television location manager is probably one of the producers. It is his or her task to oversee all the technical elements of putting together the crews, mobile units, communication, phone lines, intercoms, and recording and transmission elements necessary to create the television special. This would be someone who is familiar not only with the gear and the crews needed but the budget of the production as well.

Director

Generally speaking, the director of any event wants to know who, what, where, and when. Those questions pertain to both the artists and the venue.

1. *Who* is being shot?
   - Who are the artists involved?
   - What are they doing?
   - What's the rundown of the program?
   - What numbers are being performed and in what order? (This is answered with a show routine.)
   - Where do the performers stand/sit in relation to one another? (This is answered with a ground plan.)
   - Other notes: Do the performers go out into the audience? Are there special entrances or exits that should be covered?
2. *Where* is it taking place?
   - Which venue? Where is it?
   - What problems, limitations, or special features does the venue present?
   - Is the action on a stage, on a ball field, in a swimming pool?
   - What kind of stage or field or pool?
   - Raised platform stage?
   - End or center of the arena?
   - Dimensions of the field or pool?
   - How can the opportunities be maximized and the limitations minimized?
3. *When* is it being shot? Essentially, this is the timeline.
   - When can I see the performers?
   - When can I see and discuss the venue?
   - When are rehearsals being held and with what facilities?
   - When is there a rehearsal with equipment?
   - When is the shoot? Daytime? Dusk? Late at night?
   - When can I shoot inserts and pickups (if such can be made available)?
4. *What* else do I need to know?
   - Are there fireworks, smoke, or special effects happening at some time during the performance? When and where? How will I know about it in time to shoot it?
5. Miscellaneous questions:
   - Are there feeds to be integrated? What are they? How long are they? How are they handled?
   - Are there roll-ins? What are they? How long are they? How are they handled?
   - Are there contractual considerations? What are they? How are they to be handled?

Finally these two points must be answered:

1. What is there about this performance at this location that is special and that offers opportunities to make the most of what's happening?
2. What have I missed?

The most important questions that confront a director in preproduction are how to maximize the shooting of the performers and how to make the most of the location itself. The location, and the audience, if there is one, becomes "the set" and "the setting." If it's a stadium, then the stadium and the crowd must become a part of the televised event, just as it is in real life. By the same token, the intimacy found in a location such as a comedy club, its smaller surrounding and audience, must also be made a part of the television performance.

In order to plan the shoot, the director would like to see the performance or have worked with the performers prior to the actual television shoot. These are the fundamental tools:

1. A ground plan of the venue and, perhaps more important, a ground plan of the artist's stage area, including instruments and speaker placements
2. A sense of the performance ... musical, comedy, dance, and so on
3. A rundown of the event

Neither an actual ground plan nor a performance rundown may be available. A sketch drawn by some member of the artist's road crew may have to suffice. The danger with such a sketch is that it may leave out information that in the sketcher's opinion is irrelevant. For the sake of this chapter, let's assume that the director knows the work of a rock band, which will serve as our model. A copy of the ground plan, a probable rundown, and some tapes of prior concerts are all available. The rundown may change while the group is on stage, but any indication of the program and its order will be a help to the director. It gives the director and the lighting director a chance to establish a lighting and shooting "mood" for a number or, if they're not running that element of the program, to know what lighting and other effects are apt to be coming up.

We'll also assume that the director has been able to visit the venue where the special will be shot and has attended some of the road shows prior to shooting the special. Also, there are a few weeks between the beginning of the road show and when the special will be taped. How will the director proceed given all the who, what, where, and when information?

In a general sense, the director will consider what he or she feels is the essence of the group and how to best present that. In a very general sense, the appropriate style and way of shooting are specific

to most kinds of music. Country music usually looks different from rock and roll, which looks different from jazz or classical music. Rock and roll performances are often filled with exciting theatrical devices such as fireworks, smoke, and videos. Shooting Dutch angles, lots of moving handheld shots, and very quick cuts are appropriate to rock and roll. Even within that genre, different rock and roll groups demand different approaches. Most of the time, shooting a classical music concert with a rock and roll visual treatment would be inappropriate to both the music and the audience.

The location, too, suggests ways of being seen. A blimp, for example, would be nice for a stadium shot whether the music was classical or rock. The director might also consider the use of a cherry picker, an underwater mount, or a helicopter.

Postproduction

Once the shooting is finished, the production goes into its postproduction phase. If the production is a major one, all, or at least most, of the cameras will have been recorded individually, and a line-switched feed may also be a part of the mix. Furthermore, there may be a number of different performances, perhaps recorded in different cities, that will all be a part of the finished production. Preparation for the edit consists of the same steps as those that would be taken for a studio production.

The recordings are logged and annotated. Sometimes this is done with the director or the director and producer, and sometimes it is previewed and logged by an editor who creates a "select reel." Prior to the actual edit, the producer, or the producer and the director, as well as the talent and their representatives, go over what they think will become a part of the finished production. After a cut is finalized, the audio that will have been recorded digitally onto 24 tracks with time code is taken to an audio sweetening session. There the music is remixed and then replaced into the final show.

I asked Eric Feder, the supervisor of International Operations for *E! Entertainment*, what the tech setup would be for an imaginary Kennedy Center production. This was his reply:

It all depends on the number of cameras, and thus, the budget. I would assume that since you say it's a live show that's being edited for a later broadcast, it's being cut for timing reasons. In this case, the producers should know in advance what they can easily cut out of the show (prerecorded tape packages or a live musical number, for example) that the shorter version of the show can do without. In this case, if, for example, there were eight cameras on the show, I would guess there would be two main cameras in the back of house area, in the middle or toward the back of the audience, that have a large teleprompter underneath them. I would then add one or two jib cameras, two handheld cameras that roam the aisles for audience reaction, and two more cameras on stage for presenters walking on and off and for the musical acts. The Kennedy Center Honors may use more cameras than this, but I would consider that to be a minimum for this kind of event, with musical acts and an audience. For ISO records for a cutdown, I would choose to ISO record both of the main cameras in order to cut acceptance and presentation speeches shorter (as well as for posterity, so the footage can be used in future shows without on-screen graphics). I would then ISO record the two handheld stage cameras for the musical acts to cut them shorter, as well. As far as the two audience cameras and the jib camera, those are sort of non—time essential shots. Shots from those can probably be stolen from one part of the show to another without too many people noticing. For those, and most other cameras, I would probably do a single VTR with a subswitcher or router so the director or producer (maybe even the TD) can switch around and throw some good footage into that deck during the show.

Classical Music

In some ways classical music is very easy to shoot. The players are usually seated, and you can work from a score, so you know what instrument will be taking the lead and when. With sufficient preproduction, which includes analyzing the score, there are seldom any surprises. The rules regarding shooting remain the same as they would be for shooting in a studio. The instruments and the score are the same whether the performance is in a studio or an outdoor band shell. The key shots of the conductor, the first violin, and the wide shot are all the same. However, in a studio there is usually ample floor space for moving cameras around the orchestra, and that's not usually true in a band shell. It is possible to place a camera close to some of the instruments, the players' faces, the notes, the players' hands, and so on, but it's often impossible to get camera positions at the side of the stage or backstage. Often the shell itself is raised, and the camera position from the audience will yield a shot that looks up, missing

many of the players in the orchestra. Nevertheless, outdoor symphonies are broadcast, and the location itself offers unique shooting opportunities. A typical multiple-camera setup for the shooting of a symphony orchestra at a remote site might be designed like this:

Camera 1: At cam left. Preferably on a wheeled tripod. Electronic field production (EFP) viewing, which is to say that the viewfinder is a small monitor built onto the camera, and the zoom and focus are on the handle of the camera. The camera's responsibility is to get the following:

1. The conductor from the first violin's position
2. If possible, another shot of the conductor from over the tympani's head at the back of the band shell, as well as the audience
3. Tympani head on and from the side
4. Wind players who are seated stage left (camera right)
5. Audience
6. Side view or "down-the-line" view of the violins

Camera 2: At the front of the orchestra on a crane or jib with wheels and a moving arm. This may have its viewing, as well as its zoom and focus, at a remote location, usually at the back or base of the crane.

1. Master shots of any of the players
2. Shots past the conductor. The problem with its use is that it blocks the audience's view.

Camera 3: Even in situations where the audience is at a steep angle to the stage, a platform is almost always a necessity. Typically a platform is arranged somewhere in the middle or back of the venue. The camera on the platform is on a tripod and has a traditional EFP mounting and a long lens capable of getting close-ups at the shoulder, or at least chest shots. At the widest setting, it affords the director the second head-on shot of the orchestra with lots of audience in the foreground.

1. A wide shot
2. A shot of the conductor's back and arms as he or she is conducting
3. A head-on or three-quarters shot of selected instruments
4. Shots of the audience—both over their heads and side shots of people listening or applauding

Camera 4: A handheld camera with electronic news gathering (ENG) mounting. This camera has the zoom and focus on the lens, and the operator views the scene through an eyepiece attached to the camera. Ideally, the camera is mounted on a quick release tripod placed camera right.

1. Extreme close-ups of players head-on to the violins and profiles of wind and brass instruments
2. Dutch angles—shots in which the camera is canted so the bottom frame of the camera is off the horizontal axis and the picture appears to be going uphill on one side or the other. May be used to shoot the "gate" to the venue, or surroundings, such as the park, the front of the stadium, and so on.

Camera 5: A tripod mount camera EFP mount at the camera right position. Essentially, it has the same shots as camera 4, but it can be used to intercut with camera 4's head-on shots of the violin section. Normally, it gets the close-ups, since it's on a fixed tripod, and camera 4 gets a Dutch angle, a wide shot, or some other shot that the fixed tripod would preclude.

SPORTS: THE ULTIMATE REALITY PROGRAMS

There are no particular rules that cover the handling of all sports. Each sport is different. There are, however, some generalizations that one can make about shooting sports. Most people categorize sports as being team sports or individual sports. Sometimes they are seen as being contact or noncontact sports. Television directors add a different perspective to this kind of analysis. They must see sports as falling into one of three basic categories that relate to shooting the event:

1. *Line, or back and forth*: This includes basketball, football, hockey, soccer, and tennis, which are the major televised sports. It also includes badminton, field hockey, lacrosse, polo, water polo, and individual sports like fencing. To a lesser degree it includes sports that go in one direction such as archery, bowling, handball, jai-lai, racquet ball, and, for that matter, pool and horseshoes.

2. *Ring or circle sports*: This includes baseball, horseracing, and track.
3. *Form*: This includes gymnastics, ice skating, field events in track, as well as equestrian events, horse and dog shows, and obedience trials.

Of course, many more sports could be listed here. Perhaps poker can be included, and a sport like boxing, for example, might be considered both a ring sport (it takes place in a "ring") and a back-and-forth sport (the line of 180 degrees between the boxers). While some sports—competitive logging events, for example—don't easily fall into such categories, the consideration of sports events in terms of line, circle, or form lets the director call upon principles of presentation that are as old as the medium itself.

180 Degrees

The first major consideration might well be "the line of 180 degrees." In order to help the audience understand the opponents' relationships, the cameras have to be on one side or the other of an imaginary line passing through the participants. To achieve this, camera placement requires key camera positions on one side or the other of that imaginary line. Once it crosses oven, confusion may ensue. There are, however, even more exceptions. In some sports—baseball for example—breaking the line is common. We see the pitch from a camera in center field, and when the ball is hit, the view is changed to cover the runner. Right and left are switched, and we just accept it. In NASCAR or other such races, the profusion of cameras is so great, including shots from car-mounted cameras, that the viewer abandons the sense of direction. It becomes essential in such events to regularly include a shot that is wide enough to keep the viewer informed as to who is in the lead. In football, basketball, or any of the back-and-forth sports, we accept the shots into the dugout, the coach's area, or the close-ups that might confuse screen direction, but we see these only when "the play" is not in action.

Cross-Shooting

While the master shot for line games is almost always in profile, there are many occasions in which we'd rather see the players head-on rather than in profile. That can only be accomplished with

Figure 11.10 A typical plan for camera placement for a basketball game. This placement is used to broadcast Los Angeles Lakers games.

opposing teams by cross-shooting. Camera 1, at the far left of the field, gets the team going from right to left. Camera 3 ... (or camera 12, or whichever camera is at the far right of the field) shoots those players going the other way—from left to right.

Camera Positions

The camera positions for line sports, circle sports, or form sports are determined by the needs of the sport, the availability of the hardware, and the locations available to the production company (Figure 11.10).

Line Sports

In line sports the two key spots are high in the center of the arena, or field. One camera gets the wide shot, and another camera gets a closer shot. The next two cameras that are added are on the field and work as follows:

1. From the outside in "slash cameras," as in basketball

2. Playing back and forth from the center line to wherever the action occurs, as in football
3. Working from the center line facing the players on their side of the net, as in tennis

In tennis, the master shot, rather than being from the net at the center of the court, faces the net and is high enough to see both the near and far court, as shown in Figure 11.11.

Circle Sports

Any type of racing—a car, horse, ice, or track event—requires shooting with cameras that report the action in a wide shot. However, any shot that's wide enough to see all the action turns the competitors into nothing more than colored dots in the distance. Closer shots are needed, so cameras are placed around the track, and the sense of continuity is briefly abandoned. The audience is disoriented from the continuous line of the race and instead is offered a lot of intercut views of the race, including point-of-view shots from car-mounted cameras, as well as graphic and animated materials. Along the

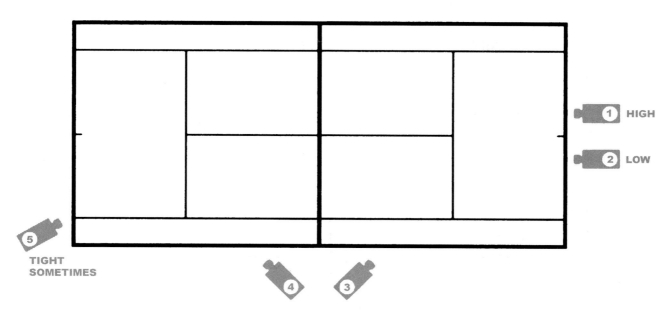

Figure 11.11 *A typical plan for camera placement for a tennis match.*

way, medium shots are included to keep the audience aware of the actual standings in the race. Finally, a "crossing-the-finish-line" shot, as the race ends, is essential.

Baseball is certainly one of the most popular sports-in-the-round. It requires a great deal of preproduction and a knowledge of the conventions that have been established. Let's look at the production of a game. Prior to going out to shoot the game, the director will have a camera assignment meeting that creates or, more likely, revisits a well-established game plan that allows him or her to call shots without having to directly ask the crew for them. Once the game begins, there is no time to assign shots, so the plan is put in place. It's based on the same logic that works for computer programs: "If . . . , then go to." If there's a right-handed pitcher and a right-handed hitter, then go to these camera assignments. If there's a right-handed pitcher but a left-handed hitter, then go to these camera assignments. Once the game has begun, the director relies on the camera assignments for each camera and situation and expects that the shots will be there when they're needed.

A typical baseball layout requires at the very least shots of the following:

1. *The pitcher* (high home): Usually from behind the catcher and high. This camera follows the ball into the field and stays wide as the cover shot.

2. The *right-handed batter* (high first): Right-handed batters are covered from high first. When the ball is hit, this camera goes to the fielder who catches (or misses) the ball. When there is more than one runner on base, this camera stays with the second runner.

3. *The left-handed batter* (high third): Sometimes the batter is left-handed and is covered by high third. This camera carries the runner to first base. If there is more than one base runner, this camera stays with the lead runner.

4. *The pitcher-batter-umpire or batter-umpire* (tight center): This shot comes from center field on a long lens.

Hardware

The hardware has gotten better. There's more of it, it's cheaper, and it can do more things. In fact, this is one area that clearly delineates the "haves" and the "have-nots." A college or high school multiple-camera crew may simply have two or three cameras for shooting the event. A major league baseball team, like the Los Angeles Dodgers, may be covered by 12 or more cameras with operators, as well as 2 or more additional robotic cameras, and 4 or more still-store or instant-replay devices. They also have two or three dedicated video sources for graphics and animation. Their audio needs include a great deal of gear in order to cover the sounds of the game, the announcers, the commercial inserts, the intercom, and so on.

Crews

Beyond the rules of the game and the hardware are the crews. Crew members start by being very responsible and by being the best or, at least, one of the best at whatever they do. Those who came before them set the bar that must now be surpassed. In their formative years, they arrive early and leave late, and if called upon, they do what no one else will. As they continue, they still arrive early and still work hard. All those around them are working in the same way, and after a while they have the advantage of working at their job for years.

Additionally, since freelance crew members work on many kinds of remotes, they bring techniques from one kind of production to the next. The solution to a problem that was encountered while working on a sporting event—for example, perhaps a way of treating graphics or animation—may be carried over to the presentation of a musical event or a live awards show. The graphic wipes and animation used in some nightly news programs are similar to the templates first seen in the presentation of sports background packages.

Finally, high on the list of crew priorities on all remotes from high school productions to major network events are those who can keep the technical operation functioning no matter what crisis occurs.

Director

Once a baseball game is underway, the director calls for the shots discussed in his earlier camera assignment meeting. These are well-planned scenarios that are designed to cover whatever situations come up. He or she doesn't give "directions" during the game. There just isn't time. The director just calls out shots and filled-in graphic templates: "Take 6. Key X, Key Y. Lose XY. Take 4. Take 1." The TD and the camera and video operators will have anticipated each of those calls. The graphics operators will have had X and Y waiting. No one will tell the graphic operator—who's keeping on-air track of balls, strikes, outs, innings and score—anything. He or she will continue with the updates. That information will remain keyed over whatever else is happening on the screen.

Producer

The producer has a list of events or material to be inserted during the pause between pitches and asks the director to run those events at appropriate times. Thus, we see the prepackaged statistics, reruns of past events, statistical graphics, and contractual events, such as shots from the blimp, field advertisements, and so forth.

Form Sports

In sports where form is essential, such as gymnastics, figure skating, and equestrian events, the rules that govern the shooting are the same as those that serve for a scripted drama. Crossing the line of 180 degrees may confuse the audience, so you should cross-shoot when possible. Always be mindful of the background so it enhances the action and isn't confusing. In a larger sense the shooting of such events, when it is intended to be more than just a record, requires a sense of what is attractive and what constitutes the drama of the situation. Figure skating is a useful sport to consider in terms of form. The director needs to show both the grace and the speed of the skater. The skater's form shows up well against the plain white of the ice. The speed shows up well against the passing faces in the audience. The director must choose a "when" and a "way" to go from shot to shot that let the audience in on the event. The choice depends on the following:

- The skaters: their strengths and weaknesses
- The routine: fast or slow, modern or classic
- The television equipment:
  What kind
  How much
  Where it's placed
  The crew

Given a gymnastic performance or an equestrian event rather than figure skating, the same criteria will exist, but the kind of isolation that white ice affords is missing. That white ice and the lone skater seen starkly against the ice create a graphic picture that is very dramatic. In its place, the director of the gymnastic or equestrian event must find those elements in the surroundings that enhance the event itself. For gymnasiums it may be the lights or the vastness of the space around a single figure working through a routine. The director's job is to find a way to tell the story and do so in a visually attractive and appropriate manner.

One thing that is common to all sports is the drama of the event. It can be seen in a close-up of a tennis player's face. That concern and drama are also evident in the face and body language of the gymnast's coach, or the coach of any ball game, for that matter. It is also in the faces of the other competitors, as well as in the actions of the spectators and their relationship to the game. The director of any sporting event is on the lookout for dramatic elements of the sport that add to the excitement of the event.

Game Rules

Inevitably, the rules of the sport, like the time spent in the huddle during a football game, or the "tempo" of the sport, such as the time between points in a tennis match, dictate some of the conventions that have become a part of our viewing experience. In order to fill those "holes," we've come to expect instant replays, graphic chalk talks, and a great deal of "color" conversation during those moments.

Ultimately, preproduction is even more critical on a remote production than in the studio because there's no place to "get stuff" —in other words, no "gimmies." You have only what you brought.

NEWS AND DOCUMENTARY EVENTS

All news events—all broadcast events, for that matter—come in one of two varieties: those events where you know what will happen and those where you don't.

The engineer-in-charge of President Nixon's trip to China in 1972, one of the earliest major remotes, was asked how long it took CBS to prepare for that broadcast. "Six months," he responded. He was then asked how long it took CBS to gear up for the Kennedy assassination in 1963. That took one half-hour, he explained, and by then every piece of equipment at the CBS network was dedicated, or ready to be dedicated, to the event.

The first part of our discussion about "event" production involves the preparation and production of major news events such as national conventions, elections, swearing-in ceremonies, NASA shuttle launches, and real-time events like funerals and disasters. The preparation and production for these kinds of broadcasts are similar to those for a graduation ceremony, a grand opening ceremony, or any similar public event.

Some news events are inevitable, and stations maintain a kind of "doomsday" library for such times. For example, at the time of his death, Pope John Paul II was 84 and had been in poor health for some time. It's safe to say that the networks had gathered biographic material to be aired immediately after he died. Other events, such as 9/11, require the massing of whatever equipment and personnel are available to cover the event as well as possible. There are no guidelines in place.

The producer's job at an anticipated news event is to make sure that whatever is needed to cover the event is available. Often two (or more) producers will be present on such a remote. One works with the staff involved in the event, such as the media liaison for the Democratic Party, or the media liason for NASA etc., and the other will work with the technical aspects of the production, serving as a link between the physical plant, the convention center, the hotel ballroom, the launch site, and so on, and the production crew and gear required for the production. They also work with engineering to set up the necessary phone and transmission links and lines. They will be responsible for creating and maintaining the Tech Book for the event.

Even in the smallest production, the producer must work with those involved with the event and work with the crews and gear required to broadcast them. Sometimes an event occurs without warning. Then the station just does whatever it can to carry the story. The newsroom becomes central headquarters. Field crews are sent out. The director and producer or producers make up the broadcast as they go along. They know they have to produce a rundown—even if it's a handwritten note scrawled on a piece of paper—that will help others such as graphics, audio, talent, and so on know what's needed and what's coming up next. As the event progresses and more staff are brought to the event and the control area, the time may come when there is some sense of organization to the broadcast. At the first moments, whoever is available takes over, and each area does the best it can with whatever is available.

Preproduction

Where the events are anticipated, the news director and/or the producer of the broadcast contact the producer of the event, perhaps a political party, for example, and the venue's staff. An appointment is then set up to survey the location—perhaps a convention center. The survey team would include representatives from nonbroadcast participants:

1. The media director of the political party or his or her assistant
2. The director of the venue or the operations director or his or her assistant
3. The chief-of-crew or crews representing stagehands and others who work at the venue and who need to be involved in the broadcast
4. A representative from whatever organization or organizations will be handling transmission issues, phone lines, up-links, and so on

The survey team also includes representatives from the broadcast group:

1. The broadcast producer and the technical producer who will be compiling the Tech Book either at the initial survey or soon after another survey takes place. The following are included in this survey:
    a. The director
    b. The engineer-in-charge
    c. An audio specialist
    d. The lighting director
    e. Chief-of-crew representing the stagehands

The concerns are universal and are based on what has to be accomplished. If it were a college production, meetings between the event coordinator and the production team would have to be arranged to work out the details of the broadcast. At a convention, some of the questions are: Is there a booth in place, or does one have to be constructed? Is there a strictly limited network feed, as might be the case for a presidential debate, or are all the stations bringing in their own hardware and crew? Sometimes the answers to these questions limit what can and cannot be done. How long is the event? A national political convention is longer than a swearing-in ceremony. How much lead time is there at the venue? If there is only a week, that may limit construction. When will there be access? Is there 24-hour access? Are there some tasks that can be accomplished while some other unrelated event is taking place? For example, can some cables be put in place at the convention center while a trade show is occupying the space? Which cables can be installed—audio, video, lighting? Where can they be installed and when? At the university graduation ceremony, the questions might revolve around

access to the gymnasium or track, but the intent would be the same.

At the networks, the director will take it for granted that audio and video, as well as proper lighting, will be delivered for the platform, the on-air correspondents, and the "house" in general. Intercom (IFB), even over the roar of the crowd, will also be taken for granted. It is likely that the director will be working from a large truck parked adjacent to the venue in line with a number of other trucks. Then the key questions become:

1. How many cameras are needed?
2. How many are available?
3. What kind of placement will be allowed?
4. What does audio need? How can its needs be fulfilled?

Often questions arise about building and placing platforms for camera mounts in the audience. Such platforms eliminate seats in the audience, which results in a conflict between the needs of the audience and the broadcast crews. The needs of each of the networks, the major cable operators, and international must be met. Everyone will want the same key positions. Some of the shots may be pool feeds, although backup positions in case of problems are very much a part of everyone's plan.

The key shots at a political convention are different from those at a space shot, which is different still from a state funeral, a royal coronation, or a college graduation. It's not the intention of this chapter to offer the procedure for every type of event, since each has its own specific requirements. What follows here is an indication of the minimum a director would try to arrange in a typical political convention, knowing that some shots may be pool feeds.

This is somewhat similar to the setup that would be appropriate for a graduation ceremony:

1. The podium in a close-up
2. The podium in a medium close-up
3. The podium in a wide shot

The director will want at least two head-on shots of the podium, perhaps a waist shot and a chest shot, in order to be able to switch from one view to the next. Isolated feeds of each camera will be very useful in the future for editing purposes.

4. A reverse over the podium to the audience and/ or a profile shot, as well as a cross-two shot featuring the graduate accepting the degree

5. A shot of the audience and a cross-two shot featuring the presenter awarding the degree, as well as:
6. Camera positions for commentators
7. Camera positions for interviews and introductions, such as "There's the delegation from Ohio" or "Also attending today's ceremony is . . ."

Recognizing that anything can change at any time, the director and producer will work out a game plan for the coverage of the event. They will go over the routine for the event and the seating chart. They'll note who speaks and in what order, as well as who will be in the audience and where they'll be seated. They'll want to determine if there is anything in the routine that might affect the recording of the event. Will a state or national seal be required? If it is a university graduation, is a university seal or mascot available? How will that be made available to the truck? What "supers" will be needed as identifiers? While the entire event may not be broadcast, the entire event will probably be recorded.

Production

During the production of the event, the director deals with the next shot. He or she will certainly be aware of events that are to unfold: "The president will be speaking tomorrow night at 8:00 EST" or "This session will end at about 10:00 P.M." or "We're going to need a station breakaway soon." But the immediate concern, as is the case with a news program, is what's happening immediately. More specifically, "air" has already happened or is in the process of unfolding. There's nothing one can do about that. So what's next? The director is relying on the producer and the producer's support staff to supply all of the relevant material in a timely fashion. Changes are handled before they get to the director, with the full awareness of the repercussions if the information doesn't get to the right people in enough time for them to do something about the changes.

Postproduction

No real postproduction is involved for live events such as these. However, the material can be of vital interest to news or documentary departments, for public relations purposes, and for historical archival needs. Thus, logging the material is essential. Time code or a time line is noted at the beginning and

end of significant speakers or events, and those notes or copies travel with the actual tapes, disks, or files. Production notes are maintained on file along with the archived material.

REVIEW

Significant remote formats are:

1. Presentational material: concerts, plays, operas, and so on
2. Sports
3. News and documentary events:
   • Television conventions such as a line of 180 degrees and those that pertain to cross-shooting are fundamental to all production whether in the studio or on location.

Remote camera positions are determined by:

1. Needs of the event
2. Availability of the hardware
3. Locations available to the production company
   • Jibs and cranes of various styles and configurations are significant directors' tools.
   • Preplanning for all remotes includes a "Tech Book," sometimes referred to as the "Production Book," which lists all the relevant crew, gear, and recording or transmission requirements.

The Tech Book answers questions about:

1. The venue: address, phone numbers, maps, directions, and so on
2. The crew: positions, phone numbers, e-mail addresses, and so on
3. The equipment: what's included, how, when, and where it functions
4. Recording or transmission requirements
5. Rehearsal and recording schedule

The two most frequent problems on all remotes are:

1. Light
2. Audio

Presentation

1. Lighting may have to augment the available light.

2. Audio, either show or broadcast, will need to work with:
   - Program audio—mixed or unmixed
   - "Foldback," which amplifies the voice of the singer to the musicians via speakers or headsets
   - "House audio" (public address—PA) for the audience
   - Private intercom for cameras, stage manager, lighting, and others related to the broadcast
   - Phone lines—sometimes
3. Generally speaking, the director of any event wants to know who, what, where, and when.

A director's fundamental tools are:

1. A ground plan of the venue and of the artist's stage area, including instruments and speaker placement
2. A rundown of the event
3. Knowledge of the remote: performance, sports, or event

Sports

A sports director sees sports as falling into one of three basic categories that relate to shooting the event:

1. Line sport
2. Circle sport

3. Form sport
   - Preproduction includes camera assignments prior to actual shooting so the director's camera and graphic instructions are kept to a minimum.

News and Documentary Events

All news events—all broadcast events, for that matter—come in one of two varieties:

1. Events in which you know what will happen
   - The producer's job at an anticipated news event is to make sure that whatever is needed to cover the event is available.
2. Events in which you don't know what will happen
   - When an event occurs without warning, the station does whatever it can to carry the story.

Logging news and documentary footage is essential:

1. Time code or the time line is noted for significant speakers or events, and those notes or copies travel with the actual tapes, disks, or files.
2. Production notes are maintained on file along with the archived material.

appendix one

Script Formatting

The following examples of the Pencil Exercise were formatted using FinalDraft 8 and FinalDraft AV. Some of the lines have been increased in length to indicate how they would be handled in a variety of formats. The layout of each script—stage plays, screenplays, daytime dramas, sitcoms, and audiovisual—is formatted in a specific way. The correct formatting is designed to facilitate the specific needs of each kind of production. The format is particularly critical to television production; there is always a large margin on the right which allows material to be written in a way that makes cues immediately identifiable, specific, and universally accepted. The sense behind the formatting of stage screen is as important. Stage directions, for which there are a number of formats, spread across an entire page. Screen formatting is critical because when it's correctly formatted, each page takes one minute of screen time. The two column formatting of AV scripts speaks for itself.

STAGE FORMAT

THE PENCIL EXERCISE - SCENE ONE

   THE SCENE: WHATEVER YOU WANT IT TO BE

                 BOY (CROSSES TO GIRL.)
I'm looking for my pencil. I'm looking for my pencil. I'm looking for my pencil.

                 GIRL
Yes.

                 BOY (CROSSES TO BAR)
I lost it.

                 GIRL
Yes.

                 BOY (CROSSES BACK TO GIRL.)
Have you seen it?... Have you seen it?... Have you seen it?

                 GIRL
No.

                 BOY (LEANS IN TOWARD GIRL.)
I thought I left it here.

                 GIRL (GETS PENCIL FROM BEHIND BOY'S
                 EAR.)
No.

                            LIGHTS OUT.

SCREENPLAY FORMAT

PENCIL EXERCISE - SCENE ONE

THE SCENE: WHATEVER YOU WANT IT TO BE

                                                    FADE IN:

BOY crosses to GIRL

                         BOY
              I'm looking for my pencil. I'm
              looking for my pencil. I'm looking
              for my pencil.

                         GIRL
              Yes.

BOY crosses to bar

                         BOY
              I lost it.

                         GIRL
              Yes.

BOY crosses back to GIRL

                         BOY
              Have you seen it?... Have you seen
              it?... Have you seen it?

                         GIRL
              No

BOY leans in toward GIRL

                         BOY
              I thought I left it here.

                         GIRL
              GIRL gets pencil from behind BOY's
              ear.

                         BOY
              No.

                                    FADE TO BLACK.

DAYTIME DRAMA - SITCOM FORMAT

THE PENCIL EXERCISE - SCENE ONE

THE SCENE: WHATEVER YOU WANT IT TO BE

FADE IN

                BOY

I'm looking for my pencil. I'm looking

for my pencil. I'm looking for my

pencil

                GIRL

Yes.

                BOY

I lost it.

                GIRL

Yes.

                BOY

Have you seen it?...Have you seen

it?...Have You seen it?...

                GIRL

No.

                BOY

I thought I left it here.

                GIRL

(GIRL GETS PENCIL FROM BEHIND BOY'S EAR.)

    No.

FADE TO BLACK

AUDIOVISUAL OR COMMERCIAL

Agency		Writer	
Client		Producer	
Project	PENCIL EXERCISE	Director	
Title		Art Director	
Subject		Medium	
Job #		Contact	
Code #		Draft	

VIDEO	AUDIO
THE SCENE WHATEVER YOU WANT IT TO BE FADE UP BOY enters and crosses to GIRL at desk	BOY: I'm looking for my pencil. I'm looking for my pencil. I'm looking for my pencil. GIRL: Yes
BOY crosses to bar	BOY: I lost it GIRL: Yes
BOY crosses back to GIRL	BOY: Have you seen it?... Have you seen it?.. Have you seen it?... GIRL: No
BOY leans in toward GIRL	BOY: I thought I left it here.
GIRL gets pencil from behind BOY'S ear. FADE TO BLACK	GIRL: No.

appendix two

Sources and Job Hunting

GUILDS, UNIONS, ASSOCIATIONS, AND INTERNET SITES

AAAA: American Association of Advertising Agencies; *aaaa.org*

Art Directors Guild: *artdirectors.org*

AFM: American Federation of Musicians; *afm.org*

AICE: Association of Creative Editors; *aice.org*

AICP: Association of Commercial Producers; *aicp.com*

AFTRA: The American Federation of Television and Radio Artists; *aftra.org*

AMPAS: The Academy of Motion Picture Arts and Sciences; *oscars.org*

AMPTP: The Alliance of Motion Picture and Television Producers; *amptp.org*

ATAS: The Academy of Television Arts and Sciences; *emmys.org*

CAB: Cable Television Advertising Bureau; *thecab.tv*

DGA: Directors Guild of America; *dga.org*

ESTA: Entertainment Services and Technology Association; *ESTA.org*

IATAS: International Television Academy of Arts and Sciences; *iemmys.tv*

MVPA: Music Video Producers Association; *mvpa.com*

NATAS: National Academy of Television Arts and Sciences; *emmyonline.org*

NATPE: National Association of Television Program Executives; *natpe.org*

NCTA: National Cable Television Association; *ncta.com*

Nielsen Media Research: *nielsen.com*

PGA: Producers Guild of America: *producersguild. org*

SAG: Screen Actors Guild; *sag.org*

SMPTE: Society of Motion Picture and Television Engineers; *smpte.org*

SOURCES

These are yearly directories that update film commissions, studios and stages, equipment, props, lighting, and costume sources, as well as listings of personnel for most production jobs. They also list associations, guilds, and unions, and serve as a "Yellow Pages" for the motion picture, television, and commercial production industry.

* Creative Industry Handbook: *creativehandbook.com*
* Debbies Book: *thesourcebookonline.com*
* Hollywood 911: *hollywood-911.com*
* Hollywood Creative Directory: *hcdonline.com*. This includes the Hollywood Creative Directory, Representation Directory, Distributors Directory, Music Directory, and the Blu-Book Production Directory.
* Motion Picture TV and Theater Directory: *mpe.net*
* Producers Master Guide: *producers. masterguide.com*

Most state film commissions publish listings that are helpful for location shooting. They can usually be found online or by contacting the particular

State Film Commission. They are also listed in the *Producer's Master Guide*.

JOB HUNTING

When it comes to job hunting, students and recent graduates have a different task from those who have been or are still in the industry. Faculty and other students make up the immediate networking pool, and networking is probably the best way to get a job or to change jobs. However, the most significant networking usually means that you've been around long enough to have a large pool with whom to network. For students, the most advantageous way to get a foot in the door and to network is to get an internship. With an internship the production company gets a college student to work at no cost. The student may prove to be valuable and, in any event, can easily be dismissed if he or she is counterproductive. Liability risks for the agency or production company are lessened or nonexistent. The student gets college credit and a great deal of knowledge about how that organization works. At the very least, while interning, professional networking opportunities abound. Along the way the student gets to know where the organization's copier is, where Joe the producer hides out, where Felicia the writer hangs out, who's who in the organization, and a great deal about how the organization works. When someone needs to be hired, the intern may be a comfortable choice because he or she is a known entity and has had the good fortune to have been at the right place at the right time.

To look for an internship, make a list of the organizations in your area. Call and explain that you want to intern at their company. Find out to whom you should apply. Write a concise cover letter and enclose a resume that includes work experience of any type. No one expects a college student to have an extensive, high-profile job history.

For help with resume writing, go to Google on the Internet and type in the word "resume." You will find millions of sites that deal with resumes. Some offer free templates, and sample cover letters are provided as well. You also might want to read *What Color Is Your Parachute?* by Dick Bolles, which is a standard job search reference source. Spell check *everything*. Most faculty members will be pleased to review your resume and cover letter.

Here is a sample cover letter for students. Make sure to include your name, address, phone number, and e-mail address.

Dear _____:

I am a student at _____ and wish to get an internship at _____. I am particularly interested in working in television production, and I have been taking as many classes as I can in related areas. I'd be glad to work in any area of your organization, as I recognize how important it would be for me to have a complete understanding of your organization's operations.

I have enclosed a resume and will call you in the next few days to discuss my qualifications in more detail. I would also appreciate any suggestions you might have for finding a position as an intern.

Sincerely yours,

Your Name

Finding a job is often a numbers game. The more contacts you make, the better your chances for success. Send out at least five letters every day, and keep track of them. Five days after you've sent a letter, call the company. Arrange an interview if possible. Expect rejections, and when that happens, just move on to the next name on the list. If you haven't had any luck after a month, start all over again, explaining that you've contacted a number of people and are still interested in a position. The situation may have changed at the company, and they may be more receptive to your inquiry. Once you get an interview, find out as much about the company as you can *before* you go to the interview. You'll make a good impression if you're knowledgeable about their operations and can ask valid questions. At the very least, they'll respect the fact that you took the time to do some research and are knowledgeable about the field. Of course, this doesn't guarantee that you'll get the job, but it has worked for many students.

If you're ready to get a job but haven't interned, you need to create a resume, and you can use a similar cover letter. If possible, include a statement that distinguishes some work you have done.

SAMPLE

Dear _____:

I recently graduated from _____ and would like to work at (Production Company name here). I am particularly interested in working in television production, and I have (majored in _____, or took a number of classes in television production, or took as many classes as I could in related areas). (Insert a sentence about any important award or recognition you've received or anything that will make you stand out.) I'd be glad to work in any area of your organization, as I recognize how important that experience would be for me.

I have enclosed my resume, and I will call you in the next few days. I hope I can meet with you and discuss working at (Production Company's name) or that you might be able to

offer some suggestions for finding a position in television production.

Sincerely yours,

Your Name,

The best advice I ever heard on the subject of successful interning came from a young director of the *Channel 5 Evening News* in Los Angeles: "Be better than average. Come early. Leave late. Do what no one else wants to do." She was a creative, intelligent, sensitive, and obviously persistent individual, and she later mentioned that she believed good time management skills were also very important.

Glossary and Jargon Buster

Many terms used in this book can have more than one meaning, depending on the country. This glossary provides explanations of terms and their equivalent British and American names as compiled by Ken Hall.

180 degree rule See *crossing the line*.

1+1 One plus one. One presenter plus one guest.

2+4 Two presenters plus four guests.

4-wire Bidirectional (two-way) communications wire.

5.1 Sound-surround sound system that has been accepted as part of the HDTV standard for the United States.

A/D Conversion converting an analog signal to a digital signal.

Actuality event Any event that is not specifically staged for television that exists in its own time scale.

Additive colors The color system that mixes colored light to create all of the various colors of the color spectrum.

Ad-lib shooting Impromptu and unrehearsed camera coverage. "Grab shots" in America.

AES/EBU (American Engineering Society/European Broadcasting Union) Standards Organizations that, among other specifications, have agreed on an industry standard digital interface. Also see *SMPTE* (US).

Algorithms Complex mathematical formulas used in defining digital compression.

Aliasing Incorrect sampling due to input frequencies exceeding one-half of the sampling rate.

Alternating current An electrical circuit through which the flow of electrons reverses itself from negative to positive, from positive to negative, and back again at a regular rate.

Amperes (amps) The unit of measurement for current.

Amplitude Maximum size of a waveform or signal.

Analog signal Electrical impulse that is analogous of the original sound or light source in terms of magnitude and/or frequency.

Anchor Main presenter in a news/current affairs program.

Angle-of-view Horizontal angle of view of a specific focal length.

Aperture correction (current term *detail*) A way of electronically compensating for distortion introduced by facets of the system including the camera, and the scanning aperture.

ASA (American Standards Association) Method of rating the speed of film. Replaced by International Standards Organization, ISO, or Exposure Index, EI.

As-directed Unrehearsed camera coverage controlled at any moment by the director.

As-live Continuous recording of a program as though it were being broadcast live.

Aspect ratio Proportion of the picture width to its height—for example, 4:3, 16:9.

Assemble edit Recording process where video, audio, and time code are recorded, in sequence, to a blank tape.

Aston (UK) Generic name for any text or caption generator.

Attenuation Reduction of the signal level.

Audio board or audio console (US) Audio device that allows you to bring several sound sources together, choose among them, mix them together, modify them through equalization (EQ), measure their strength, and hear them.

Audio mixer (UK) Audio device that allows you to bring several sound sources together, choose among them, mix them together, modify them through equalization (EQ), measure their strength, and hear them.

Audio-follows-video switcher Switcher that changes both audio and video sources with the push of one button.

Audio pot (US) Fader that controls an audio level.

Autocue (UK) UK-based manufacturer of teleprompter systems. See *teleprompter*.

Auto-gain Electronic circuit that automatically adjusts the audio recording level to keep within prescribed limits. Sometimes referred to as *automatic gain control* (AGC).

Auto-iris Automatic adjustment of the iris depending on the main subject's luminance.

Back focus (US) See *flange-back*.

Back porch Portion of the waveform scan that represents the horizontal blanking just before the start of a new line of video.

Backlight Used to separate a subject from the background by rim lighting the subject from behind.

Back timing The practice of commencing playing of closing music at start of track with volume at zero and fading music in when desired thus ensuring that music ends on cue at finish of programme, also used for closing credits in some situations.

Balance The relative level between sources in a sound or video signal.

Balanced line Connection of audio signals where the two signal paths are separate from Earth.

Bandwidth Range of frequencies required for successful transmission of audio (20 kHz) or television (PAL, 5.5 MHz).

Barndoors Lighting term: Hinged metal flaps on the front of an instrument used to control the spread of light.

Bars See *color bars*.

Bass Lower end of the audio frequency spectrum.

Battery light Small battery-powered lamp often mounted on top of a camera.

Betacam A 12.5 mm tape cassette video format recording, on two adjacent video heads, the luminance signal (Y) and a chroma signal consisting of a compressed time division multiplex of the color difference signals (R-Y and B-Y).

Big close-up (BCU) Description of the size of a shot when applied to the face. Includes the point of the chin to the midforehead.

Bit Unit of binary code.

BITC (pronounced "bitsey") Burned-in time code where the time code has been permanently printed onto the video image and is always visible on the screen. Used for tape offline editing.

Bitstream Series of binary digits.

Black balance Automatic adjustment of the black level of the camera.

Black burst Signal from the sync generator that includes all normal blanking and video cameras and players in sync in a multicamera system.

Black burst generator A device that generates a synchronizing pulse to synchronize video equipment. It provides a signal to help maintain uniform video levels and color information.

Black level Amplitude of the television video signal representing the darkest part of the picture.

Black wrap Black anodized aluminum foil used to control spill light or shaping a light beam.

Blanking The time when the electron guns in the system are turned down to a low voltage so they can return to the beginning of a new line or field without being visible on the screen.

Blanking pulses Signals from the sync generator that tells the camera's electron gun to go into blanking.

Blonde A 2000 W portable lamp.

Blue screen Choma-key background used in color separation overlay, now largely replaced with a green screen background.

BNC Twist-lock cable connector often used on monitor video cables.

Boom (or arm) mover (US) Alternative name for a sound boom swinger.

Bouncing Method of transferring audio from one track to another. Also, a method of obtaining a soft light source from a hard source.

Boom (UK) See *jib*.

B-Roll (US) Video coverage, which aids in editing and illuminates the specifics of a story.

Breaker button Automatic cutoff of power supply to electronic equipment if overload is detected.

Brightness Term often incorrectly used to mean luminance, a subjective effect, and relative to darkness.

Bus Connection point in a sound desk for a number of signals.

Bus row Row of buttons on a switcher that allows the operator to change between various video sources that are available in the system.

Butterfly Large frame to hold nets, silks, or blacks measuring 6×6 feet, 12×12 feet, or 20×20 feet.

Byte Smallest piece of computer memory that can be used as a distinct piece of information. Made up of a group of bits.

Camera angle The position of the camera relative to the main subject in the shot.

Camera control unit (CCU) The base station for a studio camera. On this (or through a remote control panel) you can adjust all of the camera and many of the engineering settings.

Camera left Left of frame as opposed to the artist's left when facing the camera.

Camera right Right of frame as opposed to the artist's right when facing the camera.

Candela The unit of measurement of the luminous intensity of a lamp.

Canting the camera Angling the camera so the horizon is not parallel to the bottom of the frame. Sometimes referred to as a *Dutch angle*.

Capgen (UK) Caption Generator creates text on screen, generating two signals: a video and a key.

Capstan servo See *vertical lock*.

Caption generator Electronic equipment that allows text to be created and manipulated on screen via a keyboard.

CCD (charge-coupled device) Analog solid-state device used instead of a pickup tube for changing light images into an electronic analog video signal.

Chroma Another name for saturation, a control usually found on monitors. Also, the color information in a TV signal.

Chroma-key An electronic process for inserting video sources, usually an artist (foreground), into a background picture. Also known as color separation overlay (CSO) in the BBC. Also, a tracking digital effect that compresses the signal from a video source into the available chroma-key window.

Chrominance The color part of a signal showing hue and saturation.

Clean feed An audio source providing a program participant with all of the audio signals but excluding his or her own audio contribution.

Clear or clearance The instruction to a cameraperson to move to his or her next position or to a stage manager regarding the end of a sequence.

Close-up (CU) A shot size that when applied to the face, the top of the frame rests slightly above the top of the head, and the bottom of the frame cuts across the chest or shoulders subject to local production standards.

C-mount Standard broadcast video lens mount.

Coaxial cable Cable with a central conductor surrounded by a sheath of screening used for video signals.

Coincident pair Two microphones in the same vertical plane arranged to pick up a stereo image.

Coloration Unpleasant effect where sound is repeated with a small time delay. Occurs when two microphones pick up the same sound.

Color balance See *white balance*.

Color bars Test signal used in color television to match monitors.

Color difference component video Video system that saves bandwidth by using the luminance (Y) of the green channel from the RGB signal and the two other color channels with the luminance removed (R-Y and B-Y).

Color separation overlay (CSO) BBC terminology for the electronic process for inserting video sources.

Color temperature Convenient way to describe the color of a light source by relating it to a black body radiator measured in Kelvins (K), named after its inventor Lord Kelvin.

Complementary color The secondary color that when added to a primary color makes white light.

Component video The individual or different signals derived from the red, blue, green, and luminance video signals.

Component switcher Video switcher that switches a signal that is composed of individual color components (red, green, and blue) of the picture rather than the encoded composite video signal.

Composite The color signals encoded (combined) with the luminance signal and sync information.

Compression (1) Process of reducing the amount of signal data that is required to be passed through a finite channel while trying to maintain the quality of the originating signal. Also a means of preventing audio signals from overmodulating. (2) Spatial video compression that takes place within an individual video frame that contributes to overall bandwidth reduction. (3) Temporal video compression that takes place between successive video frames and helps reduce overall bandwidth needs.

Condenser Type of microphone using charged plates to transfer sound pressure changes into electrical signals.

Connector (UK) In-line plugs and sockets at each end of signal cables.

Console Audio signal mixing device or a lighting console. In the United Kingdom, it usually refers to audio.

Continuous shooting (UK) When a program is shot in the order in which it will be viewed.

Contrast ratio Ratio between the brightest part of the subject and the darkest part.

Control track Regular pulse recorded on videotape to identify the position of the video signal and tape speed.

Control Room (US) Production control room, housing lighting, video, and sound control gear and associated operators. See *gallery* (UK).

Convergence The ability to converge all three television rasters (RGB) into a single raster.

Cookie or cucoloris (US) Perforated plate used to break up a light beam producing a dapple or soft shadow effect.

Crabbing 360 degree movement of a camera mount achieved by locking the wheels in the same direction.

Crash zoom Either an intentionally maximum speed zoom or an "emergency" fast zoom to recompose "on-shot."

Crib card (UK) Card attached to the side of the camera describing the planned shots and production information connected with that camera.

Cross-talk Unwanted signal picked up between adjacent audio signal cables or from one audio track to another.

Crossing the line Moving the camera to the opposite side of an imaginary line drawn between two or more subjects after recording a shot of one of the subjects, resulting in intercut faces looking out of the same side of frame and the impression that they are not in conversation with each other.

CSO (color separation overlay) See *chroma-key*.

CTDM Compressed time division multiplexed chrominance recording. Part of the Betacam method of recording.

Cue Particular lighting condition or an indication for action to start—that is, the actor to start performing or a lighting change to start.

Cursor Vertical or horizontal line that can be positioned by the cameraperson in the viewfinder as a reminder of a precise frame position or to check a vertical or horizontal visual element.

Curtains (US) Studio lead-in and lead-out of news stories.

Cut to line The video source selected as the output of the vision mixing panel.

Cutaway camera Shot that is intercut in a sequence to cover camera movement or as a means of maintaining continuity between shots. See *B-Roll* (US).

Cutter Lighting term: Similar to a flag, but long and narrow, usually used to create an edge to a beam of light.

Cyclorama Backcloth of neutral color on which light is played as a background to a shot.

D to A converter (DAC) Converts digital video or audio signals into an analog signal.

DAT Digital audiotape.

Daybook (US) Newsroom daily event diary.

DCC (dynamic contrast control) Compresses highlights of the picture to allow a greater contrast range to be recorded.

Decibel (dB) Logarithmic ratio of changes in sound intensity that mirrors the ear's response to changes in sound intensity.

Density Measure of the light transmitted by a filter.

Depth of field Zone of acceptable focus in the field of view.

Dichroic block A mix of glass layers that lets some colors through and reflects others. Used in the front of cameras to split light into its separate primary colors.

Dichroic filter Mixture of glass layers with different refractive indices, designed to reflect one color while passing other colors through.

Diffuser Material that scatters the light to create a softer light source.

Digital data Stream of individual binary numbers (zeros and ones) representing an unbroken variable (analog) value.

Digital encoding ratio Ratio that indicates the relationship between the amount of luminance (Y) and chrominance (B-Y and R-Y). Information that is contained in a digital signal—for example, 4:2:2 or 4:1:1.

Dimmer Electronic device for controlling the light output from a light source. Usually a thyristor or silicon controller rectifier (SCR), but recent developments have included the transistor dimmer. It changes the color temperature of the lighting instrument.

Direct current Electrical system in which the flow of electrons moves in only one direction and is the standard for electrical supply for many systems.

Director Responsible for selecting the images that go to air or are recorded for later broadcast.

Discharge light source Envelope that produces light by ionizing a gas contained in the bubble.

Discontinuous shooting (UK) When a program that is shot in order of locations and convenience rather than in the order in which it will be ultimately seen.

Dissolve Term for a mix between two shots.

Distortion To change from the normal. Often used to indicate unwanted damage to an analog signal that results in the output signal of a system being different from the original.

Dolby noise reduction process Used in audiorecording and playback.

Down stage Moving toward the camera or audience.

Drop frame When set in the drop frame mode, the SMPTE time code will consistently skip a number in the sequence. Since time code normally counts 30 frames a second when video really only has 29.97 frames a second, this is necessary so the time code can be consistent with the real time on a clock.

Dropout Short loss of a recorded signal due to faulty head-to-tape contact or tape imperfections.

Dry The inability of a performer either to remember or to continue with his or her presentation.

Dubbing Process of copying the electronic signal from one tape to another.

Dutch Angle (US) or Dutch shot (UK) A shot taken by a camera tilted so the horizon is not parallel to the bottom of the frame.

Dynamic range Difference between the highest and the lowest values of sound intensity or picture brightness that can be reproduced in a signal.

EBU (European Broadcasting Union) Advisory and regulatory body for broadcasting in Europe.

Edited master Final version of edited material that will be seen by the viewer.

EDL Edit decision list created to define the in and out points of an edit sequence.

Effects (FX) or (EFX) Visual or audio effects.

EFP (electronic field production) Term used to describe single-camera location video program making other than news.

Electronic shutter Electronic method of varying the length of exposure time of the CCD. Can be used to improve the slow-motion reproduction of motion.

Encode Technique of combining color information with a luminance (monochrome) signal.

ENG (electronic news gathering) Single-camera video recording of news events.

Equalization Increase or decrease in the level of chosen audio frequencies.

Establishing shot Initial shot that gives the maximum information about the subject.

EVDS (enhanced vertical definition system) Method of reducing motion blur.

Extender Additional lens that can be switched internally to extend the range of focal lengths of prime and zoom lenses.

Eyeline Direction the subject is looking within in the frame.

Face tones Signal derived from face tones, typically (average European face) about 0.5 V.

Facility (US) TV studio complex.

Fader Control for varying the level of an audio or video signal. Also a lighting fader controlling an instrument or "gang" of instruments.

Feed Either a video signal or the cable that carries the signal.

Field One Alternate line top-to-bottom scan of an image. Two fields interlaced make up one frame.

Fill light A light source used to make shadows transparent—that is, to reduce the contrast.

Filter wheels Filter holders of color correction, neutral density, or effects filters that are arranged within the camera to allow for quick selection by rotating a thumbwheel.

First generation Acquisition medium on which the video signal was first recorded.

Flag (US) Piece of metal, card, or soft black cloth in a wire frame placed near the front of a lighting instrument to give a hard edge cutoff to the light beam.

Flange-back (UK) Distance from the flange surface of the lens mount to the image plane of the pickup sensor commonly known as the back focus.

Flight kit Portable set of location lighting instruments and stands able to be packed in a compact container for easy transportation.

F-number Also *F-Stop* Method of indicating how much light is being allowed to pass through the aperture of the lens.

Focal length Distance from the principal point of a compound lens (e.g., a zoom lens) to the point at which rays from an object at infinity form the most sharply defined image.

Focus pull Moving the zone of sharpest focus to another subject.

Foldback Feed to allow artists to hear selected sound sources on loudspeakers or headphones.

Foot candle Unit of illuminance in imperial units, $1 \text{ lumen/ft}^2 = 1$ foot.

Format The video medium used to record the image (e.g., DVCPRO, S-VHS; Betacam, etc.).

Frame lock Method of stabilizing videotape playback that tries to match an even field of the playback signal to an even field coming from the sync generator and an odd field of the playback signal to an odd field coming from the sync generator.

Frame One complete television picture comprising two interlaced fields or a single video image in (US) $2 \times 262.5 = 525$ lines and (UK) $2 \times 312.5 = 625$.

Frame rate Number of images or frames per second recorded on videotape. Different frame rates pertain: (US) 29.29 (known as drop-frame) or 30 FPS and (UK) 25 FPS.

Frame store Electronic device for storing individual video frames.

Frame store synchronizer (Frame Synchronizer) Device used to lock up nonsynchronous video signals to the main system.

Free run Frame identification by time code that is set to the actual time of day when the frame was recorded.

Frequency Number of complete Hertz or cycles per second.

Frequency response Range of frequencies that a particular system can reproduce without distortion.

Fresnel Stepped lens used in lighting instruments. Named after French physicist Augustin Fresnel, who invented the lens in 1822.

Front porch Portion of the waveform scan that represents the horizontal blanking at the end of a line of video.

Fundamental Original or lowest frequency of a complex signal.

Gaffer (US) Chief lighting electrician.

Gain Amplification of a video or audio signal calibrated in dBs (e.g., +6dB of video gain is the equivalent of opening the lens iris by 1 stop).

Gallery (UK) Production control room.

Gamma Law of the transfer characteristic of a system—that is, the relationship between input and output signals.

GEO Geosynchronous orbit satellite that revolves at the same rotational speed as Earth and appears to be stationary from Earth's surface.

Gimmie (US) Any piece of a production kit that would be available in a studio-based production facility but would have to be requisitioned for a remote facility.

Gobo A stencil, often made of stainless steel, used in profile projectors to create effects—for example, windows, abstract patterns, or the moon.

Grads Abbreviation for graduated applied to front-of-lens filters that progressively filter or color the picture vertically.

Graticule Engraved calibration scale on the front of waveform monitors and vectorscopes.

Grid Area lighting suspension structure above a studio floor.

Grip (US) Supporting equipment for lighting or camera equipment. Also, the name of the technicians responsible for handling grip equipment, such as camera trucks and dollies.

GV (general view) A long-shot of the subject.

Gyroscopic time base error Time base error created when a videotape recorder is moved perpendicular to the plane of the head drum's rotation.

Handheld Operating a portable camera without a camera mounting.

Hard light Any light source, usually produced by a lens system, that casts a well-defined shadow.

Harmonic Range of frequencies that are multiples of the fundamentals that make up a complex waveform.

HDMI (High-Definition Multimedia Interface) interface for carrying uncompressed audio and video digital data signals.

Helical Method of videorecording that lays down video information at a slant to the tape's direction of travel. Also known as *slant track recording*.

Hertz Unit of frequency, 1 Hertz=1 cycle/second.

High angle Any lens height above eye level.

High key Picture with predominance of light tones and thin shadows. Originally, a high key was a light that was hung from a high grid.

Horizontal blanking Period extending from the time the electron guns are turned down to a low voltage at the end of a line until they are turned back up at the beginning of a new line.

Horizontal lock Method of stabilizing videotape playback that tries to match a horizontal sync pulse of the playback signal to each horizontal sync pulse coming from the sync generator.

Horizontal sync Signal from the sync generator that causes the electron gun to return to the other side of the screen for a new line.

Hot head (US) Remotely controlled camera pan/tilt head often on the end of a jib arm.

Hue Dominant wavelength, or color describing what we see—for example, red.

IFB interrupt foldback A sound feed (e.g., a program clean feed going to a presenter at an outside broadcast (OB)) or "remote" that someone (e.g., a director or producer) can override, usually by pressing a toggle switch or button. An easy way to speak to the presenter through a single earpiece feed.

Illuminance (illumination) (E) A unit of light measurement for incident light, lumens/m^2=lux.

Image size Image formed by the lens on the face of the CCD.

Impedance Measurement of the properties that tell whether two or more circuits will interact well, measured in ohms.

Insert edit Adding of video, audio, or time code, out of sequence.

Insert point An input/output in a system allowing the connection of other equipment.

Instrument (US) Name for a complete lighting unit—that is, light source plus its casing.

Intercom (US) System of communication between director and production staff.

Interlace Method of scanning separate parts of an image in two passes (fields) in order to reduce the bandwidth required for transmission.

Interlace scanning Process of taking a field of odd-numbered lines (1, 3, 5, 7, . . .) and combining it with a field of even-numbered lines (2, 4, 6, 8, . . .) to make a complete video frame (525).

Inverse square law Fundamental law in lighting and sound where the intensity of light and sound falls off as the inverse of the distance squared.

Invisible technique Production method that emphasizes the content of the shot rather than the production technique.

Iris Variable circular aperture in the camera used to control exposure, calculated in f-stops.

ISDN (integrated services digital network) System that allows the transfer of audio or other data via a telephone line.

Isoed (US) Recording the (isolated) output of an individual camera or cameras in a multicamera shoot in addition to the main recording.

Jib (US)/Boom (UK) Tripod mounted arm on which a camera is mounted allowing it to shoot from low and high levels.

JPEG (joint photographic experts group) Identifies a standard for the data compression of still pictures.

Kelvin (K) Unit of measurement of heat used to describe color.

Key Keying signal for chroma-key operations for graphic generation of type or other source.

Key Mood of a picture—that is, high key/low key.

Keylight or key Main source of light illuminating the subject.

Kicker (US) Light used at eye level from upstage. At eye level, to "kick" the side of the artist's head.

Knee Modified part of the transfer characteristic of a camera designed to progressively compress highlights.

Lamp (UK) Glass envelope that produces light in a lighting instrument.

Level Volume of an audio or video signal. The amount of light or sound.

Linear editing Traditional method of videotape editing in which one scene is laid down after another on tape.

Linear keys Keys in which the keyhole is not cut entirely through the background video, allowing that video to be seen through the overlying key.

Line level Reference audio level measured at 1000 Hz.

Liko (US) Hard-edged lighting instrument (or luminaire) used to illuminate areas that require a defined area of light.

Live The transmission of an event as it takes place.

Locked-off Applying the locks on a pan and tilt head to ensure that the camera setting remains in a preselected position.

Long lens Lens with a large focal length or using a zoom at or near its narrowest angle of view.

Low angle Lens height below eye height.

Low key Picture with a predominance of dark tones and strong shadows.

LS (long shot) Description of a shot when the full-length human figure fills the frame.

LTC (longitudinal time code) Recorded with a fixed head on a designated track on the tape.

Lumen Unit of quantity of light flow per second, "weighted" by the photopic curve.

Luminaire (UK) Name given for a complete lighting unit—that is, the light source plus its casing.

Luminance Monochrome or black-and-white portion of the video signal.

Luminance (L) A measure of the light reflected from a surface. A total flux reflected of 1 lumen/m^2 has a luminance of 1 Apostilb. (Imperial measurement 1 lumen/ft^2 = 1 foot lambert.) Relative brightness points of an image.

Luminance keys Keys in which the hole being cut is determined by the brightness of the video source.

Luminous intensity Measure of a lamp's capability to radiate light, measured in candelas (old term *candlepower*).

Lux A unit for illuminance; 1 lumen/m^2 = 1 lux. Also, a unit of measurement used to describe the amount of light received at a particular point.

Macro Switchable facility on a lens that allows focusing on an object placed closer to the lens than the normal minimum object distance. See *MOD*.

Master shot See *establishing shot*.

Matrix Electrical circuit for deriving "mixtures" of signals—for example, color difference signals and luminance signals from RGB signals.

Matte box Filter holder and bellows extension for the control of flare, fitted to the front of the lens.

Matte key Luminance key whereby the "hole" created by the key is filled with artificially created color from the switcher.

Medium close-up (MCU) Shot description for framing a person with the bottom of the frame cutting where a suit breast pocket would normally be.

Medium shot (MS) Description of shot size with the bottom of the frame cutting at the waist when applied to the human figure.

Megahertz (MHz) One million cycles per second.

Metal particle Videotape coating allowing a wider frequency response to be recorded and an improved signal-to-noise ratio compared to oxide tape coating.

Millisecond One-thousandth of a second.

Mired Micro-reciprocal degree value allows the relationship between a correction filter and the color temperature shift to be calculated.

Mix minus (also known as *program clean feed*) Audio of program output without one of the outside broadcast sources.

MOD Minimum object distance; the closest distance a subject in acceptable focus can be to the lens.

Modeling Action of light revealing contour and texture of a subject.

Monitor termination Switchable electronic "load" (usually 75 ohms) on the back of a monitor inserted at the end of a video cable feed to prevent the signal from "bouncing back."

Monochrome Reproduction of a single color such as a black-and-white image.

Monopod A one legged device for supporting a camera. Sometimes called a Unipod.

Movement blur Degradation of the image related to the speed of the subject movement during the exposure time of a single picture.

MPEG2 (Moving Picture Experts Group 2) Benchmark value specifying a degree of compression.

Multigeneration Numerous rerecordings of the original recording.

NAB (National Association of Broadcasters) Professional trade association for broadcasters in US, advances the interests of members in federal government, industry, and public affairs; improves the quality and profitability of broadcasting; encourages content and technology innovation; and spotlights the important and unique ways stations serve their communities.

Narrow end of the lens Longest focal length of the zoom that can be selected.

Neutral density filter Filter that reduces the amount of light transmitted without altering the color temperature.

Ni-Cad Nickel-cadmium, the constituent of rechargeable batteries widely used to power broadcast camcorders and cameras.

Nodders (US) or Noddies (UK) Cutaway shots recorded for editing purposes after an interview. Shows the interviewer listening and reacting to the interviewee's comments.

Noise reduction Method of reducing the noise on recorded or transmitted analog audio.

Nonlinear editing Method in which video information is edited.

NTSC System of color television used in the United States and other parts of the world. The system uses 525 scanning lines and 60 fields with 30 frames per second. (The field and frame rates have been rounded off.) The name is an acronym for the National Television Systems Committee, which was a group of industry experts who developed and proposed the system to the Federal Communications Commission in the early 1950s.

OB (outside broadcast) Usually a multicamera production from a nonstudio venue using a mobile control room. In the United States, it is called a *remote* broadcast.

OB van (UK) Mobile gallery used in outside broadcasts.

OFCOM (UK) Office of Communications, independent regulator for radio, television, and telecommunications industries in the UK.

Off-line editing Low-quality images that are used to produce edit lists, or a nontransmittable edited guide tape.

Off-shot The camera when its output is not selected at the vision mixing panel to be fed "to line."

On-line editing System that produces a final edited broadcast-quality program.

On-shot Also *Online* The output of the camera selected at the vision mixing panel to be fed "to line."

Opacity Reciprocal of transmission of light through a film or filter.

Open architecture Concept of using computers with highly specialized programs to replace traditional dedicated equipment. Hence, a computer could be a time base corrector, edit controller, video switcher, digital effects unit, and character generator all in one.

Oscillator Equipment to produce pure tone (sine wave) used for lining up and calibrating systems.

Oscilloscope Cathode-ray oscilloscope used to provide a visual display of video signals.

Overscanning Television set that cuts off the edges of the picture. The opposite of underscanning, which shows the entire picture into the corners of the screen.

Oxide tape Coating used in the first generation of the beta format cameras.

Pad Circuit used to reduce or attenuate the level of a signal level.

PAL (phase alternate lines) Color television system that was designed in Germany to overcome some of the problems of NTSC. Uses 625 scanning lines with 50 fields and 25 frames per second. Used in Western Europe and many other parts of the world.

PAL-M Color television system similar to PAL designed for countries that use a 60 Hz frequency for their AC power supply and therefore has 60 fields and 30 frames per second.

Pan-pot (panoramic potentiometer) Adjusts the apparent position of a sound source in a stereo image.

Peak program meter (PPM) Measures sound by averaging the peaks of intensity over a specified period and rapidly responds to high-level transients, usually calibrated from 0 to PPM 7.

Peak white Either a 100-percent video signal level or a 60-percent reflectance neutral gray surface.

Ped (pedestal) A camera mounting.

Pedestal The black level of a video camera. Also, black portions or areas of the picture on a TV screen.

Perspective Apparent position of closeness of sound in an image. Also, the optical methods used to assess or construct image depth.

PFL Prefade listen. A way of listening to an audio signal before it goes on the air. Used by sound engineer to check that an audio source is present.

Phantom power DC supply to some types of condenser microphones using the signal cable.

Phase Time delay between two signals in degrees. The actual time will vary with frequency.

Pickups Additional shots or sequences that may be recorded at any time in order to get clean material that can be edited into a seamless sequence. Pickups eliminate the need to start from the beginning of a sequence or to move away from ongoing action in a shot.

Picture monitor Good-quality viewing monitor fed with a component signal but without RF and sound.

Pink noise Random signal that appears to the human ear to contain a wide variety of frequencies.

Pipe (US) Metal tube from which luminaires are suspended. Lighting bar or barrel in the UK.

Pistol grip Hand grip controlling zoom movement that may be attached to a camera.

Pixel (picture cell) Smallest component into which a picture can be subdivided.

Planning meetings Meeting of some members of the production staff held for the exchange of information and planning decisions concerning a future program.

Playback Replaying a recorded shot or sequence of shots or audio.

PLUGE (UK) (picture line-up generating equipment) Test signal used for alignment of picture monitor contrast and brightness.

Point-of-view shot (POV) Shot from a lens position that seeks to duplicate the viewpoint of a subject depicted on the screen.

Polecat (US) Adjustable spring-loaded aluminum tubes with rubber feet that can be used vertically or horizontally to support lightweight luminaires.

Pole-operation System for remotely adjusting pan/tilt, spot/flood, and so on, of lighting instruments from the studio floor using an operating pole.

Polestar (UK) Lighting instrument that is capable of having its beam-spread, pan and tilt angles adjusted from a pole.

Postproduction Editing and other work carried on prerecorded videotape.

Practical Anything that must actually work in a shot: a lamp for a light source, a faucet that works or eggs that are to be broken on screen.

Preview monitor (UK) Picture monitor in a control room that displays the next shot to go to air.

Primary colors (television) The colors red, green, and blue.

Prime lens Fixed focal length lens.

Print-through Transfer of magnetic information from one layer of tape to another on a reel.

Production Assistant (PA) (US) There are two major types: Runners and Booth PAs. Runners are the "gophers" and run various errands for the production and the producers. Booth PAs log the takes during taping and recording and take notes.

Production Assistant (UK) Works in the gallery or control room of a TV studio, relays the shot selections of the director to camera operators and other crew during the shoot of a TV programme, and counts the programme on and off air (calls the shots).

Production control room Production areas on outside broadcasts (see *scanner*). Adjacent to studios used by production staff, lighting, and audio.

Production house (UK) Independent studio hired for production.

Production switcher (US) Video switcher.

Prompters Coated glass positioned in front of the lens to reflect text displayed on a TV monitor below the lens.

PSA (US) Public service announcement.

PSB (UK) Public service broadcast.

PSC (portable single camera) Production method of recording material on a portable single-video camera.

Pull out (UK) See *widen out*.

Pulse coded modulation (PCM) Digital audio encoding system.

Purity In a monitor, the ability of the red gun to hit only red phosphors, and so on.

Quarter-inch scale (US) Scale used (1/4"=1'-0", or 1:48) in reproducing studio plans on paper and very close to the European metric scale of 2 cm=1 m, or 1:50.

Quantize Allocation of "sample" level prior to coding in a digital system.

Quantizing Process of converting a sample of video information into digital pulses.

Racking focus or rocking focus Moving the focus zone in front of and behind the selected subject.

Radio Mic (UK) Microphone without a cable that transmits the audio to a receiver connected to the sound desk by radio or wireless frequency signals.

Readies (US) Term given to the preview shot, which is the shot that will be put on the air after the current shot.

Real time Actual running time of an event as opposed to "screen time." The compression of time achievable by editing.

Real time Time code that changes in step with the actual time of day.

Recces The inspection of a location by production staff to assess the practicalities involved in its use as a setting for a program or program insert.

Receptacle (US) See *connector*.

Recorded-as-live Continuous recording with no recording breaks.

Record-run Time code that only records frame identification when the camera is recording.

Redhead (UK) 800 W portable lightweight luminaire.

Redundancy In signal compression, the part that can be determined from the signal already received and that therefore need not be sent.

Reflector Any white or silvered surface that can be used to reflect light.

Remote (US) Usually a multicamera production from a nonstudio venue.

Remote truck (US) Vision and sound-mixing facility for a remote multicamera production.

Rental facility (US) Studio hired for production by day, week, month, or series.

Reverberation Gradual decay of reflected sound.

Reverse angle When applied to a standard two-person interview, a camera repositioned 180 degrees to the immediate shot being recorded to provide a complementary shot of the opposite subject.

RF mic (US) Radio-controlled battery-operated microphone used with a transmitter and receiver.

RMS (root mean square) Method of calculating the effective value of an audio signal.

Robotic (US) A camera head in which pan/tilt, zoom, focus, and sometimes position and height can be remotely controlled. Also full robotic action including dolly moves.

Room Tone (US) Ambient background of recording location.

Routine (US) Program running order.

Rule of Thirds Method of picture composition that divides the 4:3 screen into nine boxes allowing the camera operator to position the main elements of the image appropriately within the boxes.

Rundown (US) Program running order.

S/PDIF Consumer version of the digital interface agreed by Sony and Philips (Sony-Philips digital interface).

Sample rate Number of measurement points over time that a continuously variable signal is measured.

Sampling Process of "grabbing" a piece of analog video information so it can be quantized or converted into binary code zeros and ones.

Saturation Measure of the purity of a color—for example, pale red or deep red.

Scoop Soft light or flood.

Scope (UK) See *talescope*.

SDTV (standard definition digital television) Digital equal to the analog color standard.

SECAM (sequential couleur a memoire) French-developed method of encoding color.

Secondary colors Cyan, magenta, and yellow, which are created by mixing any two primary colors (red, green, and blue).

Self-fill key Luminance key in which the hole cut is filled by the video that cut the hole.

Shot box Preset control on a camera that remembers a range of shots and moves.

Shot number Number assigned to a specific shot as detailed in a camera script or camera rehearsal.

Shot Sheets (US) Card attached to the camera describing the planned shots and production information connected with that camera.

Shooting Ratio Ratio of shot footage to final footage actually used in a program.

Shuttling Rapidly reviewing videotape to determine content or edit point.

Signal to noise ratio Difference in dB between the signal and the inherent background system noise.

Simple PAL Monitor mode that enables the eye to average out color errors—that is, no delay line used. Also enables phase errors to be seen.

Single shot technique Discontinuous recording by a single camera of a number of shots that are later edited in postproduction.

Sitcom ("situation comedy") Minidrama (usually of approximately 30 minutes duration) often performed before an audience.

Slo-mo replay Replaying a prerecorded material at a slower speed.

Slug Blank footage inserted into the film or video to represent a portion of the program that is to be added later (a placeholder). The slug will be the exact length of the forthcoming footage so that it matches the final piece.

SMPTE (Society of Motion Picture and Television Engineers) Professional organization of electrical engineers that focuses on motion picture and broadcast technology. See *AES/EBU* (UK).

SNG (satellite news gathering) Technique of relaying video location news reports or news material via a satellite to a base station.

Soaps (UK) Refered to as daytime dramas (examples: *Eastenders, Coronation Street, Emmerdale*).

Soft light Light source that produces a soft-edged shadow.

SOT Sound on tape.

Sound board (US) Audio mixing desk.

SOVT Sound on videotape.

SPL Sound pressure level expressed in dB where the reference is the threshold of hearing.

Spot effects Sounds that relate to short actions, door knocks, gunfire, telephone ring, usually in vision.

Stage Left The talent's left when on a set.

Stage manager (US) Person responsible to the director for production issues and activities on the studio floor.

Stage Right The talent's right when on set.

Star quad Four-core sound cable designed to reduce unwanted electromagnetic noise pickup.

Station out Program output being fed to a transmitter, satellite, or cable distribution system.

Stereo System of reproducing a spatial sound image using two channels.

Stop The f-number or aperture of the lens.

Stringer (US) A video stringer is a freelance video journalist who works predominantly in the evening hours, when station crews are slim or nonexistent, covering events he or she hears about by listening to police and fire department transmissions on radio scanners. In UK a **freelancer**.

Studio manager Person who deals with studio/management issues.

Studio out Output of the vision mixing panel.

Super Abbreviation for Superimpose. Key a source over a background video.

Switcher (US) Vision control desk in a studio control room for selecting and manipulating the shots or images that are recorded or go to air.

Sync generator Device that provides various sync signals (drive pulses, blanking pulses, and sync pulses) to keep all of the equipment in a video system working together.

Sync pulse Signal from the sync generator that causes the electron guns to return to the beginning of a new video line or field.

Synchronous Vision source that can be used on air because it starts each field at the same time as all the other sources.

Talent (US) Anyone who works in front of the camera.

Talescope Vertical access ladder on a wheeled frame used to focus luminaires fixed on the grid of a studio.

Talkback Intercommunication by microphone and headset between a television control room and other operational areas.

Talking heads Close-up shots of talent intercut with each other as in a panel show.

Tally light Vision mixers can send simple signals (tallies) to equipment—for example, cameras telling them when they have been cut on-air.

TBU (telephone balance unit) Device connected to telephone lines that enables presenters to have a phone conversation live on the air.

Tech Book (US) Production manual or folder specific to each program.

Technical director (US) Operator of the video board who also oversees picture quality.

Teleprompter (US) or Autocue (UK) Display device that prompts the person speaking with an electronic visual text of the script. Similar to cue cards.

Termination A 75-ohm resistor included across the video cable at the end of a transmission chain. Inclusion of 75-ohm termination ensures no reflection of energy and that the signal level is correct.

Tight in/out An edit point with little space or time between the "in" and/or the "out" point of a sequence.

Tight lens Long focal length primary lens or zoom lens setting.

Time base error Instability of a videotape playback signal created by the machine's inability to play back at exactly the same speed at which the tape was recorded.

Time code The means by which every recorded frame of video is able to be numbered.

T-number Also *T stop* Indicates the amount of light transmitted by a lens at a specific iris setting. Unlike f-numbers, identical T-numbers on lenses will transmit the same amount of light independent of lens design.

T-piece BNC connectors to allow teeing of video connectors: connecting two video cables to one video socket.

Transformer Device made with two coils wound around a core that can be magnetized to isolate a signal or change its voltage.

Transient response Ability of equipment to respond to fast changes in level.

Transient Signal that changes very quickly.

Translucent Semitransparent. Usually some form of light diffuser.

Trucking (US) or Dollying (UK) Movement of camera mount toward or away from talent.

Tungsten filament Material in a light envelope producing light by heat.

Turtle Very low-lighting stand for rigging instruments at floor level.

Tweak Term used for small adjustments to lighting rig or operational settings—for example, black level or iris setting.

TX Transmission.

Unipod (US) Another name for a *monopod*.

Upstage Moving farther away from the camera or audience.

User-bit ID system that allows up to ten digits and an A to F (hexadecimal) code to be programmed into the code word that is recorded on every frame.

User-bit-code Programmable identification code compiled by the "user" of the camera that is recorded as part of the time code on each video frame.

Vectorscope Special oscilloscope designed to display the chrominance information in an easily recognizable way—that is, hue and saturation.

Vertical sync Signal from the sync generator that tells the electron beams to return to the top of the screen for the start of a new video field.

Vertical blanking Period from when the electron beam is turned down at the end of a video field until it is turned back up at the start of a new field.

Vertical interval Period when the electron beam is in vertical blanking.

Vertical interval switcher Switcher that delays cuts between video sources until the entire system is in vertical blanking.

Vertical lock Method of stabilizing videotape playback that tries to match the control track pulses of the playback signal to vertical sync pulses coming from the sync generator. Also called *capstan servo*.

VGA Voltage controlled amplifier.

Video barrel (US) Small in-line adaptor designed to connect two BNC video sources.

Video board (US) The equipment that selects and routes video signals to one output.

Video compression Technology that allows digital video information to be compressed into a smaller space, thereby requiring less bandwidth or memory space for transmission or storage.

Video contrast range Relationship between the brightest part of the scene and the darkest part.

Video operator (US) Person who adjusts camera exposure, color, gamma, and so on in a multicamera production. Also applied to the area where the person performs this function.

Video stringers (US) Video journalists who work independently and sell their stories across the networks.

Video wall Several individual TV screens that are often stacked in a rectangle, displaying multiple, individual, or composite images.

Vignette Shading of the edges of the picture area.

Virtual reality System of chroma-key where the background is computer generated. Size and positioning of the background are controlled by the foreground camera movements.

Vision control (UK) Person who adjusts camera exposure, color, gamma, and so on in a multicamera production. Also applied to the area where the person performs this function.

Vision mixer (UK) The person who switches between video sources. Also applied to the pieces of equipment the person uses to perform this function.

Vision mixer (UK) Video switching unit used to select camera images in a multicamera program.

VITC (vertical interval time code) Time code numbers recorded in one or more of the unused lines in the TV signal. Can be read when the tape is in still frame.

Voice-over (VO) Commentary mixed with effects or music as part of a sound track.

VOVT Voice-over videotape.

Vox pops (vox populi) Voice of the people, usually consists of a series of edited impromptu answers to a question recorded on the street with members of the public. Man on the Street in the US.

VTR Videotape recorder.

VU meter Volume unit meter, indicates average level of sound.

Waveform monitor Oscilloscope with appropriate time-base for displaying the television waveform. Usually includes a face-plate graticule to indicate sync level, black level, peak white, and percentage signal level.

Wavelength Length between adjacent peaks of a signal.

White balance Electronic process of defining a reference white that is lit by a light source of a specific color temperature.

White noise Random noise containing an equal level of the audio frequency spectrum.

Wide angle Horizontal field of view of a lens greater than approximately 40 degrees.

Wide shot (WS) Description of shot size that includes objects greater than the size of the human figure.

Widen out (US) or Pull out (UK) Movement of zoom lens in or out rather than moving the camera mount.

Working behind the camera Operating the camera using remote lens controls attached to pan bars and a nonmonocular viewfinder.

Working-as-live Continuous recording with no opportunity for recording breaks or retakes.

Wow and flutter Variations in speed of a mechanical system, audible as frequency variations in an analog recording. "Wow" is a slow form of flutter.

XLR connectors (UK) Type of connector used with microphones.

Zebra exposure indicator Black-and-white striped pattern that appears in the viewfinder at points in the picture corresponding to a preset video level as an aid to manual exposure.

Zero-level voltage Standard reference audio signal of 0.775 V at 1000 Hz used for audio equipment lineup.

Zoom Variable focal length lens achieved by internally moving elements of the lens.

Zoom ratio Ratio of the longest focal length to the shortest focal length a specific zoom lens can achieve.

Zoom tracking Lens prefocused on a distant subject will stay in focus for its entire zoom movement toward (or away from) that subject, provided that the back focus (flange back) has been correctly aligned.

Index